The Beauty and the Terror

The Beauty and the Terror

The Italian Renaissance and the Rise of the West

CATHERINE FLETCHER

OXFORD

UNIVERSITY PRESS

Oxford University Press is a department of the University of Oxford.
It furthers the University's objective of excellence in research, scholarship,
and education by publishing worldwide. Oxford is a registered trade mark of
Oxford University Press in the UK and in certain other countries.

Published in the United States of America by Oxford University Press
198 Madison Avenue, New York, NY 10016, United States of America.

First published in the UK by The Bodley Head in 2020

Library of Congress Cataloging-in-Publication information
is available.

ISBN 978-0-19-090849-2

1 3 5 7 9 8 6 4 2

Printed by Sheridan Books, Inc., United States of America

To my students

Contents

Map ix

Introduction: *1492* I

1 *The Fifteenth Century* 15
2 *Beyond the Alps* 29
3 *1494: The French Descent* 39
4 *The Borgias vs Savonarola* 55
5 *The Art of War* 69
6 *Soldiers and Society* 79
7 *Wars for the New World* 91
8 *Popes, Princes and Republics* 107
9 *The Run-up to the Reformation* 125
10 *The League of Cambrai* 137
11 *Women and Power* 149
12 *The Ghetto and the Politics of Venice* 159
13 *The Battle for the Church* 173
14 *The High Renaissance* 185
15 *From Pavia to Mohács* 197
16 *Wars of Words* 207
17 *The Invention of Pornography* 221
18 *The Sack of Rome* 235
19 *Courtiers and the Art of Power in Italy and Beyond* 247
20 *The Empire at War* 259
21 *Weapons of War* 271
22 *The Council of Trent* 281
23 *Art, Science and Reform* 293

24 *The Peace of Cateau-Cambrésis*   307
25 *The Index and the Inquisition*   321
26 *The Battle of Lepanto*   333

    Epilogue: *From Hard Power to Soft*   343

    Acknowledgements   351
    Bibliography   353
    Endnotes   379
    Index   395

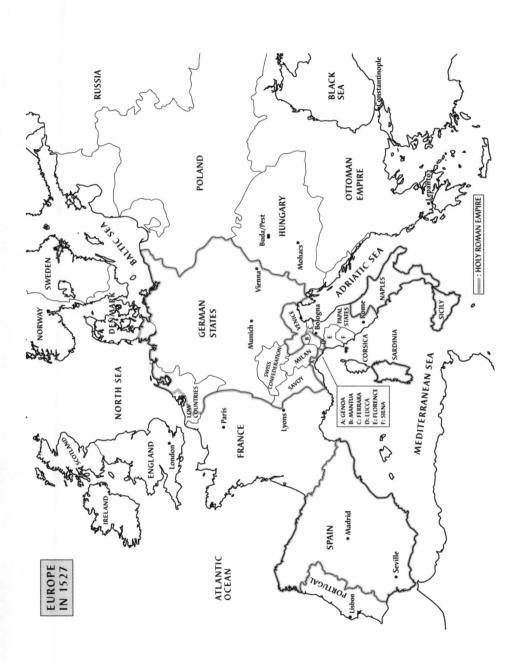

EUROPE
IN 1527

RUSSIA

NORWAY

SWEDEN

BALTIC SEA

DENMARK

POLAND

GERMAN
STATES

NORTH SEA

SCOTLAND

IRELAND

ENGLAND

London

Paris

FRANCE

Munich

Vienna

Buda/Pest

HUNGARY

Mohács

SWISS
CONFEDERATION

SAVOY

MILAN

VENICE

B

E

F

Bologna

PAPAL
STATES

Rome

ADRIATIC SEA

NAPLES

OTTOMAN
EMPIRE

BLACK
SEA

Constantinople

Lepanto

LOW
COUNTRIES

Lyons

CORSICA

SARDINIA

SICILY

MEDITERRANEAN SEA

ATLANTIC
OCEAN

SPAIN

Madrid

Seville

PORTUGAL

Lisbon

A: GENOA
B: MANTUA
C: FERRARA
D: LUCCA
E: FLORENCE
F: SIENA

: HOLY ROMAN EMPIRE

Introduction

1492

In the days before the death of Lorenzo the Magnificent de' Medici there had been bad omens in Florence. A bolt of lightning had hit the cathedral dome. Two of the lions in the palace lion-house had been fighting. And when on the night of 8 April 1492 the first citizen of Florence and great patron of Renaissance arts and letters died at his hillside villa in Careggi, three miles to the city's north, there were the inevitable rumours of poison. A messenger rode overnight to bring the news to Rome, and to his son, Cardinal Giovanni de' Medici.

By the time of Lorenzo, the Medici family had risen from wealthy merchants and leading oligarchs of the city of Florence to its de facto lords. Lorenzo had not matched his grandfather's skills in banking. The Medici bank – fount of the family's wealth – had suffered losses in the 1470s and 80s. Income from the Florentine state had therefore become ever more important in sustaining the family finances: or, to put it another way, the Medici had their hands in the till. Lorenzo left a fabulous collection of books and antiquities and a luxurious set of country villas, as well as a poetic legacy of his own, though he regretted, on his deathbed at the age of forty-three, that he had not seen his 'marvellous Greek and Latin library done'. Looking back on his death some decades later, the Florentine statesman and historian Francesco Guicciardini would describe it as 'a grievous stroke to his country'. Lorenzo's 'reputation, prudence and genius' had helped maintain a 'long and secure peace' in Italy. He had kept in check the ambitions of King Ferdinand of Naples and Ludovico Sforza, regent of Milan.

This was at best rose-tinted and at worst entirely misleading: Lorenzo had his family's political interests at heart, and his quest to secure their own position had done damage to the peninsula's equilibrium.[4] As part of that strategy, his daughter Maddalena had wed a nephew of Pope Innocent VIII, and his heir, Piero had been married to a Neapolitan heiress, Alfonsina Orsini. (Piero was soon to be known as 'the Unfortunate' for his disastrous tenure at the head of the Medici and Florence; the closer the Medici came to dynastic power, the more they fell prey to that curse of dynasties, that the eldest son could not always be relied upon.) Lorenzo's greatest coup, however, had been to obtain for his second son Giovanni a position as cardinal: this was in 1489, when Giovanni had been only thirteen. He was sixteen, now, at his father's death.

Lorenzo had advised his son to live modestly in the 'sink of all iniquity' that was Rome.

> A handsome house and a well-ordered family will be preferable to a great retinue and a splendid residence [he wrote]. Your taste will be better shown in the acquisition of a few elegant remains of antiquity, or in the collecting of handsome books, and by your attendants being learned and well-bred rather than numerous.

Giovanni's role as a cardinal was, of course, a religious one.

> You are now devoted to God and the church: on which account you ought to aim at being a good ecclesiastic, and to show that you prefer the honour and state of the church and of the apostolic see to every other consideration. Nor, while you keep this in view, will it be difficult for you to favour your family and your native place [...] observing, however, that you are always to prefer the interests of the church.[5]

It is doubtful Lorenzo intended his son to take this advice literally, and he did not. Cardinal Giovanni's nepotism would do no favours for a church in need of reform, though it proved the saving of his family's fortunes.

Italy at this time was entering a period of remarkable turbulence. Like the area we now know as Germany, the Italian peninsula of the late fifteenth century was not a unified country – nor would it be until the latter half of the nineteenth century – but was divided into multiple small states. The five largest of these were two republics, Venice and Florence, and three princely states: the kingdom of Naples, the duchy of Milan, and the Papal States, of which the pope was effectively the monarch, alongside his religious status as the vicar of Christ on earth. (The Italian kingdoms, duchies and marquisates all had a single hereditary ruler, the different titles indicating different degrees of grandeur.) The political balance between these states was already precarious, and the death of a second in the space of three months now threatened it further.

On 25 July 1492, Pope Innocent VIII died, Just a few months earlier he had presided over great celebrations in Rome. On Sunday 5 February, dressed in white vestments, he had made his way through constant, miserable rain from his apartments at the Vatican to the church of St James on Piazza Navona, centre of worship for Rome's Spanish community. There, before bishops and cardinals, he had given thanks to God for the victory of the king and queen of Spain against the Muslim city of Granada. Since the year 711 the 'Moors', as Christians called them, had ruled large parts of the Iberian peninsula. Its history had been one of coexistence, sometimes tolerance, and often outbursts of persecution. In the early years political alliances had periodic crossed religious lines, but the Muslims had gradually been pushed back in what became known by their Christian rivals as the *Reconquista* or Reconquest of Spain. In the face of increasingly brutal tactics, King Boabdil – Mohammed XII of Granada – had tried compromise, working with the Spanish monarchs Ferdinand of Aragon and Isabella of Castile against rivals in his own family. It did not save him. On 2 January 1492, amid splendid but humiliating ceremony, he handed the keys to his city to the king and queen, ending more than seven centuries of Muslim rule in Western Europe.

For their commitment to the Christianisation of Spain – and the conversion of people beyond – Ferdinand and Isabella would be honoured with the title of the Catholic Monarchs. They had married in 1469 and after the deaths of Isabella's brother and half-brother had seen off a challenge to her throne from a niece. Among their instruments as they worked to build a new Spanish monarchy the most notorious was the Spanish Inquisition. Licensed by Innocent's predecessor, Pope Sixtus IV, it had begun as a campaign against heresy. It had focused at first on Spain's *conversos*, former Jews who had converted to Christianity but who were accused of faking their commitment to the new religion. The Inquisition's campaign against Jews and 'Judaisers' ran in parallel with the campaign against the Moors.

Military victories were always an excuse for festivities in Rome, and such an explicitly religious success was irresistible. After Mass, the cardinals processed through the city. Cardinal Rodrigo Borgia, vice-chancellor of the Church (the most senior office-holder in church administration after the pope), and himself of Spanish descent, organised a bullfight to celebrate his nation's triumph over the infidels. The Spanish ambassadors put up a tableau in the street, with a mock castle standing in for the captured city of Granada. Borgia's was only the first of the contests: over the next few weeks Piazza Navona was packed with spectators as one after another Spanish prelate put up bulls for killing. Cardinal Raffaele Riario, the pope's nephew, donated a prize worth two hundred ducats. It was Carnival season, and the celebrations continued until Lent with games and races for 'old men, young men, boys, Jews, donkeys and buffaloes'.[1]

It is telling that the papal master of ceremonies who wrote down that list put the Roman runners in that order. The Jews of Rome were second-class citizens, as they were across Europe. Ferdinand and Isabella followed their victory against the Muslims of Granada with a decree that all Jews must leave Spain by the end of July. The Inquisition, they said, had firm evidence that Jews were 'soliciting and corrupting Christians': expulsion was the only way to put an end to 'heresy and apostasy'. Proclaimed in Aragon on 29 April, and in Castile on 1 May, their edict allowed a bare three months for the sale of property, a formula for a collapse in prices; Jews were banned from removing gold or silver or coins from the realm. The confiscated gold and silver would fund Columbus' second voyage to the Americas the following year.

The Jews of Spain scattered. It is hard to calculate exactly how many were expelled: probably tens of thousands.[2] Some went to Portugal, some to North Africa; some to papal lands in Avignon and Provence. Others went to Italy, some to the kingdom of Naples, ruled by a bastard branch of the Aragonese royal family (located in north-eastern Spain, Aragon was one of multiple kingdoms now being consolidated into Ferdinand and Isabella's realm). A ship from the eastern ports of Spain could reach Italy in about a week: far worse were the voyages of those forced to flee from the northern ports on the Bay of Biscay and back through the Strait of Gibraltar. Rome, Venice and Mantua were relatively, if not unconditionally, welcoming.

Elsewhere in Italy, however, cities such as Milan, Perugia and Lucca had pre-empted the Spanish move, expelling their Jews in the 1480s.[3]

Meanwhile in Rome, Cardinal Giovanni de' Medici was among those now called upon for the most important political task facing any Renaissance cardinal: a conclave in which he and his fellows would elect the new pope. The Sistine Chapel was partitioned into cubicles, equipped with candles, clothes, and cooking equipment: all manner of necessary goods for what might prove a lengthy stay. The cardinals and their personal servants arrived; the doors were locked, and guards were placed on each one to keep them closed, and keep spies out, until the men inside had chosen a successor.

There were four candidates in play: Cardinal Costa of Portugal, Cardinal Zen of Venice, Oliviero Carafa, Cardinal of Naples, and Cardinal Borgia. Rodrigo Borgia was not the leading contender, and his enemies would claim that he bought the papacy with four mule-loads of silver. The truth is more mundane, though the politics still worldly enough. The cardinals were split into two parties, each with backing from different Italian states and players. One group, headed by Cardinal Giuliano della Rovere (himself a future pope), had backing from the king of Naples, from the Venetian and Genoese cardinals, and from the Colonna, a powerful baronial family in Rome. They would be happy with either Costa or Zen. The other, headed by Cardinal Ascanio Sforza, was supported by the duke of Milan, and backed Cardinal Carafa. The silver, so the story goes, went to Sforza, to buy him off. The tallies of votes, however, suggest Borgia already had significant support in the early rounds. By the third scrutiny Borgia had eight and Carafa ten, and the della Rovere party looked to have momentum. When Cardinal Sforza realised that he had a better chance with Borgia than with Carafa, he switched his votes. No bribery was necessary: this was politics. If it had come down simply to money, the richly backed della Rovere could have outbid Borgia, but he could not summon enough votes.[6]

It was thus that on 11 August 1492 Rodrigo Borgia was elected pope. He was crowned on the 26th, taking the name Alexander VI, with the usual splendid ceremony. As a senior cardinal, he had held many rich benefices – bringing incomes from church and abbey lands – that could be redistributed now he was pope, not least to reward his supporters. He made his nephew, Juan Borgia Lanzol, a cardinal, and his son, Cesare Borgia, archbishop of Valencia. Yet from his papal throne, Alexander VI looked out on a rocky prospect. The government of Florence was insecure. The balance of power between Milan, Florence and Naples that had kept Italy largely peaceful over several decades was at risk of collapse. Innocent's death, as Guicciardini would put it, had 'laid the foundation of further calamities'. The political task facing the pope was vast, and his responsibilities were about to extend in a quite unexpected direction.[7]

For it was in the early hours of Friday, 12 October that same year that the sailing crew under the command of explorer Christopher Columbus (Cristoforo Colombo) saw land. They believed they were somewhere off the eastern coast of Japan. They had been at sea for almost two months, and Columbus had concealed from his men their true distance from Spain, for fear of sparking alarm. He waited until dawn to disembark and step onto the island that he would learn was called Guanahaní. He saw 'trees, very green, many streams and a large variety of fruits'. His captains unfurled two banners of the green cross, with an F and a Y, initials of the Spanish monarchs Ferdinand and Ysabella [Isabella], his patrons. Columbus recounted his first meeting with the Taíno people of this island in optimistic terms: 'I could see that they were a people who could more easily be won over and converted to our holy faith by kindness than by force.' He began to barter with them: red hats, glass beads and hawks' bells, in return for parrots, balls of cotton thread, and spears. 'They took and gave everything they had with good will,' he wrote, 'but it seemed to me that they were a people who were very poor in everything.'[8]

Columbus had been born (like Innocent VIII) in Genoa, on the north-west coast of Italy, in about 1451. His father was a weaver, though more fanciful histories accorded him a university education and ancient Roman ancestry.[9] Columbus was far from the only young man of the city who made a career in seafaring and exploration: John (Giovanni) Cabot, who 'discovered' the North American continent in 1497, was a contemporary. Columbus had studied the maps made by a Florentine cosmographer, Paolo dal Pozzo Toscanelli; in his twenties he moved to Lisbon, by which time he had sailed east to the Genoese colony of Chios in the Eastern Mediterranean, perhaps to England and certainly south to Madeira.[10] He had tried to convince the king of Portugal to support a voyage west; having no success he turned instead to the neighbouring realm of Castile and its queen, Isabella, where he spent six years at court before he convinced her of his grandiose plan for a voyage to the Indies. They did not know it, but it was a voyage that would, for more than a century, shift the balance of power in Europe. When the ambassadors of Spain came to Rome to pledge the obedience of Ferdinand and Isabella to the new Pope Alexander VI, their countryman, they proudly announced the discovery and conquest of 'four enormous islands'.[11]

Thus, as 1492 turned to 1493 on the Italian peninsula, its people looked to a world of uncertainty. They contemplated Spanish Christian victories: against King Boabdil, against Spain's own Jews, and – as they would soon learn – in this strange place that Europeans had never before seen. Rodrigo Borgia, who some forty years earlier had moved from Spain to Italy, had been elected pope: his cardinals waited to see how he might rule. The government of Florence, meanwhile, was in the shaky hands of Lorenzo de' Medici's son Piero and his long-standing but untrustworthy allies. The scene was set for a conflict that would engulf the Italian peninsula for the next eighty years.

The history of Italy has long been a subject of fascination. The courses in 'Western Civilisation' that were established in North American universities at the end of the nineteenth century began with the ancient world – Greece and Rome, primarily, perhaps Egypt – and then jumped the 'Dark Ages' to arrive at the splendours of the Renaissance and the rebirth of great classical ideas before marching on to the world of Enlightenment. 'Western civilisation' was a term rarely used before that point: it is a nineteenth-century invention that emerged in a very particular context of European empires and of racial segregation in the USA. In this story of the West, Italy has occupied a central place, and if that history is no longer invariably told with the moral self-confidence it once was, the significance of 'the Renaissance' has kept its grip.[12] Every year thousands of overseas students flock to Italy on study abroad programmes. And not only from the West: growth in tourism to Florence comes now less from Europe than from Japan, China, India and Brazil. It has become a world city. Or perhaps, I should say, has become a world city again. For it was in the context of global trade, exploration, colonisation and exploitation – of New

World riches and Old World finery – that some of Renaissance Italy's most celebrated artists and thinkers worked.

This is a book about those connections, about the links between people and stories that are told as part of 'Western history', some of them expected, some of them not. I imagine many readers will have heard of Michelangelo and Machiavelli, of Columbus and Cabot, of the Medici and Borgias. There are many stars of the later Italian Renaissance, and their lives are often told one by one. I want to try and arrange them into their galaxy, and to think not only about the great Renaissance cities of Venice, Florence and Rome, but also about the rest of the Italian peninsula: the city of Genoa that made explorers and popes; the tiny courts of Urbino and Mantua, home to a model of 'the courtier' that would spread through Europe; the southern realm of Naples and its Spanish rulers. Moreover, that Italy was not a peninsula in isolation: far from it. Rome was the centre of European diplomacy; the southern kingdom of Naples was ruled by a branch of the Aragonese royal family and later directly by Spanish viceroys. Some of the northern states owed allegiance to the Holy Roman Emperor. (This empire, it is often said, was neither Roman nor holy: rather, it was a complex of territories of different types that owed allegiance to a ruler chosen by a select group of prince-electors.) I want to think, as well, about the people whose lives often do not feature in the usual narrative: the women writers and artists, the soldiers and citizens who lived through sieges and scorched earth, the men who behind the scenes made fortunes as bankers to the new imperialists, not to mention as suppliers of arms: Beretta, first documented selling firearms in 1526, offers a direct link between this past and our present world but rarely makes its way into the popular image of the period.

This is also a book about war and its consequences. From 1494 to 1559 the Italian peninsula was the setting for a ferocious series of conflicts between the princes of Europe, known commonly as the Italian Wars: a battle between the Spanish monarchs and their great rivals at this time, the French, for supremacy in Italy. The Mediterranean, meanwhile, was a theatre of conflict with the Ottoman Empire that lasted still longer, whose most famous engagement was perhaps the Battle of Lepanto in 1571. Lives and livelihoods were destroyed; but war also prompted creation and invention, new military techniques and technologies. If we know Leonardo da Vinci now for the Mona

Lisa's smile, his contemporaries knew him, too, as a designer of military maps, and of fortifications and weaponry. And war also drew soldiers and diplomats from across Europe to the Italian peninsula. Among them was Thomas Cromwell, later Henry VIII's chief minister.

The centrality of Italy in European conflict and peacemaking over these eight decades made it a melting pot for ideas about politics and culture: arguments over the ethics of republican versus princely rule, over the enslavement of Native Americans, over religious belief, over sexual morality. Venetian printers found new markets for ancient learning, and for more modern ideas too. Italian navigators sailed not only to the New World, but sought out new routes to the East. Yet between the drama of 1492 and the unexpected Christian naval victory against the Ottomans at Lepanto, Italy's place in the world shifted. As the geography of the globe became clearer, the peninsula's city states could no longer assume their centrality at the crossroads of the Mediterranean. Italians watched the rise of Spain and a Spanish effort (not always successful) to dominate Italian politics and institutions; thereafter the centres of European power would be elsewhere, to Italy's north and west. The Roman Catholic Church, meanwhile, saw the greatest challenge to its authority it has ever faced. In 1511, the German monk Martin Luther visited Rome on business for the Augustinian Order, and later told of his shock at the city's corruption, quoting an Italian proverb: 'If there is a Hell, Rome is built over it.'[13] Over the next decades, the challenge from Protestantism to which Luther gave birth would give major impetus to the Catholic movement for reform.

The importance attached today to the culture of the Italian Renaissance is easily illustrated with a look at the UNESCO World Heritage list of sites considered to be of cultural significance for humankind. Take the entry for the historic centre of Florence, inscribed in 1982:

> Built on the site of an Etruscan settlement, Florence, the symbol of the Renaissance, rose to economic and cultural pre-eminence under the Medici in the 15th and 16th centuries. Its 600 years of extraordinary artistic activity can be seen above all in the 13th-century cathedral (Santa Maria del Fiore), the Church of Santa Croce, the Uffizi and the Pitti Palace, the work of great masters such as Giotto, Brunelleschi, Botticelli and Michelangelo.

Many other Renaissance masterpieces make UNESCO's list too: the church of Santa Maria delle Grazie with Leonardo's *Last Supper*; Ferrara, City of the Renaissance, and its Po Delta; Ippolito d'Este's villa in Tivoli; the Medici Villas and Gardens in Tuscany; the Venetian Works of Defence built between the sixteenth and seventeenth centuries; the botanical garden of Padua made in 1545. The historic towns of Mantua and Sabbioneta are listed: so are the centres of Urbino, Pisa, Venice, Naples and Siena. As I write this in 2019, Italy has more inscriptions on the World Heritage list than any other country, narrowly beating the far larger China. That is partly an indication of past biases, of course, but it gives a sense of just how strongly Italian and Renaissance culture more broadly was valued among the cultural and diplomatic decision-makers of the late twentieth century.

This is not without reason. The culture of fourteenth- and fifteenth-century Italy – and the city of Florence in particular – left a substantial legacy in the worlds of the arts, education and political thought. The use of the term 'Renaissance' to describe this period is (like the use of 'Western Civilisation') a nineteenth-century phenomenon, and many details of the world conjured by the Swiss scholar Jacob Burckhardt's 1860 *Civilization of the Renaissance in Italy* – a foundational text in the study of Renaissance history – have since been challenged. Yet the idea of the Renaissance, and the popular use of the term, remains persistent for good reason, and I use it here for convenience. There is no doubt that the developments of this period were important, and that influential intellectuals of the time saw themselves as engaged in a revival of the ancient Greek and Roman classics.* This Renaissance saw the rise of the self-promoting scholar, dedicated to book-collecting: three of Italy's major libraries today (the Vatican, the Biblioteca Medicea Laurenziana in Florence and the Biblioteca Marciana in Venice) are its products. It saw the rise of the individual named artist, and important developments in secular art, including paintings based on classical myth. It saw the rise of a new liberal arts curriculum in universities, and its debates about 'republicanism', 'liberty' and 'reason of state' – while often more rhetoric than fact

---

* This tale somewhat glosses over the significance of ninth-century scholars who produced the copies of Latin texts on which they relied; it is a more convincing story so far as it concerns Greek literature.

when it came to Renaissance regimes – had a long-lasting influence in politics.

In many narratives of the Italian Renaissance, the year 1492 (or sometimes 1494, when French troops descended into Italy) marks the beginning of the end, a period in which foreigners began to dominate the peninsula and war overtook civility. Yet some of the most iconic 'Renaissance' artworks – the *Mona Lisa*, the Sistine Chapel ceiling and *Last Judgement*, the *Venus of Urbino* – are products of the war-torn sixteenth century. In art history works of the later Renaissance are sometimes described as 'mannerist', referring to the way artists moved away from more naturalistic representations to a more sophisticated but also more artificial style. These years were also characterised by some decidedly 'modern' phenomena, as opposed to those looking back to the ancients: European contact with the New World, the proliferation of gunpowder technology, and the rise of printing. For me, one of the fascinations of the sixteenth century is the way that it teeters between old and new.

When I first began studying Renaissance history, almost two decades ago, I did so in part because I wanted a change from the world of present-day politics. I always found parallels, of course: I would laugh over sixteenth-century letters that unwittingly foreshadowed the voices of politicians I knew, but I was firm in my mind that the past was a foreign country. When I made jokes comparing those supra-national centres of Europe – fifteenth-century Rome and twenty-first-century Brussels – they got a laugh, but I was sure I was being flippant. As I went on, however, the past seemed to become less foreign. I would read 'tech revolution' stories and think about the history of printing; read about the election of Pope Francis and think about the global sixteenth-century Catholic Church; read about a refugee crisis in the Mediterranean and think about the expulsion of Jews and Muslims from Spain. This is not to say that nothing has changed: as we will see, there are many differences between that society and our own. But precisely because the legacy of this Renaissance (or Age of Reform, or Age of Exploration, if we prefer) has become so important in Western culture, in defining who 'we' are (and who 'we' are not), it is worth getting to know it better.

This is all the more important because the popular story of the Renaissance – like many versions of modern Western history – tends to focus on the genius and glory at the expense of the atrocities. Machiavelli's ideas about power, for example, become a set of timeless aphorisms rather than emerging, as in fact they did, from a specific setting. The fact that all these people coexisted with the early European voyages to the Americas, to which some of them had very personal connections, and that Italians provided personnel, finance and write-ups of the subsequent colonisation, is not unknown, exactly. The bloody side of the Renaissance has always been part of the period's fascination. It is more often told, however, in the fashion of TV's *The Borgias* as the glamorous, sexy violence of the rich-and-famous murdering one other in pursuit of power (the viewer consoling herself that most of them deserve their fate), and far less the violence of war, exile and colonisation, nor yet domestic abuse. This is the narrative that makes of the Medici a family of mafia godfathers, and it is about as connected to the reality of Florence in the sixteenth century as gangster movies are to actual life in a town run by organised crime today. I have no objection to people enjoying a bloody tale of vendetta: I've told the gory story of the Baglioni wedding massacre at Perugia in 1500 to tour groups myself. Yet too much of this masks the brutal realities behind Renaissance works of art. Take the *Mona Lisa*: Lisa Gherardini, the woman of the mysterious smile, was married to a slave-trader. One possible model for the *Venus of Urbino* – Angela Zaffetta – was gang-raped. The Florentine Republic that commissioned and was symbolised by Michelangelo's *David* came to a brutal end with a sack of 'unheard-of cruelty' in which thousands of men were massacred in just a few hours.

As I was finishing this book in March 2019, forty-nine people were killed in a gun attack on two mosques in Christchurch, New Zealand. The perpetrator, a right-wing extremist, posted on social media numerous historical precedents that he claimed for his actions, including notable Christian victories against Muslim forces. One was the 1571 Battle of Lepanto, the subject of my final chapter. Sixteenth-century history has rarely been so explicitly appropriated by the far-right as have, say, the Crusades or the myth of an all-white medieval West. More commonly, Renaissance history has played a more subtle, if no less pernicious role, the mythologies of its great men reinforcing ideas about European and Christian and white superiority without ever being so vulgar as to say so outright. That is not to say it is wrong to appreciate or enjoy the artistic innovation of sixteenth-century Europe: there is plenty to wonder at. And by exploring how the people of this world thought about their own media revolution, or considered questions of gender and sexuality, or responded to changing weapons technology, we can better understand our own world too, and the ways in which then as now brilliant cultural innovation can exist alongside – indeed, is often intertwined with – all manner of atrocity.

Chapter One

The Fifteenth Century

Forty years before Columbus' voyage, in 1452, the citizens of Rome had witnessed a fabulous spectacle when Pope Nicholas V crowned Frederick III Holy Roman Emperor in St Peter's Basilica. This was the old St Peter's, dating back to the fourth century, with its colonnaded entrance and columns arranged along a long nave: the new basilica with its dome lay more than a century in the future. Its location above the site of the saint's tomb conjured the symbolism of the apostolic succession, the line of popes that had begun with Christ's disciple, St Peter. The coronation was a triumph for both pope and emperor. Only five years before, Nicholas had made his entry to Rome, established as the single recognised pontiff after decades of schism in the Church that had at one point seen three men claim to be the rightful pope. Nicholas himself had been born a Roman and for him now to preside over the coronation of an emperor was a sign of both his own status and his city's. His papacy promised, moreover, stability and wealth for Rome. For Frederick, the first of the house of Habsburg to be elected emperor, the coronation cemented his role as the most senior Christian monarch in Europe. In his long reign (he died in 1493), he would establish the continent's most powerful dynasty. Although the emperor was elected, the Habsburgs held the title for over four hundred years, until their main line became extinct in 1740. Frederick was also to be crowned king of Italy (this did not refer to lordship over the whole of the peninsula, but rather recognised that some of the northern states had the emperor for an overlord, albeit usually a distant one).

Frederick's coronation, inevitably, did not lack for controversy. There was nervousness in the Italian states about his decision to travel to Italy, and the risk to the delicate politics of the peninsula should he decide to ally himself with any rebels or challengers for power in the various regimes. His decision to take a sightseeing tour of Rome prior to his coronation led to raised eyebrows from the city's traditionalists, who considered it a violation of protocol. The ambassadors of Milan objected to his coronation as king of Italy altogether, and their lord Francesco Sforza had made sure Frederick could not get his hands on the Iron Crown of Lombardy, normally used for that purpose. Frederick, not to be outmanoeuvred, had himself crowned king of Italy with a German crown instead; his marriage to Eleanor, daughter of the king of Portugal, took place the same afternoon, and three days later, on the anniversary of Pope Nicholas' own coronation, Frederick was anointed and crowned Holy Roman Emperor at Saint Peter's.[1]

Among the observers of the ceremony was Poggio Bracciolini, one of the most prominent scholars of Renaissance Florence and one of the new breed of 'humanists' in Italy. The word 'humanist' initially meant simply a student of the humanities, or liberal arts, a new curriculum that had grown up in the context of a revived study of classical texts. Though these ancient Greek and Roman texts were not Christian, Renaissance humanists generally were (and found in late antique writers like St Augustine of Hippo people who directly integrated the two cultures). Humanism did not yet refer to secularism or atheism, though it did emphasise the importance of human action and values, which created some tension with aspects of Christian theology. In particular, its exponents advocated a new intellectual method of textual criticism, which helped open up challenges to church authority, notably in the debate over the veracity of the Donation of Constantine, a document purporting be a fourth-century decree of the Emperor Constantine which handed authority over the Western Roman Empire to the pope. Following centuries of rumour as to its authenticity, humanist techniques helped to expose it as a forgery. The implications were enormous. This was the document on which papal authority rested and now it had been proved a fake.

The idea of humanism also encompassed a more practically applied 'civic humanism', most commonly associated with Florence, which emphasised the importance of active engagement in the political life of the republic, not merely contemplative study. In practical terms the rise of humanists to positions of political power ensured sponsorship for the new intellectual trend through, for example, the creation of a Professorship of Greek at the University of Florence. Humanism's interest in the classical world is apparent in Bracciolini's citation of ancient precedents for the coronation ceremony.[2]

Indeed, it was not just Bracciolini's account of Frederick's coronation that highlighted the antiquity of the ceremony and the surroundings.[3] This was an opportunity for Rome once again to assert its centrality in European politics, not only in Christianity but in the approbation of temporal rulers too. It was also a chance to show off the city's splendours to visitors. Nikolaus Muffel, a German counsellor who attended the coronation, took the opportunity to visit Rome's wealth of pilgrim sites, from the Scala Sancta at Aracoeli with its twenty-eight marble steps, to the relic of St Peter's chains at San Pietro in Vincoli, and to write up a description of his visit.[4] For all that there were challenges to the authority of the fifteenth-century Church, devotion was deeply embedded in the lives of individual Christians. To them, 1452 must surely have seemed an auspicious year for Christendom.

Yet the following year proved quite the opposite when Constantinople, the ancient eastern capital of the Roman Empire and the second-largest city in the world, was conquered by the Ottoman Turks.[*] The end of the Byzantine Empire after more than a millennium was an enormous psychological shock not just for its Greek Christian populace but for Christian powers everywhere, a 'great terror', in the words of the later Venetian historian Marin Sanudo (1466–1536). The news arrived in Venice on 29 June and from the council meeting men rushed to spread the word that on 28 May Pera, the Genoese colony in Constantinople and home to many Italian merchants, had been captured by the sultan, who had ordered the slaughter of everyone – male and female – bar the tiniest children. Only by a miracle had two Venetian galleys escaped. For a few weeks people hoped this was false rumour, but the tale of the city's fall, if not every brutal detail, proved all too true.[5]

Nicolò Barbaro, a Venetian eyewitness to the events, wrote an account of what happened. There had been a long build-up to the conquest. Sultan Mehmed II, nicknamed with good reason 'the

---

[*] The Ottoman Empire was by no means exclusively Turkish, but Italian writers of this period commonly identified its rulers and armies as 'the Turks'.

Conqueror', built a castle some six miles from Constantinople in the summer of 1452, and in August that year he took two ambassadors from the Byzantine Emperor hostage. (The empire had shrunk dramatically over the past two and a half centuries, and consisted of little more than the city of Constantinople itself and the Peloponnese in southern Greece.) Theories of diplomatic immunity were not fully formed in the fifteenth century but even so Mehmed overstepped a widely agreed mark when he had the pair executed. It prompted war. The Ottomans began to assemble an army of perhaps 50,000 men.[6] There was a long process of skirmishing and embassies before the siege began in earnest, during which time Venetian and Genoese ships arrived to offer aid to the city. There were, however, tensions between the trading interests of merchants from these states and loyalty to the Greek Christians of Constantinople (the Byzantine Empire was, in any case, Orthodox rather than part of the Catholic Church). When the Greek rulers of the city sought their help, the Venetian merchants gathered in a city church to debate their tactics: should they stay and support the Greeks, as requested? They resolved to offer five galleys for the city's defence, but did not balk at charging the city authorities 400 ducats a month plus a supply of food for the crews. The Emperor was concerned that the Venetian merchants might abandon the city in the face of an Ottoman assault and refused to allow them to load their merchandise – a cargo of silk, wax, copper and carmine – onto the galleys lest they flee in the night. Still, some Venetian ships, including six from Candia (Crete, then a Venetian colony) managed to get out, leaving their remaining countrymen to help fortify the palace in anticipation of an attack. A bridge was built between the walled city of Constantinople on one side of the harbour and the enclave of Pera on the other.[7]

The siege proper began on 5 April 1453, by which time, on Barbaro's estimate, Mehmed's troops numbered about 160,000 men. Other accounts put the actual total of fighting men lower, around sixty thousand, up to two-thirds of whom were cavalry.[8] Either way, they wholly outnumbered the people inside. The key for the attackers was to identify the weakest parts of the city walls: from then on it was a matter of bombardment (the Ottoman cannon, which proved decisive, were said to use a thousand pounds of gunpowder a day).[9] There was the occasional skirmish besides; on 20 April the Ottoman fleet attacked some Genoese ships that had been becalmed. The Christians were victorious, beneficiaries of a lucky change in the wind, a victory that Barbaro attributed to their prayers to God. The Turks turned back to focus on the land war and the following day they succeeded in breaching the city walls. Prompt repairs were vital to defending a besieged city and those inside improvised, filling barrels with whatever rubble they could find to reinforce the walls, and digging trenches to provide an extra line of defence. They had not, however, been well prepared, and by the beginning of May the city was beginning to feel the lack of provisions: bread and wine were already running short. There was short-lived relief when overnight a Venetian ship raised the Sultan's flag, dressed its sailors in the Turkish fashion and managed to fool the enemy into allowing them access with supplies. Still, the siege went on. The Ottomans tried to tunnel into the city; the Greeks foiled them. The Ottomans built a tower that topped the walls, and their own bridge made of barrels that stretched across the harbour from Pera to Constantinople itself. Finally, on 29 May, three hours before daybreak, Mehmed ordered his soldiers to begin the assault. The city fell. For Barbaro, this was God's will, but also the fulfilment of an ancient prophecy made to the Emperor Constantine, for whom the city was named. There was now nothing for it but to hope for the mercy of Christ and his Mother.[10]

Barbaro described in horrific detail the Turkish enslavement of Christian prisoners, the looting and the hostage taking, the rape and abuse of women, nuns among them, and then a 'great slaughter of Christians through the city', which left blood flowing 'like rainwater in the gutters after a sudden storm'.[11] Some people tried to swim for freedom; those wealthy Venetian noblemen of Barbaro's acquaintance who were unfortunate enough to be captured were obliged to pay ransoms ranging from 800 to 2,000 ducats. More, perhaps, than anything else, Barbaro's diary gives us a sense of Christian hostility towards the Turks in these years. They were 'faithless' or 'infidel', 'treacherous', 'evil', 'wicked and evil'; the Sultan was an 'evil pagan' and 'a dog'. Particular ire was reserved for the high-ranking Christians in the Sultan's service.[12] Not that the westerners were necessarily much better. The Ottomans had no monopoly on enslaving prisoners of war, nor on wartime cruelty. Barbaro accused the Genoese of being 'enemies of the Christian faith' and 'treacherous dogs' who made a secret deal with the Turks to frustrate Greek and Venetian plans to burn the sultan's fleet.[13] The Genoese countered with their own version of events, one senior official in Pera insisting that he had done everything he could to defend the city, bringing mercenaries from the Mediterranean colony of Chios, as well as from Genoa itself.[14] The rivalry between the Italian city states was never far distant. But as the French diplomat Philippe de Commynes recorded in his memoirs the point was the humiliation: it was 'a great disgrace to all Christendom to suffer that city to be lost'.[15]

For the Ottomans, this was a glorious victory. One historian wrote of 'guns as big as dragons' and described how the soldiers breached the fortress, entered Constantinople, plundered its wealth (they were given licence to loot for three days) and seized its inhabitants for slaves; another wrote of the 'rays of the light of Islam' now falling on the city. Greek refugees fled west in an effort to raise ransoms to free relatives, or for fear of persecution; some returned, while others stayed abroad long-term.[16] Yet trade went on, and the Venetians had an economy to run. They dispatched an envoy to the new rulers, and within a year they and the Ottomans had made peace.[17]

The loss of Constantinople concentrated the minds of the men the Ottoman historians called 'despicable infidels'.[18] The Italian states had been at war among themselves, but faced with such calamity, in 1454 they agreed a peace (the Peace of Lodi), and the following year formed a mutual defence pact known as the Italian League. Pope Pius II (Enea Silvio Piccolomini), a member of a prominent Sienese family who was elected in 1458, spent much of his papacy trying to organise a crusade to recover the lost lands. Pius II was an unexpected sort of pope, whose early career gives an idea of the lifestyle a high-ranking young man might enjoy in these years. He had made his name as a writer of rather amorous poetry and a lover of women. His witty *Memoirs* – whole sections of them in code, the better to conceal his acerbic comments on his adversaries – tell wonderful tales of his travels. Before his rise to the throne of St Peter he had been a diplomat, in which capacity he had visited King James II of Scotland; while on embassy, he recorded, he had turned down a proposition of two young women who had been planning to sleep with him, 'as was the custom of the country'.[19] He had a fondness for the spa baths that his predecessor Nicholas V had had built in the papal city of Viterbo, north of Rome, and used to greet visitors in the garden, accompanied by his lapdog, Musetta. His life and works are immortalised in a stunning fresco series in the Piccolomini Library in Siena's cathedral, which shows him as diplomat, poet laureate, and then pope.

Yet at his death in 1464, Pius' papacy ended in disappointment. In 1459 he had called a congress at Mantua and announced a crusade; he had dispatched legates across Europe to seek support for it, but the European powers were no more than lukewarm at the prospect, and when Pius died, he was waiting at the Adriatic port city of Ancona in the forlorn hope of launching ships. The princes of Europe had more pressing concerns. The French had only just won the Hundred Years War (1337–1453), in which their ruling house of Valois had contended with the English Plantagenets for the right to rule France. Rival branches of the Plantagenet dynasty subsequently fought for power in England in the Wars of the Roses, resolved only with Henry VII's victory over Richard III at the Battle of Bosworth Field in 1485. Spain was not yet unified and had dynastic troubles to navigate before it would be; the Holy Roman Empire's interest lay in defending its eastern borders from Ottoman incursion, and not so much in a naval campaign.

On the other hand, the consequences of the Turkish conquests had undoubtedly stimulating effects for Italian scholarship. There was already a lively interest in the study of Greek in learned circles and Italy provided a home for Greek-speaking refugees like John Argyropoulos, who took up a chair of Latin and Greek at the University of Florence in 1456. Argyropoulos had already spent time in Italy at the Council of Florence (in 1439, which discussed unity between the Eastern and Western churches) and at Padua, but now the peninsula became his home; he was made a citizen of Florence in 1466 and also spent extended periods in Rome.[20] More commonly, educated refugees from the Byzantine Empire found work copying manuscripts or as agents supplying texts for the libraries of elite humanists.[21] Translations of Greek scholarship influenced Columbus, whose notes include references to the work of the ancient Greek geographer Strabo (64/63 BC–AD 24).[22]

In the face of an external threat, for the next forty years there was relative, if not absolute, peace on the Italian peninsula. This became an age of renovation and renewal for the church, and for political stability that allowed merchants to continue capitalising on Italy's geographic position at the crossroads of the Mediterranean; this was, moreover, the middle stage of a Renaissance in the visual arts: the age of artists such as Sandro Botticelli in Florence, of Andrea Mantegna's frescoes for the *Camera degli Sposi* in Mantua, and the restoration of the Sistine Chapel (its wall paintings, though not its ceiling, were complete by 1482). This had followed the earlier work of painters including Giotto (1267–1337), whose innovations had included the development of more lifelike figures, emphasising the importance of observation, of conveying emotion and of techniques such as foreshortening to convey a sense of depth.

The artistic efforts of the Renaissance benefited from economic developments in Italy, and in particular from the growing disposable income of a new wealthy class of merchants. There is much debate about how to judge the economic performance of the Italian states in the later fifteenth century and through the sixteenth. In 1300, Italy had been the most advanced economic area of Europe, notable for the number of its towns and cities. From 1500, however, while in absolute terms the Italian states still made economic progress, their growth did not keep up with the most dynamic regions of Europe (initially Flanders, the Rhineland and Castile, later England and the Netherlands). Besides the impact of war, the political division of Italy was a factor here: there was no obvious reason for an Italian city state to cooperate with others on the peninsula when there were greater opportunities to be found by working with the larger foreign powers. Italian unification was still three and a half centuries away.[23]

Italy was covered by a patchwork of political regimes and wider European power struggles over Italian territory were nothing new. In the south, the kingdom of Naples was ruled by a line of princes from the kingdom of Aragon, in north-eastern Spain. From 1268 to 1435 it had been under the control of the Angevins or house of Anjou (a dynasty related to the kings of France) who maintained a claim to Naples that would become important as the Italian Wars began in the 1490s. However, the last of the Angevin rulers, Queen Giovanna (r. 1414–1435), had fallen out with the realm's barons and adopted Alfonso V of Aragon as her heir (before unadopting him a decade later, when they in turn fell out). This did not prevent Alfonso pressing ahead with a claim to the kingdom after her death. He had a rival in René d'Anjou, but despite enjoying support from the pope and other Italian states, not to mention a share of the local barons, René's claim was thwarted largely because until 1438 he was held prisoner by the duke of Burgundy. Alfonso's fleet was defeated by the Genoese, commercial rivals to Naples and the Aragonese in the Mediterranean, but thanks to a nifty deal with Milan against the French he secured power in Naples by 1442, becoming King Alfonso I; he made a triumphal entry in to the city the following year. He found praise from Florentine writer Vespasiano da Bisticci, who commented on 'his extraordinary compassion and kindness joined to exceeding liberality' and 'the integrity and justice with which he treated all his subjects, small as well as great';[24] he was regarded as pious and became known as 'Alfonso the Magnanimous'. By the time of his death in 1458, his rule had been carefully secured thanks to judicious delegation of power to the barons (power being what barons liked), and a diplomatic deal that secured papal recognition.[25] Yet, he had also stored up problems for the future. He had been rather fickle in his foreign alliances and in buying off the barons he had equipped them with the means to challenge his successor, King Ferrante.

After an initial scrap with the popes for recognition of his rule, Ferrante was recognised by Pius II as king of Naples and Jerusalem (the latter title a relic of the eleventh-century Crusader conquest of the city). After half a dozen years of conflict with a group of Neapolitan barons who supported rival claimant John of Anjou (drawing in Milan, the Papacy, Aragon and Albania) he had established himself in power. During his reign from 1458 to 1494 he built a splendid court in the city, which became a home to poets and artists, although he never acquired the cultural reputation of a Lorenzo the Magnificent or an Isabella d'Este,[26] perhaps because less of Naples' early building survives for modern visitors, who make their way instead through its baroque palaces or down to the ruins of Pompeii and the picture-postcard Amalfi coast. Yet this was a spectacular Renaissance court and prominent citizens of Naples included the humanist Lorenzo Valla, one of the debunkers of the Donation of Constantine. No less than Florence or Venice, Naples could produce 'Renaissance men' like Ferrante's chief minister Giovanni Gioviano Pontano, memorialised in the Borgia apartment frescoes, a distinguished poet and scholar besides his political roles.[27]

Ferrante survived the challenge of pretenders to the throne, and extended a range of privileges to the realm's towns to provide an alternative power base to the barons.[28] Indeed, by 1471 a history of Naples could make the case for its superiority to all other cities with its mountains, plains, sea and waters; its walls, streets, houses, churches and fountains; its fine nobility.[29] The pope was overlord of Naples, and Ferrante owed him tribute, which could be substantial or token depending on the political situation, but the king secured his interests in Rome by offering *condotte* (contracts for the supply of mercenary troops) to selected Roman barons, which meant that for the period of the contract at least he could use them as a threat against the popes.[30] Ferrante acquired a brutal reputation as a ruler. In response to a barons' conspiracy in 1485 he had the participants arrested during a wedding at the Castel Nuovo and subsequently murdered in jail; whether or not it is true that he had his enemies embalmed and their mummies on display in a museum, he certainly struck contemporaries as a nasty piece of work. Philippe de Commynes wrote that 'no man had ever been more cruel' than Alfonso II, Ferrante's son, 'nor more wicked, nor more vicious and vile', but that Ferrante himself had been more dangerous still.[31]

If the king had been establishing a dynasty, Ferrante's neighbours to the north, the popes, were re-establishing one after decades of schism with a campaign of renovation and renewal of both the city of Rome and the Church that aimed to restore them to their proper glory.[32] Over the course of the later fifteenth century, Rome became ever more a European centre. Representatives of Christian rulers lived and worked there, seeing to church business. On occasion they handled secular business too. The popes at first resisted long-term embassies, but gradually accommodated to them so that by the turn of the fifteenth to the sixteenth century Rome was clearly the major diplomatic centre of Europe, attracting ambassadors from Western and Eastern states, from Muscovy in the north, and from Ethiopia. Domestically, too, a pope's concerns were not only religious. As ruler of one of Italy's five large states his lands provided him with resources, but they also made him a temporal ruler with all the usual challenges of government: maintaining social order, ensuring taxes were paid, and if need be raising armies to defend his territory. In that sense he was a monarch very much like those of Milan and Naples. Moreover, with the exception of the Aragonese Pope Calixtus III (r. 1455–1458), the fifteenth-century popes were Italian, and their elections a matter of Italian politicking. Calixtus' successor Pius II was followed by Paul II (Pietro Barbo), a Venetian; then Sixtus IV (Francesco della Rovere,) of Liguria; and Innocent VIII (Innocenzo Cibo), of Genoa. The parties in the curia (or papal court) were fluid but tended to align with one or other large foreign power, either France or the Holy Roman Empire. Within Rome itself two principal families, the Orsini and the Colonna, were also important players. Over the course of the fifteenth century, the curia became increasingly dominated by Italian families, and more aristocratic, as the small states of Italy secured their representation.[33] The Gonzaga, rulers of Mantua, obtained for one of their sons an appointment as cardinal in 1461, as did the Este of Ferrara in 1493. The tradition of ensuring posts in the College of Cardinals for non-Italian nations rather dwindled during this period, and a new fashion arose: the appointment of papal nephews, known from the Italian *nepote* (meaning nephew or grandson) as 'nepotism'.

Outside the aristocracy, Italian families on the rise likewise sought curia positions for their sons, and marriage alliances with papal families for their daughters. The most starry among them were the Medici who, three generations before, had made their fortune as bankers to the popes. The founder of the family, Giovanni di Bicci de' Medici, had built a power base in Florence thanks to wealth from the wool trade and banking, though the family did not lack for challengers. In 1433 opponents managed, through political manoeuvres, to force Giovanni's son Cosimo ('Cosimo the Elder') into a short exile, but the Medici emerged to establish themselves as the republic's first family (though not as yet hereditary lords). In 1440, Florence beat Milan at the Battle of Anghiari, an iconic victory in confirming the city state's power. Being banker to the pope – or to royalty – was a role that might bring wealth but also brought considerable risks. In 1478, Giovanni di Bicci's great-grandson, Lorenzo the Magnificent, fell out with Pope Sixtus IV. By this time, the Medici and their allies were increasingly reliant on their role in city government for power, as their banking fortunes floundered. In response, they strengthened their grip on the city's institutions. They set up special committees to vet candidates for office, and used military emergencies to justify creating structures that functioned outside the normal rules, relying to maintain their power on a network of allies and increasingly dubious tactics of candidate selection whenever an election came along.

Opposition to the Medici was wide: from other, rival, oligarchs who sought to replace them at the helm of Florentine politics; from the lower classes. It was not surprising, then, that at this time their opponents, chief among them the Pazzi family, looked to overthrow the regime by conspiracy and murder. Their hand was strengthened by the backing of Pope Sixtus IV, who was in conflict with the Medici over a deal to purchase the city of Imola. Yet while the conspirators succeeded in murdering Giuliano de' Medici, Lorenzo's brother, at Mass in Florence's cathedral, their hopes of killing Lorenzo too were dashed. Sixtus had hoped the Pazzi Conspiracy would be followed by a Neapolitan attack on Florence. Lorenzo, however, circumvented that with a spectacular piece of personal diplomacy: he sailed to Naples and convinced King Ferrante not to go ahead. Florence and Naples settled for some years into a political alliance and Lorenzo followed the other ruling families of Italy in seeking representation in Rome, securing the election of his son Giovanni to the cardinalate. Giovanni, who at thirteen was well below the canonical age for such an appointment, went on to become Pope Leo X.

The Sforza of Milan, another dynasty on the rise, also got their cardinal.[34] Ascanio Sforza was promoted in 1484. He was the brother of Galeazzo Maria Sforza, duke of Milan, whose assassination in 1476 (at the age of thirty-two) probably inspired the Pazzi conspirators in Florence. Dynastic states were all very well, but dynasties were peculiarly susceptible to the mortality of their rulers. At the time of Ascanio's appointment the duchy was held by his teenage nephew, Gian Galeazzo, while the cardinal's brother Ludovico 'il Moro' acted as regent. In the words of the sixteenth-century Florentine historian Francesco Guicciardini, Ludovico was a 'restless and ambitious' man, and the arrangement would explode into conflict ten years on.[35]

Alongside these five large states were the numerous small states of Italy: principalities like the marquisates of Mantua and Monferrato and the duchies of Ferrara and Urbino; republics like Genoa and the Tuscan city states of Siena and Lucca. As the Milanese objections to Frederick's coronation show, the relations between these states were complex and often hostile. Most historians now are rather sceptical about the claim of Guicciardini, who wrote with hindsight that 'Italy had never enjoyed such prosperity, or known so favourable a situation as that in which it found itself so securely at rest in the year of our Christian salvation 1490, and the years immediately before and after'. Besides the 1478 wobble in Florence after the Pazzi Conspiracy there had been the Ottoman incursion of 1480 (see Chapter Three) and the Salt War of 1482–4, a conflict between the papacy, backed by Venice, and the duchy of Ferrara. Guicciardini was a Florentine statesman who also served in the papal administration, and one of most important historians of the early Italian Wars. His rosy view of the fifteenth century and an Italy that 'deservedly enjoyed amongst all other nations a most brilliant reputation' only serves to underline the deterioration of the ensuing years.[36] Nonetheless, the image has persisted, and it is fair to say that the conflicts of the fifteenth century were substantially smaller-scale than the wars that were to come.

Chapter Two

Beyond the Alps

Guicciardini speaks of 'Italy' in his history, which may surprise us, given that Italy was not unified as a nation until the later nineteenth century. It is certainly the case that the people of the peninsula might have had a strong identification with their home village, town or city: what is known even today as *campanilismo* or allegiance to the local bell-tower. But in the context of the Italian Wars of the sixteenth century, and in terms of what we might call 'national character', it is common to find references in the literature and letters of the period to Italians (and indeed also to Germans, who likewise did not have a unified political nation-state until the nineteenth century). If this was an affirmation of identity, it was perhaps as much a negative as a positive one: a way of distinguishing those on the Italian peninsula from the barbarians to the north, known as 'ultramontani' or 'those from beyond the mountains'.

Plenty of Italians ventured beyond the mountains, of course. One of the most famous portraits of a fifteenth-century Italian was painted not in Italy at all, but in Flanders. It shows Giovanni Arnolfini, a merchant from Lucca living in Bruges, and Giovanna Cenami his wife, standing in a richly furnished chamber, greeting guests who can just be glimpsed in the mirror behind them. The artist, Jan van Eyck (*c.*1390–1441), was court painter to Philip the Good, duke of Burgundy. The Arnolfini portrait is a very early example of European oil painting (most panel works of this period were painted in tempera), and an early secular portrait too; it is notable for the artist's prominent signature, which ensures his identity is clear. His fate is not to be labelled 'the Master of the Arnolfini Portrait', as an earlier painter might have been: van Eyck will be remembered by name. His reflection may even appear in the mirror which, like the splendid chandelier, allows van Eyck to play with the effects of light from the window (the glass itself testimony to the wealth of the pair). Between the rich fur of Arnolfini's gown, the fine lace of Cenami's headdress, her gold necklace and the splendid red fabric of the bed-curtains, this is a commission that in its drapery and detail drips not only with artistic innovation but also with mercantile pride.

Lucca, the home city of the Arnolfini and Cenami, lay about fifty miles west of Florence. It was an independent city state, in that it had its own government and ran its own affairs; at the time the painting was completed, in 1434, its citizens were no doubt hearing news of the turmoil facing their larger neighbour as the Medici contended for rulership of the city. Giovanni and Giovanna, however, were hundreds of miles away, their families well established in Bruges; the Cenami had been there for half a century. They played their part in the local Lucchese networks: foreign merchants across Europe in this period arranged themselves into 'nations', community organisations that negotiated collectively with the host city on their duties and privileges. Back in Lucca, their relatives held high office: Giovanni was related on his mother's side to the Guinigi, Lucca's ruling family. Both he and Giovanna had a grandfather who had held the prestigious city post of Gonfaloniere (standard-bearer) of Justice. These merchants traded all manner of goods: from buttons and ribbons, cheap and accessible for purchase by a wide section of society, to luxurious cloth of gold and silver, velvets, furs and satins, and desirable food imports such as almonds, oranges and ginger. Others of Giovanna's relatives were bankers in Paris, Antwerp and Bruges; before the Medici opened their own Bruges branch in 1436, they had entrusted their affairs there to Lucchese bankers. Indeed, art historians speculate on the symbolism of Giovanna's green dress in relation to banking: green cloth adorned bankers' tables (the word *bank* comes from the Italian *banco* for stall or bench, the table from which bankers did their business in the market or street).[1] Giovanni would become a leading supplier of silks to the Burgundian court in the decades after this picture was painted.[2] There are traces of their extra-European trade networks in the portrait, in the glimpse of Turkish carpet, a fashionable commodity for fifteenth-century Italians, typically imported from the Ottoman Empire. (In some Western museums today a tradition persists of categorising Turkish carpets not by their origins but by the names of the artists who depicted each type,[3] the celebrity of the painters trumping the identity of the artisans who produced the textiles in the first place, testament to the biases of art collection and classification.) This is, in short, not only a painting full of artistic marvels but one that tells a story of continental merchant networks, of trade, and of families far from their roots and the importance of marriage alliances among the Italian elite. A story of Italy in the fifteenth century is not only a story of the Italian peninsula, but a story that stretches across Europe and beyond.

The painting's fate is instructive too: it ended up in the collection of the Habsburg grande dame Margaret of Austria, before passing to Mary of Hungary.[4] Both women had their courts in the Low Countries where in the fifteenth century the small state of Burgundy (incorporating parts of what are now Belgium, the Netherlands, Luxembourg, Germany and France) had grown into a spectacular cultural centre. It was, moreover, enjoying a distinctive northern Renaissance with leading artists including not only van Eyck but his contemporary Rogier van der Weyden and later Hieronymous Bosch and Pieter Bruegel the Elder. Their style was artistically very different from the Renaissance fashions developing in Italy, but it was just as innovative: Italy was far from the only source of cultural developments in this period. The Burgundian court was a significant source of ideas about chivalry, warfare and princely patronage, and the Italian Wars became something of a melting pot, in which its culture (and others of Western Europe) mixed with those of the Italian peninsula.[5] The Holy Roman Emperor Charles V, who came to power in 1519 and would be one of the great protagonists of those wars, was himself descended from the Burgundian dukes. We are accustomed to think of Italian Renaissance trends being exported to the rest of Europe – and they were – but other ideas were imported to Italy too. Flemish musicians, for example, proved hugely in demand at the Italian courts.

Meanwhile, as the Ottomans took Constantinople, the Hundred Years War between England and France was coming to an end. France had won: England had lost the vast bulk of its French territory and was left with only a toehold on the Continent in the form of Calais. Conflict between the houses of York and Lancaster ensued in the Wars of the Roses, finally settled only when Henry Tudor came to power in 1485. The new Henry VII ensured his claim to the throne was recognised by Pope Innocent VIII, sending an embassy to Rome for the purpose. In 1492 he and Charles VIII of France signed the Treaty of Étaples, with which Charles agreed to end his backing for Perkin Warbeck, a pretender to the English throne, and to offer a generous pension in return for Henry's promise not to invade France.[6] The English court was more directly influenced by developments in Burgundy than by Italian fashions, but it was in the fifteenth century that we see the first significant humanist patron in the person of Humphrey, duke of Gloucester (1390–1447). Through his connection with an Italian bishop of Bayeux, Zano Castiglione, Duke Humphrey corresponded with luminaries of the Italian Renaissance including Leonardo Bruni, chancellor of Florence. He is memorialised today by his library in Oxford. The early Tudors also had Italian cultural and trading connections. Henry VII's tomb was sculpted by a Florentine, Pietro Torrigiano, and significant numbers of English students attended Italian universities, particularly Padua: while numbers there dropped following Henry VIII's break with Rome they were already picking up before the accession of his Catholic daughter Mary and continued on a more modest scale even after her Protestant sister Elizabeth came to power.[7] So far as the Italian Wars were concerned, the major English interventions (occasional subsidies aside) were invasions in the north of France that served to pull troops away from the peninsula.

Having seen off the English claims, by the mid fifteenth century France was the greatest of the European states; its ruler at the time of that triumph, Charles VII, could justly call himself 'the Victorious'. By 1500 it had a population of some fifteen million, notably higher than the eleven million who lived in Italy and almost four times the 3.75 million in England and Wales; Spain, by comparison, had 6.5 million. Charles was succeeded in 1461 by his son Louis XI, 'the Prudent', who ruled until 1483. After the death of Charles the Bold of Burgundy at the Battle of Nancy (1477), his line became extinct, and Louis contrived to seize Burgundian territory. There was further consolidation under his successor, Charles VIII, whose marriage to Anne of Brittany (a dubious business, since she was already contracted to marry the Holy Roman Emperor) was a step on the way to incorporating the duchy of Brittany into France. And Charles, as we will

see, had ambitions in Italy, specifically to revive the old French claim
to the kingdom of Naples.

Spain was consolidating too: with the marriage of Ferdinand of
Aragon to Isabella of Castile in 1469 and the slow union of their
kingdoms that followed, it started to take on its modern shape. Isabella
had come to power against considerable odds. Only after first a
half-brother and then a brother had died had she come into the line
of succession; even then her rise was challenged by a niece, Juana 'la
Beltraneja', with a solid claim to the Castilian throne. Isabella and her
allies threw doubt on Juana's legitimacy and – after a long campaign
– succeeded in cloistering her in a convent. In 1478, with licence from
Pope Sixtus IV, she established an Inquisition in Castile. It initially
focused on heresy among Andalusian *conversos* (Christians who had
converted from Judaism) but subsequently acquired a much wider
Christianising remit.[8] In later years the Spanish Inquisition would
become a byword for persecution, although some of this reputation
is attributable to the subsequent 'Black Legend' of Spain (a myth that
the Spanish were innately cruel and which linked that to their alleged
non-Christian roots). It should not be inferred that the Spanish were
worse than any other nation.[9] It was more a matter of opportunity:
what was distinctive about Spain in the European context was the
historic size of its non-Christian populations, and the way that its
Christian rulers Ferdinand and Isabella pursued an active policy of
Christianisation as they sought to unite the realm. The 1492 expulsion
of the Jews was preceded by a long campaign against Jewish influence
in Spain that was a part of this strategy and, as we have seen, was
accompanied by another conquest of land: the region of Granada,
the southernmost part of Spain. Territorial expansionism was nothing
unusual in Europe; nor indeed was the significance of Christianity in
ideologies of conquest (the Crusades being a case in point). In the
sixteenth century the Spanish monarchs also went on to conquer much
of Navarre, which lay on their border with France.

Spain's neighbour Portugal was building an empire, too. For much
of the fifteenth century it sought to conquer Morocco; its merchants
raided the Canary Islands for slaves in competition with Castile. In
the face of Castilian superiority, the Portuguese switched their
interest to Madeira and the Azores, which were uninhabited, establishing colonies to which farmers and fishermen chose to migrate

and enslaved people were forcibly transported. Italians, and especially the Genoese, played important roles in this early colonisation,[10] which was largely motivated by a desire to find both labour and a source of gold that avoided trade with North African enemies or payments to Ottoman or Mamluk middlemen (on the Mamluks, see below). In the 1450s, Portuguese explorers established trading posts in West Africa and acquired an effective monopoly on the seaborne trade in enslaved Africans. The right of the Portuguese to enslave non-Christians had been secured in 1452 with a papal bull from Nicholas V;[11] the process was justified by the prospect of conversion. There had long been a slave trade in the Mediterranean: Genoese merchants had a central role in importing enslaved people to Italy from the Black Sea ports. The Portuguese expansion, however, laid the groundwork for what became the transatlantic slave trade. Portuguese traders went east, too, rounding the Cape of Good Hope in 1498 to reach the Indian Ocean. There, gunpowder weapons enabled them to become the dominant maritime power; in 1509 they beat an allied Mamluk–Gujarati fleet at the Battle of Diu.[12] The Portuguese benefited from the Chinese abandonment of exploration and trading in the Indian Ocean and on the east coast of Africa after the last voyage of Zheng He in 1433. So determined were Chinese court opponents of the expansionist strategy that in 1525 the government had all ocean-going ships destroyed.

The most famous Italian traveller to China was Marco Polo (1254–1324), whose tales of his journey, the *Books of the Marvels of the World*, brought a new level of knowledge of China to Europeans. The single largest state in the world, China had been ruled by the Ming dynasty since 1368 via a centralised civil service on a scale unknown in Europe. Its goods travelled to Italy along the Silk Roads, effectively controlled by the Ottoman Empire. Silk was not the only commodity to travel. So did lapis lazuli; so did precious stones and hand-crafted carpets, to arrive in households like that of the Arnolfini. The influence of Islamic art in particular can be seen clearly in the architecture of Venice and in the colourful maiolica ceramics produced in Italy, not to mention in numerous paintings depicting saints in cloaks of luxurious imported textiles, or in portraits where carpets are laid on the sitter's table. These international trade links were essential to the development of Italian Renaissance art and craft.[13]

African history from the twelfth to the sixteenth century was characterised by three major trends. First, there was an expansion of Islam;
second, thanks in part to the networks that the wider Islamic world
offered, there was an expansion of trade in commodities including
gold, ivory and agricultural produce, as well as in enslaved people.
Third, kingdoms and empires rose: the Mamluk Empire, from 1250,
was centred on Egypt, and benefited from its location on the pilgrim
routes to Jerusalem and Mecca. In West Africa, the kingdom of Mali
was superseded by the Songhai Empire in the late fifteenth century;
other key centres included Benin and Zimbabwe, where there was an
important royal capital. Besides trade on the new Portuguese routes,
Italian contacts with Africa in this period arose primarily in relation to
its Ethiopian Christians. There were Ethiopians living in Rome at the
church of San Stefano degli Abissini, and Italians at the court of the
Ethiopian emperor in Barata.[14] Beyond the documented history, North
Africa was a short sail across the Mediterranean from southern Italy,
the sort of trip that could be done in a fishing boat, and no doubt
many people made the crossing without leaving any trace in the records.
One who did was a man named Giovanni the Ethiopian or Zuan Bianco
('Bianco', which means 'white', was probably an ironic nickname;
around the same time another black man, at the English court, went
by the name of John Blanke). Described by the writer Marin Sanudo
as 'a most valiant Saracen', Zuan was killed in Venetian service in the
1490s and his widow awarded a house in Verona and a generous pension
of 72 ducats a year (significantly more than a skilled worker's wage).[15]

Then there were parts of the world about which Europeans still
knew almost nothing, even if an occasional gift might make its way
along the trade routes. A white cockatoo travelled from Australasia
(most likely Indonesia) to the court of the Emperor Frederick II in
Sicily as a gift of the 'Sultan of Babylon' and is shown in a manuscript
of the 1240s,[16] though there was no European map of the period on
which its owner might have placed its origin. Much of the knowledge
fifteenth-century Italians had of India came not from eyewitnesses but
from the accounts of classical writers such as Pliny the Elder (AD
23–79), whose *Natural History*, incorporating accounts of life in Africa
and Asia, was one of the first classical texts to appear in a printed
edition, in 1469. More unknown still to Europeans were the Aztec and
Inca civilisations of the Americas.

Central and Eastern Europe were more familiar. On the borders of the Holy Roman Empire, Matthias Corvinus, king of Hungary from 1458 to 1490, and his wife Beatrice of Aragon (daughter of King Ferdinand I of Naples), whom he married in 1476, established another important centre for the arts. Numerous Italians followed Beatrice to Hungary, among them Bernardo Vespucci,[17] brother to Amerigo, after whom America was named. The Italians also traded with the Grand Duchy of Muscovy but the relationship was looser than with Western European states because of the lack of a direct tie with Rome. The Orthodox Church had split with the western Roman Catholic Church in the Great Schism of the eleventh century after multiple controversies between the two churches, so there was not the same need for Eastern Europeans to engage with Rome as there was for the rulers, bishops and pilgrims of the West. On the other hand, there was demand for luxury furs from Muscovy, which were supplied via Novgorod (south of the future St Petersburg and connected by river to the Baltic Sea), as well as other forest commodities, particularly wax and honey.[18] Yet not all of what we now think of as Eastern Europe was Orthodox: Poland, for example, then and now was Catholic; likewise Hungary and Bohemia. Lithuania had officially adopted Christianity as recently as 1387. Hungary was not the only court to attract an Italian bride: in 1518 Bona Sforza of Milan married the king of Poland-Lithuania.

Squeezed between the Habsburg and Ottoman Empires, Hungary's position would become precarious as both empires sought to expand and its own nobility played off one against the other. Indeed, the Ottomans put pressure on all their neighbours, including the Mamluks, who had dominated Egypt for centuries, and the Safavid (Persian) Empire, on the Ottomans' eastern front. No less than the western princes, the Ottoman rulers saw military expansion as fundamental to kingship, and a generation after the conquest of Constantinople, their empire was the dominant political force in the Eastern Mediterranean and the Balkans. In 1480, Mehmed II, having captured the old eastern capital of the Roman Empire twenty-eight years before, now set his sights on the western one: Rome itself.

In the summer of that year, with apparent agreement from Venice not to intervene, his forces invaded Puglia and succeeded in occupying the town of Otranto, which lies at the very tip of Italy's heel, across the sea from what is now Albania. Otranto's location at the entrance to the Adriatic was strategically important and its invasion matters to the story of Italy in these years because it illustrates first that the prospect of Turkish invasion was no idle threat but a practical reality, and second, why it prompted such alarm among Italians. Otranto fell on 11 August 1480 to an army led by Gedik Ahmed Pasha, and such was the fear in Rome that Pope Sixtus IV started planning an evacuation to the city of Avignon in southern France. The Ottomans held Otranto for a year, but what became inscribed in collective memory were two infamous atrocities. The first was the murder of the city's archbishop, Stefano Pendinelli, at the high altar of the cathedral. (The Pazzi Conspiracy in Florence, two years before, had involved murder in a cathedral too, but when committed by the 'infidel' the symbolism was very different.) The second was the massacre on Monte Minerva in which eight hundred townspeople were killed for their refusal to convert to Islam. For a year Duke Alfonso of Calabria, son of the king of Naples, besieged the city. In the end it was not so much Italian military strategy that enabled the recapture of Otranto in September 1481, nor the Hungarian force sent for relief, but rather the political confusion in Constantinople that had followed the death of Mehmed II at the age of around fifty, four months earlier.[19] Otranto's most important legacy was, in fact, the myth that grew up around it. The eight hundred murdered Christians were beatified as martyrs in 1771 and canonised in 2013, an indication of their continuing symbolism in Italy, in the Catholic faith, and in wider narratives about a 'clash of civilisations' between Christianity and Islam.[20]

The late fifteenth-century scholar Laura Cereta was unusual in her dissension from the mainstream narrative of Italian writers, who typically urged readers to fight the Turks. Although in her public letters she discussed the Ottoman outrages, she pointed too to the impact of Italian military misconduct on women, who were vulnerable to rape and murder for resisting.[21] In fact, for the most part populations in areas conquered by the Ottoman Empire made no great statement of principle against their conquerors. Prior to the conquest of Constantinople the Byzantine first minister Loukas Notaras is said to have observed: 'Rather the Turkish turban than a Roman cardinal's hat.'[22] For all the rhetoric, when it came to real life, people swapped sides. Many of the men labelled 'Turks' by the Italians were in fact from the Balkans. Like their Italian counterparts they were motivated as much by the prospect of booty as any religious consideration when it came to their treatment of civilians; the same might be said of the Hungarian relievers of Otranto.[23]

Thus at the end of the fifteenth century, the Italian peninsula was home to rich trading powers with leading positions in the economy of Europe and links far beyond. It was, however, vulnerable not only to incursions from the east, but to the claims of monarchs from the north and west. In 1494, the temptation to exploit one such claim would tip Italy into more than six decades of war.

Chapter Three

1494: *The French Descent*

In 1494, Leonardo da Vinci was working in Milan for the city's ruler Ludovico Sforza, where among his tasks was the production of a spectacular sculpture: an equestrian monument to Francesco Sforza, Ludovico's father and the first of his house to rule Milan. The size of it alone posed huge technical challenges, and Leonardo's notebooks show how he planned to tackle the problems of first casting the bronze and then removing the cast from its mould. In 1493 he had completed a model of the sculpture for the wedding celebrations of Ludovico's niece Bianca Maria Sforza and the Holy Roman Emperor Maximilian, but there were doubts about whether the casting could even be done, and indeed whether Leonardo even intended to finish it. He had been established in Milan since 1482, when he had visited on a peace mission from Florence, and got himself head-hunted by the appreciative Sforza. He had been thirty at the time, and a master in the Guild of St Luke (the guild of artists and doctors of medicine) for ten years. 'The greatest gifts', wrote Giorgio Vasari, 'are often seen, in the course of nature, rained by celestial influences on human creatures; and sometimes, in supernatural fashion, beauty, grace and talent are united beyond measure in one single person.'[1] Vasari, whose *Lives of the Artists* is a founding text of western art history, was looking back on the career of Leonardo da Vinci from a vantage point later in the century, and his description of Leonardo as an almost super-human genius has stuck.

Leonardo had been born some four decades earlier, in 1452, in a small town called Vinci which lay in Florentine territory, the illegitimate son of a notary, Ser Piero, and an orphaned teenager, Caterina di Meo Lippi.[2] He had been apprenticed at the age of fourteen to the leading Florentine artist Andrea del Verrocchio (who had also supervised the work of Ghirlandaio, Perugino and Botticelli). Leonardo had gained guild recognition as a master in his trade by 1472, and collaborated with his teacher on a very beautiful *Annunciation*. The later 1470s, however, saw both personal and political troubles. In 1476 Leonardo, along with three others, was charged with sodomy, but the case was not pursued and the incident did not harm his career. There is no recorded detail of Leonardo's subsequent sexual relationships, which suggests he learned caution or discretion or both. (The accusation he faced was far from unusual: the police records show that the majority of men in later fifteenth-century Florence had or were denounced for having sex with other men on at least one occasion.[3]) Political troubles came in the turbulent months following the Pazzi Conspiracy of 1478: in December of that year Leonardo sketched the hanged corpse of one of the conspirators, Bernardo di Bandino Baroncelli.[4] All in all, a move to Milan may well have been attractive, and many of Leonardo's most famous works were completed in his years there, including the *Virgin of the Rocks* and his celebrated *Last Supper* for the refectory of the Dominican friars at Santa Maria delle Grazie. Leonardo was not only a painter: he worked on architectural designs for the duomo in Milan, produced many ephemeral works for Ludovico's public festivals and studied with the geographer Paolo Toscanelli, whose work was also familiar to Columbus.[5] Indeed, his appointment to Milan had been preceded by his writing a ten-point letter setting out his skills, in which points one to nine focused on the 'secrets' he might bring having 'considered the proofs of all those who count themselves masters and inventors of instruments of war'. These included plans for bridges, for sieges, for bombardment, mortars, secret passages, covered cars (effectively tanks), cannon, mortars and light ordnance, catapults and 'other engines of wonderful efficacy'. Only in point ten did he add that in peacetime he could 'give perfect satisfaction' in architecture and canal design, and that he could also contribute sculpture and painting. Moreover, he could take the bronze horse in hand.[6] As it happened, the argument over the horse's feasibility was never settled, because when war broke out the bronze intended for the statue was diverted to Ludovico's father-in-law, Ercole d'Este, duke of Ferrara, to make cannon: as we will see, the Este dukes were prominent in military experimentation.

Leonardo, however, had had good reason to emphasise his military skills. As with so many conflicts, the Italian Wars of 1494–1559 began with an apparently small disagreement. We saw in Chapter One how the rulers of Milan and Naples had united in 1442 to oppose French military ambitions in Italy – particularly the long-standing claim of the house of Anjou to the kingdom of Naples. For Milan the next fifty years proved torrid ones. Milan was the northernmost of the great Italian cities and, like so many of them, had once been a Roman centre. It had been a duchy since the end of the twelfth century but when in 1447 the last of the Visconti dukes, Filippo Maria, died, the city opted to continue without a lord, and its artisans enjoyed a rare degree of political influence in the Ambrosian Republic (so named for Milan's patron saint Ambrose, who according to legend had been elected bishop by popular acclaim). The republic, however, did not last, and after three years Francesco Sforza, husband of Filippo Maria's illegitimate daughter Bianca Maria, succeeded in establishing himself as duke. Such contests, setting the desire of citizens for broader-based regimes against the preference of rulers for tighter control, were a motif of Italian politics through the fifteenth and sixteenth centuries, from the popes trying to see off the threat of councils to the continued struggles for liberty in Florence and Siena.

The Sforza regime found it hard to maintain its grip after the death of its founder. The notorious cruelty of the second duke, Galeazzo Maria, who inherited in 1466, proved a factor in his assassination ten years later, and his son Gian Galeazzo became duke at the age of just seven. After a struggle for power Ludovico Sforza, Gian Galeazzo's uncle, eventually ousted the boy's mother, Bona of Savoy, to become regent. As Gian Galeazzo approached adulthood, however, Ludovico's influence began to wane. In 1489, aged nineteen, Gian Galeazzo married his cousin Isabella of Naples, granddaughter of King Ferrante, and (on Commynes' account at least) a 'very courageous' young lady, whose husband by contrast was a 'weak prince'. Despite Gian Galeazzo's shortcomings, the match secured Neapolitan backing for him to rule in Milan, which was bad news for his uncle. Ludovico turned to the French for backing, dispatching an embassy to Paris to persuade Charles VIII that the time was right to assert the French Crown's long-standing claim to Naples against Gian Galeazzo's in-laws.[7]

It was not the first time a regent had ambitions to rule in his own right, nor was it the first time that a larger power took advantage of dissension within a ruling family. The situation was complicated further by conflict between Ferrante and Pope Innocent (to the extent that Innocent at one point in 1489 declared Ferrante deposed as ruler of Naples in favour of Charles VIII of France) and by negotiations between Milan and France over Genoa.[8]

There were good economic reasons for French acquisitiveness over Italian territory and over Naples in particular. Italy was an agricultural producer; her port towns served the trading centre of Europe: the Mediterranean, with its connections south and east. Naples had grown substantially in the fifteenth century as smaller Italian towns declined in size.[9] With a population of over 150,000, it was the Italian peninsula's largest city.[10] Royal pride and chivalry were adequate reasons for conquest, but there might be good financial motives for territorial expansion too, and with ancient claims lingering in the memory of European monarchs they could easily be dusted off to provide an excuse for invasion.

In 1491, as Ludovico Sforza negotiated for a French alliance, Innocent VIII decided to settle his differences with Ferrante, and the king of Naples finally received papal recognition. The death of Lorenzo de' Medici in 1492 added a new layer of tension to these manoeuvrings, as his son Piero confirmed that the Medici family's friendship (and by extension that of Florence) lay with Naples, which in turn left Ludovico further isolated in Milan. The election of Rodrigo Borgia as Pope Alexander VI should have reassured the Milanese that a political equalibrium could be maintained (a key ally in the conclave had been Cardinal Ascanio Sforza, Ludovico's brother). However, the new pope promptly fell out with the Neapolitans over an apparent attempt by Ferrante to strengthen his influence in the Papal States, and offered discreet backing to the French claim to Naples, effectively inviting an invasion. In short, there was no single political factor in the 1490s that accounted for the events of 1494. The death of Lorenzo de' Medici might have reconfigured matters a little, but that was only one part of a larger set of changes in the delicate balance of power between the Italian states, where even marginal shifts of policy might tip the peninsula into war. And in fact the events of 1492 would affect the situation in other ways, too: though no one knew it at the time, New

World wealth, expropriated in the years following Columbus's voyage west, would turn out to be enormously important in financing the coming wars.

That was Italy. But what of the invader? Guicciardini's verdict on the character of Charles VIII, king of France, was predictably harsh: the king lacked learning; he 'knew not how to preserve either majesty or authority' with his courtiers; he tended to impulsiveness; he was 'liberal but inconsiderate', and 'if anything appeared in him worthy of praise, if thoroughly examined, it was yet farther from virtue than vice'.[11] Charles was twenty-four when he embarked on his first campaign in France. He had come to the throne at the age of thirteen; his elder sister and her husband had acted (in practice, though not officially) as regents until he came of age in 1491, seeing off an attempt by Charles' cousin, Louis of Orléans, to replace him. As we saw in Chapter Two, his father Louis XI had begun the process of consolidating France with seizures of Burgundian territory; under Charles that had continued with an invasion of the duchy of Brittany and his marriage to Anne, its heiress. This effectively incorporated the duchy into France but it won Charles no favour with the Habsburg rulers of the Holy Roman Empire: Anne had been meant to marry the Emperor Maximilian, and in order to wed her himself Charles had ditched plans for his own marriage to Maximilian's daughter Margaret. On the other hand, the French monarchy was as secure as any king might hope in this world, and the country's economy was doing well (better access to Mediterranean ports could only improve it further). Perhaps more to the point, Charles was the only one of the Western European monarchs to feel quite such stability. In England the Battle of Bosworth Field was less than a decade past, and Henry VII had work to do to secure himself and his descendants in power. In Spain, Ferdinand and Isabella had succeeded in their Reconquest of Granada, but victories took time to consolidate. Moreover, King Ferrante of Naples had died at the beginning of 1494, leaving his son Alfonso to contend with rebellious barons. It was, in short, an auspicious time for Charles VIII to launch an invasion, and for all that he was arguably invited by Ludovico Sforza, he had his own historic rights to assert, and was more than content to assert them.

This was a pivotal moment for kingship in Europe. Although courts were becoming more settled with growing households replacing the old military bands of followers (and new palaces built to accommodate them) it was still a matter of princely honour to go to war in person, to conquer land, to seize the territory of rivals. King Richard III of England had died on the battlefield only nine years before Charles' descent into Italy, and King Ferdinand of Aragon also led his army. It was a matter of masculinity but also of duty, and whereas later monarchs might happily take the credit for the conquests of others, at this time direct involvement was still expected, and training in the arts of war by way of jousting on the tournament field or hunting in the countryside was all part of a prince's preparation for this martial role. Charles, who had a history of ill health, perhaps had more reason than some to insist on proving himself in war. While other aspects of life at the turn of the fifteenth to sixteenth century may look new and even 'modern' (such as print and gunpowder technologies), when it comes to kingship there was a great deal of continuity with older fashions and ideals. Questions of honour would tie in Charles and his successors – and their imperial rivals – to a conflict that continued far longer than anyone anticipated in 1494.

Thus Charles assembled his troops (the numbers were intended to reach over twenty thousand) at the foot of the Alps. His courtiers had plenty of concerns about his plans: in the words of Commynes,

> it was warmly debated whether he should go or not, for by all persons of experience and wisdom it was looked upon as a very dangerous undertaking; nor indeed was anybody in favour of it but himself and one man ... of mean extraction, and who had never seen or had the least knowledge of military affairs.[12]

Charles, for all his kingdom's relative stability, was short of cash and supplies, and despite domestic troubles with the barons his opponent King Alfonso II, the reliever of Otranto and newly succeeded to the throne of Naples, was formidable. Charles, however, boasted of religious visions promising success. Alessandro Benedetti, a Venetian physician who wrote a diary of this first Italian war, dismissed the sincerity of Charles' claim that this was a crusade against the Turk and described him rather as 'seized with a desire for power'.[13] Any campaign to secure Naples would inevitably take a toll in money and in lives. Yet Charles proved stubborn and on 2 September his troops made the crossing into Italy. There were two principal routes for an invading army to enter the peninsula by land. Both old Roman roads, they were well known to travellers and couriers, and had long been pilgrim routes for travellers from Northern Europe to Rome. The lower of the two crossings traversed the Alps near Susa (now on Italy's western border with France), then made the descent via Turin to nearby Milan, passing through the flat plain of the River Po to Bologna, steep over the Apennines to Florence and back to the more level ground on the final road to Rome. Another way, for soldiers coming from the German States, would bring troops down from Bavaria, through Innsbruck and over the Brenner Pass, now at Italy's northern border with Austria, through the bishop's seat at Bressanone (Brixen) to Bolzano and Trent (the city that would later become famous for its Church Council), then to Verona, Mantua and joining the other road at Modena, a little way from Bologna. Managing supplies along these routes was a challenge, not least when the French had to bring cannon over the Alps, a feat achieved only thanks to impressive teams of Swiss mountaineers, who roped themselves together to drag the artillery up paths barely passable by mules.[14]

Charles' march down the peninsula proved unexpectedly smooth, though his army of mercenaries – Swiss, Scots and Germans among them – faced accusations of 'great cruelty' as they sacked villages. The key to the success of the French in this early stage of the Italian Wars was their impressive artillery. Since their victories against the English in the wars of the mid fifteenth century, the French had further improved their artillery design, shifting to bronze rather than iron, which allowed for lighter and more manoeuvrable weapons. Combined with better carriages, highly trained horses to draw them and expert gunners, this made for a devastating impact.[15] It would take another generation of the arms race before effective defences were developed to combat these great guns.

The French were not always unwelcome. The politics of the Italian states were complex: Tuscan territories delighted in an alternative to their usual overlords. In Florence, opponents of the ruling Medici family – among them one Niccolò Machiavelli – seized the chance of the French invasion to expel their former oligarchs. Piero de' Medici, son of Lorenzo the Magnificent, gained the soubriquet 'the

Unfortunate' from his dealings with Charles. He had tried to make an agreement with the king, but it proved so unpopular that he was forced from the city, apparently in fear for his life, and Charles made a grand entrance as Florence's effective conqueror on 17 November 1494. Aware that he needed Florentine support for his campaign to succeed, he made a deal with the city's new rulers that allowed him to take over a number of Florentine fortresses, including that of Pisa, with a promise that they would be returned at the end of his Neapolitan expedition. The Florentines paid a subsidy of 120,000 florins to Charles and agreed that his representatives in the city could be present at any debates on France or Naples. Charles did not get his way on everything: he tried to restore the Medici but that was pushing the citizens too far, and they refused. The agreement concluded, in late November Charles left to travel south via Siena to Rome. His men preceded him on the traditional triumphal route from the north, over Monte Mario and down the hill past the church of San Lazzaro to the fields around the Castel Sant'Angelo, and on 31 December the king himself made his entrance, greeted by the city's leading dignitaries and cardinals. There followed a series of formal visits from churchmen and citizens, while the Romans tutted at vandalism carried out by the soldiers in the French entourage, who had been left kicking their heels with little to do except cause trouble. Five of the offenders were swiftly hanged, presumably as an example to others. On 16 January 1495, the king attended papal Mass and was accorded a tour of the newly decorated apartments of Pope Alexander VI, 'a most beautiful residence, so well supplied with everything that you never saw a palace or castle to compare'.[16]

Meanwhile, intensive diplomatic discussions had been taking place, in which the pope agreed to give the French free passage to Naples and to hand over his long-standing hostage Prince Djem, brother of the Ottoman Sultan Bayezid II, to Charles. A man of 'very great courage and a vigorous mind'[17] and a potential claimant to the Ottoman throne, Djem had proved a useful bargaining counter for the pope (not to mention the Hungarians and other Christian powers), who had threatened the sultan with the provision of military backing for Djem's claim. Djem and his brother were sons of Mehmed II, the conqueror of Constantinople, and their rivalry had arisen in the aftermath of their father's death in 1481, by which time thanks to his conquests the empire was a rich prize. Mehmed had not designated an heir and it was no surprise that the 21-year-old Djem, governor of the city of Karaman in central Anatolia, aspired to rule it himself. He had secured the backing of the Ottomans' grand vizier, but Djem's elder brother Bayezid had other ideas, as well as (more importantly) his own network among the influential officials of Istanbul and backing from the Janissaries, the Sultan's elite household troops. After a bloody rebellion in which the grand vizier was lynched, Bayezid entered the city and was proclaimed sultan on 21 May 1481. Djem proposed the division of the empire, but Bayezid refused and after a brief war Djem fled to the neighbouring Mamluk Empire, where he was welcomed in the city of Cairo. A pilgrimage to Mecca and a failed invasion of Anatolia later, he arrived in Rhodes to seek the protection of the Knights of St John, an old crusading order who had long provided hospitality for pilgrims en route to Jerusalem. The Knights double-crossed him, made peace with Bayezid instead, and with considerable pragmatism agreed on an annual payment of 45,000 ducats from the sultan in return for keeping Djem hostage. He was later transferred to various locations in France and Savoy, and became something of a pawn in European diplomacy with the Ottomans. In 1489 Pope Innocent VIII became Djem's new host/captor, securing from Bayezid ongoing pension payments as well as a relic of the Holy Lance, relics being much in demand in the churches of Italy not least as attractions for pilgrims.[18]

Six years later, as the French army left Rome in January 1495, they took custody of Djem from Pope Alexander VI. Within a month the Ottoman prince was dead. The usual rumours of poison circulated (as they did for almost any untimely death of a high-profile figure in the period) but it was just as likely pneumonia: as a hostage Djem was more useful alive than dead. Bayezid requested the return of Djem's body for an Islamic funeral (Djem himself had expressed a wish to die in his homeland). That did not stop the Christian powers attempting to extort more money from the Ottoman Empire in return for Djem's corpse, which was not returned for burial for another four years.

Meanwhile in Naples, King Alfonso had not lived up to expectations, proving so unpopular that within a year of his accession he had abdicated in favour of his son Ferrandino, who promised reforms.

Guicciardini's account of Alfonso's decision to quit has his father's ghost appearing to the court surgeon and ordering him to tell Alfonso that his progeny were doomed first to lose the realm and then to die; Alfonso, haunted by the ghosts of barons he had secretly murdered, packed his ships with treasure and fled to Sicily, where he died in 1495.[19] It was, therefore, the 25-year-old Ferrandino who – barely a month into his rule – faced Charles VIII's invasion. It did not go well. The people of Rome were unenthused by Ferrandino and reluctant to take on the French; he took refuge first in the seafront fortresses, Castel Nuovo and the Castel dell'Ovo, and then on the islands in the Bay of Naples, Procida and Ischia, even as his troops still held the castles and as the harbour filled with burning ships, set alight so that the French could not seize them (as was the city arsenal). It was not enough to hold off Charles' troops, but ongoing exchanges of fire were sufficient to ensure that plans for a grand ceremony around Charles' arrival were scaled down in favour of a modest entry, the king arriving as if he were returning from a pleasant day's hunting rather than with the military might of a conqueror.[20]

Anticipating by a good decade Machiavelli's observation in *The Prince* that fortresses would not save a prince who was hated by his citizens, Isabella d'Este, marchioness of Mantua and a granddaughter of King Ferrante, wrote to her husband: 'This should be an admonition to all rulers to esteem the hearts of their subjects more than fortresses, treasure and men-at-arms, because the discontent of subjects wages worse war than the enemy in the field.'[21] Charles VIII, however, did no better than Ferrandino in relations with the citizens and struggled to consolidate his conquest.

Meanwhile, the other Italian powers were busily forming a league against him, and Charles headed north, home to France to contrive a response, leaving Naples in the charge of a viceroy. Charles hoped to persuade Pope Alexander VI to invest him formally with the realm, but the pope was reluctant to commit himself so firmly to one side of the war, declined to meet Charles and decamped to Orvieto instead, which was both a pleasant retreat with a fine bishop's palace and, thanks to its hilltop location, easily defended against attack. As King Charles pursued him, he moved on from city to city; a French sack of the town of Toscanella near Bologna, in which perhaps eight hundred people died, 'left all Italy trembling at the cruelty'.[22] Not only the pope but all the rulers of the Italian states were now realising that Ludovico Sforza had opened a Pandora's box: even Ludovico himself had second thoughts. (Ludovico was now definitively ruler of Milan following the death of his nephew Gian Galeazzo in October 1494. Guicciardini reported the rumour that Gian Galeazzo had died owing to 'immoderate coitus', along with the more plausible suggestion that he had been poisoned.[23]) On 31 March 1495 the League of Venice was formed, uniting the major northern states (Milan, Venice, Florence, Mantua) against the French, with the support besides of Naples, Spain and the Holy Roman Empire. Back in the north, near the town of Fornovo (about twenty miles south-west of Parma and sixty miles west of Bologna) in July 1495 the two sides faced off in the first substantive battle of the Italian Wars.

Leading the army of the League was Isabella's husband Francesco Gonzaga, marquis of Mantua. His army, predominantly Venetian, was almost double the size of the French force, and the Venetian authorities were hoping they could avoid a fight. Still, skirmishes began early in the month: as the French approached the Venetian camp the stradiots (mercenary cavalry from the Balkans) were sent forward in an unexpected – and successful – attack. Benedetti, the Venetian diarist, described their return to the camp: 'exulting over the first clash, [they] affixed the heads of the enemy to their light lances [...] and were welcomed with great enthusiasm'.[24] The Frenchman Commynes judged that 'they did it on purpose to terrify us, and indeed so they did', though he boasted that the French artillery had a comparable effect.[25] When the battle itself came, it took place in a muddy mire and with much disorder and confusion. Soldiers found themselves 'bogged down in the swamp and slain there', while rain put paid to the use of artillery.[26] It was not much of a triumph for anyone.

Charles made his escape, and the French lost nearly all the booty from their campaign as the soldiers divided among themselves gold, silver, jewels and textiles, not to mention (on Benedetti's account) 'a book in which were painted various nude images of the king's mistresses', which Charles carried about with him as a souvenir of his various sexual encounters on campaign.[27] Sanudo was rather blunter about Charles' conduct, writing that the king was 'one of the most lascivious men in France' who abused his power to coerce virgins and married women into sex.[28] All this, however, must have been poor consolation for the king as his troops withdrew to France. In between the salacious tales, Benedetti's diary gives a vivid account of the squalor of the battlefield after the plunder. As he surveyed the dead, he saw 'no blood, for the rain had bathed their gaping wounds'.[29] He found injured men stripped of their clothing, left 'naked among the corpses, some begging aid, some half-dead [...] weakened by hunger and loss of blood and wearied by the heat of the sun and thirst'. He and his fellow Venetian surgeons treated French wounded too, whom they found 'begrimed with mud and blood and looking like slaves'. More had been killed by wounds to the neck or head than by artillery.[30] Both sides claimed victory; in the longer term it was the Italians whom had prevented another French offensive. Paolo Giovio, a historian and close adviser to the Medici popes, knew whom he blamed for the 'present sorrow and these miseries': Ludovico Sforza, who had been 'provoked by the monstrous arrogance of King Alfonso', along with 'the Venetians, more ambitious than was befitting a free people; and likewise Pope Alexander VI, the worst of men'.[31]

So far as civilians were concerned, the impact of war was highly varied. The poet Matteo Maria Boiardo, who in 1494 was working on a grand chivalric romance, *Orlando innamorato* (Orlando in Love), found his own attempts to write of love overwhelmed by the 'flame and fire' of the French invasion.[32] More prosaically, locals often clashed with soldiers over access to supplies: feeding troops was expensive and could quickly exhaust land where an army passed. Commynes complained that even while the locals had welcomed the French army to Fornovo, the only available bread was 'small and black, and they sold it very dear, and their wine was three parts water'. He was concerned, moreover, that the 'good store of provision' they found abandoned in the town might be a trap, intended to poison the French.[33] In the absence of adequate financing soldiers were often permitted (tacitly or explicitly) to loot captured cities, or else money was extorted from city authorities with the threat of a sack should it not be forthcoming. Benedetti describes how Charles' troops went 'wandering at will through Campania, Puglia, Calabria, and the Abruzzi, ravaging private homes, despoiling churches, and abstaining not even from nuns in their terrible lust'.[34]

The 1490s also saw another unwelcome development in Italy with the arrival of what Italians came to call 'the French disease'. This is often identified as syphilis, although the term was not used at the time, and trying to be specific about five-hundred-year-old pathogens and their origin is a tricky business. (Early opinion leant towards France as a source but as time went on there was more speculation about the vaguely defined 'Ethiopia' or 'the Indies', and more modern accounts often speculate on a New World origin.) In contrast, there was a fair, if not complete, consensus about the symptoms: boils and aching limbs first, rotting flesh later, but also the possibility of remission. Whatever the cause, the French invasion of 1494 provided the backdrop for the rise of this pox. It was exacerbated by the perennial problem of poor harvests which, combined with a growing population and particularly severe weather in the winter of 1495–6, would have caused enough trouble without the demands of thousands of troops. The Florentine physician Antonio Benivieni, whose treatise on the pox was published in 1528, observed:

> During the year 1496 almost all Italy was stricken with such widespread and enormous hunger that everywhere many people died in the streets and public squares, and many others fell prey to various diseases as a result of having consumed bad and unhealthy food. [...] We also saw women who passed away along with, and because of, the infected children they nursed.[35]

Among the earliest identified victims of the new disease was Bernard Stuart (c.1447–1508), lieutenant general of the French army, whose illness was recorded by eyewitnesses to the French retreat from Calabria in late 1496. The following year it became public that Alfonso d'Este, eldest son of the duke of Ferrara, had the *mal francese*; others said to have suffered with it include his brother Cardinal Ippolito d'Este, and Ippolito's fellow cardinals Ascanio Sforza, Cesare Borgia and Giuliano della Rovere (the future Pope Julius II). That said, social status and access to resources for good quality care probably made a difference, especially after the first few years of the epidemic when it appeared to become less ferocious. Francesco Gonzaga, marquis of Mantua, survived for twenty-three years after his initial symptoms. In 1515 Pope Leo X refounded the hospital of San Giacomo for people suffering from the pox.[36]

Many interpreted the disease – as indeed they interpreted wars, poor harvests and natural disasters – as God's punishment for ill living. They found references to it in old prophecies and apparitions.[37] The people of fifteenth-century Italy took a great deal of interest in portents and omens, and the appearance of comets or other astronomical phenomena prompted wide comment. When the wars broke out there were reports of people seeing three suns in the sky, of sweating statues and of monstrous births.[38] Such beliefs were not confined to the uneducated: the dukes of Milan, for example, consulted astrologers on their political implications, as well as on such matters as the prospect of an enemy's death.[39] (That is not to say there was never scepticism: the historian Giovio observed that horoscopes of kings were often wrong, and 'we received far truer answers from sensible men'.[40])

This was a world in which for most people commonplace illnesses were likely to be treated at home, or with purchases from a pharmacy. Medical professionals included physicians, who were licensed and often university-educated, and barber-surgeons who were usually not, although skilled surgeons gradually began to differentiate themselves from barbers. At the bottom of the medical hierarchy came herbalists and apothecaries.[41] When prostitutes were expelled from cities in response to the epidemic, that was not necessarily because the pox was understood as a venereal disease (although it was one, and as time went on its spread was increasingly attributed to promiscuous women), but rather because of a more general understanding that by purging the city of sin it might once again become healthy.[42]

That the people of Italy turned to religion to understand the pox is no surprise. Christianity permeated life at the turn of the sixteenth century in a way that seems quite unusual now. In the twenty-first-century West, the existence of atheists is an ordinary matter. In the sixteenth century there was almost no one who did not believe in God. Some intellectuals may have taken an interest in the arguments of ancient writers who saw their ancient gods as rather powerless – more a soap opera than a matter of fact – but atheist ideas were not commonplace in this society, and nor was religion the rather abstract, intellectual set of beliefs it can be now. It is best explained as a set of practices embedded in everyday life, as a world of ritual that framed the life cycle and the year, contact with the Church following the routine of the seasons. In a community of vine-growers, for example, there would be feasts for the grape harvest in November on St Martin's Day. There were processions through the streets, images of the local patron saint borne aloft for her feast day. Key events in the life cycle were marked with religious ceremony: baptism for the birth of a child, marriage, ordination, the last rites. Especially at Easter, villagers and townspeople confessed their sins and partook of Communion. Mothers were responsible for the religious upbringing of their children, though as boys grew older they were likely to receive wider education from tutors.

No one in this period carried out opinion polls on the population's religious belief, so it is hard to know how far the average person appreciated theological nuances. Later in the sixteenth century, after the Reformation, when more careful inquiries were undertaken, investigators found popular ignorance worrying. That, however, may simply reflect the gap between their own attitude towards religion and that of the people they were researching. Probably many people had a rather vague grasp of the details, beyond a belief in God and the Devil (both regarded as exercising real and immediate influence in the world), and in the Virgin Mary and Christ, and the few saints of immediate relevance to their town, trade or profession. In practice, official religion accommodated many local saints and beliefs. People might ask priests to bless objects or bring gifts to a statue of the Virgin known for her intercession on behalf of the sick. There was quite a shading between traditional folk belief and the formal teaching of the Bible; in a world where literacy was restricted, the imagery of churches combined with preaching to communicate the word of God to listeners. This was, in short, a world of bright and constant religious life.

Christian beliefs in 'good works' and salvation were important factors in the patronage of art. Over a lifetime, a person could be expected to sin – and correspondingly expect to spend a period in Purgatory atoning – but those sins might be expiated (to some extent at least) by giving to charity, or beautifying a local church, or donating for Masses to be said for one's soul. Among the sins that particularly concerned merchants at this time was usury: Christians were officially forbidden to lend money at interest, though by this time many were making fortunes in banking doing precisely that. Some investment in good works to offset the sin was thought wise, hence the many elaborately decorated family chapels in Renaissance churches. As the merchants of Italy grew wealthier, they spent money on art, and not only art but all sorts of material goods, creating a striking culture of images.[43]

The priest oversaw their spiritual lives: sometimes well and sometimes badly. Absenteeism, poorly educated clergy and lax moral standards were well-known problems and a matter of considerable debate within the Church. It is a paradox that even while the Church was becoming a more political organisation in terms of the government of Italian affairs, it was simultaneously engaged in extensive discussions about its own reform and renewal. After the end of the schism, the re-establishment of a single pope at the Vatican, and the return of many churchmen to Rome in the middle of the fifteenth century, there was plenty of talk of 'renovation' both spiritual and physical (of church buildings long neglected, for example).[44] The project that eventually resulted in the creation of the present-day St Peter's got under way in 1505 under Pope Julius II, although initially the plans were largely for restoration and updating, not for the entirely new basilica that would come to pass.[45]

These two phenomena – a lively Christianity that structured everyday life and thought, and a papacy aware of reform demands but increasingly concerned with temporal government – would be central to the next stage of Italy's conflicts, as one of the most notorious popes in history clashed with a reformer who had a dramatically different vision of the Church.

Chapter Four

The Borgias vs Savonarola

The single most infamous family in Renaissance Italy, the Borgias get a famously bad press.[1] Guicciardini's observations on the Borgia pope Alexander VI sum him up as a man of 'wonderful acuteness and extraordinary sagacity', an expert politician, but a man whose virtues were far outweighed by his vices: 'very impure manners, insincere, shameless, false, faithless and irreligious, without probity, insatiably covetous [...] barbarously cruel, and ardently solicitous to exalt his children, who were numerous and amongst them some (that he might not want instruments to execute his villainous designs) as bad as himself'.[2] It did not help that they were of Spanish origin, foreign and suspect among Italians. Yet by the time of Rodrigo Borgia's election as Pope Alexander VI in 1492 he was hardly new to Rome; nor was he as Spanish as one might think. The family name had been Italianised from 'Borja' over Rodrigo's long residence at the court of Rome. He had arrived during the short pontificate of his uncle, Pope Calixtus III, who in 1456 had made him a cardinal; from there he had risen to the office of vice-chancellor, the most powerful role in the secular hierarchy of the Church, and one that many other nephews of popes and future popes occupied in the decades to come. In that role his conduct was, for the most part, respectable and unexceptional. He did, at one point, get a telling off from Pope Pius II after a rather lively party with Cardinal d'Estouteville: 'You behaved,' wrote Pius, 'as if you were one of a group of young laymen'. But three days later Pius wrote another letter admitting that perhaps he overreacted, and were it not for Rodrigo's subsequent notoriety the incident would probably have passed without notice.[3]

Rodrigo's strategy for the papacy was similarly unexceptional: he aimed for peace and equilibrium and focused on opposition to the

Turks. His private life as pope, however, was far more contentious, although he was by no means the first pope to have, or promote, illegitimate children. Innocent VIII had married his son into the Medici family and promoted other relatives to the cardinalate, but Rodrigo's openness about his family was unusual (Innocent's son Franceschetto had been born before his church career began). Rodrigo had at least nine children, of whom the most politically significant were the four born in the 1470s and 1480s to his mistress Vannozza de' Cattanei, a woman probably of Mantuan family who in her later life amassed a significant property portfolio in Rome, including an inn called 'La Vacca' ('The Cow').[4] These children were Cesare, who as Rodrigo's second son was initially destined for an ecclesiastical career; Juan, who became second duke of Gandia (in Spain) after the early death of an elder brother; Lucrezia, who was initially expected to marry into the Spanish nobility; and Jofrè, who like Cesare was slated for a career in the Church. However, all those expectations shifted when Rodrigo's election to the papacy allowed for more splendid ambitions.

In June 1493 Lucrezia was married instead to Giovanni Sforza, a cousin of Ludovico Sforza of Milan. (The ceremony took place at the Vatican, itself a provocation: it was one thing for a pope to have illegitimate children, quite another to parade them so publicly.) The following year, on 10 June 1494, the 14-year-old Lucrezia was in the city of Pesaro, on the Adriatic coast, from where she wrote to the pope. She had arrived with her husband safe and sound and 'despite the rain, which disturbed us, we were greeted with great festivity', though hearing of the prospect of a French invasion she was worried: 'We have learned', she wrote, 'that things are going very badly in Rome at the present moment, which causes us great distress and worry [...] I entreat Your Blessedness as much as I am able, to get out of Rome, and if it is not convenient to leave, to be most vigilant and take great care.'[5] Lucrezia was not the only one whose fortunes had been improved by the new pope. Her brother Jofrè married into the aristocracy of Naples with a wedding to Sancia, an illegitimate daughter of the future King Alfonso II; he became a Neapolitan grandee, prince of Squillace (a town in the far south of Italy). Juan, duke of Gandia, married María Enríquez de Luna, a cousin of Ferdinand of Aragon, with the aim of consolidating the family fortunes in that realm. This pattern of dynastic marriage to secure alliances was entirely typical of a Renaissance ruler, and Alexander VI's successors would do very much the same. Indeed one of those successors, Alessandro Farnese, the future Pope Paul III, was himself promoted to the cardinalate by Alexander. Alessandro happened to be the brother of the pope's mistress, Giulia Farnese, and as a consequence acquired the nickname 'the Petticoat Cardinal'. Cesare Borgia was also made a cardinal; he held the office of governor of the papal city of Orvieto from 1493. Juan took up a role within the Church too, as captain general of its armies, in which capacity he led a campaign against the Orsini, Roman barons allied to the French. His troops were defeated at the Battle of Soriano in January 1497 but two months later, in a joint campaign with the Spanish, succeeded in capturing the port of Ostia from a French garrison. For all that Alexander VI had had to accommodate the French descent into Italy he had no intention of allowing Charles VIII's sphere of influence to expand too far.

Meanwhile, Lucrezia's marriage to Giovanni Sforza was floundering. The diplomatic alliance with Milan was no longer helpful to the Borgias and moreover Sforza's loyalty was under question. Divorce proceedings began in 1497 and in the absence of any technical problems with the paperwork (one convenient route to a divorce in this period), Alexander fell back on the device of an annulment for non-consummation. The suggestion that Sforza was unable to perform was predictably humiliating for him, and he responded with a counterclaim of incestuous relations within the Borgia family. There is no reason to think this was anything more than mud-slinging, and indeed as mud-slinging it had some metaphorical weight. The infamous emperors Nero and Caligula had been accused of incest in Suetonius' *Lives of the Caesars*, the latter with three of his sisters; Suetonius, a classical writer, was a fashionable source for Renaissance authors and editions of his work were widely available in Rome. The household, moreover, was a popular metaphor for government: a man who tolerated or indeed fomented sexual perversity at home was bound to be a poor ruler when it came to the state. None of that, however, mattered to later Protestant writers who delighted in taking literally these tales of popish outrages.

Eventually Ludovico Sforza persuaded his cousin to agree to the annulment, and the divorce went through. In June 1498 Lucrezia was married to Alfonso, duke of Bisceglie, an illegitimate son of Alfonso

II of Naples and brother of Sancia. She brought with her a dowry of 41,000 ducats (here we head towards the category of super-rich) and during the marriage went on to carry out significant administrative responsibilities in the Papal States, including as governor of Spoleto. In 1499–1500, while Alexander VI was on a tour of some former Colonna properties, he left Lucrezia in charge of the Vatican. Such an arrangement would have been entirely unexceptional for a secular ruler (as we will see in Chapter Eleven, female relatives frequently acted as regents) but the pope was supposed to play by different rules.

If accusations of incest were not awkward enough, on 14 June 1497, Lucrezia's brother Juan was murdered. His body, covered in stab wounds, was found floating in the Tiber. The number of possible suspects is worthy of an Agatha Christie novel. They included Lucrezia's former husband Giovanni Sforza; Guidobaldo da Montefeltro, duke of Urbino; the Orsini family, whose troops had defeated Juan at Soriano; Gonzalo Fernández de Córdoba, a Spanish commander, and Cardinal Ascanio Sforza, who had a personal axe to grind with the victim. Other rumours pointed to Count Antonio Maria della Mirandola, supposedly motivated by Juan's seduction of his daughter. Alexander made public that he did not blame either of the Sforza suspects – this was undoubtedly diplomatic – and further exculpated the duke of Urbino and Jofrè, Juan's youngest brother. Only nine months later did reports begin to point to the middle brother, Cesare. The truth is that no one knows who did it: perhaps the Orsini – whom Alexander pointedly did not absolve – or perhaps not.[6] The reason dramatists have such fun with the Borgias is that there are so many possibilities.

The French also had dynastic troubles, if somewhat less dramatic: in April 1498 the 27-year-old Charles VIII died and, in the absence of heirs, his cousin Louis of Orléans inherited, becoming King Louis XII. (Charles's death was actually not as heroic as his stature might suggest: he hit his head on a door lintel at the Château d'Amboise, and died of the injury.) This made for a brief hiatus in the wars. The new King Louis XII intended to marry Charles's widow, Anne of Brittany. However, this required an annulment and special dispensation from the pope, from which Alexander extracted maximum political capital. The young Lucrezia might have fretted about her father's safety in the face of a French army, but four years on the pope now enjoyed a diplomatic advantage with France, and exercised it, as ever, in his family's favour. In return for the permission he required, Louis made Cesare, who in 1498 renounced the cardinalate to seek his fortune in the wars, duke of Valence – hence Duke Valentino in Italian – a name echoing his previous title, cardinal of Valencia. Cesare was now nearly 23 and leaving the cardinalate was quite a sacrifice: he was giving up benefices worth 35,000 ducats a year in search of secular, military power. On the other hand, his father was 67, and that might not leave a great deal of time for Cesare to establish himself as a prince while he still had papal patronage. A dynastic marriage was an obvious first step and in 1499 Cesare wed Charlotte d'Albret, sister of the king of Navarre in northern Spain. Louis also promised him a military force to assist in the Romagna where Cesare hoped to make himself duke, in return for Cesare's service in the campaign against Milan that Louis launched in the autumn of the same year. No less than any other young man he saw in war an opportunity.

Lucrezia's fortunes took a further painful twist the following year, when her husband Alfonso was murdered – a crime for which Cesare was blamed. That Alfonso was killed on Cesare's orders seems clear but again this is a murky tale. On 15 July 1500, someone had tried to assassinate Alfonso on the steps of St Peter's – a surprisingly public choice when there were poisons available. Cesare was not clearly to blame for that, and fingers were pointed at the Orsini. But it was certainly Cesare's lieutenant Michele Corella, known as Don Michelotto, who strangled Alfonso in his bed a month later. It may have been a matter of revenge after Alfonso had tried to kill Cesare but either way Cesare's murderous reputation was confirmed, and the whispers picked up about Juan's murder three years before. In any case, the murder did no harm to papal strategy: Lucrezia's marriage to the ruling family of Naples served no political purpose now that Alexander had allied himself with France. Tempting as it is to see the Borgia murders as a domestic tale of family jealousies, they were as much – if not more so – a matter of geopolitical interests and military alliances.

Lucrezia was by now onto her third marriage. She was twenty-one, and her new husband was Alfonso d'Este, heir to the duchy of Ferrara. Lucrezia, her reputation already clouded by the fate of her previous husband, the tales of incest and rumours about an illegitimate child, was not a high matrimonial prize, but Alexander VI had one useful card to play: the prospect of papal recognition for the Este family's claim to be lords of Ferrara (which, though long-standing, had never been fully accepted by the popes). He also had money, though Lucrezia's hundred thousand ducat dowry put considerable strain on the papal coffers. A proxy wedding ceremony took place on 30 December 1501, and Lucrezia set out for Ferrara on 6 January with an entourage of over seven hundred courtiers and servants, where she was married in a ceremony that dazzled with its cloth of gold.[7] As she settled into her new role, her husband became an important military commander and innovator in the Italian Wars, following in the footsteps of his father Ercole.

The salacious tales of Borgia private lives are only a part of the story of this papacy, however. Alexander VI was also the pope who had to deal with the immediate consequences of Columbus' voyages to the New World. As we have seen, popes in this period were a source of supranational judicial authority, so it was not surprising that the new conquering powers turned to Alexander for official approval of their activities. Just as Pope Nicholas V had authorised the Portuguese expansion, so in 1493 did Alexander issue a papal bull that settled a dispute between the Spanish and Portuguese by declaring all lands 100 leagues south and to the west of the Azores as being under Spanish sovereignty (predictably, there were then fierce arguments as to precisely what this meant). Along with the Treaty of Tordesillas, agreed by Spain and Portugal the following year, the bull effectively divided the world between East and West, granting rights in the West to Spain and in the East to Portugal. (Brazil fell east of the line.) The bull praised Ferdinand and Isabella's 'recovery of the kingdom of Granada from the tyranny of the Saracens' and described their intent to 'seek out distant and unknown mainlands and islands'. We 'command you by virtue of holy obedience,' the pope went on,

> that just as you have promised (and on account of your very great devotion and royal magnanimity we do not doubt that you will do it), you should send to the said mainlands and islands prudent and God-fearing men, learned, skilled, and proven, to instruct the said natives and inhabitants in the Catholic faith and to instill good morals in them.

That extensive justification, however, was not the primary purpose of the bull: that was to address the demarcation of territory between Spain and Portugal.[8]

The frescoes of the Borgia apartments may even include the first European representation of Native Americans. Painted in 1494, but uncovered only during a 2013 restoration, the artwork includes a detail of dancing naked men in feathered headdresses, with a man on horseback beside them, an image consistent with Columbus' description of the people he encountered.[9] This fresco series – which can be seen today in the Vatican Museums – tells us much more about Alexander's papacy. His patronage of art was typical for a ruler of his time. His chosen artist, Pinturicchio (Bernardino di Betto), was long disparaged by art historians influenced by Giorgio Vasari, who had criticised his use of stucco and understanding of perspective, and claimed the artist 'enjoyed a much greater reputation than his works deserved'.[10] That assessment continued to affect judgements until very recently, despite the fact that the artist's contemporaries had more subtle opinions and praised his work. Like the Borgias themselves, Pinturicchio is now getting some rehabilitation. Along with Andrea Mantegna, the artist had been commissioned to work on the Belvedere casino ('little house') in the Vatican gardens, to which he contributed painted ceilings in imitation of ancient Roman style; he painted fake 'marble' columns and his other trompe l'oeil work included an image of a parrot in its cage that hung on the casino wall. His designs for the Borgia apartments likewise included trompe l'oeil cupboards, a fashionable motif used a generation earlier in the studiolo of the Ducal Palace in Urbino.

The schemes that Pinturicchio designed for the six rooms and two cubicula (cubicles or small rooms) give a good indication of the ways that the art of these years brought together Christian and pagan subjects. The rooms told a story of salvation, beginning with the sibyls (prophetesses of classical myth) and the prophets of the Old Testament; along the way to the final scene of Christ's redemption, the frescoes featured the planets and the signs of the zodiac. A 'Room of the Saints' here could sit alongside a 'Room of the Sibyls', and for the design of the latter room Pinturicchio drew on a 1481 Dominican treatise that linked the prophecies of these ancient figures with those of the first years of Christ.

This combination – of sibyls with figures from Christian sources – had precedents. The pulpit at Pisa Cathedral, sculpted by Giovanni Pisano early in the fourteenth century, included images of sibyls and the liberal arts as well as the more usual Christian figures. The prophets-and-sibyls motif can also be seen in Michelangelo's designs for the ceiling of the Sistine Chapel and Filippino Lippi's work on the vault of the Carafa Chapel in the church of Santa Maria sopra Minerva in Rome, though the earliest example seems to have been the Sassetti Chapel in Santa Trinità, Florence, by Domenico Ghirlandaio, completed in 1485; a couple of years later Perugino (Pietro Vannucci) completed his own version for the money-changers' guild of Perugia. Painted to a design by the humanist Francesco Maturanzio, who had taught at the universities of Vicenza and Venice before returning to a role in the Perugian civil service, it includes a ceiling fresco featuring the moon, Mercury, Mars, Saturn, Jupiter and Venus; the theme is man's perfection on earth achieved by accord between ancient virtues and Christian revelation.

Pinturicchio's scheme for the Borgia apartments also incorporated the surviving landmarks of ancient Rome. The arch of Constantine sits behind an image of the dispute of St Catherine and the Colosseum appears in an image of the martyrdom of St Sebastian,[11] while the decor for the Sala dei Misteri della Fede (Room of the Mysteries of Faith) featured Borgia heraldic devices, including gilded bulls, the double crown of Aragon and a half-dozen fluttering flames on an ultramarine ground.[12]

Nor were contemporary concerns far away. Prominent intellectuals of the present day featured in Pinturicchio's design too, among them Giovanni Pontano (the former prime minister of Naples) and Pico della Mirandola (a leading philosopher). Elsewhere, Pinturicchio's sequence includes multiple allusions to conflict with the Ottomans, and the decorations were gratifying enough to the pope that he granted Pinturicchio two pieces of land and gave him a second commission to work on a tower and loggia in the Castel Sant'Angelo.[13] There he painted scenes of the meeting of Alexander VI and Charles VIII (now lost), perhaps in similar style to his later frescoes for the Piccolomini Library in Siena Cathedral glorifying the diplomacy of Pope Pius II.[14] The importance of this sequence in the wider culture of the period, though, lies in its combination of a dual ancient inheritance – that of

Christian Europe and pagan Rome – with contemporary comment
that emphasised the superiority of Christian heritage over ferocious
Turkish invaders on the one hand and naked, playful people of the
New World on the other.

So far as religious matters were concerned, the major challenge of
Alexander's papacy came from Florence in the person of Girolamo
Savonarola, a charismatic preacher who had arrived in the city a
decade earlier. Born in Ferrara in 1452 to a middling sort of family
(his grandfather had been a doctor), Savonarola graduated from
university and began to read medicine, but in his early twenties, after
a dramatic vocation, he took religious orders and joined the Dominican priory at Bologna.[15] In a letter to his father, he wrote of his
reasons for leaving the family home. He was moved by the 'great
misery of the world, the wickedness of men, the rapes, the adulteries,
the thefts, the pride, the idolatry, the vile curses'. Unable to bear the
iniquities of Italy, he had thought to flee the 'filth of this world', and
daily he prayed to Christ to raise him from the mire. He had left the
family home almost in secret to devote himself to religion; he hoped
that his father's grief would soon pass, and begged him to comfort
his mother.[16]

Savonarola's concerns for the state of the church are apparent
from his poem 'On the Decline of the Church', written in 1475, in
which he described it as perverted by a demon, and locusts (a
metaphor for false friars) grabbing it by the roots.[17] While this was
no doubt harsh criticism, anticlerical writing was nothing new.
Dante's *Inferno*, written in the first decade of the fourteenth century,
saw plenty of clerics in hell; Boccaccio's *Decameron*, thirty years or
so later, had them breaking all manner of vows. Besides the literary
classics there was a large tradition of anticlerical writing in both
popular and more serious vein, and there was a long history of
demands for Church reform. The Church was a major landowner
in this period and it would not have been at all unusual for a peasant
family to find themselves tenants of an abbot or bishop, and to moan
at the hypocrisy of their landlords. Indeed, when the popes had
returned to Rome in the middle of the fifteenth century they had
done so with many promises of renewal for the Church and engaged
happily with the idea that reform was both necessary and desirable

– a piece of rhetoric that politicians have echoed in all sorts of contexts in the centuries since.

Savonarola proved a promising monk and in 1482 he was dispatched to preach at Florence, a city with a very lively lay religious life. There he took up residence at the Dominican convent of San Marco. The Dominicans, the Order of Preachers, were one of several rival monastic orders in Italy at this time. Their great rivals were the Franciscans, who had their base in Assisi; other orders included the Augustinians and Benedictines. As the 'OP' suggests, the Dominicans saw their role as reaching out and preaching. They were now almost three hundred years old, and a mendicant order, that is, one that depended for survival on donations from well-wishers. The Florentine Dominicans had attracted some substantial followers, not least the late Lorenzo the Magnificent, who had often been a guest in their convent, and his grandfather Cosimo the Elder, who had financed the restoration of the worn-out Benedictine monastery of San Marco to house the Dominican order. It was decorated with strange and beautiful artwork, completed some thirty years before by Fra Angelico: a great Annunciation, featuring an angel with stunning feathered wings, greeted visitors at the top of the stairs, and each cell of the dormitory held a curious painted reference to the life of Christ or St Dominic on which the monks might meditate. Fra Angelico was noted for his devotion: in Vasari's words 'the saints he painted possess more of the expression and the appearance of saints than those of any other artist'.[18] Savonarola, meanwhile, was increasingly in demand as a preacher elsewhere in Italy; he travelled to Brescia, where in 1486 he preached on the Book of Revelation, and he became ever more preoccupied with ideas about the coming apocalypse. He was far from alone in this: the 'millenarian' idea that the year 1500 might prove a cataclysmic moment was a common one. Columbus had similar thoughts.[19] Such widespread beliefs made for a receptive audience for sermons that demanded urgent moral reform to avoid imminent damnation. In 1489 Savonarola returned to Florence and in August of the following year began a series of sermons (in San Marco) on this theme. The Medici tolerated his preaching against the worldly and wealthy provided he did not name names.[20] The death of Lorenzo de' Medici in Easter Week of 1492 was, Savonarola asserted, a portent, and later he claimed to have had a vision, on Good Friday, showing first the Cross of the

Wrath of God rising over Rome, then the Cross of the Mercy of God rising over Jerusalem.[21] (Visions of the cross were a motif of Christian tradition: some forty years before, Piero della Francesca had completed a dramatic series of frescoes showing *The Legend of the True Cross* for the Basilica of San Francesco in nearby Arezzo, highlighting the vision seen by the first Christian Emperor, Constantine, in Rome prior to his victory over his pagan rival Maxentius at the Battle of the Milvian Bridge.)

It was inevitable that the power shift following the death of Lorenzo de' Medici would be difficult. His son Piero was not a convincing successor and in the formally republican system it was not enough simply to rely on the dynastic tie. Piero's Neapolitan wife Alfonsina – a politically influential woman *and* a foreigner – was unpopular. Meanwhile, the Tuscan monasteries obtained Pope Alexander's approval to form an independent congregation within the Dominican Order, and Savonarola became its vicar general. He set in place a vigorous reform of monastic life, promoting austere living, which proved an attractive prospect to some young men of Florence, and the number of vocations at San Marco soared. His influence was felt beyond Florence, too: Savonarola corresponded extensively with the admiring Ercole d'Este, duke of Ferrara and disapproving father-in-law of Lucrezia Borgia, from 1495 to 1497.[22] Guicciardini described Savonarola as a man of 'unusual erudition'.[23] In his sermons Savonarola excoriated the Florentines for their immorality, targeting pagan (that is, classical) books and art and sexual depravity as well as the tyrannical rule of the Medici. Late in the year, he had another vision, this time of the Sword of God, on which he preached in Advent.[24]

The vision took some time to come to pass, but Savonarola was convinced that the judgment of God was approaching, and as the prospect of a French invasion grew closer he began to conceive of Charles VIII as a potential avenger who might impose Church reform. He repeatedly criticised the princes of Italy and the clergy's obsession with classical learning over the Bible. It was a long way from the clever combination of prophets and sibyls to be found in the Borgia apartments, or just over the Tuscan border in Perugia. When the French troops finally arrived, Savonarola welcomed them. The invasion was to his advantage. He met Charles several times, and the fact that

Charles refrained from sacking Florence only confirmed Savonarola's favourable prophecies about the king. (Philippe de Commynes, the diplomat and memoirist, later pointed out that Savonarola had got several of his predictions right, including the deaths of the king and his son.[25])

Capitalising on Charles' support for the expulsion of the Medici, who were now exiled from their home city, Savonarola established a virtual theocratic regime, with a new constitution for Florence that recognised Christ as the city's king, and set up a great council (of almost three thousand, compared to the previous three hundred). Savonarola's exercise of power was indirect: just like the Medici he did not take city office himself. The new constitution, however, alienated a faction of the office-holding class, which preferred a narrower – albeit still republican – form of government; moreover the wealthiest Florentines, predictably, disliked Savonarola's taxes on the rich. His austere theology was a challenge not only to a substantial section of Florentine society but also to the Borgias.

While Pope Alexander VI had not prevented Charles VIII's progress to Naples, he did not share the French king's political priorities. The city state of Florence and its dominions was – after all – one of the five large powers of Italy and, in alliance with France, might (from the pope's point of view) do considerable damage to both papal and private Borgia interests. Thus the pope's considerations here were not only religious. Savonarola was now attacking the papacy in ever more virulent terms, but with Charles' return to France in 1495 he had lost the military presence of an ally. On 21 July that year, he was commanded to come to Rome and explain to the pope his claims to 'divine revelation'. Savonarola demurred, pleaded 'infirmity of the body', specifically 'fevers and dysentery', as well as the scheming of his enemies, who 'are vehemently angry with me and hold enmity toward me for no reason; often, also, they plot my destruction'.[26] His pleas did not convince the pope, who in September banned him from preaching and revoked the independence that he had previously granted San Marco; the following month – after a response from Savonarola – he backtracked on the latter ruling but the ban on preaching remained in place.

Savonarola ignored it in October 1495 when he preached against Piero de' Medici and other enemies of the republic (though claiming merely to be 'talking', not preaching),[27] and in February the following year returned to outright disobedience of papal orders (albeit with the encouragement of the Florentine authorities). In a series of sermons for Lent of 1496 he repeatedly criticised the papacy, which prompted another revocation of San Marco's independence later that same year. Meanwhile, he and his supporters organised 'bonfires of the vanities' in which playing cards, ornaments, and classical poetry books were burnt. Botticelli, a supporter of Savonarola, is sometimes said to have burnt his paintings, but Vasari's account is rather less dramatic, and has the artist merely abandoning his work.[28] There was certainly pressure to conform. Members of confraternities went door to door, cracking down on gambling by confiscating dice and cards, and browbeating women whom they regarded as too extravagantly dressed. Yet while Florentines may have endorsed the rhetoric of moral renewal, such heavy-handed policing of daily lives aroused resentment, and soon attracted further attention from the pope. In May 1497, against the backdrop of rising discontent in the city, an unfavourable election result in the *Signoria* – Florence's governing authority – and more inflammatory publications from Savonarola, the preacher was excommunicated.

Alexander VI, a more subtle and interesting politician than the popular image of the Borgias would suggest, responded quite seriously to Savonarola's challenge, beyond simply excluding the preacher himself from the Church. He set up a reform commission of six cardinals, which worked with considerable involvement from the pope himself in the second half of 1497.[29] There was, however, significant institutional resistance at the curia to reforms that might have limited the incomes of cardinals and officials, and the commission struggled to make an impact. In turn, Savonarola ignored the papal sentences. Reform in Florence continued, and became ever more visible in the city's material culture: in November 1497 the crucifix was removed from the Duomo's high altar, to be replaced with a simple wooden tabernacle containing the bread and wine that in Christian ritual represent (and in Catholic ritual are understood to become) the body and blood of Christ.[30] On 11 February 1498 Savonarola defied his excommunication to resume his preaching at the Cathedral.

He hoped to win the support of European rulers for a Council to oppose the pope. General Councils – international conferences of theologians and senior clergy convoked to settle disputes on doctrine and reform – had been outlawed under Pius II in favour of papal decision-making,[31] so this was a high-risk strategy, but it was not altogether implausible if he could win the backing of Charles VIII.[32] But his authority in Florence was beginning to wane. The Franciscans, old rivals of the Dominicans, called for an ordeal by fire to settle matters, in which representatives of either side would walk through flame to establish the truth or falsehood of Savonarola's doctrine. It was arranged for 7 April but then cancelled, for which Savonarola blamed the Franciscans. Infuriated supporters of both sides took to the streets. Riots broke out; houses were sacked; there were multiple deaths and woundings in the clashes that followed. Eventually the city authorities ordered Savonarola to leave Florence; when he did not, he was arrested.[33] The crucifix was restored to the cathedral and under extensive torture Savonarola confessed to being a false prophet, driven by personal ambition, interested only in worldly glory.[34] Whether he was in fact persuaded to make the confession or whether the records were falsified remains an open question, but the confession served a purpose: it helped the civic authorities prevent a cult building around him. With two colleagues, Savonarola was condemned to death and burnt at the stake on 23 May 1498.

For all that discussions of some moderate reform might be acceptable at the papal court, changes to Church structures inevitably ran up against substantial vested interests. The pope was not about to tolerate a radical theocracy on his doorstep, nor did Savonarola's brand of hellfire preaching eventually endear him to the Florentines: rhetoric was one thing, policing quite another. With Savonarola dead, the city returned to a more conventional form of republican government. The Medici remained in exile, but the artists at least could be welcomed back.

Chapter Five

The Art of War

As the wars gathered pace on the Italian peninsula, many artists and architects doubled as military engineers, designing fortifications and weapons in between their famous works. While many of Leonardo da Vinci's designs – for parachutes, gliders and armoured vehicles – were speculative, he also took a practical military role. In the later years of the fifteenth century he had made his home in Milan, and thus saw at first hand the struggle for control of the city. Following the death of Charles VIII in April 1498 the new king of France, Charles' cousin Louis XII, who had a tenuous claim to Milan via his paternal grandmother, set his sights on conquering the city from Ludovico Sforza, in which he succeeded the following year. (Ludovico, who must have cursed himself for ever having the idea of turning to the French, briefly recaptured Milan in 1500, but was betrayed by his own Swiss mercenaries and spent the next eight years a French prisoner. He died in 1508.) Amid all this, observing that Ludovico had 'lost his state, his personal possessions and his liberty, and none of his enterprises has been completed',[1] Leonardo fled to Venice. There he was employed as a military architect and engineer and designed defences aimed at protecting the Friuli region from a possible Turkish invasion. His Venetian stay was short-lived, however: he swiftly returned to Florence, where he was once again in demand as a painter; the agents of Isabella d'Este, marchioness of Mantua, reported on his activities there as she pursued her interest in a Leonardo portrait. In Florence, however, no one of Leonardo's prominence could avoid being drawn into city politicking, which was probably how he found himself in the company of both Cesare Borgia and a Florentine envoy, Niccolò Machiavelli.

In his capacity as secretary to a committee known as the 'Ten of War', Machiavelli, now in his early thirties, had carried out a range of military and diplomatic roles, as we will see below, although he never reached the rank of ambassador.[2] In July 1499 he had been dispatched by the Florentines to the court of Caterina Riario Sforza, regent of the town of Imola and nearby Forlì, both of which lay on the important strategic route from Bologna to the Adriatic ports of Pesaro and Ancona, for negotiations regarding her son Ottaviano's role in Florentine military service. (Caterina's role here points to the important part played by women in the conduct of these wars.) Three years on, in June 1502, Machiavelli arrived in Urbino for meetings with Cesare Borgia, whose commanders had been involved in a rebellion in Arezzo, a town subject to Florentine rule. Urbino lay in the hills close to the Adriatic coast, the northern part of the Marche, and was bordered by the dominions of Florence to its west and the Papal States to its south. Ruled by the Montefeltro family, Urbino had a fine ducal palace and was a centre of Renaissance culture and learning. Among its architectural detailing is a design of a garter, a reference to the Order of the Garter that its previous ruler Duke Federico da Montefeltro, a *condottiere* of high reputation, had received in 1474 from King Edward IV of England.[3] Cesare had seized the city with a highly impressive surprise attack, and Machiavelli reported his impressions of the pope's son in a letter to the Florentine government:

> This Lord is truly splendid and magnificent, and in war there is no enterprise so great that it does not appear small to him; in the pursuit of glory and lands he never rests nor recognizes fatigue or danger. He arrives in one place before it is known that he has left another; he is popular with his soldiers and he has collected the best men in Italy; these things make him victorious and formidable particularly when added to perpetual good fortune.[4]

It is possible that while in Urbino Machiavelli and the ambassador whom he was accompanying offered Leonardo's services to Borgia.[5]

Cesare's French-backed campaign to create a state for himself in the Romagna had been largely successful: he ended up with Caterina Riario Sforza, regent of Forlì, as a hostage and made a victorious entry into Rome on 25 February 1500. Later that year there followed the murder of his brother-in-law Alfonso. Cesare, meanwhile, was continuing his campaign in the Romagna, with an overwhelming vote of confidence in his efforts from the Venetian Great Council: murder did not count badly against him as long as military alliances were confirmed. Not that Cesare was a great respecter of the honourable norms of war, as Astorre Manfredi, lord of Faenza, discovered after he was taken prisoner: in June 1502 his body turned up floating in the Tiber, just as Juan Borgia's had done five years before. But by this time Cesare enjoyed the title of duke of the Romagna and not only could he get away with murder, he could also command advice from the starriest of military architects.

Leonardo da Vinci is sometimes portrayed as a man who disliked military conflict. His description of war as 'brutal madness', however, needs to be read in context: it comes from his *Treatise on Painting*, in which he was discussing history paintings. He noted that in battle scenes (such as the one he himself went on to design in Florence) 'many shortenings and contortions of figures happen, amongst such an enraged multitude of actors, possessed, as it were, of a brutal madness'.[6] This is not, therefore, a general observation on contemporary warfare, but a specific comment on what an image of soldiers in battle should look like. On 18 August 1502 Cesare Borgia granted Leonardo the title of Architect and General Engineer, and among his work in this capacity was a plan of Imola, taking a revolutionary bird's-eye view of the town that offered an unprecedented level of precision for military planners.[7] (By comparison, Barbari's view of Venice, made a year or two before, showed the city from an oblique angle.[8]) Leonardo also made a sketch of Borgia himself, showing the commander bearded and grim.

In October 1502 Machiavelli began a longer mission to Borgia, and his path must have crossed with Leonardo's in Imola. This was a fine, fortified town in low country, the view from the top of its fortress tower stretching for miles, while the castle itself – low, square and moated with a neat double drawbridge arrangement – was equipped with comfortable lodgings for its lords. Here Machiavelli went on to witness Cesare's ruthless countermove against a conspiracy among his own men, and wrote an account of it. He described the fears of Borgia's lieutenants that their master was becoming too powerful, and that if he succeeded in his aim of conquering Bologna he might then move against them. The Florentines, who had their own reasons for disliking certain of the plotters, offered Borgia assistance. On

26 December, Machiavelli wrote from Cesena (a town not far from the Adriatic coast, on the main road south-east from Bologna) with an account of the murder of Don Ramiro de Lorqua, a Spanish captain whom Cesare had once entrusted with significant responsibility, but whom he had now thrown in jail for his part in the conspiracy.

> Messer Rimirro this morning was found in two pieces on the public square, where he still is; and all the people have been able to see him. Nobody feels sure of the cause of his death, except that so it has pleased the Prince, who shows that he can make and unmake men as he likes, according to their deserts.[9]

Borgia, meanwhile, had left the town of Cesena for Fano, and tricked the conspirators, led by men of the Vitelli and Orsini families, into waiting for him in Senigallia, about thirteen miles down the coast. Machiavelli's dry tone belies the drama of events; he later wrote up a literary account of how the affair had played out, with Borgia subsequently giving licence to his own soldiers to attack those of the conspirators: 'And when night came on,' he wrote, 'and the disturbances had stopped, the Duke [Borgia] decided to have Vitellozzo and Liverotto killed; and taking them into a place together, he had them strangled.'[10] His letter of 8 January sums up his impression of Borgia: 'Duke Valentino exhibits a fortune unheard of, a courage and a confidence more than human that he can attain all his desires.'[11]

Meanwhile, as the reality of the chaos unleashed by the invasions of Italy became apparent, Alexander VI was trying to pursue an alliance with Venice in an effort to check the expansion of both Spain and France. 'Although Spaniards by birth,' he told the Venetian ambassador, 'and temporarily allied with France, we are Italians and it is in Italy that our fortune lies.'[12] Fortunes, however, could change very quickly in the Italian Wars, and it soon suited the pope's interests to turn towards a Spanish alliance instead. Cesare's huge military success meant he could afford to dispense with French support for the Romagna campaign, and conflict had broken out again in the realm of Naples, where the Spanish were close to vanquishing the French. When the pope appointed nine new cardinals, five of them were Spaniards, bringing the number of Spanish cardinals to sixteen (more than a quarter of the College), a potentially powerful faction in a future papal election.

Yet these fine prospects for the Borgias did not last. On 12 August 1503 both Alexander and Cesare were struck down by fever. Amid rumours of poison, including one that he had accidentally poisoned himself while trying to poison his guests,[13] Alexander died six days later, leaving his son in a precarious position. When the conclave opened on 16 September, Cardinal Piccolomini, a compromise candidate in serious ill health, was elected as Pius III. Pius might have allowed Cesare to retain his Romagna territories but the new pope lived only until 18 October. There would have to be a new conclave, and with Giuliano della Rovere the only credible candidate, Cesare agreed to support him in return for his own continuation in the offices he currently held in the Papal States. On 1 November Giuliano was elected Pope Julius II, but it quickly became clear that he was preparing to double-cross Cesare.

Cesare now found himself the victim of a deal between the Spanish monarchs Ferdinand and Isabella and Julius II. For all that Alexander might have hoped for loyalty from the nation of his birth and in return for his creation of Spanish cardinals, Ferdinand and Isabella declined to support Cesare against the pope. When the last of his Romagna strongholds surrendered, the Spanish governor of Naples (which by that time had been recaptured from the French) sent Cesare as a prisoner to Spain. He escaped in 1506 and found refuge with his brother-in-law, the king of Navarre, for whom in 1507 he died fighting in a skirmish during civil war. If there was any redeeming feature to Cesare's years in power it was in his government of the Romagna, which was generally (if not universally) seen as popular; on the other hand his notoriety was confirmed not only by his brutal disposal of the lieutenants who crossed him but by salacious rumours about his sex life, not least the infamous Vatican 'banquet of the chestnuts' on All Saints' Eve, 1501, in which naked courtesans were said to have competed to pick chestnuts from the floor.

With Cesare's patronage gone, Leonardo looked to other options. In February 1503 he drew up project proposals for Sultan Bayezid II, including a design for a bridge across the Golden Horn, the inlet of the Bosphorus dividing the historic centre of Constantinople from the district of Pera, home to the city's foreign traders.[14] For all the religious hostility to the Ottoman Turks in Italy, they remained important trading partners, and for all that Leonardo had previously planned defences *against* the Turks while in Venetian service, a job was a job, and it was not only mercenaries who might switch sides. The scheme, however, never came to fruition and with Milan now under French control, Leonardo opted for employment with the government of Florence. Here too his roles were various. Between 1503 and 1505 he drew a number of plans of the river Arno, exploring the possibility of making it navigable between Florence and the sea; he was involved in a military scheme to divert the Arno from its usual path near Pisa in 1504 when that city was under siege.[15] His skills in art and engineering had wide application in warfare. It is no surprise that in his *Book of the Courtier* (to which we will come in more detail), Baldassare Castiglione would note that

> from painting, which is in itself a most worthy and noble art, many useful skills can be derived, and not least for military purposes: thus a knowledge of the art gives one the facility to sketch towns, rivers, bridges, citadels, fortresses and similar things, which otherwise cannot be shown to others even if, with a great deal of effort, the details are memorised.[16]

This was a period of extensive debate and experimentation as to how best to improve fortifications to withstand the new artillery that had done so much destruction in the initial French descent of 1494. (One can overplay the significance of artillery: a lack of supplies or relief could and did prompt surrender too; nonetheless, the technological developments mattered.[17]) Some of the early initiatives were remarkably simple: for example, digging a trench behind an existing city wall so that even if it were breached the troops outside had a further barrier to overcome. Besieging troops, on the other hand, also had to deal with an increasing use of artillery from inside towns under siege, which prevented the besiegers moving closer towards the walls (at least without the use of trenches). It was rare for a siege to be broken by bombardment alone, though sometimes multiple breaches might work. More often victory resulted from a combination of starving out the participants, tunnelling under walls and setting mines. Perhaps most importantly a new style of fortification now came into its own. This was the *trace italienne*. Established in Italy by 1515 it featured pointed bastions at the corners of a fortress from which fire could be directed back along its walls, and ditches on either side of the wall. The ditches meant the walls could be built thick but relatively low (as opposed to the old-fashioned high, thin walls that made an excellent target for artillery fire), and in combination with gunfire from the bastions protected them from assault by scaling.[18] It was a means of fortification that significantly improved the chances for a small city state of protecting itself from attack.[19]

After the fall of Savonarola in 1498, the city of Florence returned to a more moderate form of republican government, rejecting the radical Savonarolan elements and electing Piero Soderini *gonfaloniere* for life. The 'gonfaloniere' was literally the standard-bearer of the city, and in some ways this role echoed the Venetian practice of electing a doge for life. Like any government of this period, the Florentine *Signoria* saw art as a means of glorifying the city's achievements, and in 1503–4 they commissioned first Leonardo then Michelangelo to paint a pair of frescoes in the Hall of the Five Hundred in Florence's Palazzo Vecchio, depicting the fourteenth- and fifteenth-century battles of Cascina and Anghiari. Both were significant in Florentine history. The Battle of Anghiari (which Leonardo was to paint) had taken place in 1440 between Florence and Milan. The Florentines had won, and their victory established their dominance in central Italy. The Battle of Cascina had likewise been a Florentine victory, over Pisa in 1364, and Michelangelo's depiction drew directly on a *History of the Florentine People* by Leonardo Bruni, a distinguished humanist thinker who in the fifteenth century had served as chancellor of Florence.[20] Neither of these paintings survives, although there has long been fascination about whether some remnants – or perhaps more than remnants – live on behind the works that covered them over when the palazzo was remodelled in the middle of the sixteenth century. Both artists, however, produced preparatory drawings (known as cartoons) that were later copied. Rubens copied a part of Leonardo's *Anghiari*; Aristotele del Sangallo the cartoon for Michelangelo's *Cascina*. Benvenuto Cellini, an artist, goldsmith and writer, saw the work for himself:

> The splendid Leonardo had chosen to show a battle-scene, with horsemen fighting together and standards being captured, and he had drawn it magnificently. In his cartoon, Michelangelo depicted a number of infantrymen who because of the summer heat had gone down to

bathe in the river Arno: he caught in his drawing the moment when the alarm is sounded and the naked soldiers rush for their arms. He showed all their actions and gestures so wonderfully that no ancient or modern artist has ever reached such a high standard. Leonardo's as well, as I said, was wonderfully beautiful. One of these cartoons was in the Medici palace, and the other in the Pope's hall: and while they remained intact they served as a school for all the world.[21]

Perhaps most importantly, they sum up the importance of rivalry in the Renaissance, of competition between artists for commissions, of competition among patrons for an artist's service.[22] And if the modern significance of these works is primarily for their artistic value, they are a reminder that military conquest and victory were very much at the forefront of government. Indeed, they were intended specifically to inspire the citizens as they met in the council hall to deliberate on policy. At the time of the commission, Florence was still trying to recover the port city of Pisa, which had rebelled during the French descent of 1494. As the campaign was dragging on, Leonardo's fresco might remind them of the heroics of battle, while Michelangelo's was a reminder that no smart soldier should be caught unprepared.[23]

Michelangelo (1475–1564) was, like Leonardo, born in Tuscany and had been raised in Florence where he was apprenticed to Domenico Ghirlandaio at the age of thirteen. He swiftly secured Medici patronage and sculpted his early relief works, *Madonna of the Steps* and *Battle of the Centaurs* while still in his teens. For much of the period of Savonarola's rule he lived away from Florence: his most famous project of this period was the *Pietà*, now in St Peter's, sculpted for a French cardinal and showing the dead Christ draped in a remarkably naturalistic mode across the lap of his mother Mary. Michelangelo returned to Florence after the fall of Savonarola and it was for the Soderini regime that he produced his most iconic sculpture, the statue of *David*, a symbol of Florentine struggle against tyranny. The political dynamics of city life were rarely absent from artistic commissions: during this second period in Florence, Leonardo also painted a *Virgin and Child with St Anne*. For all the warmth and humanity of the composition, it had a political message too. In the mid fourteenth century the Florentines had risen up against the tyrannical duke of Athens – on St Anne's Day. Even a seemingly religious work, such as this one for the church of the Servite Order, might have civic significance. Leonardo also made drawings for a *Hercules* and a *Salvator Mundi* (Saviour of the World), subjects that via feats of strength (the former) and the coincidence of the 1494 expulsion of the Medici with the feast day of St Saviour (the latter) fitted the symbolism of the republic.[24]

Here in Florence Leonardo also began work on his single most celebrated painting, the *Mona Lisa*, the woman with 'a smile so pleasing,' in Vasari's words, 'that it seems more divine than human, and it was considered a wondrous thing that it was as lively as the smile of the living original.'[25] The sitter, Lisa Gherardini, was the wife of a ruthless and upwardly mobile silk merchant, Francesco del Giocondo. She had been born in 1479 to an old city family; she was the second wife of Francesco, who was fourteen years her senior. Such age gaps were not unusual for wealthy couples, whose marriages were often as much about property transactions as about any affectionate relationship. In this case, as part of her dowry Lisa brought to the marriage an estate in Chianti, San Silvestro. The choice of Lisa as model has always been a little mysterious: Leonardo rejected the demands of very much more famous patrons to paint their portraits, but as far as it is possible to tell, this was a simple commercial commission. Debate about the identity of Mona Lisa has often been prompted by the assertion that the woman in the portrait was painted 'at the behest of the late Magnificent Giuliano de' Medici' (a son of Lorenzo the Magnificent). The most recent research, however, suggests that once at the French court – and as he reworked the painting from a simple portrait into a more philosophical, abstract piece – Leonardo opted to highlight his influential patron in preference to the lesser-known Florentine merchant who had originally commissioned him to paint his wife.[26]

Like many Florentine traders, Francesco had connections well beyond Italy. His family had business interests in Lisbon and in the sugar trade of Portugal's colony of Madeira, an island a few hundred miles off the coast of Morocco; Lisa's brother made his home in the Castilian colony of the Canary Islands to its south. Alvise Cadamosto of Venice, who visited the West African coast as early as 1455, described the production in Madeira of wheat and wine as well as sugar and timber (*madeira* is Portuguese for wood). Prior to his departure he had been presented in Portugal with samples of sugar from Madeira, as well as a substance called 'dragon's blood', in fact the resin of the dragon tree *Dracaena draco*, used at the time in medicinal remedies. Cadamosto's narrative of his voyage describes quite cold-bloodedly how the early Portuguese settlers on the wooded island burnt its trees to the ground, the fires burning with such ferocity that they were forced to spend two days and nights in the sea to escape the flames. Those clearances, however, freed the ground for cultivation: Madeira, Cadamosto wrote, was 'one large garden, and everyone reaps golden rewards'.[27]

Golden rewards, however, came not only at environmental but also at human cost. Francesco del Giocondo was very likely a slave trader too. He brought a series of enslaved people, mostly women, to be baptised in Florence during the 1480s and 1490s. One of them, a twelve-year-old boy named Giovanbattista, had come via Portugal; three of the women – given the names Silla, Grazia and Caterina – were described as 'Moors', an unspecific term which might indicate either North or sub-Saharan African ancestry; another woman had the name Cumba, which has West African associations.[28] The commissioning of a portrait from Florence's leading painter was just the sort of thing a merchant might do to establish himself as a cultural patron, but the back story of Francesco's finances puts a new and less marvellous perspective on the Mona Lisa's famous smile. This later Renaissance art was entangled not only with war, but also with colonialism, and these wider phenomena did not only affect the cultural world, but Italian society as a whole.

Chapter Six

Soldiers and Society

While Florence was occupied by the drama of Savonarola, and the Romagna by Cesare's machinations, further south the conflict over Naples played out to a conclusion, in the process illustrating many of the factors that would characterise the next decades of the Italian Wars. As we saw in Chapter Three, in 1494 Charles VIII had succeeded in seizing the city without much opposition. Holding power, however, was a different matter: the troublesome Neapolitan barons had no more love for Charles than the alternatives, including King Ferrandino, who had been left in power when Charles had withdrawn to the north.

Charles' first move to secure his newly acquired territory was to try for an alliance, very much the usual tactic in this war of multiple states. On 9 October 1495 he came to terms with Milan in the Peace of Vercelli, hoping to gain some assistance from the Sforza for the defence of Naples. His opponent in Naples was doing exactly the same thing: Ferrandino had secured backing from Spain and Venice against Charles' viceroy and his forces. Moreover, as so often in these wars, while the major forces were those of the French and Spanish, local tensions came into play too, so this was as much a war between factions of the Neapolitan barons as an attempt at conquest by either of the larger European powers. The war for Naples was also typical in its combination of pitched battles and local uprisings. In the summer of 1495 there had already been some flashpoints: the French had won at Seminara on 28 June, their heavy cavalry and Swiss pikes outdoing the more lightly armed Spanish;[1] there had then been an uprising in Naples on 6–7 July and thanks to help from barons of the Colonna family Ferrandino temporarily regained power. By early 1496 he had secured both the city's key fortresses, the Castel Nuovo and the Castel dell'Ovo. Meanwhile, the Spanish commander Gonzalo

Fernández de Córdoba, nicknamed 'el Gran Capitán' and a star tac-
tician of this conflict, carefully delayed further fighting until he had
the necessary reinforcements.[2] Choosing your battles – both in terms
of timing and terrain – was all-important. No surprise that Giovio
described Córdoba, who had made his name in the war for Granada,
as the most noble and successful of the foreign commanders in Italy.[3]

Just as Cesare Borgia's illness had prevented him from asserting his
rule in the Romagna at a crucial moment, so the Aragonese rulers of
Naples found themselves at the mercy of poor health. On 7 September
1496 Ferrandino died and his uncle Federico inherited. Meanwhile,
King Ferdinand of Aragon (of the legitimate line of Ferrante's family)
decided to claim the Neapolitan Crown for himself, and opened negotiations with the French to partition the territory. Ferdinand's proposal
for partition was welcomed by Louis XII of France, whose military
priority was at this point to seize the duchy of Milan (in which, as
we saw above, he succeeded in 1499, ousting Ludovico Sforza in the
process). The decision to limit fights to one front was a feature of
strategising throughout these wars. In 1500 Louis and Ferdinand and
Isabella signed the Treaty of Granada, in which they divided Naples
between them, deposing Federico in the process. But the Spanish then
turned on their former allies and took the kingdom for themselves,
extending their reach east into the Mediterranean. These were brutal
conflicts. After one three-month siege, only half of a ten-thousand-
strong garrison survived. The French practice of burning buildings
after their sacks and massacres had not been seen in Italy for centuries,
and 'filled all the kingdom with the greatest terror'.[4]

Those historians who wrote accounts of the wars while they were
still going on, such as the Florentines Niccolò Machiavelli and Francesco Guicciardini, tended to highlight their novelty, and to posit 1494
as a dramatic watershed in the conduct of war. Modern historians are
more sensitive to the continuities, though there is no doubt that, as
one puts it, the wars were also 'a bloody laboratory of experimentation'.[5] So far as technology and tactics are concerned, the innovations
of these wars did not come from nowhere. Men from the countryside
around Lucca, for example, were invited to join the city's crossbow
competitions as early as the 1440s in the hope of improving the city's
preparedness for war, and by the end of the century, as gunpowder
weapons became increasingly important, the authorities added

shooting competitions to ensure the local men were equipped to fight with arquebuses.[6] The Swiss had gradually been changing infantry tactics since their defeat by the Milanese at Arbedo in 1422, after which they began to swap halberds (pole weapons about six feet long, topped with an axe-head and spike) for pikes of almost three times the length, which were more effective against cavalry. Unlike the halberd, which was a useful individual weapon, the unwieldy pike worked best for formation fighting, and the Swiss developed ferocious 'hedgehogs' of infantry, as well – through careful training – as the ability to manoeuvre them effectively in the field. The camaraderie needed between the men in these formations was vital: for all that the popular image of the Renaissance tends to focus on the individual great genius, Italian warfare was a lot about teamwork.[7] The soldiers would form a square, their pikes protruding six feet from each side. In between the pikemen, arquebusiers would point their weapons out. Having fired their one shot, they would fall back to be replaced by a second line of arque-busiers for the minute or two it took to reload. It was a tactic that required training and discipline, to create what was in effect a human machine gun. It was this shift from cavalry to the infantry 'pike-and-shot' formation that – along with siege warfare – came to characterise these conflicts.

Gonzalo de Córdoba's innovative strategy was particularly apparent in his use of arquebusiers, not least at the Battle of Cerignola on 28 April 1503, perhaps the first in which firearms were decisive. The Spanish – who had arrived first at Cerignola, a small town near the Adriatic coast – had the advantage. Their commander had his men dig a ditch and embankment, behind which he stationed his forces, using his arquebusiers to cover both cavalry and infantry. The French arrived late in the day and debated whether to attack or wait for the morning. Deciding to advance, they soon reached the ditch, found their horses could not cross it and, as confusion mounted, rounds of fire from the Spanish arquebuses hit. The battle lasted less than an hour, and it left two thousand French soldiers dead.[8] The speed of the Spanish victory was well enough known that some years later it was the basis for a joke in Baldassare Castiglione's *The Book of the Courtier* in which one of the commanders turns up late to find he's missed the action.[9] 'Spanish affairs are prospering,' observed the Vene-tian ambassador in Rome.[10]

Few soldiers of these wars wrote any detailed descriptions of the battlefield, and the diplomatic reports are typically curt, but hints at the experience of battle survive thanks to Leonardo da Vinci, who consistently stressed the importance of observation and wrote detailed notes in preparation for making battle paintings. 'Represent first', he wrote, 'the smoke of the artillery, mingled in the air with the dust tossed up by the movement of the horses and combatants.' Amid the guidance on colour and light, his text is full of observations of the realities of battle:

> Let the air be full of arrows in every direction, some shooting upwards, some falling, some flying level. The balls from the guns must have a train of smoke following their course [...] And if you make anyone fallen you must make the mark where he has slipped on the dust turned into bloodstained mire; and round about in the half-liquid earth show the print of the trampling of men and horses who have passed that way. Make a horse dragging the dead body of his master [...] Make the conquered and beaten pale, with brows raised and knit [...] Show someone using one hand as a shield for his terrified eyes with the palm turned towards the enemy; while the other rests on the ground to support his half-raised body. Represent others shouting with their mouths wide open, and running away. Put all sorts of arms between the feet of the combatants, such as broken shields, lances, broken swords and other such objects. Make the dead partly or entirely covered with dust, which is mingled with the oozing blood and changed into crimson mire, and let the blood be seen by its colour flowing in a sinuous stream from the corpse to the dust.[11]

Peace negotiations in the late spring of 1503 came to nothing. In June that year the Spanish seized the Castel Nuovo in Naples by dint of mining then blowing up the walls.[12] There was another success for the Spanish at the Battle of Garigliano late in December, when once again smart tactics (in this case a surprise attack) proved crucial. The French were forced to abandon their artillery and, after a brief siege of the nearby town of Gaeta, the Spanish triumphed in a victory that put an end to French ambitions in Naples.[13]

Over the next two decades, the Spanish infantry was transformed with a wholehearted adoption of the pike-and-shot tactics that had proved so successful here. Yet for all that Gonzalo de Córdoba's lead-ership made a difference, the stoicism of the Spanish soldiers was also essential to their victory. In the late spring heat at Cerignola they marched in 'burning sun' and several soldiers died en route. Wintering at Garigliano, they had to endure storms and rain.[14] Until the last couple of decades, this experience – of the soldiers who actually fought these wars – had been rather little studied. More recently, historians have begun to look in greater depth at the question of what it was actually like to fight.

The writers of the period were often rather scathing about the quality of the troops. In his dialogue on the *Art of War*, Machiavelli had his protagonist observe that foreigners who embarked on military service were typically 'among the most wicked of a province', those who were 'scandalous, idle, without restraint, without religion, fugi-tives from their father's rule, blasphemers, gamblers, in every part badly raised'.[15] This was an unexceptional view so far as intellectuals were concerned: the military commanders in Giovio's dialogue on *Notable Men and Women* also fretted that things had 'become dreadfully slack – in vain will anyone either seek obedience from a soldier, or expect leadership and diligence from a commander'.[16] Only a handful of soldiers wrote about their experiences at war (reflective diaries are a phenomenon of later history), but the contemporary sources point to financial hardship as the biggest motivating factor to sign up.[17] Among the Spanish armies, most recruits came from the larger urban centres of Iberia. They may have been rural migrants to those centres, which had large numbers of unemployed and poor men for whom military service might have promised stability at worst and wealth at best. The armies also drew in young noblemen, especially those with money troubles: these were a modest percentage of the total but were entitled to a larger stipend on grounds of rank.[18] Some foreigners (Portuguese, Flemish and Burgundian) joined up, and some reports refer to the presence of Moors and Jews in the armies too, although they most often do so in order to blame the non-Christians for the worst wartime atrocities. That said, armies probably did include some members (or converted members) of religious minorities; moreover, a painting by Paris Bordon of a man in armour, produced in the middle of the sixteenth century when Bordon was living in Milan, shows him with two pages, one black and one white.[19] Most recruits

were in their twenties: some served only for a year or so, while others
remained for two decades. The Italian Wars in particular seem to have
attracted men who planned to stay for the longer term.[20]

In relation to the organisation of its army, Spain was an unusual
case: its troops were more permanent, more professional and its
recruitment more centralised and state-controlled than most other
armies'. Elsewhere in Europe, by contrast, there were much larger
roles for individual feudal lords and foreign mercenaries.[21] These came
from a wide variety of places. The Swiss cantons, for example, had a
long tradition of mercenary service that had emerged (rather para-
doxically) from the practice of raising citizen militias for defence. Over
time supplying troops became fundamental to the local economies;
these soldiers earned roughly the wage of a skilled craftsman, twice
what they might have had from agricultural work, and could hope
for bonuses on top, while a clutch of noble families provided commanders expert against a range of opponents.[22] The other major group
of mercenaries at this time were the German landsknechts, who came
into their own under the Emperor Maximilian when he realised he
needed a permanent and well-trained force to beat the Swiss.[23]

While the individual companies (which varied in size) of the French
and Spanish armies were often made up of soldiers of a single nation,
the wars themselves were very international and brought numerous
men – of all ranks – into contact with Italian peoples and customs.
The first French army to march into Italy was predominantly French,
but both the French and Spanish soon began to recruit Italians, to
whom were added Swiss and German infantry, Balkan stradiots and
adventurers from all across the continent of Europe – including from
England, perhaps its most famous example being Thomas Cromwell,
later chief minister to Henry VIII. Others made their way south to
Italy from the Netherlands or Burgundy via the trade routes of the
Holy Roman Empire.

Across Europe, un- and under-employment was enough of a
problem that it was straightforward to recruit troops, not least because
soldiers were paid a signing-on fee. Beyond that, soldiers could expect
to be paid on a standard scale. During the Italian Wars, pike infantry
received about three ducats a month: some elite troops could insist
on more, notably the Swiss and Germans. The Swiss were sufficiently
in demand that their pay was delivered monthly; other less fortunate

soldiers might wait months before any wages materialised. Men-at-arms (cavalry) were paid rather more, but their 90–110 ducats a year had to cover the costs of three men. Captains were often obliged to extend credit to their men until funds arrived from the central administration to cover the costs.[24] All this was, however, subject to deductions for supplies. Arquebusiers, whose supplies of match, powder and bullets were more costly, were paid extra to compensate. Spanish arquebusiers, for example, received a third more than did pikemen, while there were additional payments to men of noble rank. But all too often soldiers went without the money that was due – sometimes because of fraud by captains, sometimes because the promised royal subsidy simply did not arrive on time.[25] Unpaid wages were often compensated for by the promise of booty. Beyond the prospect of a wage – or the opportunities for looting and ransom – perhaps some men valued the prospect of seeing a world beyond their usual sphere; others may have sought an escape from unhappy circumstances of one sort or another.[26]

The Italian states struggled to match this approach. Italy had a different socioeconomic structure which made long-term recruitment of troops tricky, and no history of organised military service in the style of the German landsknechts or the Swiss militias. Instead, as we will see, it had a long tradition of employing mercenaries to fight its wars. The new tactics required training, larger numbers of men and cohesion, and so the Italian states had all the more reason to collaborate with larger powers, with their own troops taking supporting and complementary roles.[27] This was, in part, a product of Italy's dynamic economy: unlike in other more economically deprived parts of Europe, where soldiering held a greater financial attraction, it made little sense for Italians to leave a decent artisan job in order to fight. That economy, meanwhile, was the product of a host of demographic and social factors – factors that affected the ways the war was fought, but which were affected in turn by the conflict.

At the time of the French invasion, there were about eleven million people living in Italy. It was one of two heavily urbanised regions of Europe, the other being the Netherlands. Venice and Milan had populations of about 100,000. Genoa had 60,000 people; Bologna and Rome about 55,000 each; Florence had about 70,000.[28] Some of these cities had been substantially larger before the Black Death of 1348: Florence had had over 100,000 inhabitants in 1300. The basic impact of the Black Death – which killed around a third of the Italian population – had been to create labour shortages and force up wages.[29] Despite the relative urbanisation, Italy's largest employment sector by some distance remained agriculture, while in the cities trades ranged from blacksmithing to carpentry to weaving. There were local specialisms: textiles from Lucca were valued, as was glass from Venice. Elsewhere, firms produced jewellery, furniture, pottery, books and musical instruments besides the heavier industries such as shipbuilding and mining. There was a sophisticated banking sector that facilitated trade across Europe and beyond through bills of exchange, while on a more modest level pawnbrokers catered to the needs of farmers who needed short-term loans to buy seeds or city artisans with a cashflow problem.

The economic life of cities was organised around guilds, which regulated craft production, and guild membership was often associated with political rights. In Florence, for example, different guilds represented wool and silk manufacturers and merchants, physicians and pharmacists; judges, lawyers and notaries; blacksmiths; stonemasons; saddlers; armourers and so on. To become a master craftsman, a boy had to serve an apprenticeship conforming to the guild regulations before progressing to the status of worker and then (if he was fortunate) master. Not everyone succeeded in this aim, but outside the guild structure there were other opportunities for casual work. A man with the necessary skills might become a journeyman (day labourer) in his trade; if those skills were not in demand, he could work in unskilled labouring or agriculture. Because religion and its rituals imbued this society, members of a guild might well also be members of a confraternity or brotherhood, a lay religious organisation that undertook charitable work like the distribution of food and alms, cared for the sick and might also be patrons of culture. Many celebrated Renaissance artworks were commissioned by confraternities, and engagement with them was an integral part of their rituals: they became the focus for meditation on the suffering of Christ, for example, sometimes in combination with practices including self-flagellation.[30] Confraternities were also important social networks, and through their charitable and religious activities members might gain useful contacts for work and public life.[31] Access to credit depended on such social networks and on personal assessments of one's honour and reputation. In short, this was a world in which there were many more attractive options and incentives for work than time spent at war.

A significant percentage of Italians spent time in domestic service. Servants accounted for just over twelve per cent of the population in Verona in 1502; numbers grew higher in Florence later in the century (16.7 per cent in 1552) but remained lower in Venice (7.65 per cent in 1563). In Venice, households, even wealthy ones, were relatively small, with just two or three servants, though that changed gradually as aristocratic fashions from elsewhere in Italy and Europe, which favoured larger, grander establishments, took hold (not least thanks to contact during the Italian Wars). For many young women a period of domestic service offered a means of raising a dowry.[32]

Unless manumission documents survive, it is often hard to distinguish in records between enslaved and free domestic servants, who did very similar household jobs, but about one per cent of people in fifteenth-century Italy were enslaved, the majority of whom came from the areas around the Black Sea. As the century wore on those markets came to be dominated by Ottoman traders, and the Venetians and Genoese sought enslaved people instead from the Balkans and West Africa. There was supposedly a prohibition on enslaving Christians, but it was not always respected, and conversion did not automatically gain a slave freedom. The enslaved people in late fifteenth- and sixteenth-century Italy were ethnically diverse, and gaining freedom at some point in their lives was a genuine prospect for a minority: the racialised system of chattel slavery in the Americas, and its outright contempt for the lives and humanity of the enslaved, was yet to come. On the other hand, Italian merchants were very familiar with the profits to be made from trafficking in people, and they took that knowledge with them when they travelled further afield.

All but the poorest of households in Italy had more than one room. Typically there was a *sala* or reception room, which over the course of the sixteenth century took on a more public function of welcoming guests. This would be furnished with portable trestle tables, benches, stools and perhaps rush chairs. A sideboard or *credenza* in a more modest house might simply have a basin and ewer on top, but in wealthier households silver or gilt plate would be displayed to guests here. There are cases of aspirational families hiring additional plate when entertaining to ensure a lavish impression of wealth. Only the finest of palaces had running water via a wall-fountain in the dining room. Portraits of saints hung over doorways; there would be candles to give some light in the dusk and fire irons to ensure the fire was kept burning. Chambers were used for sleeping. Beds came with a variety of hanging arrangement: some were four-poster, some had curtains hung from a single point in the ceiling. The basic storage unit was the chest or *cassone*: wealthy girls would have these painted with scenes for their trousseaux. Even the most celebrated Italian artists painted on furniture: Botticelli was among those whose panels (known as *spalliere*) might have acted as headboards or backboards for a bed or chest.[33] If there was one thing to distinguish the houses of the rich it was the quality of their textiles: wall-hangings, Turkish carpets placed over tables, superior bedlinen. In both middle- and upper-class households the selection of furnishings said something about the people who lived there, even if in the former case the number of valuable objects might be small: 'one gilded marble bowl, one maiolica plate, or two crystal drinking cups'.[34] Michelangelo's illustrated menus, sketched on the back of a letter from 1518, give an impression of the available food: 'two breads, a pitcher of wine, a herring, tortelli' or 'a salad, four breads, a pitcher of sweet wine and a quarter dry wine, a little plate of spinach, four anchovies and tortelli', or 'six breads, two fennel soups, a herring, a pitcher of sweet wine'.[35]

In wartime, however, it was not so easy to come by good supplies. The wars also demanded an enormous effort so far as logistics were concerned, and if they extended economic opportunity to some, they also imposed enormous costs on others. The large numbers of troops fighting on the Italian peninsula had to be accommodated somewhere. Typically, they were billeted in the countryside. In winter their commanders may have requisitioned inns or private houses; in summertime they would camp or even sleep outdoors. For officers, especially on long campaigns, the camp experience might well be deluxe. A fresco in the Castello di Issogne shows the castle guard in rather privileged surroundings, eating, drinking and playing backgammon at table, their weapons hanging on the wall behind them; the comfort does not prevent three coming to blows.[36] Campaigns at a distance, however, also posed problems of supply: food for the soldiers; fodder for their horses; and indeed the horses themselves. Merchants in northern and central Italy shifted from supplying cities to supplying armies; over the course of the wars the role of the quartermaster became more established in army structures. Spain had the advantage of shipping produce by sea, not only from its mainland but thanks to its control of Sicily.

Shortages of money contributed to shortages of food, as at times did 'scorched earth' policies in which a retreating army destroyed the mills that would have processed grain for bread. Soldiers routinely resorted to stealing livestock from the local population and as we will see siege situations could be even more desperate. Poor weather made soldiers' lives miserable too: northern Italy in particular had freezing winters and for men sleeping in tents hypothermia and frostbite were real risks. There were no uniforms: soldiers wore what they could find, buy or steal, and they might well go a month without changing their clothes; even when supplies were available scarcity might drive prices out of an average infantryman's reach. The landsknechts in particular were known for colourful costume, while after their commander's death the troops of Giovanni de' Medici (the son of Caterina Riario Sforza) adopted permanent mourning sashes. Leather coats provided some protection from knife or sword cuts.[37] Armour might be decorated with religious symbols, as might weapons. Surviving luxury firearms from the period incorporate religious, hunting and erotic scenes, and it is not hard to imagine that lower down the ranks one might have found carved onto weapons the equivalents of the pin-up girls who in the twentieth century were painted on the noses of warplanes.

Armies on the march struggled to maintain adequate supplies; in bad weather they might be forced to ford rivers. This was the 'Little Ice Age' when European temperatures seem to have been generally low. On sea voyages between Spain and Italy poor weather could stretch the voyage to a point where food supplies ran out; worse, there was the risk of shipwreck, as German soldiers sailing to Genoa discovered in October 1535 when their carrack was holed, leaving out of the hundreds aboard only thirty survivors.[38] If that were not bad enough, armies also contended with the threat of disease – typhus, plague, dysentery, typhoid and smallpox – which combined with poor nutrition and inadequate sanitation could easily prove deadly. Those who had money to pay for treatment (or goods to pawn for it) might manage a little better if they could get themselves to a nearby hospital, but that was a private matter, not the army's responsibility, although barber-surgeons were employed to accompany military companies, as were chaplains, to provide spiritual consolation to those men facing illness or death.

In fact at times in the Italian Wars soldiers were more likely to die from hunger or disease than from injuries in combat. It has been calculated that following campaigns in 1527 and 1536 the Spanish forces lost between a third and a half of their soldiers to non-combat-related causes.[39] All that said, the majority of sixteenth-century people were accustomed to famine, disease and deprivation in their everyday lives,[40] and some clearly reckoned that joining up was still a risk worth taking.

On the other hand, soldiering evidently had its attractions. It is from the Spanish army that we get the modern word 'camaraderie', from the institution of the *camarada*, an informal group of soldiers who lived, ate and socialised together on campaign. Camp followers included soldiers' wives and children as well as numerous people to service the armies – cooks, nurses and prostitutes. Liaisons with local women were officially prohibited but certainly went on in practice, as did gambling, which was officially restricted to betting for modest food prizes in games like chess, crossbow shooting or quoits (but not dice or cards). Wine was drunk routinely as part of the diet but intoxication no doubt helped with the stresses of war.[41]

War, moreover, prompted the imposition of extraordinary taxes or forced loans to fund defence, which weighed yet further on incomes. Where populations were forced to flee or men left for the wars it could be enormously disruptive to agricultural production. On the other hand, for some people a war economy created new employment opportunities, whether directly as soldiers or indirectly, as for example rope makers produced fuses for cannon and matchlocks, or scrap metal merchants sold their wares to arms makers; there was demand for wood to shore up fortifications, while carters and bakers (women among them) were drawn into servicing armies in place of – or as well as – their old domestic customers. In the ten years 1495–1504, the Spanish spent 2.73 million ducats on the war in Naples alone.[42] Brutal, distressing and deadly it might be, but war was big business.

Chapter Seven

Wars for the New World

There were business opportunities in the New World too, and in the growing Iberian empires. Bartolomeo Marchionni was one of the men who exploited them. Born in Florence around 1450 he joined a firm of merchant bankers (likely while still in his teens) and subsequently became their agent in Lisbon, where he enjoyed considerable favour from the Crown and was naturalised in 1482. Like Columbus and Leonardo da Vinci, he knew of Paolo dal Pozzo Toscanelli's maps, and had apparently shown one to Portugal's King Alfonso V. A wealthy merchant, his business interests stretched from Flanders in the north via England and Ireland, south to Madeira and east to the Levant. He imported luxury Italian objects to Portugal, including crystal glass and books, as well as dealing in saltpetre (an essential ingredient for gunpowder). He had major trading interests in West Africa, from where he was licensed to import ivory and precious metals; he imported melegueta pepper – the so-called 'grains of paradise' – in huge quantities, as well as North African textiles and sugar from Madeira. Like his fellow sugar trader, Mona Lisa's husband Francesco del Giocondo, he also dealt in slaves, including to the Tuscan ports, to which he dispatched two enslaved women, Luza and Margherita, in 1478.[1]

While Marchionni did not have a monopoly on enslaving Africans (as some sources suggest), he did have a very large interest in the trade, which had expanded after the conquest of Constantinople cut off key eastern slave-trading routes. He purchased an exclusive licence for slave-trading in a large zone of the West African coast, and it is estimated that between 1486 and 1493 alone, Marchionni imported almost half the slaves brought to Lisbon, 1,648 out of a total of 3,589. (Lisbon was the single most important European centre for the trade in enslaved Africans in these years.) On the backs of these people, whom he subsequently sold on, Marchionni raked in a profit that likely ranged from 20 to 40 per cent of his initial investment. He is known to have imported slaves from Brazil, and to have exported them from Lisbon on to Valencia, to Seville (including to Columbus' Florentine associate Giannotto Berardi) and to Genoese merchants in Granada. Marchionni's unscrupulousness is illustrated by the case of an 8-year-old girl, Catarina (Christian names were typically imposed on enslaved people), whom Marchionni sold sometime in the late 1480s to a Jew named Guedelha Guoallite. The child converted to Christianity and was subsequently manumitted; she returned to Marchionni as a free servant only to have him claim that he had never sold her at all and that she remained his slave. The authorities evidently disagreed, because in 1492 Catarina was issued with official confirm-ation of her liberty.[2]

Marchionni was among the people who saw the commercial potential of Columbus' discoveries. He may have promoted Amerigo Vespucci's voyage in 1501–2 as well as a number of others. He was certainly involved in the voyage of the ship *Bretoa* in 1511 to Brazil, where it went to obtain Brazilwood (pernambuco), a source of red dye. This ship returned to Lisbon with a cargo including thirty-six enslaved indigenous people as well as a selection of animals and birds that were much in demand at European courts for their 'exotic' appeal: jaguars, parrots, macaques and other monkeys.[3] Marchionni did not, however, restrict himself to the new West. He also had extensive involvement in trade to the East, especially in spices such as pepper, cinnamon, ginger, nutmeg and cloves, as well as the Sappanwood for which Brazilwood became an alternative source of dye. He had, moreover, a significant role in the first Portuguese efforts at conquest and colonisation in East Africa and India, and was one of the financiers of the second voyage of Vasco da Gama in 1502; nor was he the only Italian involved. Marchionni's ship the *St Vincent* was part of the fleet that set out with the Portuguese naval commander Tristão da Cunha to India in 1506.[4] The extent of his international networks is illustrated by the fact that he attracted German investment for this voyage from the Welser, one of the two leading banking families of the German states, who went on to be governors of Venezuela.[5] The author of a recent book on Marchionni sums him up as a 'typical Renaissance merchant',[6] a point well made: Marchionni may have done particularly well for himself as an individual, but among Italian traders his interests were far from exceptional.

Like Bartolomeo Marchionni, Christopher Columbus had connections to Madeira: he had travelled there as a sugar-trader, part of a larger role in the service of the Centurione family of Genoa.[7] Though the details of Columbus' early life are slender, he had likely also visited the Genoese colony of Chios in the Eastern Mediterranean; he also plausibly claimed to have travelled to the Portuguese trading post of São Jorge da Mina in West Africa.[8] Columbus' early crews included Venetians, both from Venice itself and from Venice's Greek colonies.[9] After the removal of Columbus' monopoly on transatlantic voyages in 1499, Amerigo Vespucci joined the next ship across the Atlantic to be authorised by the Spanish monarchs Ferdinand and Isabella.[10] Vespucci was by no means rich, but he was an extremely well-connected Florentine, with links to both the Medici family (via his tutor) and to Sandro Botticelli, from whom the family commissioned work. There is much speculation about Simonetta Vespucci, wife of a distant cousin of his, who is said to have been a lover of Lorenzo the Magnificent's brother Giuliano and to have modelled for several portraits. Amerigo himself got a job as a clerk in the Medici Bank and in 1492, at the age of thirty-eight, was sent to deal with problems in its branch at the port of Cádiz in south-western Spain. He and Columbus are connected by the figure of Giannotto Berardi, a Florentine slave-trader whom Vespucci recommended to the Medici as a suitable agent in Seville and who became one of the backers of Columbus' first voyage.[11] In Seville Vespucci met other Italian merchants, especially the Genoese, the city's single most prominent community of foreign traders.

Indeed, the Italian – and particularly the Genoese – history of enslavement provides an essential context for the activities of these early voyagers. Genoa had a centuries-long history of enslaving people in the Black Sea region and importing them to Italy to work in domestic service, craft and agriculture. There was also plenty of history of sharp practice as regards the law of the time: not everyone respected the papal bulls that banned the enslavement of Christians. The scope for enslavement in Hispaniola, Columbus' newly established colony in the Caribbean, would have been immediately apparent, and indeed in 1495 Columbus' colleague Torres returned from there to Spain with

five hundred enslaved indigenous people.[12] Canon law (the internationally applicable law of the Church) had three justifications for
slavery. Captives of a just war could be enslaved (a good excuse for
slave-traders who could offer assurances that the people they were
selling had indeed been seized in the course of warfare). So could
people who transgressed so-called 'natural law': these included can-
nibals (reports of New World cannibalism served an economic
purpose) and sodomites, that is, anyone engaged in deviant sexual
practices (which could have covered a substantial section of Florence's
own population). Enslavement was also permitted when the alternative
was worse (for example, human sacrifice). These laws were not mere
window-dressing but had in very recent memory been enforced:
clerical opposition to unjust enslavement had led in 1488 to the freeing
of hundreds of people wrongly enslaved during the Spanish conquest
of the Canary Islands.[13] Hence there was an incentive for those hoping
to profit from the slave trade to emphasise any or all of justified conflict, cannibalism and sexual deviance – including incest, which in
Church doctrine encompassed not only relations with blood kin but
marriage to in-laws – in their reports on the New World.[14] Italian
impressions of the peoples of the New World were strongly shaped
by the early descriptions of Columbus, who highlighted both such
deviant conduct and, in contrast, a level of innocence that might
indicate suitability for conversion.[15]

Vespucci's specific role on his first voyage is unknown but his
expertise in pearl-trading may have proved attractive to its promoters,
though so far as pearls were concerned the enterprise was not a
success. The crew compensated by enslaving indigenous people
instead. They took two hundred captives, of whom thirty-two died
on the voyage to Europe.[16] Vespucci himself was a slave-owner; in a
will of 1511 (the year before he died) he listed four enslaved women
and a man as his property. Two of the women were from West Africa
and one from the Canary Islands; the latter had two children. It is
impossible to say for certain whether they were Vespucci's – as scholars
have speculated – but the sexual exploitation of enslaved women was
all too common.[17]

As the voyages went on, it became increasingly apparent to
Columbus and Vespucci that they had found not only islands off the
east coast of the known world but an entire new land mass.[18] Initially

it was assumed that this was Asia, but in 1513 the first sighting by a European of the Pacific raised questions, resolved within a decade by the first circumnavigation of the globe in 1522.[19] Antonio Pigafetta of Vicenza accompanied the leader of that circumnavigation, the Portuguese Fernão de Magalhães (known to English-speakers as Ferdinand Magellan), and as one of just eighteen survivors of the complete voyage produced the main account of the events, incorporating descriptions of the people they encountered and their customs, their food and land. His account vividly conveys the hardships that these voyages involved: 'We were three months and twenty days without getting any kind of fresh food,' he wrote, describing the passage around Cape Horn.

> We ate biscuit, which was no longer biscuit, but powder of biscuits swarming with worms, for they had eaten the good. It stank strongly of the urine of rats [...] Rats were sold for one-half ducado apiece, and even then we could not get them. But above all the other misfortunes the following was the worst. The gums of both the lower and upper teeth of some of our men swelled, so that they could not eat under any circumstances and therefore died.[20]

Two accounts of Vespucci's voyages were published, although whether Vespucci was the author (or sole author) is disputed: at a minimum there was some significant editorial intervention, and one of them (known as the *Soderini Letter*) may in fact have been reworked from published accounts of Columbus' voyages. In any case, Vespucci's *Mundus Novus* (*New World*) was a huge success and went through twenty-three editions between 1504 and 1506.[21] The significance of these and other texts on the New World lies more in the way that they publicised the new continent to Europe than in their precise descriptions of it. Right from the start, they highlighted the practice of cannibalism: the 1505 Augsburg edition of the *Mundus Novus*, for example, was accompanied by an engraving depicting it. In 1507, Martin Waldseemüller, a German cosmographer, and his collaborator Matthias Ringmann published a map naming the new continent 'America' after the man they later described as being 'of sagacious genius'. Yet although the attribution stuck it was not without controversy. Waldseemüller dropped the name from a 1513 map, and credited

Columbus with the discovery instead, while Sebastian Cabot pointed out that in fact his father had crossed the Atlantic before Vespucci.[22]

The father in question, John Cabot, was another Italian explorer sponsored by a foreign power – in his case, England. Born around the middle of the fifteenth century (his birthplace is uncertain), he was a Venetian citizen and gained a commission from King Henry VII. He undertook three voyages in the last years of the fifteenth century for which the support of Italians in London, including a papal official, seems to have been crucial in raising funds. Cabot's backers included the Bardi bankers of Florence, who were closely connected to the Medici; a little later the Bardi and Cavalcanti firm was involved in supplying the English Crown with a range of goods, from luxury textiles to weapons.[23] Cabot may also have had connections to the papacy in the person of Adriano Castellesi (absentee bishop of Hereford, secretary to Alexander VI and future cardinal), whose deputy Giovanni Antonio de Carbonariis perhaps introduced Cabot to Henry VII and went on to participate in Cabot's 1498 voyage himself. Cabot is known to have landed on the coast of North America, perhaps near Cape Bonavista, Cape Dégrat or Cape Bauld on the island of Newfoundland, and he was successful in identifying the fisheries that backers in Bristol had been hoping to find.[24] In England as elsewhere, Italians played a key role in the early transatlantic voyages and in their financing.

As the potential for exploitation of the new lands and peoples became apparent, other Italians joined the enterprise. Sebastian Cabot, who had probably joined his father on that north-western voyage, later entered the service of the Spanish Crown, in which capacity he acted as negotiator over the delimitation of Spanish and Portuguese colonial territories.[25] In 1524, Giovanni da Verrazzano led a French expedition seeking a western passage to Asia, and ended up in what is now Maine, on the east coast of North America. Other Italians still went east. In 1511, the Portuguese had conquered Melaka (Malacca), in what is now Malaysia but was then loyal to the Ming dynasty of China; there they benefited from the abandonment of Chinese voyages in the previous century. Italians, among them the Florentine Giovanni da Empoli, travelled to Malacca, returning with 'great riches and great honour': his cargo included pearls, diamonds, rubies and sapphires. He described in a letter to his father how he had met merchants from two Chinese junks, and enthused about the prospects for trade with China. He went on to travel there himself, with the first official Portuguese embassy to China in 1517, but died on arrival.[26] In short, while it was Portugal and Spain, not the Italian states, that made the running in European imperial expansion, individual Italians were involved in significant numbers and in high-profile roles. That was possible because people in this period were accustomed to the idea that experts – whether soldiers, sailors or secretaries – might enter the service of a foreign monarch. It was not considered unpatriotic to do so.

Moreover, Italian finance was to prove central to the transatlantic colonisation projects of the Iberian monarchs. Two factors militated against Italian involvement: Iberian monopolies on direct exploration, and reluctance to abandon existing Eastern Mediterranean patterns of trade. On the other hand, there was what one historian has described as a symbiotic relationship between Iberia and Genoa in terms of their pursuit of power and profit, and Italian experience in the Eastern Mediterranean and then on the islands off northwestern Africa (the Canaries and Madeira) fed directly into colonial projects in the New World.[27] By halfway through the fifteenth century the Genoese were the most important group of foreign entrepreneurs in Spain (Florentines, in contrast, like Francesco del Giocondo, preferred Lisbon), and the importance of Spain to Italian merchants grew yet further after the loss of Constantinople. In Italy, the rise of Genoese bankers had been favoured by the election of two popes, Sixtus IV and Julius II, whose families were both from Genoese territory and who in turn had favoured relatives and co-nationals.[28]

These men had connections throughout Europe: in Lyons, Marseilles, and further across France, to Flanders and Brussels as well as Nuremberg, Frankfurt, Hamburg and Geneva. Many opened branches in Seville, a key centre for the import and export of African gold. All sorts of goods were traded through Spain – dried fruit was shipped from Málaga to England and Flanders, while textiles went in the other direction – and Genoese merchants were at the heart of this trade. They also played a vital role in financing the Spanish conquest of the Canary Islands (an enterprise in which the Florentine Giannotto Berardi had also been involved). One such Genoese merchant based in Spain, Francesco Pinello, used wealth from the Canaries to help finance

Columbus' first expedition; other Genoese joined him, including a member of the prominent Grimaldi family, Bernardo. In 1503 Pinello drew on connections in Andalusia and Portugal to expand his financial interests into West Africa and Brazil; he bought wood from the latter. As early as 1505, barely a decade after Columbus' first voyage, Pinello sold enslaved Africans to the Spanish Crown: they would be transported across the Atlantic to work in the newly colonised lands, and in particular in the silver mines. Some of these merchants became naturalised as Spanish (a route around the monopoly that otherwise excluded Italians), while others used connections in Spanish Italy, especially Naples, as a jumping-off point for expansion. Commercial networks could stretch not only across Europe but well beyond, west to the Americas and east to the remaining Genoese colony of Chios. In 1508, the state monopoly in Spain on trade with America was lifted, which gave a new impetus to private enterprise. In 1519 a group of Genoese merchants paid 25,000 ducats for a licence to import 4,000 enslaved Africans to America.[29]

It is hardly surprising that a proportion of this money went to fund the single biggest cost of any monarch in the period: warfare. Among the people who received loans from these bankers was 'el Gran Capitán' Gonzalo Fernández de Córdoba, he of the victories in Naples, who in 1497 was lent 3,500 ducats to pay his troops.[30] And as money flowed east from the colonies, so the experience of war flowed west in return: at least some of the colonisers must have known of the developments in tactics that had enabled Spanish victories in Naples.[31] And though they could not be straightforwardly applied in the very different context of war in the New World, and most conquistadors did not have direct experience of Italian conflict[32] – for young Spanish adventurers it was generally a choice of Italy or the New World, not both – even so, where they might learn from the Italian experience was in the practice of alliances: numerous small states of Italy survived and even thrived by aligning themselves with larger powers, just as the Spanish in the New World gained by strategically allying with one or other side in the indigenous conflicts they encountered. Worlds apart, these two theatres of combat were nonetheless entwined.

Besides financing voyages, Italian scholarship and learning provided an intellectual underpinning for understanding the lands and peoples that were being encountered. Many Italians approached the New

World primarily as observers, gathering and disseminating information about the new discoveries. Although these days the term 'discovery' is understandably challenged, it effectively sums up the way that many Europeans experienced their encounter with the New World – real or via news sources – at the time. Similarly, though the New World was anything but new to its inhabitants, it was decidedly novel to Europeans. Lucrezia Borgia's father-in-law, Ercole d'Este, duke of Ferrara, even sent a spy, Alberto Cantino to Lisbon to try to find out more. The first map of the Brazilian coast is now to be found in the Este library at Modena: this Cantino map of 1503, named after the secret agent, is also one of the first maps to show North America's east coast.[33]

Italian writers, unsurprisingly, were proud of the achievements of their compatriots. Columbus' voyage was 'a remarkable feat of nautical art and cosmography', wrote Battista Fregoso, a former doge of Genoa.[34] Chronicler Antonio Gallo, also Genoese, noted Columbus' plebeian upbringing but his attainment nonetheless of 'great celebrity throughout all Europe by a very brave feat of daring, a remarkable novelty in human affairs'.[35] The name Venezuela most likely comes from a diminutive of Venice, because the houses built on lakes there reminded Vespucci of the city.[36]

The New World, however, posed a challenge to European scientific thinkers. As Guicciardini pointed out, the discoveries had 'given some cause for alarm to interpreters of the Holy Scriptures', not least as it became clear that Christianity had not – as the Psalms implied – reached all the peoples of the world.[37] They were troubling, too, for those who in the context of Renaissance humanism were inclined to turn to classical scholarship. Until the late fifteenth century they had relied on the treatises by the likes of Ptolemy (c. AD 100–170) and Pliny the Elder (AD 23–79) to understand their world. Ptolemy's Geography was in print by 1475, and went through numerous editions; Leonardo da Vinci was among his readers.[38] Yet these works made no mention of the new lands. Scholars now had to consider how to reimagine the world, or make it fit the old categories.

Even prior to the first transatlantic voyages there had already been discussion about the possibility of a western route to Asia and on the question of whether the Indian Ocean was linked to other seas.[39] Still, such debates relied heavily on the ancient authorities, which divided the world into three continents (Europe, Asia and Africa). One way of getting round this division was to regard the New World as an earthly paradise (as Columbus did), while some scholars tried to relate it to an idea of the edge of the known world. It took some time, therefore, for the full impact of the discoveries to filter through into European understanding.

When it did so, the new writers had a range of models from which to choose, but the most important of these was, perhaps, that of the humanists, who had already made a case for the superiority of their own intellectual methods over their rivals'. The humanists adopted the historical and ethnographic approaches of the classical texts. Among these, the works of Plato, Herodotus, Strabo and Tacitus all offered different approaches to the study of the world beyond their own – sometimes in positive terms, sometimes not – but they held in common an underlying presumption of the superiority of the Greeks or Romans over the peoples they encountered.[40]

Nicolò Scillacio, a lecturer at the University of Padua, drew on classical metaphor in his 1494 descriptions of the New World: 'Flutists and guitarists,' he wrote, 'held even the Nereids, Nymphs, and Sirens themselves rapt with their melodious tunes.' He described King Ferdinand of Aragon, with some geographical confusion, 'taming the savage Libyans, beyond the Pillars of Hercules and following his example, he added the unknown Ethiopians to the empire of the Spains.'[41] Early accounts of the New World became, in turn, sources for more polished syntheses: Peter Martyr (Pietro Martire d'Anghiera), an Italian historian in Spanish service, wrote a series of accounts of the Spanish discoveries, beginning in 1511 and continuing over the next two and a half decades. The whole collection was published together in 1530 as De Orbo Novo (On the New World). Based in part on Columbus and in part on government documents as well as the testimony of indigenous travellers and explorers who visited the court, it drew extensively on classical literature to contextualise the discoveries.[42]

The Venetian authorities also took considerable interest in news from further east. In 1508 Ludovico de Varthema of Bologna reported the details of his travels to India to the Venetian Senate: his Itinerary was published two years later and went through several editions. Whether the details are reliable is another question: some of it has the ring of the storyteller (he claimed to have had a fling with the wife of the Yemeni sultan), and other details could have been acquired at second hand. What was no doubt most of interest to the Venetians was the assessment of the city of Vijayanagara in southern India, then the second largest in the world after Beijing. Amid praise for the city as a 'second paradise', not to mention its fine hunting and beautiful location, Ludovico did not neglect the essential details of size, fortifications and trade prospects. 'The said city of Bisinagar,' he reported,

> belongs to the king of Narsinga, and is very large and strongly walled. It is situated on the side of a mountain, and is seven miles in circumference. It has three circles of walls. It is a place of great merchandise, is extremely fertile, and is endowed with all possible kinds of delicacies.[43]

None of this, of course, was solely an Italian affair: German printmakers were important in producing such publications; so were the Spanish themselves. Italian accounts of the New World, however, soon started to draw a distinction between the activities of the honourable Columbus and the more dubious activities they attributed to the Spanish. Alessandro Zorzi, a Venetian, praised the decision of Bartolomé Columbus (brother of Christopher) to take with him to the New World 'friars learned in philosophy, theology and sacred Scripture', and noted that there 'one could easily convert very many people to the Christian faith with honour and profit'.[44] As early as 1504, Angelo Trevisan, a secretary to the Venetian ambassador in Spain, began to hint at the New World 'misdeeds of the Spanish'.[45] It was convenient for Italian authors that Columbus' personal triumph could be distinguished from the subsequent conduct of the Spanish colonisers. It was rather a case of 'we are explorers, you are colonisers, they are exploiters and oppressors'.

Alessandro Geraldini (1455–1525), a priest who travelled to the New World, is a good example of the trend. He wrote that: 'Christopher Columbus, most holy Father, was Italian by birth, from the city of Genoa in Liguria, and was well-known for his knowledge of cosmography, mathematics, and techniques for measuring the sky and land, but was famous most of all for the greatness of his spirit.'[46] In a letter to Pope Leo X, Geraldini denounced the Spanish, but in the process absolved Columbus:

The Spaniards, after the death of the Ligurian Columbus, discoverer
of the equatorial zone, killed over a million of these people by various
kinds of death, even though they were good people and should have
been led with great care to our faith; and because many of the criminals
are secretly conscience-stricken to this day over the crimes they have
committed, but confessors of all the religious orders openly refuse to
absolve them unless they return the goods they earned from the labor
of those people whom they everywhere exterminated; therefore I
humbly beg that a sum of that money be set aside for the construction
of a larger cathedral, by which these men may be freely absolved from
all subsequent penance.[47]

On Geraldini's proposed cathedral an inscription was to be carved
noting the 'cruel slaughter' and 'cursed crimes'. Only a half-century
after Columbus' first voyage would anyone break from a wholly
positive analysis of the 'discoverer' himself: as we will see, that was
Bartolomé de Las Casas.

As the sixteenth century went on, many more Italians took an
interest in the new discoveries of the world and had pivotal roles in
writing them up for public consumption. The circulation of objects
from the New World no doubt helped to prompt that interest. Pope
Clement VII owned a pre-conquest Mesoamerican manuscript (the
Codex Vindobonensis Mexicanus I, now in the National Library in
Vienna), a gift from King Manuel of Portugal, brother-in-law of
Charles V; the king also sent Clement a blanket made of parrot
feathers, and he further acquired turquoise masks.[48] Benvenuto Cellini,
the artist and goldsmith, borrowed from the Medici Aztec animal
heads made from agate and amethyst.[49] Gasparo Contarini, an ambassador, praised the featherwork he saw at the papal court, but so far
as the New World was concerned he, like most Venetians, was
probably more interested in the economic impact on his city of the
Portuguese and Spanish exploration. Still, he drafted a new geography
book (now lost) and wrote in horror at the Spanish treatment of
American Indians.[50]

Much of Contarini's knowledge of the New World came from conversations with Pietro Martire d'Anghiera. Born in 1457, Martire was
one of many intellectuals that the Italian states exported to other courts
of Europe in the later fifteenth and early sixteenth centuries. His modern

biographer describes Contarini's beliefs about the conquered peoples of the New World as 'conventional', although Contarini was sufficiently critical to note that the 'cruel treatment of the Spaniards' was driving indigenous women in Hispaniola and Jamaica to kill their own children. Returning from an embassy to Spain in the 1520s, he reported that there had been a million people on the islands of Hispaniola and Jamaica when Columbus arrived, but now thanks to the 'cruel treatment' of the Spaniards, who had forced them to mine for gold, and to the desperation that had led to island mothers killing their own children rather than allow them to be enslaved, there were now only about seven thousand.[51] His observations were repeated by an anonymous Mantuan correspondent who explained that they would rather they did not live than be subjected to Spanish servitude.[52] Venice was particularly hostile to the Spanish, and as far back as 1504 Angelo Trevisan, secretary to the Venetian ambassador in Spain, had been deducing from the reports he heard at court that there had been considerable 'misdeeds' on the part of the Spanish.[53] (Reports such as this, incidentally, give the lie to anyone who argues that colonial projects did not attract criticism from Europeans at the time, although it is perhaps more to the point that the voices of the people most likely to object – those who were being colonised – are largely lost.)

Contarini's interest in the New World did not extend to the patronage of actual projects. He was one of the Venetian senators who turned down an approach by Sebastian Cabot (son of Giovanni) for funds for his voyage; Cabot turned to the English Crown (unsuccessfully) and to the Spanish Crown (successfully) for patronage instead.[54] Contarini's attitude arguably made sense for small and already wealthy Italian states. The regimes that eventually patronised exploration of the New World were not those with existing wealth and power but monarchies on the up, who might expect both monetary reward and territorial gains, not to mention personal status. Nor did the ongoing wars in Italy – politically distracting and financially draining – lend themselves to direct involvement in colonisation projects.

That said, there were plenty of individual Italians besides Contarini who took an interest both in the Americas and in the colonisation of Africa. Historian Paolo Giovio later drew on the work of Pigafetta, who documented Magellan's voyage, and Peter Martyr to write his own account of the New World in his *Historiae Sui Temporis* (1530):[55] by this time news of the discoveries and associated commentary made it into all sorts of contemporary histories. Another was Guicciardini's *History of Italy*, which also echoed some of the later criticisms of Las Casas:

> Worthy, indeed, are those Portuguese and Spaniards, and particularly Columbus, the first undertaker of this wonderful and most dangerous navigation, to be celebrated with eternal praises, for their skill and industry, for their boldness, vigilance and hardiness, which have enlightened our age with the knowledge of such great and marvellous things that were hitherto buried in obscurity. But yet more worthy would they be to be celebrated for their undertaking, had they not been induced to undergo such great perils and fatigues by an immoderate thirst after gold and riches, but by a desire to improve themselves or others in knowledge, or to propagate the Christian faith.[55]

Other Italians, among them Pietro Bembo, worried about the economic impact of the discoveries and the consequent shift in trade, even while Venetian printers profited from publishing about the New World.[56]

For all their criticism of the Spanish, though, there were Italians whose writing about the New World helped to justify aspects of their exploitation. Alessandro Geraldini, a papal envoy to the Spanish court who later became bishop of Santo Domingo (now capital of the Dominican Republic), was a fierce critic of Spanish treatment of the Indians, but when it came to Africans his attitude was rather different, as is evident from his account of his travels along the coast of West Africa. He wrote to Pope Leo X:

> I hated the idea of visiting the kingdom of Gambia because of the savagery of its people, and completely avoided the infidel shores of Guinea, where the people live without religion: for there brothers and other relations even sell one another, with a hateful kind of treachery, to foreign merchants from the most distant nations.[57]

This was just a year after the first transatlantic slave voyage to depart directly from West Africa for the Americas, and even as Geraldini criticised enslavement in the New World, his hostility to Africans was the sort of rhetoric that helped to justify the enslavement of black Africans specifically. Other Italians followed. Giulio Landi, a gentleman of letters, wrote a description of the island of Madeira; published in the mid 1530s it was probably based on personal observation, and described Madeira's black residents as 'of blunt intelligence'.[58] Niccolò Machiavelli discussed colonisation in general terms in *The Prince*: as a means to securing new territory it was preferable to dispatching and maintaining troops, which was expensive.

> Colonies do not cost much, [he wrote] and with little or no expense a prince can send and maintain them; and in doing so he hurts only those whose fields and houses have been taken and given to the new inhabitants, who are only a small part of that state; and those that he hurts, being dispersed and poor, can never be a threat to him, and all others remain on the one side unharmed (and because of this, they should remain silent), and on the other afraid of making a mistake, for fear that what happened to those who were dispossessed might happen to them.[59]

The fact is that there was huge scope for profit in New World silver mining, and that gave all manner of people a motive to explain away (and indeed legitimise) the development of colonies, and the enslavement of both Amerindian and African labourers.[60]

Italian engagement in this new world of exploration and exploitation was, then, initially a matter of individual entrepreneurs, though individuals were supported by a long-standing infrastructure of international mercantile networks. Columbus, Vespucci and Cabot all fall into this category. They benefited from a long history of Italian seafaring: one of the very first maritime law tables was drawn up in Amalfi in the eleventh or twelfth century. Italy had two substantial republics – Venice and Genoa – that based their wealth on maritime trading, and the peninsula's wealth had grown precisely because of its place at the heart of the Mediterranean. On the other hand, Italian states did not sponsor these voyages themselves: that took the larger powers of Europe, and in particular Spain which as a newly consolidated state had more of a motive for territorial and trade expansion, not to mention a strong ideology of Christianisation to justify its conquests. (They wanted, moreover, to cut out Italian and Ottoman middlemen.) Venice continued instead to look to old trade routes in the East. Even had an Italian state been inclined to sponsor voyages, the demands of the wars would probably have prevented it. Yet out of Italy came finance, individuals, a history of enslavement and ideas about running colonies, a framework for understanding the conquered lands, and – from the papacy – religious legitimisation for colonial projects via papal bulls and interpretation of canon law.

Chapter Eight

Popes, Princes and Republics

If the Spanish were facing criticism for their activities in the New World, Italian antipathy to Spain was also levelled against the late Pope Alexander VI. Within weeks of the pope's death, Francesco Gonzaga, marquis of Mantua, was writing to his wife Isabella d'Este that Alexander had made a pact with the Devil. 'There are others,' Francesco went on, 'who affirm having seen seven devils around him at the moment of his death; at once his body began to boil and his mouth to foam, like a cauldron on a fire.' Promoted by supporters of Savonarola, such tales were accompanied by claims that Alexander VI was a converted Jew – in the offensive slang of the day a 'marrano', which may mean 'pig'. In fact, such claims first appeared as early as 1493, after the Pope allowed Jewish refugees from Spain to come to Italy; his son Cesare was labelled a 'Jewish dog'.[1] These tales were a precursor to the later 'Black Legend' of Spain, promoted by Protestant propagandists who pointed to the non-Christian heritage of many Spaniards to imply that the nation was backward, superstitious and cruel. In Italy, where the presence of Spanish troops was directly experienced, the myths quickly gained ground.

Alexander's successor, Pope Julius II, only fanned the flames of rumour. He moved out of the Borgia apartments of the papal palace into an alternative set upstairs, telling Paride Grassi, the master of papal ceremonies, 'that he didn't want to see the image of his predecessor and enemy every hour, whom he called *marrano*, a Jew, and circumcised'.[2] Grassi noted in his diary that he did not believe the rumours, but nonetheless Julius' suggestion that he did not wish to live surrounded by the 'worst, wicked memory' of the Borgia pope stuck, and as time went on, the tales of Borgia excess only grew. In the 1530s Martin Luther picked up on the myth of Alexander as a converted Jew, 'who believed in nothing', adding the salacious detail of the Pope's naked serving girls. In 1550 Francesco Negri of Bassano, an Italian Protestant, published a work that described Alexander's pact with the Devil, and in 1558, John Bale, an English Protestant exile, reworked a 1506 Italian commentary on the Borgias to add in descriptions of prostitutes and rent boys, delete praise for Cesare, and – perhaps most spectacularly – tell the tale of how Pedro Mendoza, the cardinal of Valencia, 'married' one of the Borgia sons.[3]

It is easy to see why the Borgia myth would be propagated by admirers of Savonarola, and indeed by Protestants. Moreover, in Italy itself – as Spanish influence on the peninsula increased in the course of the wars – the Borgia papacy could be read as the start of an unwelcome Spanish presence in many of the Italian states. Despite the fact that Rodrigo Borgia had spent only his childhood in Spain, in Italy the Borgias could always be labelled dubiously foreign. That was not a claim that could be levelled against his successor. Elected in 1503, Pope Julius II was a member of the della Rovere family, relatives of the earlier Pope Sixtus IV. He played on the family name in his propaganda: in Italian 'rovere' means oak, and the tree was used widely as a symbol for the pope. His own arms included a golden oak, representing vigour and power, and hinting at the prospect of a revived 'golden age'.[4] Julius, like his predecessor, had an illegitimate daughter, but – perhaps aware of the controversy that dogged the high profile Lucrezia – Felice della Rovere married one of the Orsini barons of Rome and contrived to stay out of the limelight.

Like the Borgias, Pope Julius had military ambitions, but while Alexander VI had concentrated on familial advantage, Julius' focus was on the lands that belonged to the Church, and taking control of rebellious subject cities such as Bologna. His reputation as 'chief defender of ecclesiastical dignity and liberty' had won him friends in Rome, despite his being 'notoriously very difficult by nature'.[5] The image of a warrior cleric might seem a little strange in the West now but it had a long pedigree through military orders like the Knights Templar, and it was not uncommon for popes to present their military activity in terms of crusading, or in terms of peace – which sounds ironic, but 'peacemaking' continues to be a justification for military intervention to this day.

Among Julius' early challenges was the decision about whether to recognise the Spanish victory in Naples and invest King Ferdinand of Aragon with the kingdom. Not to do so would offend the Spanish; to do so would invite revenge from the French. The matter came to a head in 1505, on the feast of Sts Peter and Paul, when it was customary for the pope to receive tribute from the ruler of Naples in the form of a white horse. This caused no little stress to Julius' master of ceremonies, who fretted about the potential for 'horrendous scandal' at court if both Spanish and French ambassadors turned up with their gifts. Despite guards being posted on the doors, the Spanish envoy – whom the ceremonialist described as 'a most importunate man, lacking modesty and eloquence' – contrived to get his palfrey onto the premises and then tried to ambush the pope on the stairs. Julius eventually conceded that he would accept both horses, without prejudice to either side.[6]

Julius ruled at a high point of papal secularisation.[7] He actively sought to expand and consolidate the popes' territorial holdings, which stretched from Rome, through Bologna (a city for which he fought twice), to Ravenna on Italy's Adriatic coast. His warlike activities required justification, and the question of what made a just war lay at the heart of the swirl of argument that surrounded this pontificate. Besides the imagery of his family name, Giuliano della Rovere's choice of Julius as his papal name facilitated comparisons with Julius Caesar. Parallels were drawn between Caesar's conquests in Gaul and Julius' own conflict with the French. Some disapproved, notably the Dutch humanist Erasmus of Rotterdam and Paride Grassi. Historians disagree on whether Julius really saw himself as Caesar, but there is no doubt that the imagery featured widely in his propaganda. That said, when it suited Julius he also used the rhetoric of peacemaking (as would his successor Leo X), though all too often his peace was to be achieved by force of arms.[8]

One way to think about the papacies of Alexander VI and Julius II is that they shifted incrementally towards a model in which cardinals were treated not as the pope's senators, but as his courtiers,[9] with the pope becoming ever more a prince, concerned – like Louis XII or Ferdinand of Aragon – with expansion of territorial power. This is not, however, to say that Julius was entirely preoccupied with his own military image and conquests. As we will see, in the last year of his papacy the Lateran Council met to oversee a series of reforms to the Church. He also began to consider serious plans for the rebuilding of St Peter's, not least because parts of the ancient building were in serious danger of collapse; these plans began rather modestly, encompassing restoration and repair of specific sections; only a century later was the decision taken to demolish all that remained of the old basilica.[10] So far as art was concerned, by far Julius' most famous commission was that entrusted to Michelangelo for work on the Sistine Chapel ceiling: the image of the hand of God reaching out to Adam at its heart is now an international icon. Michelangelo received his first payment for the chapel project in 1508 and brought in a team of assistants from Florence to begin the work (later claims that this was the maestro's solo achievement were wide of the mark).[11] Julius also commissioned Michelangelo to sculpt his tomb, now in San Pietro in Vincoli. The pope's reach as patron ranged broadly: he collected ancient sculpture, including the celebrated *Laocoön*, a statue of the Trojan priest and his sons being attacked by sea serpents. Excavated on Rome's Esquiline Hill in 1506, the sculpture formed part of a new garden at the Vatican Belvedere. Like many popes Julius took the opportunity to endow building projects in his home town (in this case Savona); whether or not his schemes were a conscious effort to reflect the glories of ancient Rome, and if so whether that was more Julius' initiative or his architects', remains an open question.[12]

So far as military activity is concerned, Julius' most significant action within the ongoing wars was to assert his authority over Perugia and Bologna. Both were significant cities in the Papal States, Perugia on the borders with Florence and Bologna further north, close to the small lordships of the Po Valley such as Ferrara and Mantua. Both were ruled by independent-minded families (not as lords, but somewhat like the Medici in Florence as the most prominent private citizens). The Baglioni dominated Perugia, while in Bologna the Bentivoglio family had built up an elegant court society over several decades. In the context of the Italian Wars, however, their independence proved a nuisance: they were in the habit of making private agreements to provide troops and supplies rather than checking first with Julius, and this was fundamentally unhelpful to a papacy that was strapped enough for defence and decent military leadership in the first place.[13]

It was in this context that on 26 August 1506 Julius embarked on his own military expedition north, leading the papal court in a procession of thousands of men and horses. This threat of action prompted Gianpaolo Baglioni of Perugia to cut a deal with the pope before he arrived and accept the appointment of a papal governor. Machiavelli later observed that had Baglioni taken the opportunity to assassinate the pope (who would enter Perugia unarmed, following their agreement), he would have enjoyed 'immortal fame' for it. Baglioni, however, failed to be 'splendidly wicked', and the governor, Cardinal Antonio Ferreri, went on to replace Baglioni's appointees on a major city council with his own men.[14]

With Perugia under papal control, that left Bologna, where Giovanni Bentivoglio, dissatisfied with Julius' efforts to restrict his sons' military contracting, made an effort to negotiate but to no avail: Julius was determined that he, and not the Bentivoglio, should be the arbiter of power in the city. Julius continued preparations for an assault on the Bentivoglio even while still travelling, should they take up arms against him, securing the promise of troops from both Florence (a negotiation in which Machiavelli was, once again, involved) and the French.[15] Early in October he held talks with envoys from Bologna, but they found Julius quite implacable, preparing bulls for an interdict against the city and the excommunication of Giovanni Bentivoglio. In the end there was no need to attack. The cost that Bentivoglio's provisions for defence imposed on the Bolognese citizens was a source of resentment, and pressure from the French proved sufficient to convince Giovanni and his sons to leave the city. Julius was free to celebrate his liberation of the Bolognese from tyranny.[16]

Further military campaigns to secure the claims of the Papal States, however, prompted considerable antagonism. In 1510, Julius excommunicated Alfonso d'Este, duke of Ferrara, after Alfonso refused to submit to papal authority (the Este claim to Ferrara had been acknowledged on Alfonso's marriage to Lucrezia Borgia, but Julius showed no inclination to honour his predecessor's agreements). Julius subsequently broke with his former allies, the French (on account of their backing for Alfonso), and after failed attempts to attack French-occupied Genoa he made his base in Bologna. In January 1511 he succeeded in capturing the lordship of Mirandola (located about thirty miles from Ferrara and a little further from Bologna), but the French camp stood in the way of his route to Ferrara. There followed peace talks involving several of the allied powers, but these failed, and in May the people of Bologna rebelled against their papal governor and the Bentivoglio returned to power. Julius blamed Cardinal Alidosi (papal legate to the city), and his own nephew Duke Francesco Maria della Rovere of Urbino (captain general of the papal armies) for the loss of Bologna. While Alidosi was on his way to an audience with the pope, Francesco Maria and his men dragged him from his mule and stabbed him to death, an act justified by reference to the cardinal's treachery.[17] 'His great dignity as a cardinal,' Guicciardini observed, 'ought perhaps to have preserved his person inviolable, but, with regard to his infinite and enormous vices, he deserved the worst of punishments.'[18]

The bloody reality of war found its metaphorical counterpart in the propaganda produced by both sides. Bolognese opponents accused Julius of homosexuality (here most likely intended as a metaphor for military impotence). His legate was the subject of a vicious satirical poem that not only called him a killer, tyrant and thief, but also compared him to a Turk, a Jew, and a range of wild animals. Michelangelo's nine-foot-tall bronze statue of the pope was dragged down from the church façade (given its weight the tale that its head was used as a football seems unlikely to be true), and to add insult to injury Alfonso d'Este had it melted down and remade into a gun; he called it 'La Giulia', a feminised nickname that again questioned the pope's masculinity.[19] The cruel punishments imposed by the papal regime in Bologna for seditious speech became the target of Julius' opponents in Ferrara.[20] Ferrarese propaganda once again compared papal backers to Jews, while Julius accused his enemies of being in league with the Ottoman Empire. Papal propaganda showed Venetian senators dressed in 'Moorish' style, while in Bologna Julius' opponents turned that on its head, calling his troops 'Moors, Saracens and Turks'. On the contrary, Julius insisted, he was a liberator of Italy from foreign domination, a powerful idea that gained a hold not only in learned discussion but also in the piazza. In 1512 he excommunicated King Louis XII of France, and the 1513 Carnival procession through Rome opened with a depiction of *Italia liberata*: Italy liberated. But the reality of the wars, as Francesco Guicciardini would point out, was French and Spanish domination.[21]

Louis XII retaliated with his own propaganda campaign. Having previously portrayed himself as a latter-day Caesar, employing classical triumph imagery, Louis rethought his strategy following his excommunication and in light of public opposition to spending on warfare, and styled himself instead as a 'humble Christian soldier'. Official initiatives to promote this image were accompanied by a wave of popular pamphlets, courtly poems and even street theatre that helped to justify war against a pope, emphasising the principle of self-defence and suggesting that Julius was unfit for office.[22] In England, meanwhile, the new king, Henry VIII, sided with Julius against the French. (In the aftermath of Henry's break with Rome in the 1530s, many of the English texts published in defence of the papacy fell into obscurity, and printers turned instead to translating and publishing propaganda against Julius that had been produced by their French enemies.) The most celebrated propaganda take on Julius, however, must be the anonymous but thoroughly hostile dialogue *Julius Exclusus*, in which the deceased pontiff arrives at the Pearly Gates only to be denied entrance by St Peter, who declares himself unimpressed with the pontiff's 'sumptuous crown' and his accompanying army, who stink of 'brothels, booze and gunpowder'.[23] Written in 1514 (most likely by the prominent Catholic reformer Erasmus of Rotterdam[24]) it was printed as a pamphlet in 1517, defining a negative image of Julius that would gain ground in a new religious climate.

The pope was far from alone in his turn against the French. January 1512 saw a revolt against French rule in Brescia, a city some sixty miles east of Milan. Led by a Brescian nobleman with backing from Venetian troops (Brescia had been a subject city of Venice since 1426), it prompted further rebellions in the surrounding provinces and in the city of Bergamo. In response the French marched troops rapidly up from Bologna, and on the night of 18/19 February, led by Gaston de Foix, they mounted a surprise attack via an underground corridor that led up into the city's castle, located on a high hill above the town. In his *Cronichetta* ('Little Chronicle'), first published in 1555 but added to in subsequent editions, Bernardino Vallabio gave a dry account of what happened next.

Then, on 19 February they streamed down from the castle to the city, to find the Venetian army, and were valorously repulsed, but meanwhile half the stradiots, who were on the Venetian side, opened the gate of San Nazzaro to flee, and thereby the French cavalry entered, and routed the Venetian army; there died, between one side and the other, more than 13,000 people; messer Andrea Gritti, the Venetian proveditor, was captured and taken to France; and the city was sacked and the citizens taken prisoner and held to ransom.[25]

The diarist Sanudo, noting down reports of the atrocities as they trickled into Venice, gave only the barest details, relating that the French 'have done things that are horrendous and disturbing to hear.[26]

This was a considerable victory for the French, but success was a poisoned chalice, for such was the booty it prompted numerous French soldiers to retire on their winnings. Louis XII, meanwhile, was keen to capitalise on his victories with a decisive besting of the Spanish (not least because he was conscious of Henry VIII's enthusiasm for an invasion of his northern territories). Less than two months later, on Easter Sunday, 11 April 1512, at the Battle of Ravenna, the French got their opportunity. They took advantage of support from their ally Alfonso d'Este, duke of Ferrara and of a squabble between the multiple Holy League powers (the Papal States were now allied in this league with Venice, Spain, the Holy Roman Empire and England, but the papal commander Francesco Maria della Rovere was refusing to take orders from the Spanish commander Ramón de Cardona). Stronger both in numbers and weaponry, and vividly portrayed in an engraving showing the massed pikemen, artillery ominous in the foreground, the French triumphed in one of the bloodiest single battles of the Italian Wars, in which 'the flower of the soldiery was savagely killed by the artillery'.[27] It was, in Guicciardini's words, 'a miserable spectacle to behold [...] men and horses [...] with horrible cries falling dead to the ground, sometimes heads and arms struck off from the rest of the body, and bounding in the air'.[28] Estimates of the casualties range from ten to twenty thousand dead, the majority of them from the League. Among the French casualties – no doubt to the satisfaction of the citizens of Brescia – was Gaston de Foix. (Brescia itself subsequently passed to the Spanish before returning to Venetian rule in 1516.)

For all that the Italian Wars were primarily a conflict between France and Spain for hegemony on the Italian peninsula, they also provided extensive opportunities for regime change in the individual city states. In the Battle of Ravenna, the papal legate, Cardinal Giovanni de' Medici, had been captured, alongside several senior Spanish commanders, among them the marquis of Pescara, Fernando Francesco d'Avalos, whose wife Vittoria Colonna wrote a poem (as we will see) to mourn his capture.[29] Cardinal de' Medici was quickly freed, however, which enabled him to turn his attention to his own family affairs, namely, returning Florence to Medici rule. (Less fortunate were the citizens of Ravenna, whose city was cruelly sacked by soldiers from the losing side, in 'a spirit of revenge for the loss they had sustained in the battle'.[30]) The intense complexity of these wars is illustrated by the fact that as Julius was trying to reassert papal rule over Bologna, the cardinal was planning an attack on Florence with the help of Spanish troops that would allow his family to retake the city after eighteen years of exile. In Rome, the Medici and their allies had built up the wealth they needed, and they had gradually accumulated friends within the republic as well.[31] The Medici, at this point, did not envisage becoming princes of Florence. 'First citizens', yes, but the rhetoric of the republic gave them cover for more difficult diplomacy and policy making, enabling them to blame others in government where a prince would have to stand alone.

The Spanish alliance was something of a novelty for the Medici. Florence's historic trade links were with France and indeed the fleur-de-lis on the Medici arms had been granted to Piero de' Medici by King Louis XI of France in 1465, testament to the strength of the relationship (and further playing on the wider historic use of the lily as a civic symbol in Florence).[32] Yet with Italy dominated by the two major European powers, rulers (and aspiring rulers) could not always afford to stick with tradition, and the Medici could promise the Spanish a stable, friendly regime in Florence. Indeed, in the years to come Florentine 'liberty' would come to mean something rather different from what it had previously: no longer was this the people's liberty from tyranny in the city, but the city's freedom from direct foreign rule, obtained through careful diplomacy and accommodation with the kings of Europe.[33]

Having attempted diplomacy with the republican regime in Florence (and predictably been turned down), Cardinal de' Medici, his brother Giuliano de' Medici and a Spanish army under the viceroy

Ramón de Cardona marched down through the Mugello hills outside Florence, spreading such 'terror and fear' that the inhabitants fled. Some – and with them some Florentines – took refuge in the town of Prato, about fourteen miles to the north-west. The Spanish followed, and on 28 August 1512 began an assault on the city – perhaps not least to avenge their losses at the Battle of Ravenna a few months before.[34] Jacopo Modesti, who wrote an account of the 'miserable sack', described how – having battered the walls with artillery and handguns – the Spanish scaled them 'like mad dogs'. Florentine soldiers who tried to make an escape from inside the city were caught by cavalry beyond its bounds, while the enemy 'without the slightest pity' ran through, 'killing women, men great and small, old and young, priests and friars, and every sort of person'. There were multiple rapes, including of children; citizens were tortured into revealing the location of their valuables. One method of torture involved stripping the skin from the soles of a victim's feet, then dowsing them with salt and vinegar. Bodies piled up even in the churches – over two hundred dead in the principal church and forty in San Domenico, according to the news in Florence – while the soldiers took the opportunity to seize money, jewels and church plate. There were few limits, though stories tell of some: when one soldier tried to steal the silver crown from a marble statue of the Madonna in the church of La Cintola, the figure of the Christ Child in her arms reached up to his mother's head, while the statue began to sweat. The soldiers quickly repented, returned the stolen jewels and killed the comrade responsible.[35] The sack lasted twenty-one days: hearing of events, Michelangelo wrote from Rome to his brother in Florence on 5 September 1512, encouraging the family to leave Florence – even at the price of abandoning property – for somewhere they might be safe.[36] It is hardly surprising that the Florentine regime was persuaded to surrender. The new rulers moved swiftly to assert their power. Machiavelli was dismissed and his handling of city finances investigated. After being linked to an anti-Medici conspiracy he was arrested, imprisoned and tortured, but had sufficiently influential friends to gain his freedom.[37]

While Julius II and Cardinal Giovanni de' Medici were busy ensuring their authority over Bologna and Florence, other Italian states contrived to prevent ambitious noblemen imposing themselves as hereditary lords. The peculiarities of Italian republican government were well known to other Europeans. When the Spanish conquistador Hernán Cortés described a Tlaxcalán city (in what is now central Mexico), he compared its system of government to that of Venice, Genoa and Pisa.[38] The Italian republics were not by any means democratic in the modern sense: there were strict limits on who was eligible to hold office, although the boundaries of this elite of citizens could and did shift according to political circumstances from a tight or even closed list of nobility to a relatively broader base.

Genoa, on the western coast of Italy, was the home city of Columbus, and like Venice (of which it had once been an equal) depended for its wealth on seafaring and trade, although it did not have an equivalent of Venice's Eastern empire. It had lost many of its holdings in the latter part of the fifteenth century to Ottoman conquest: Phocaea, Lesbos, Famagusta, Cyprus, Caffa; only Chios (an island in the Aegean Sea off Anatolia, now part of Greece) was held until 1566. Its trade with the east was worth only around a quarter of Venice's; while its rival provided state protection for convoys of galleys, Genoa did not, and from the later fifteenth century its economy was significantly more dependent on industry,[39] although as we have seen individual Genoese made the most of opportunities in Spanish and Portuguese service. In the early years of the wars, Genoa fell largely under the control of the French, who ruled from 1499 to 1512 (apart from a brief rebellion which declared a republic in 1507). The Spanish succeeded in overthrowing them in 1512 but the French were not yet done and retook the city, holding it from 1515 to 1522 when a Spanish-sponsored sack left Genoa heavily impoverished. However, a few years later (when his contract with the French expired, and as their fortunes in the wars began to fade) Andrea Doria, who became the city's de facto ruler, switched his allegiance to the new Holy Roman Emperor, Charles V (Charles I of Spain). Doria was the leading naval commander of his generation: 'an unparalleled and prescient observer of the sea and the clouds [...] always vigorous and successful in all his expeditions and battles'.[40] Although under Doria Genoa became a much more aristocratic version of a republic than it had been, it was not a closed system and there remained scope for families to be declared noble and become eligible for high office, though such opportunities were limited.[41] From now on, the price of Genoa's independence was alliance with Spain. It would not be the only Italian state to pay it, though the fortunes that Genoese bankers extracted in their service to the Spanish may have been some consolation.

Lucca, to the west of Florence, was another small city state that maintained its independence in the long term in the face of an invading French army. Like Genoa, its trajectory was towards a narrower and more aristocratic ruling council. The republic had been established in 1430 and the city had a thriving silk industry – supplied by Genoese merchants, who had an important role in supplying raw materials to other Italian states – with customers including the Crown of France. Lucca's location on the principal road from Paris to Rome, the Via Francigena, ensured it was a regular stopping-point for travellers, traders and pilgrims.[42] As we saw in the case of Giovanni Arnolfini, there were many Lucchese merchants who made careers internationally. Another was Benedetto Buonvisi, based in London, whose family business developed over several decades from the import/export of cloth and alum, to land investments in Italy, to the provision of banking services to the English Crown.[43] Members of the Buonvisi family lived in Crosby Hall, London, originally on Bishopsgate but subsequently moved to Cheyne Walk, Chelsea, where it still stands. Another Lucchese merchant family, the Gigli, secured posts at the turn of the fifteenth to sixteenth century as bishops of the English diocese of Worcester: they did not live there themselves but retained income from the diocese in return for acting as diplomatic agents for the English Crown in Rome.[44] Indeed, knowledge of the papal curia – because of its international role – was important currency for many Italians overseas. Lucca itself maintained its independence until 1799, two years longer than Venice.

Siena was another independent city state that, like Lucca, benefited from a location on the Via Francigena, this time to the south of Florence. This hilltop town had traditionally been allied with the Holy Roman emperors in preference to the popes, though some Sienese had illustrious church careers, including Pope Pius II. It had been a lively medieval centre, but had suffered economic decline from the later fourteenth century and after 1455 was ruled not by its

1. By an unknown artist, the *Tavola Strozzi* shows the city of Naples in the second half of the fifteenth century.

2. Jan van Eyck's painting of the Arnolfini in Bruges is testament to the range of Italian mercantile networks.

3. Pinturicchio's fresco in the Borgia Apartments incorporates an image of the Arch of Constantine in the background; the figure of St Catherine is said to be a portrait of Lucrezia Borgia.

4. Isabella d'Este hoped that Leonardo da Vinci would paint her portrait, but he completed only this drawing.

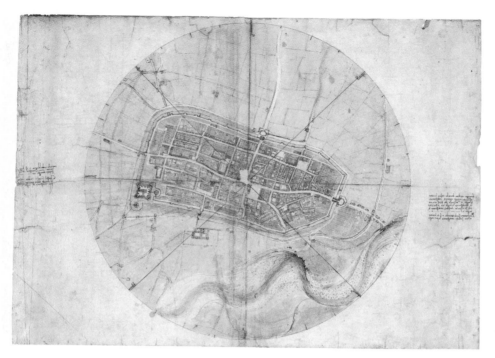

5. Leonardo da Vinci's plan of Imola was revolutionary in its bird's-eye approach to mapping.

6. This engraving by Daniel Hopfer shows the characteristic slashed dress
of German landsknechts.

7. The identity of the people in this painting by Paris Bordon (1500-71) is unknown, but Africans certainly participated in the Italian Wars.

8. Dosso Dossi's portrait of Alfonso d'Este, duke of Ferrara features in the background the 1509 Ferrarese attack on the Venetian fleet.

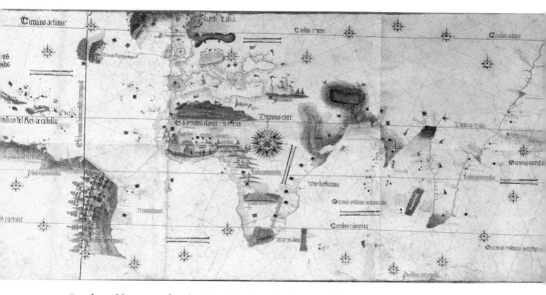

9. Produced by a spy for the Este family, this is one of the first maps to show North America's east coast.

10. The plants in this relief of Adam and Eve from the workshop of Giovanni della Robbia have sometimes been interpreted as New World maize.

11. Vasari said Raphael's portrait of Julius II was so lifelike as to make viewers 'shrink in fear'.

12. Published in 1521, Lucas Cranach's illustrations for Luther's *Passional Christi und Antichristi* contrasted the life of Christ with that of the pope, labelled here the Antichrist.

13. Piero di Cosimo's *Building of a Palace* was produced for the Florentine guild of master stonemasons and wood-carvers.

14. Testimony to Venetian trade with the Mamluk Empire, this painting may show an embassy linked to a spying scandal in 1510.

15. The capture of Francis I by imperial forces at Pavia was memorialised in this tapestry by Bernard van Orley.

16. Pope Adrian VI's brief rule is marked by this portrayal on a sixteenth-century Netherlandish coin.

traditional communal institutions but instead by an emergency committee known a *Balìa*, that had gradually become permanent. Once
again the trend was towards a more exclusive political elite,[45] and
also towards resentment of its imperial allies' high-handed demands
on the city.

Venice was a curious hybrid. It had an elected head of state, known
as the doge, which in the rankings of Italian powers enabled it to be
classed as a duchy (in the world of diplomatic ceremony, republics
were at the bottom of the political pecking order). The city was run
by a series of councils: the Senate (with 120 permanent members) was
responsible for most legislation, but there was also a Large Council
(made up of all the noblemen who had reached the qualifying age)
and a Small Council (a select group of the doge's counsellors). There
were also two judicial councils, with forty members each (still
noblemen), that heard civil and criminal cases respectively. A range
of magistracies dealt with issues such as public order and taxation.
Although it was officially forbidden to buy and sell offices in these
institutions, the rules were frequently ignored.[46]

Italy was not the only part of Europe to have this mix of governmental systems. The Holy Roman Empire, spreading from northern
Italy through what is now Austria and the German lands to the Low
Countries, had a similar variety of counties and duchies ruled by lords,
as well as a number of free imperial cities that governed themselves.
In terms of the competition for power in Europe, however, none of
these small states could compete with the wealth of France, nor with
the growing revenues that Spanish colonisation was securing in the
New World.

This Italy, with its multiple states and multiple structures of government, and indeed debates about their relative success, was the
background against which Niccolò Machiavelli, now exiled from Florence, had written and continued to write his works: his most famous,
The Prince; his lesser-known but arguably more important study of
republics, framed as *Discourses on the First Decade of Titus Livy* (the
Roman historian); his *Florentine Histories*, and three fine comic plays
and many shorter works, among them an *Art of War*. *The Prince* became
notorious, but it was only one of many texts penned in the arguments
over government and politics that flourished in sixteenth-century Italy
and would fuel debate for centuries to come. The idea of the republic

became a defining idea of the West: it was refined here, in the age of the Italian Wars.

Machiavelli had been born in Florence in 1469; in an earlier generation, Machiavelli cousins had opposed the rise of the Medici as rulers of the city, and had faced death and exile for it. Niccolò's father, whose debts (probably inherited) excluded him from city office, kept his distance from politics. Although he was qualified as a lawyer, he lived largely on the rents from a cluster of farms and a tavern. Young Niccolò got a respectable education, beginning with Latin grammar at the age of seven and acquiring a wide-ranging knowledge of the classics, although he would write his chief works in Italian. What we know of Machiavelli's youth comes largely from his father's *ricordi*, a matter-of-fact diary recording purchases, contracts and moments of family importance. The *ricordi* end in 1487, and the details of Machiavelli's life from the age of eighteen to twenty-eight remain mysterious: did he study at the university in Florence? Did he work, and, if so, what did he do?

Machiavelli reappears in the records in 1497 during the Savonarola regime, and in early 1498 he stood for election for the office of First Secretary of the *Signoria* (Florence's city council). He was not a supporter of Savonarola, and that probably cost him the election, but following Savonarola's execution Machiavelli became secretary of the Second Chancellery of the Republic. It was in this role that he made his name, carrying out diplomatic missions. On the return of the Medici in 1512, he was forced from the city but subsequently worked for the Medici and their allies; following financial trouble, the patronage of the Strozzi family, in-laws of the Medici, helped convince them to make use of Machiavelli's skills.[47] Popes Leo X and Clement VII (successive heads of the family) commissioned Machiavelli to write an opinion on the government of Florence and a history of the city. Clement, in fact, licensed the first printed editions of Machiavelli's works after the author's death; their notoriety came later, and in 1559 they were placed on the Index of Prohibited Books. More importantly, though, Machiavelli was part of the humanist tradition that saw political advice and political engagement as civic virtues: that is, it was the duty of a man to try to improve government, and if advising the Medici was his only route to doing that (which, given his exclusion from office-holding in the structures of the republic, it was) then that is what he would do.

The meaning of Machiavelli's work and the trajectory of his thought over his lifetime have long been subjects for debate among scholars. There are many interpretations of *The Prince* as a text. Its fame and reuse down the centuries in different contexts is explained in part by its ambiguities. Some would have Machiavelli a lifelong, committed republican, and *The Prince* a satire. How else might one account for the references to Cesare Borgia's 'extraordinary *virtù*' and at the same time the praise of his use of cruelty? (*Virtù*, a central concept in *The Prince*, which can be translated as 'skill', 'ingenuity' or 'power', among other options, has connotations both of virtue in the modern sense and of virility.) More recent commentary has tended to rule out the idea of *The Prince* as outright satire in favour of the idea that this is an ironic text, at once advising on potential tactics for princes while at the same time assessing how they might go wrong: perhaps it is a study of *failed* princes (which would make sense of the Borgia example).[48] It is generally agreed that *The Prince* was not intended as a set of tips on turning Florence into a principality. Florence was a city with a history of republican government, albeit a poorly ordered one which typically ended up with an unbalanced regime that tilted too far towards the interests of one social class.[49] At this point, almost no one thought changing that was a good idea (though opinions differed on how matters might be improved). Other interpretations of *The Prince* have focused on Machiavelli's interest in the prince as redeemer (perhaps echoing his own desire for redemption following exile), and on the rhetorical qualities of his work: that is, that the texts need to be read in light of whom they were designed to persuade. He was interested in establishing and maintaining the rule of law, and in different scenarios that required different actors: a prince, perhaps, to establish a legal system, but the people to maintain it.[50]

The Prince was written in the context of Machiavelli's exile from Florence and his attempt to regain some role in government; it was also written following his torture, the long-term effects of which are debated,[51] and may have been as much an effort to secure his financial interests (he was now lacking any income from government office) as anything else. *The Prince* should also be read, however, in the context of the ongoing wars, and especially in light of the French defeat at Novara (of which more below), not to mention the wider

Mediterranean conflicts. Machiavelli had previously regarded the French as potential saviours of Italy (not through conquest but as a counterweight against the Spanish), but by the 1510s that looked a less likely prospect. Instead, perhaps the prince of the book's title might prevail.[52] Indeed, the book as a whole gives a notably negative view both of the state of play in Italy and more widely. He observed that Ferdinand of Aragon, for example, was 'always using religion for his own purposes [...] hunting down and clearing out the Moors from his kingdom: no example could be more pathetic or more unusual than this.' In his view, Ferdinand similarly used the 'cloak of religion' to justify a series of attacks on the North African coast that established Spanish outposts there.[53] Nonetheless, Machiavelli was impressed with Ferdinand, and credited him with 'great deeds': the king's story is told in the chapter on how a prince should act to acquire esteem.

By the time he came to finish the *Discourses*, late in 1519 (he had begun them much earlier, shortly after his encounter with Cesare Borgia), Machiavelli's views had shifted somewhat from the argument of *The Prince*. For a start, the work is more clearly humanist in its engagement with the classics: just as scholars of the New World saw the writings of the ancients as a lens through which to view their discoveries, so Machiavelli found in them the keys to good government in the present.[54] The *Discourses* are also more clearly pro-republican, explicitly condemning tyranny and monarchy, arguing that two weak princes in a row spelled disaster for a polity. In the context of a Florence that was by now back under Medici rule, a regime that looked increasingly autocratic, it was also a text that was hostile to the ruling family, though the text's criticism of the Medici is sometimes veiled.[55]

Opposed to the feudal nobility, Machiavelli was also highly critical of the papacy, observing in the *Discourses* that 'those peoples who are near the church of Rome, the head of our religion, are the least religious'. He praised Gianpaolo Baglioni, observing that had he managed to murder Julius II in 1506, 'he would have led everyone to admire his courage and have gained immortal fame as the first to show prelates who live and rule as they do how little they are respected'.[56] This is not to say that Machiavelli was entirely hostile to religion: while being extraordinarily critical of it, he thought religion was politically necessary.[57] On the other hand, the extensive role accorded to Fortune in his work (as opposed to, say, the will of God), as well as his willingness to criticise the popes, later made him a target for censorship by the Church.

But if Machiavelli was one threat to the Medici and their papacy, another far more serious was about to enter the political scene: Martin Luther.

Chapter Nine

The Run-up to the Reformation

At the time of Martin Luther's first visit to the Eternal City in 1511 no one (least of all Luther himself) anticipated how his antipathy to the papacy might develop. In the popular version of this tale, Luther spent his visit being positively shocked by the outrageous conduct of the papal court, his observations feeding his later passion for reform. However, the claim does not fit so easily with the limited available sources.

What we do know is that in the winter of 1510–11 Luther, an Augustinian monk in his late twenties, travelled with a colleague to Rome from their monastery in Erfurt, in the centre of what is now Germany. Their journey south and across the Alps along an old pilgrim route (and in winter at that) took two months each way. They had gone to deal with a dispute about the reform of the Augustinian Order – the sort of church business that regularly drew clerics of all sorts to Rome – and there they met its prior general, Egidio da Viterbo (known in English as Giles of Viterbo), whose commitment to reform Luther later commended. The details of the visit are sketchy, and can only be pieced together from works written much later. Luther could not have seen Pope Julius, who was off on his Bologna campaign, but he did as much as could be expected of any pilgrim to Rome: visiting the city's seven most important churches, including St Peter's and St John Lateran, as well as the catacombs; he saw the Pantheon and the Colosseum too. He ascended the Scala Sancta or Holy Staircase on his knees, an act of devotion still undertaken by pilgrims today.[1]

Only much later, after 1525 and once Luther had been excommunicated, did he vent his criticism of Rome. It was no surprise to Luther that the pope resided in Italy, he wrote, 'for the Italians can make out many things to be real and true, which in truth are not so: they have

crafty and subtle brains'. He described the assassination of two Augustinian monks in Rome, who had dared to criticise Julius' successor,
Pope Leo X, in their sermons, and cited internal critics of the Church
against it, among them Pietro Bembo, later a cardinal.

> Bembo [Luther wrote], an exceeding learned man, who had thoroughly
> investigated Rome, said: Rome is a filthy, stinking puddle, full of the
> wickedest wretches in the world. [... Yet] the pope and his crew can
> in nowise endure the idea of reformation; the mere word creates more
> alarm at Rome, than thunderbolts from heaven, or the day of judgment.
> A cardinal said, the other day: Let them eat, and drink, and do what
> they will; but as to reforming us, we think that is a vain idea; we will
> not endure it.

Here, it must be acknowledged, Luther is concerned as much with
the subsequent formation of a Protestant image of Rome as his own
personal reaction. Moreover, Luther in telling his tales of wicked Rome
was not inspired solely by his own experience: one of his stories draws
on the *Decameron* of the celebrated medieval poet Boccaccio. His
personal opinions, however, were blunt. 'They show at Rome,' he
wrote, 'the head of St John the Baptist, though 'tis well known that
the Saracens opened his tomb, and burned his remains to ashes. These
impostures of the papists cannot be too seriously reprehended.'[2]
(Should you wish to see the head that prompted Luther's complaint,
it is still at the Church of San Silvestro in Capite, a short walk from
the Pantheon, today.)

Historians disagree about the precise consequences of Luther's visit
to Rome for his later thinking: on the one hand his subsequent writings
show a hostility to Italians that can only have been directly acquired
on this trip; on the other much of what he had to say in later life was
written with hindsight. At the time of his visit to Rome he sought
for his father the very 'indulgences' (the purchase of a reduction of
one's time in Purgatory) that would later be the butt of his criticism.[3]
Much of what Luther said about Rome, in fact, could easily have been
said by a critical loyalist. Anticlerical writing had a long history. Besides
Boccaccio there is plenty of it in the work of the poet Dante, not to
mention in less famous ballads – and anticlerical is not a synonym for
Protestant. In a 1525 play, *La Cortigiana*, Pietro Aretino (to whose

fascinating career we will come) described Rome as *coda mundi*: the tail of the world, an inversion of the idea of Rome as *caput mundi*, the head of the world.[4] Michelangelo, possibly frustrated at the progress of the Sistine Chapel project, observed of Julius II's court:

> They make a sword or helmet from a chalice,
> And sell the blood of Christ here by the load,
> And cross and thorn become a shield, a blade,
> And even Christ is being stripped of patience.[5]

Erasmus, on the other hand, despite his negative opinion of Julius II, had spent time in Rome and liked it. He had ample praise for its libraries and scholars, and for the generosity of cardinals, quite apart from the 'bright light, the noble setting of the most famous city in the world'.[6]

There were many calls for reform and (as we saw in the case of Savonarola) many of them were taken seriously. Alexander VI had initiated a reform commission in 1497, the proposals from which not only called for more modest lifestyles but would have substantially limited cardinals' incomes through restrictions on holding multiple benefices, and on the sale of offices. One of its members proposed a limit on the fees cardinals received from foreign powers for such tasks as proposing candidates for bishoprics, which could in some cases enhance a cardinal's income by 5,000 ducats a year.[7] The idea of reform and renewal had gained particular significance in the Church since the return of the popes to Rome in the mid fifteenth century, manifesting itself both in theological debate and in the built environment of the city, where it was made visible through the restoration of churches. The campaign for a new St Peter's that later prompted Luther's ire was indeed all about fundraising, but it was prompted by the reasonable recognition that the Church deserved a building in respectable condition to mark the tomb of the apostle.* To make sense of the architectural grandeur, it is worth knowing that in the Renaissance 'magnificence' was considered a princely virtue. Whereas in

---

* The most likely explanation for the orientation of St Peter's, which faces west rather than east, is that its founders wanted to place the altar over what they believed to be Peter's tomb but owing to the difficult terrain could only do so by reversing the usual layout.

later centuries people might well look at this splendour and think it rather excessive, spending money on ostentatious projects was simply understood as the type of thing that a prince ought to do. It was, moreover, part of a complex socioeconomic structure in which buyers and sellers were typically known to one another and in which it was expected that princes were to support the artisans of the area.[8] The renewal of Rome was important on account of the city's symbolism: Rome was often portrayed as the Church's bride, and when the popes had left Rome for Avignon between 1309 and 1376, the image of the city became instead that of a weeping widow (or, in the bawdier version, a bride abandoned while the pope consorted with his whore).[9] Renewal and renovation were political projects aimed at underlining the majesty of the papacy and might involve all sorts of places in Rome. Indeed, this glorious new papal Rome would be an even greater city than its ancient predecessor, because while classical Rome had been only a worldly capital, Renaissance Rome under the popes was leading the peoples of the world to heaven.[10]

That was, at least, the theory. The practice looked rather different. As we have seen, the papal curia was gradually shifting to become less of a senate and more of a court, and cardinals' own miniature courts matched the lavish lifestyles of their secular counterparts. Not every cardinal was an extravagant spender, by any means: those who spent their time hunting and feasting were more typically the scions of Italian princely families, appointed for political motives, than the men chosen for their theological or legal expertise. Yet by comparison to the average individual they were very well off indeed: those in the senior offices of vice-chancellor and penitentiary had salaries of 6,000 ducats a year. On the other hand, there was an expectation that cardinals should offer hospitality appropriate to their rank as princes of the Church, and as the size of the College of Cardinals increased, there was less money in the central pot to share between them, which led to numerous complaints.[11]

This is not the place to give an exhaustive account of Luther's rise. But the challenge of his theology can only be understood fully in light of the nature of the sixteenth-century Church leadership and the longer-term contexts of reform and war. Luther's beliefs eventually had three key tenets. One was the priesthood of all believers – priests were not, he maintained, a special caste peculiarly able to mediate the word of God. This was, in practice, abandoned quite quickly by many Protestant churches but its egalitarian implication persisted. The second was justification through faith: the idea that one need not do good works on earth to lessen one's time in Purgatory but that good works were the natural behaviour of godly people. The third was that only scripture mattered – ideas that were the product of Church tradition should be set aside in favour of reference to the word of God.

The connection of Luther's ideas to the earlier work of humanists in Renaissance Italy (and elsewhere) is not straightforward. Although he attended a university where there was lively discussion about humanist ideas, he does not seem to have been close to that intellectual circle.[12] Nonetheless, developments in Bible scholarship were important for critical scrutiny of church practices. Humanist scholars produced new editions of important Christian texts including the writings of St Augustine (interpretation of whose work was central to debates between Protestants and Catholics about justification through faith); they also retranslated the Bible itself, turning back to Greek texts. This process of retranslation produced important new glosses on theological questions. For example, the standard Latin translation of the Bible, the Vulgate (produced by St Jerome in the late fourth or early fifth century) had for Matthew 4:17 'Do penance, for the Kingdom of Heaven is at hand', while in Erasmus' 1516 translation it became 'Repent, for the Kingdom of Heaven is at hand'.[13] This internal turn to mental repentance rather than external action would be reflected in Protestantism, although Erasmus himself did not become a Protestant. On the other hand some later Protestant leaders – among them notably Heinrich Zwingli and Philip Melanchthon – did have significant backgrounds in the Christian humanist tradition.

The longer term context for the events that would so anger Luther was a large shift in papal finances. In 1462 alum, a vital ingredient for the textile industry, had been discovered in the Tolfa mountains which lay within the Papal States, on which the Church capitalised by banning the import of alum from the Ottoman Empire.[14] By 1480 this monopoly was contributing almost twenty per cent of total papal income. Significant sums also came from the sale of indulgences and church offices, while the importance of routine taxes dwindled. Temporal revenues (that is, from non-ecclesiastical sources including customs duty, taxes and rents) made up half the papacy's income in the early sixteenth century, though it was spending around the same amount on defence.[15] However, as a large and wealthy institution, the Church inevitably attracted power-seekers alongside those with a genuine commitment to religious life (and many monks, nuns and clerics undoubtedly combined a bit of both). For aspiring families, positions in the papal civil service were valued, and the dispatch of a nephew to Rome to make a curial career was a handy strategy for advancement; this in turn made the curia ever more Italian in focus. Besides the high echelons of the papal court, local bishops and arch-bishops might have substantial entourages, and as we have seen in the case of San Marco in Florence, convents and monasteries could provide a power base for an ambitious preacher, not to mention a noble abbot or abbess as interested in lavish art and architectural patronage as religious devotion. Even a modest position as village priest offered the incumbent a certain authority within a community. In finances and in lifestyle, the popes seemed very much like secular princes. They had learned few lessons from the Savonarola experience. The Italian Wars made the situation worse: wartime was far from the most propitious moment to focus on internal reform of institu-tions. However, Julius II must be given credit for trying, although his efforts were (to some extent at least) forced by opponents who in 1511 called a 'Little Council' at Pisa. They swiftly moved this *concili-abulum*, however: first to Milan and then to France, before finally abandoning it because, in response, Julius had decided to call a reforming council of his own.

This was the Fifth Lateran Council, and it opened in May 1512 with an address from Egidio da Viterbo; it ran until March 1517, with par-ticipants from across Europe and perhaps as far away as Syria (whose Maronite Christians are thought to have been represented). Besides the ecclesiastical representatives, most European powers sent ambas-sadors, an indication of the extent to which church decisions were a matter of general governmental interest.[16]

Overshadowed by subsequent events, the Council's dealings have often been ignored, but it laid down markers for reform that informed subsequent responses to the Protestant challenge, not least those of the Council of Trent some thirty years later. Among its outcomes were reforms to university education as well as tighter provisions for the quality of priests, who should be 'of mature age, learning and serious character'.[17] (Some wit must surely have pointed to the appointment of Giovanni de' Medici, now a senior cardinal, while still a teenager.) There were to be improvements, too, to the running of religious institutions, with greater provision for bishops to visit and inspect monasteries, convents and churches run by holy orders as well as a clampdown on absentee abbots and on dubious claims of miracles.[18] There was criticism of extravagant lifestyles at the curia: cardinals were urged to avoid excessive 'display or splendour' in their households, and to be 'mirrors of moderation and frugality'.[19]

All in all, the trend of the Lateran decisions was towards more centralised power for the ecclesiastical hierarchy, and it is hard to avoid the observation that such provisions would also have allowed more oversight of the likes of Savonarola. Some of the proposed reforms were significant and notable. For example, the requirement for competence in preaching was a matter that would concern both Protestant and Catholic clergy later in the century. The Council was also concerned about printing, and especially about those books that included 'errors opposed to the faith as well as pernicious views contrary to the Christian religion and to the reputation of prominent persons of rank'.[20] It hoped, moreover, for a crusade – a 'holy and necessary expedition against the frenzy of the infidels, panting to have their fill of Christian blood'.[21] In any case, the Lateran Council and its reforms highlight that for all the evident worldly interests of the Renaissance popes they could also be seriously engaged with religious reform and desire improvements to the Church. It also puts paid to any simple idea that the later and more famous reforms of the Council of Trent were only a response to Protestantism. Scholars today are much more likely to find long continuities in the process of Catholic reform.

Julius II did not see the outcome of his Council. He died on 21 February 1513, and the conclave to choose his replacement began in March. With St Peter's Basilica still in the process of renovation – as it would remain for some time – the opening Mass was held instead in the Chapel of St Andrew, while small furnished cells, eight feet long, for the cardinals and their servants (each cardinal was permitted two attendants) were set up in the Sistine Chapel. Relatives of the late pope and the 'palatine' cardinals entitled to reside in the Vatican

Palace had purple hangings around their cells; other cardinals got green ones. They took their oath in the small chapel of St Nicholas in the Vatican Palace. There were thirty-one men eligible to vote in the election (Julius II had excommunicated four over the schismatic Little Council); twenty-four arrived on time while latecomers including Cardinal Adriano Castellesi, bishop of Hereford, had to negotiate to be allowed entry. Custodians were appointed to guard each exit, and the masters of ceremonies kept a close eye on the keys to ensure no one got in or out. That said, the drains of the temporary latrines provided a means – if a rather unpleasant one – for secret discussions, as did messages scratched onto plates (though these were inspected before being allowed through the doors). Cardinal Giovanni de' Medici made a slow and painful journey to the conclave. He was suffering from an anal fistula, and a surgeon had to be on hand to attend to him throughout. Despite (or perhaps because of) his illness, which promised a relatively short papacy, Giovanni was one of the two leading candidates for election. The other was Raffaele Riario, a relative of the late Pope Julius. In the end – despite delays caused by a dispute over money among the cardinals' attendants, and a hiatus to allow an inauspicious solar eclipse to pass – the conclave was a relatively brief affair and after negotiations between the leading candidates, Giovanni de' Medici was elected as Pope Leo X on 10 March 1513.[22]

There was considerable enthusiasm for Leo's papacy in Florentine circles, not least because of the prospects for curia jobs that came with it,[23] and as usual for a newly elected pope, Leo appointed cardinals from among his circle. They included his cousin, Giulio de' Medici, and Innocenzo Cibo, a nephew. Leo hoped that the marriage of his younger brother Giuliano to a Savoyard bride would seal an alliance with the French. In September 1513, he held a grand ceremony to grant the citizenship of Rome to Giuliano and the senior Medici nephew, Lorenzo. Pope Leo X had grand ambitions. Like the Borgia Pope Alexander VI before him, he sought a state for his family: specifically, Urbino, a city state near the Adriatic coast, where he was planning to install Lorenzo as duke in place of Francesco Maria della Rovere, relative of Pope Julius II and thus a member of the family whose rivalry with the Medici stretched back to the Pazzi Conspiracy some thirty-odd years before. What transpired was, so far as the Italian Wars were concerned, a relatively rapid conflict. Leo secured 130,000 ducats in a loan from Florence to finance the invasion (secured by grants of territory).[24] Recruitment of troops began in mid April 1516; six weeks later the city had surrendered, and by the autumn Lorenzo had been invested as duke of Urbino and was looking forward to a French marriage. Two years later, he married Madeleine de la Tour d'Auvergne, an heiress and distant relative of French royalty.[25]

The rulership of Florence, however, proved more troublesome. After the return of the Medici in 1512, Leo's brother Giuliano (whom in 1515 he had appointed head of the papal troops in place, once again, of Francesco Maria della Rovere) had become the city's leader, but Giuliano died unexpectedly at the age of thirty-seven in 1516, and to add to the difficulties his marriage to Filiberta of Savoy had been childless. Giuliano had a bastard son, Ippolito, but the Medici were now left with only one legitimate, marriageable heir: Duke Lorenzo of Urbino. Worse was to come. In the summer of 1516, Leo himself became seriously ill. He had not been the healthiest of candidates three years before and now his troublesome fistula was again causing grief. To compensate, Leo worked hard to consolidate his power in Rome, promoting record numbers of friends and relatives to the cardinalate. He also moved against potential rivals to the Medici in the College of Cardinals.

Known as the 'Cardinals' Conspiracy' of 1517, the affair might better be called the 'Papal Frame-Up'.[26] In the late spring and early summer of that year, five cardinals were accused of plotting to poison Leo. The early stages of the investigation targeted the suspects' servants: they were more easily bribed, coerced or intimidated than their masters. The appointed prosecutor had a notorious reputation for brutality and it did not take long for the investigators to find a link – albeit a tenuous one – to one of Leo X's doctors (a man in a position to administer poison) around which to construct a case. The pope now needed to decide what to do with the conspirators.

One of them, Cardinal Petrucci, came from the Tuscan city of Siena, famously a rival of the pope's home city of Florence. The previous year, Leo had ousted Petrucci's relatives from the rulership of the city and brought it under the 'protection' of the papacy, part of his broad strategy to join papal interests with those of his Florentine family. Petrucci was understandably unhappy, and spent several months negotiating an alliance to retake Siena, behaviour that Leo regarded as *lèse majesté*. Naturally enough, Petrucci turned for support to the man ousted by the Medici from Urbino and from his role as captain general of the papal troops, Francesco Maria della Rovere (whom we previously encountered murdering Cardinal Alidosi). He also worked with the Baglioni family of Perugia, a border city traditionally hostile both to the popes and to Florence, and with the Spanish, traditional supporters of Siena against a French-backed Florence.

Another of the accused, Cardinal Sauli, came from a Genoese banking family. His motives for joining Petrucci were less obvious. He seems to have been close to Petrucci, and may have resented the loss of a key papal banking post and certain benefices to Medici relatives after Leo's election. A third, Raffaele Riario, was the longest-serving cardinal in the College. He had been appointed at the age of seventeen by his great-uncle, Pope Sixtus IV, and thanks to his long service in the curia had acquired an impressive tranche of benefices. Like the banking scion Sauli, he was rich. The fourth, Cardinal Francesco Soderini, was from an old Florentine family who were well-known rivals of the Medici. It was agreed that he and the fifth, Cardinal Adriano Castellesi, were really witnesses to the plot, and there is some suggestion that Cardinal Castellesi's real problem was that he had incurred the enmity of Cardinal Thomas Wolsey, who had his eye on Castellesi's English benefices.

In light of Leo's failing health in the summer of 1516, there may well have been loose talk about who would succeed him. Yet the line between speculation on what might happen should the pope die and the conclusion that his death was desirable proved a fine one, and it was that fine line that sent the cardinals to their fates. The political rival, Cardinal Alfonso Petrucci, was executed on 4 July 1517, strangled in his cell in the Castel Sant'Angelo, Rome. He was twenty-six and had been a prisoner in the papal fortress for six weeks, his fatal mistake having been to trust Leo's promise of a safe conduct to Rome. Three of the lower-ranking 'conspirators' were executed too. The remaining cardinals were fined: 12,500 ducats apiece for Soderini and Castellesi, who were found guilty by their fellow cardinals of failing to reveal the plot; 25,000 ducats for Sauli and a staggering 150,000 ducats for Riario, who was exiled to Naples. Moreover, Leo was now able to resell the benefices he had confiscated from the so-called plotters. The

Venetian diarist Marin Sanudo reckoned Leo had made half a million ducats from the business. That was ten times the annual income of the richest cardinal, and 250 times the income of the poorest.

The most likely explanation of the whole affair is one suggested by Paolo Giovio, an intimate observer of the Medici circle. In Giovio's account, Petrucci really did threaten to kill the pope; the other cardinals laughed and made fun of him. Said one way, 'I'm going to kill the pope' can be an empty boast. Said another, it can be a genuine threat. In an atmosphere of high tension – as this certainly was after Giuliano de' Medici's death and Leo's illness – such comments could easily be interpreted as conspiracy to murder. Students of English history might well be reminded of the way that careless talk about a ruler's death provided vital evidence in the 1536 trial of Queen Anne Boleyn. In her case, she admitted to a conversation with the courtier Henry Norris about what might happen should Henry VIII die. It is not so hard to imagine the 'Cardinals' Conspiracy' emanating from similarly loose talk.

Leo topped the whole affair with an astonishing appointment of no fewer than thirty-one new cardinals, more than doubling the size of the College. Since the re-establishment of a single papacy in Rome some seventy years before, the record for a single creation had been twelve. Four of the new men were Florentines; others were Medici allies and in-laws; two were Sienese, including Raffaele Petrucci, from a rival branch of Cardinal Alfonso's family. The influence of the old guard was permanently diluted; the new men owed Leo for their appointments, so the pope had the compliant College he wanted. If ever there was an auspicious time for reformers to point at a pope's focus on politics and family at the expense of Christian faith, good works and piety, this was it. When, almost four months later, Martin Luther published his 'Ninety-Five Theses' on indulgences, he was probably not thinking of politics in Rome. The timing, however, could not have been better.

Chapter Ten

The League of Cambrai

The conflicts over reform in the Church intersected not only with the family strategies of the popes but also with wider developments in the Italian Wars that dated back some ten years. If Leo was trying to rescue his dynastic fortunes plenty of others had similar interests, as became apparent in the 'War of the League of Cambrai'. Their target, this time, was Venice.

In 1494, Milan had been the catalyst for the French descent into Italy. They had captured it in 1499, and King Louis XII now hoped to incorporate more territory into its holdings. In 1507 he met King Ferdinand of Aragon at Savona, a port city to the west of Genoa on the Ligurian coast. Summit meetings between monarchs were a novelty of this period, and would feature in multiple contexts over the coming years. They required a level of trust that one king would not take the other hostage and were one of a number of important developments in diplomacy, another being the increasing use of permanent embassies instead of reliance solely on shorter-term missions by special envoys. What Louis and Ferdinand had in common – and shared with the Holy Roman Emperor Maximilian – was an antipathy to Venice. The maritime republic had substantial landholdings on the Italian *terraferma* (mainland), many of which were desirable to other rulers. Ferdinand had his eye on Venice's Apulian ports in the southern Adriatic, which were rivals for his own ports in the kingdom of Naples; the popes disputed territory with the Venetians in the Romagna; the Holy Roman Empire was embroiled in border disputes with them in Austria, not to mention having a legitimate claim over cities such as Verona and Vicenza which Venice held without imperial permission. Pope, king and emperor could also count on the support of the rulers of the small northern states of Mantua and Ferrara, which had lost territory to Venice during the expansion of the previous century.

The first step towards forming a league against Venice was to settle potential disputes between the parties, for which purpose talks were convened at Cambrai (conveniently situated between Paris and the cities of the Low Countries) late the following year. Among the key representatives were Margaret of Austria, Maximilian's daughter and regent in the Netherlands on behalf of her nephew Charles, and – for Louis – Cardinal d'Amboise. (We will see more of Margaret, one of the important women in the conduct of the Italian Wars, below; the cardinal was one of a number of princes of the Church who in this period held high office in their home countries: others included Thomas Wolsey of England and Antoine du Prat of France.) Their negotiations were a success, and concluded with agreements on the future of Navarre and several cities of the Low Countries, as well as acknowledging Louis and his heirs as the rightful rulers of Milan. They also made a secret treaty for a league to attack Venice in April 1509, aiming to capture the entirety of Venice's *terraferma*. These were relatively recent annexations dating from the fifteenth century, when Venice had expanded its empire to encompass the cities of Treviso, Vicenza, Verona, Padua, then the region of Friuli as well as Brescia and Bergamo, this last only thirty miles from Milan and over a hundred and forty from Venice.

The stage was thus set for a battle between France and Venice, though as ever mercenaries were important on both sides: there were Swiss troops fighting with the French and stradiots (cavalry from the Balkans) with Venice. The armies looked more or less evenly matched in the run-up to the engagement. Louis had initially mishandled the negotiations for Swiss mercenaries and had to make do with informal recruitment of volunteers rather than the trained bands that were provided through the official mechanisms, but the numbers proved more than sufficient. The Venetians opted for a defensive strategy, aiming to avoid engagement, but it failed. As they were moving camp in mid May 1509 the French advance guard attacked the Venetian rearguard at Agnadello, about twenty miles east of Milan and almost at the western limit of Venetian holdings on the mainland. It was a brutal battle: Louis had ordered his troops to take no prisoners, and they responded with a massacre of their enemies. The Venetians did take prisoners, among them Bartolomeo d'Alviano, their own second in command, who had to account for the disaster.

As the news trickled into Venice in letter after letter, the scale of the humiliation became clear. Of Andrea Gritti, proveditor general (and later doge of Venice), Sanudo recorded: 'he writes the ugly news and wishes he were dead.' The commissioner of artillery wrote describing how he had suffered a head wound and been thrown from his horse; he had contrived to find another mount and escaped the scene. From the point of view of military tactics or technology, Agnadello was not a particularly significant battle, but it changed the geopolitics of Italy, because with the defeat Venice lost almost all its mainland territories. (The flight of Jewish refugees from the *terraferma* to Venice after 1509 was also one of the factors in the creation of the city's ghetto.) It was, as a letter from Brescia declared, a 'most unhappy day'.[1]

The Venetians subsequently saw significant losses to Ferrara, to Mantua and to France (including Brescia and Crema, the latter about equidistant between Brescia and Milan). They lost less to the imperial forces who made modest gains to Venice's east, including the city of Trieste on the Adriatic (close to the modern Italian border with Slovenia). On the other hand Venice managed to hold Udine and nearby Cividale in Friuli, along with Treviso, just north of the lagoon. Even Guicciardini, who thought the Venetians a nation 'hated' for their reputation of 'natural pride and haughtiness, observed that the speed of Venetian decline was 'a violent and astonishing shock'.[2] A fierce debate followed within Venice as its rulers considered the failure of the mainland expansion: perhaps it had been a bad idea after all. On the *terraferma* there was likewise a variety of opinion. The elites of the subject towns and cities looked with envy at the hands-off approach of the emperor to the free imperial cities of Germany and had reason to prefer a distant overlord to close Venetian scrutiny. Rural communities, on the other hand, tended to prefer the more distant Venetians to the prospect of closer interference from rulers in a town nearby. These were wars in which 'the Italians' as a group had few common interests. In an attempt to settle with at least part of the League of Cambrai, the Venetians handed back lands in the Romagna to Julius II, who at this point still had four more years as pope ahead of him, and the Neapolitan ports to Ferdinand of Aragon. This was wise diplomacy because neither the pope nor the king of Spain was keen to see either France or the Empire gaining too much territory in northern Italy. Venice then retook Padua and in August captured Francesco Gonzaga, marquis of Mantua. The Emperor Maximilian besieged Padua but got nowhere; the Venetians also got Vicenza back, though not Verona.[3]

In 1510 Julius withdrew his excommunication of Venice, but there was still further drama in the campaign that year; the League's armies took back again the strategic town of Vicenza on the road between Venice and Milan, as well as Polesine near the River Po; the French took Legnago on the River Adige; the League also captured Bassano and Belluno but by late summer problems in Genoa and Milan proved more pressing and the Venetians recovered virtually everything as their opponents withdrew; only the fortresses of Verona and Legnago remained under French control.[4] It was at this point that Julius switched sides against the French, declaring (so tradition has it) 'barbarians out'. Whether in fact he said these precise words is a moot point, but his sentiment was clear.[5] He then began the campaign that temporarily lost him control of Bologna, and was defeated again in 1512, at the Battle of Ravenna, when a joint French and Ferrarese force beat the Spanish and Papal armies.[6] The complex back-and-forth of these gains and losses and the accompanying changes of alliance were typical of the Italian Wars, where this year's friend could easily become next year's enemy.

One of the most important small states in these northern wars was Ferrara. Located on a tributary of the River Po, it benefited from rich farmland. Flowing eastwards across Italy via Turin and Piacenza, and lying in a wide, flat river plain, the Po was both a vital agricultural resource and a natural line of defence that repeatedly featured in the Italian Wars, its banks dotted with castles and fortifications. The duke of Ferrara, who was so significant in the conflict with Julius II, was Alfonso d'Este, the third husband of Lucrezia Borgia and a brother to Isabella d'Este, marchioness of Mantua. Lucrezia, who was twenty-one at the time of their marriage in 1501, had a famous rivalry with her sister-in-law, and was rumoured to have had an affair with Isabella's husband Francesco (the historical evidence for this is not reliable, and her other celebrated affair, with the future cardinal Pietro Bembo, is also unlikely to have been more than a passionate correspondence). From 1505, when Alfonso became duke, Lucrezia turned her attention to a variety of projects. On the one hand she remodelled the ducal apartments, incorporating new history paintings, a bathroom and grotto as well as silk draperies for the walls and tapestries featuring the story of Susanna and the Elders.[7] (This Old Testament narrative both alluded to the virtue of a woman falsely accused – perhaps appropriate for Lucrezia – and offered scope for a sexy portrayal of a woman bathing.) On the other she built something of a business empire, with drainage projects in the Po valley to improve the local grazing land* as well as the establishment of a mozzarella factory.[8]

Duke Alfonso, meanwhile, took a personal interest in the design of artillery, working alongside his artisans to perfect new types of cannon, to the point that he was nicknamed 'il duca artigliere' or 'the Gunner Duke'. Paolo Giovio, a member of the Medici circle who observed the politics of these years at first hand, wrote Alfonso's biography, noting that he was in the habit of going down to the foundry dressed as a smith to cast items in bronze, among them great artillery pieces.[9] Francesco Sperulo, who had been a mercenary in Cesare Borgia's service, wrote a poem that gave a dramatic account of Alfonso's intervention at the Battle of Ravenna, describing the duke turning to the craft from which his father had dissuaded him, 'always busy among lifeless instruments of death, bronze mouths, heaps of sulphur and nitre'. There was little enthusiasm for such pursuits, but as Sperulo observed, 'the Fates had decreed that by these arts contests of state would be decided.'[10] And indeed they were, most spectacularly when a Venetian fleet moored overnight on the River Po during the Battle of Polesella in December 1509: the Ferrarese set up their guns behind embankments on either side of the river, hidden from the unsuspecting crews, and calculated the trajectory so that when – just before dawn – they fired, the cannonballs (almost literally) blew the fleet out of the water.[11] Alfonso was sufficiently proud of his achievement to have it commemorated in a portrait by Dosso Dossi. Lucrezia, too, was more than capable of handling military affairs in her husband's

---

* Leonardo da Vinci's extensive studies of water can be understood against the backdrop of such practical interest in its diversion and exploitation.

absence, liaising both with her brother-in-law Cardinal Ippolito I d'Este and with local officials to ensure the provision of supplies.[12]

In his *History of Italy*, Guicciardini explained how the development of new, lighter-weight cannon had begun to shift the course of the wars. Cannon in general had 'rendered ridiculous all former weapons of attack which had been used by the ancients', but the French version was 'more manoeuvrable' and its iron shot, replacing the previous stone balls, 'incomparably larger and heavier'. By employing horses in place of oxen to draw the gun-carriages, meanwhile, the army became more agile: the horses could keep pace with the troops, who would shift the artillery right up to the city walls, 'and set into position there with incredible speed'. Conquests that had once taken days could now be achieved within hours. No wonder, then, that Guicciardini thought this a weapon more 'diabolical than human'.[13] Machiavelli complained that the Italian princes had been complacent, thinking their command of arts and letters, their splendour and deceit, sufficient protection.

> Nor [he wrote] did these wretches perceive that they were preparing themselves to be the prey of whoever assaulted them. From here then arose in 1494 great terrors, sudden flights, and miraculous losses; and thus three very powerful states that were in Italy have been sacked and wasted. But what is worse, those who are left persist in the same error and disorder.[14]

However, for both these Florentine historians a dramatic turning point in 1494 served rhetorical purpose more than it did historical accuracy. The real-life shift from the predominance of cavalry to infantry, and the rise of artillery, was a slow process that took place over decades, not an overnight event.[15] That said, technology did matter: Ferrarese guns, for example, were significant to the French victory over Venice at Legnago in 1510.[16] And if Guicciardini thought the new technology was devilish, others linked it to a more specific problem of the period: the pox, to which Alfonso fell victim. Ferrarese court physician Coradino Gilino was among them:

> We see then that the Creator on high, being angered with us at this time for our impious deeds, is afflicting us with this most terrible

distemper that is raging not only in Italy but throughout the whole of Christendom. Everywhere the blare of trumpets is sounding, everywhere is heard the clash of arms, everywhere are being constructed military weapons, bombards, instruments and a great many engines of war, moreover instead of the spherical stones, which have been in use up to the present time they are now making iron balls, a hitherto unheard-of thing. The Turks are called into Italy, and would that I would deny how many conflagrations, how many depradations, how many massacres of wretched human beings we have already seen, how many and how great we are yet to see! [...] Such then I deem to be the cause of this raging epidemic.[17]

Alfonso's encounter with the pox was evidently unpleasant, but he outlived his wife by fifteen years, dying at the age of fifty-eight.

While not everyone got their hands dirty in quite the direct way Alfonso did, military conquest mattered to all rulers. In 1515, a new king of France, Francis I, launched a revived assault to recover the territories lost in the previous years. Francis' predecessor, his cousin and father-in-law Louis XII, had died at New Year without a direct heir. Francis' inheritance was not unexpected: he had been heir presumptive since Louis had come to the throne in 1498; Louis and his wife Anne of Brittany's only surviving children were daughters and by 1512 it was clear that Francis would succeed. Provided with an excellent humanist education by his mother Louise of Savoy as well as the customary training in the military arts, Francis was well prepared for his coronation at the age of twenty.[18] He was praised in Castiglione's *The Courtier* for his 'noble courtesy, his magnanimity, his valour and his generous spirit'; Guicciardini observed that it had been many years since a prince 'of greater expectations' had ascended the throne.[19]

Francis had a competitor in England, his contemporary Henry VIII (Castiglione again: 'in a single body enough virtues for a host of men');[20] and from 1516 he acquired a second rival in Charles, king of Spain from that year and Holy Roman Emperor Charles V from 1519. Charles had inherited the duchy of Burgundy following the death of his father, Philip the Handsome, in 1506. To those he had added in 1516 the crown of Aragon, inherited from his maternal grandfather

Ferdinand (his grandmother, Isabella of Castile, had died in 1504). Technically, his Spanish lands were ruled jointly with his mother Joanna (or Juana) of Castile: she, however, had been declared insane and imprisoned. (Historians continue to debate whether or not she was in fact mentally ill and/or incompetent to rule.) On the death of his paternal grandfather the Emperor Maximilian in 1519 Charles gained the Habsburg inheritance in Austria and the German states too. Later that year, he was elected Holy Roman Emperor. Charles' election was not a foregone conclusion. He offered bribes to secure it, including to Pope Leo X. He was not the only candidate: in England Cardinal Wolsey had thought Henry VIII might be an alternative, and Francis I had ambitions as well, but the Habsburgs prevailed. Thanks to the spread of his territories, Charles became the most powerful man in Europe and overlord of the Spanish Empire in the Americas too. The significance of the personal rivalry between these three – and from 1520 a fourth, the Ottoman Sultan Süleyman – should not be underestimated.

For the twenty-one-year-old Francis, military victory, and reclaiming France's lost territories in northern Italy, was a matter of honour. The French had failed to consolidate their 1509 victory at Agnadello, and four years later had lost Milan at the Battle of Novara, which had put the Sforza back in power. In 1515, the year before Charles ascended the Spanish throne, Francis faced an alliance including the duke of Milan, the pope, King Ferdinand of Aragon and the Emperor Maximilian. By sneaking his army into Italy over a small Alpine pass rather than any of the predictable major routes, he evaded the Swiss mercenaries waiting for him. At Villlafranca, not far from Verona, the French vanguard sprang a surprise attack on the duke of Milan's cavalry, prompting Swiss infantry in Milanese service to retreat. Francis sent agents to try to buy them off; the Swiss negotiated hard and extracted the promise of a million écus as the price of their withdrawal. They were, however, divided, and men from certain cantons opted to fight on in what became the Battle of Marignano, which took place about halfway between Parma and Piacenza on 13–14 September 1515. The Swiss might well have prevailed, were it not for the arrival of Venetian reinforcements, who together with the French triumphed in one of the bloodiest battles of the Italian Wars, a 'battle of giants' that made others look like children's games. As the French chronicler

Martin du Bellay wrote, it was a 'glorious victory' for the 21-year-old king.[21] The retreating Swiss tried their best to hide in trees, streams and marshes, but, as one delighted Venetian correspondent reported from the camp (the memory of Agnadello no doubt still bruising) they were pursued and 'cut to pieces'.[22] Massimiliano Sforza, son of Ludovico and now duke of Milan, accepted the offer of a pension and retired to France, leaving the city in Francis' hands.[23]

It was a spectacular beginning to Francis' reign, in an age when battlefield prowess could still make a royal reputation. Even his rival Charles had to praise the 'beautiful and great victory that God had given him'.[24] The word 'honour' is not widely used now, but it was a central concept in early modern Europe at all levels of society. While these days an individual's 'credit score' at the bank is generally determined by a computer algorithm, until very recently it rested much more on social reputation within a community, of which in the sixteenth century 'honour' was a key component. For a king, honour might be achieved on the battlefield; it might be conveyed through splendour and spectacle. Lower down the social ranks, it might be linked to a man's proper management of household and family: nothing was worse for a man's honour than being cuckolded. Female honour, on the other hand, was closely linked to chastity. The legacy of these ideas is apparent in many societies to this day, for example, in pejorative insults that focus on women's (perceived) promiscuity: son of a bitch; son of a whore. Yet though military campaigns were important to establish a new ruler's credentials, they were also expensive. In 1517, the French Chancellor Antoine du Prat said the campaign to recover Milan (including Marignano) had cost France about 3,700,000 ducats, or about seventy-five per cent of total French revenue for the two-year campaign (taking into account both long- and short-term costs). This was well in excess of the proportion a state would normally spend on war and defence: a more typical figure was 50 per cent, which still gives an indication of the importance of warfare in the early modern period.[25]

If new military technologies were contentious, the Italian wars also prompted debate about the use of mercenaries. As we have seen, mercenaries – Swiss pikemen and German landsknechts – were vital to military success in this world of privatised companies and captains for hire. This system has more in common with modern warfare than one might think: today's private military companies go by names like Blackwater, contractors in Iraq, or the earlier Sandline in Papua New Guinea, Sierra Leone and Liberia. In Italy at this time, instead of corporations, it was individuals – often well-known members of aristocratic families – who received a contract (or *condotta*) to raise a company and fight for a defined period on behalf of a particular state. Military contracting was an important source of income for rulers of small states like Ferrara, which were not strong enough alone to lead a campaign by this time but might have a significant role in an alliance. The system was long-standing but not without its critics.

Guicciardini, for example, contrasted the mercenary captains of the Italian armies unfavourably to the French captains who typically served the French king:

> The captains [that is, those of the Italian armies] were very seldom subjects of the prince they served, but had often a different interest, and separate views, were full of piques and jealousies; their service not commonly limited to a certain time, and being entirely masters of their own companies, they seldom kept the number they were paid for complete. Nor were they were satisfied with what was just, but took all occasions to impose upon their masters by exorbitant accounts; never long settled, but when tired with one service they passed into another, and tempted by ambition, avarice, or any thing that concerned their interest, were not only unsettled but often treacherous.[26]

Many heads were shaken at the inadequacies of mercenaries as compared to a citizen militia, more likely to be loyal to the state in question, and numerous Italian cities took measures to develop their militias in the first half of the sixteenth century. Machiavelli took charge of doing so in Florence. He was attacked by German mercenaries himself, and was a particularly harsh critic:

> Mercenaries and auxiliaries are useless and dangerous; and if one holds his state based on these arms, he will stand neither firm nor safe; for they are disunited, ambitious and without discipline, unfaithful, valiant before friends, cowardly before enemies; they have neither the fear of God nor fidelity to men, and destruction is deferred only so long as

the attack is; for in peace one is robbed by them, and in war by the enemy. The fact is, they have no other attraction or reason for keeping the field than a trifle of stipend, which is not sufficient to make them willing to die for you. They are ready enough to be your soldiers whilst you do not make war, but if war comes they take themselves off or run from the foe; which I should have little trouble to prove, for the ruin of Italy has been caused by nothing else than by resting all her hopes for many years on mercenaries, and although they formerly made some display and appeared valiant amongst themselves, yet when the foreigners came they showed what they were.[27]

Some of this was reasonable criticism: mercenaries did indeed switch sides, hold out for more money and avoid conflict. But some of it was unfair. Discontent with mercenaries was not sufficient reason to dispense with their services and on the battlefield they were valued, to the point that other troops borrowed their techniques.[28] Their engagements were regulated by contracts between their commander and the state he was serving: these varied widely in their detail but generally allowed for a specified period of service, the option of an extension and part payment in advance.[29] No European ruler had the resources to support a large permanent army, although they did employ some troops on an ongoing basis, regulated by military ordinances. A series of these were published through the fifteenth and early sixteenth centuries. Ferdinand and Isabella issued them in 1495, 1496 and 1503, Louis XII in 1498, and Francis I in 1515, with a further ordinance establishing infantry legions in 1534.[30]

In fact, it is often hard to distinguish in this period who are the mercenaries and who are not. Troops might switch between national and mercenary service. For example, a Spanish unit who had received their final pay-off in Italy might opt to fight for an Italian commander: this happened during the 1517 campaign in Urbino.[31] 'Italy', as we have seen, was not a single country; nor was the Holy Roman Empire (which itself incorporated parts of Italy), and it is far from clear that 'Spanish' troops had more of an allegiance to their newly united polity than to its constituent parts of Castile, Aragon, Granada or León. Nor is fighting for money a particularly helpful definition: plenty of soldiers who joined the army of their local ruler did so with the hope of booty, or at least some improvement on their current lot.

Among the most famous mercenaries of the Italian Wars was Thomas Cromwell, who fought with the French at the Battle of Garigliano shortly after the death of Pope Alexander VI in 1503. He ended up on the losing side and subsequently made his way to Florence, where he met Francesco Frescobaldi, a banker, for whom he began working. While there is no evidence that Cromwell and Machiavelli met, the timing of Cromwell's stay in Florence has long invited speculation. He subsequently spent time in the Low Countries where there were ample Italian trade connections, and returned to Italy in 1514, staying at the English Hospital in Rome which provided accommodation to visiting pilgrims (it is now the Venerable English College, a seminary). He was in Rome again in 1517–18, to secure indulgences for the Guild of Our Lady in Boston, and there he is supposed to have won over Pope Leo X with a gift of sweetmeats, quickly obtaining the paperwork he needed. He also had the opportunity, during that stay, to observe the drama surrounding the 'Cardinals' Conspiracy'. If Cromwell is an unusually prominent example of a mercenary who rose to power, his career also shows the variety of connections a man might acquire from a stint in the Italian Wars.[32] At all levels of the wars, allegiances could shift and change, and alliances be made and dropped, to suit the needs of individual and state. The League of Cambrai would last only as long as it served the interests of those involved, just as on a battlefield a soldier abandoned without pay by his captain might easily decide to switch sides.

Chapter Eleven

Women and Power

The Italian Wars had a critical impact on the lives of women at all levels of society. They left women in charge of many Renaissance states while their sons or husbands fought: Lucrezia Borgia in Ferrara, her sister-in-law Isabella d'Este in Mantua, and Alfonsina Orsini in Florence. Although women in general were formally subject to the control of their fathers or husbands, records suggest they were often far from submissive in that role; moreover, gender roles were not consistent across Italy and as we will see there is a paradox that in court societies, which we might tend to think of as less 'democratic', women could exercise greater power than they could in the republics, where they were excluded from political office.

There has been much argument over whether women had a Renaissance. In the 1970s, feminist scholar Joan Kelly used the example of the Renaissance to illustrate the problems of historical periods for women's history. Not many women, she pointed out, had in fact participated in the key aspects of this celebrated western artistic and cultural movement. For the most part, it had passed by some half of the population. (One might make a similar argument about lower-ranking men.) That critique still largely stands, but more recently scholars have pointed to a number of cases suggesting that some women did engage in 'Renaissance' activities, especially in the realm of literature, as we will see below. The typical expectation of women, however, can be summed up by the treatise of Leonardo Bruni, humanist and chancellor of Florence, praising Bice de' Medici: 'The excellence of a woman's life are reckoned to be (unless I am mistaken), good family, a good appearance, modesty, fertility, children, riches and above all virtue and a good name'.[1] In practice, however, the concept of 'riches' might encompass a significant amount of work and initiative on a woman's part. Supervision of a large household could entail administration of a substantial estate and extensive decision-making, as we saw in the case of Lucrezia Borgia. Women could be praised in similar terms to men for such virtues as liberality, prudence and household management, and even business acumen.[2]

For better-off families, marriage was a means of allying property and business interests, and parents had a strong financial motive to arrange their children's marriages. Those without property likely had more freedom of choice. Marriage patterns varied enormously depending on social class and location: elite girls might be wed very young to men a decade senior, while a girl from a farming family might work for several years first to save a dowry.[3] Affection between the partners mattered, and people did marry for love: few historians now hold to the view that romantic marriage was a later invention. Sex with one's spouse was an obligation under Catholic doctrine (and one that applied to both husband and wife). That said, as always with human behaviour, the details of any individual marriage are more complex than such overarching analysis can ever account for. On the one hand, there is ample evidence for forced marriage in Renaissance Italy. On the other, we also find clandestine marriages and sons and daughters defying parental authority to insist on their own right to consent to marriage. In theory (legal and theological), a woman's consent was required for marriage: in practice there was plenty of scope for coercion.[4] So far as dynastic marriages were concerned, companionship was not particularly a consideration. If the couple got on well, so much the better, but it is perhaps more helpful to think of them as business partners. The men involved, at least, could seek romantic or sexual liaisons elsewhere; women had to do so more cautiously.

Very few women exercised power in Italy in this period by virtue of their own independent status as rulers, although in a handful of cases women successfully contrived to hold and pass on hereditary property in the absence of male heirs. Caterina Cibo, a niece of popes Leo X (on her mother's side) and Innocent VIII (on her father's) married the duke of Camerino, a tiny state in the mountains of the Marche about forty miles from the Adriatic coast and a hundred and ten miles north of Rome. Their sole surviving child was a daughter, Giulia Varano, and after the duke's death in 1527 Caterina waged a fierce fight to protect Giulia's interest in the duchy until the girl was old enough to marry. Further north, in the lands around Parma and Piacenza, branches of the Pallavicino family spent decades in legal proceedings around the question of whether land could be passed down the female line.[5] In practice sometimes it was, but rarely without difficulty.

Women who had political power, then, gained it primarily through their relationships to men, and they held it as intercessors who could lobby husbands, sons or fathers, and in some cases stand in for them directly, ruling the aristocratic city states of Italy as regents. Two well-known early examples are Lucrezia Borgia, as duchess of Ferrara, and her sister-in-law Isabella d'Este, wife of Francesco Gonzaga, marquis of Mantua. In the ecclesiastical context, it was controversial for Lucrezia to act as her father Alexander VI's representative in the papal town of Spoleto: it was much less so for her to take a political role as duchess of Ferrara. The next papal daughter – Julius II's child Felice della Rovere Orsini – was more guarded in her public activities, though Giovio thought her 'incredibly vigilant and exceptionally diligent [...] suited to running the family and to governing towns'.[6] She did on occasion act as a diplomatic intermediary, most notably around 1509 when she helped settle a dispute between her husband's family, the Orsini, and another prominent Roman house, the Savelli; she subsequently manoeuvred to avoid the Orsini entering into a diplomatic alliance with Venice that did not suit her father's interests.[7] Like the Borgia and della Rovere popes, the Medici popes also used their positions to secure advantageous diplomatic matches for female relatives, including the marriage of Emilia Ridolfi, daughter of Contessina de' Medici Ridolfi, to the lord of Piombino in 1514; other husbands of Medici women were granted landholdings and titles.

There is no doubt that aristocratic women had considerable scope to exercise agency in the context of war. In *The Courtier* Castiglione has Giuliano de' Medici (the future duke of Nemours) point to the fact that

> if you study ancient and modern history (although men have always been very sparing in their praises of women) you will find that women as well as men have constantly given proof of their worth; and also

that there have been some women who have waged wars and won glorious victories, governed kingdoms with the greatest prudence and justice, and done all that men have done.[8]

Other participants in Castiglione's imagined conversations were not so enthusiastic, but in practice, although leading troops into battle was out of the question, almost nothing else was. When her husband Francesco was captured by the Venetians in August 1509, Isabella d'Este took over the government of Mantua for the eleven months of his imprisonment, reassuring local officials while lobbying internationally to secure his release and maintaining a tricky balance between the self-interested offers of both the emperor and the king of France to intervene. In a letter to Count Lodovico della Mirandola, she said (using the royal 'we') that she was 'beside ourself and unable to think'; none-theless, she had 'not neglected to take necessary measures either for the safety of our state or for the liberation of our lord'.[9] Managing her state in this context was far from easy, and involved a clever perform-ance of taking advice from her brother-in-law, Cardinal Sigismondo Gonzaga, to reassure courtiers and correspondents that she had good manly counsel, as well as public demonstrations of her heir Federico's good health; the whole business put a great deal of strain on her rela-tions with the imprisoned Francesco.[10] Like most powerful women in the period she was the subject of misogynist comment, including from Pietro Aretino, who described the 'monstrous marchesa of Mantua' as 'immorally ugly and even more immorally painted with make-up'.[11]

Isabella is probably the best-known example of a 'Renaissance woman'. Described by court poet Niccolò da Correggio as the *prima donna del mundo* – 'first lady of the world' – she was a daughter of the duke of Ferrara, and on her mother's side a granddaughter of the king of Naples. Her siblings made marriage alliances not only with the Borgias but also with the duke of Milan, and she in turn facilitated impressive careers for her children: her daughter Eleonora married the duke of Urbino, Francesco Maria della Rovere in a match that was politically useful but domestically brutal; more happily her youngest son Ercole became a cardinal and an important figure in Church reform. Her husband, like many princes of smaller Italian states, made his career as a *condottiere* during the wars, and during his absences Isabella was an effective regent. She was also famous as an art collector, trying for six years to convince Leonardo da Vinci to paint her portrait, though the reluctant artist never delivered more than a charcoal drawing; a portrait from Raphael also eluded her, but she commissioned both Mantegna and Perugino, as well as collecting works by Michelangelo and Titian among others. Her *studiolo* (little study) with its fine *trompe l'oeil* marquetry, gilded ceiling and ceramic floor tiles was unprecedented for a woman in this period, and offered a space where she could both display her refined artistic taste – it featured paintings on classical themes by Mantegna and Perugino – and receive select visitors.[12] In government, Isabella developed a network of correspondents across the Italian peninsula, building on Mantua's history as a diplomatic player that punched above its weight thanks to its access to superior information and willingness to share that with others.[13] Isabella also travelled. In 1515 she was at the papal court, where Leo X staged a hunt in her honour.[14] She demanded high-quality accommodation, much to the irritation of her staff, who in 1530 were to be found struggling to obtain suitable lodgings in Venice.[15] She was also in Rome twelve years later, when her palace became a refuge during the sack of 1527.

Caterina Riario Sforza, whose biographer nicknamed her the 'Renaissance Virago', is another well-known example of a prominent lady at war. A decade older than Isabella, Caterina was a bastard daughter of Galeazzo Maria Sforza, duke of Milan and Lucrezia Landriani, though she was subsequently adopted into the Sforza family and brought up with her half-siblings. While illegitimate children were not perceived to be equal to legitimate ones, this or similar processes were common: so far as aristocratic families were concerned it was often helpful to have additional children in play for marriage alliances, and there was not such stigma attached to bastardy at this stage as there would be a century later.[16] In 1477 the 14-year-old Caterina married Girolamo Riario, a nephew of the then pope, Sixtus IV, who was granted the lordship of Imola. In the conclave of 1484 that followed Sixtus' death, the heavily pregnant Caterina led an occupation of the Castel Sant'Angelo in Rome to secure her family's property. After Girolamo's assassination at the hands of a rival family in 1488, Caterina and her children were taken prisoner. Tricking her captors into allowing her to leave for negotiations with her castellan, who had secured the city's fortress on her orders, once inside the castle she is famously said to have stood atop its walls, raised her skirts and challenged the men who had killed her husband to kill her children as well: after all, she had the mould to make more. In fact, she did no more than to assert – probably falsely – that she was pregnant (because a new heir would scupper any advantage her captors might have gained from murdering her children, not to mention securing future revenge). The skirt-lifting story is in fact an invention of Machiavelli, derived from classical sources (including Plutarch), and obscures Sforza's actual diplomatic ploy.[17]

A second, secret, marriage to Giacomo Feo, brother of Caterina's castellan, ended in disaster when he was murdered by supporters of her son (who were convinced that Feo was usurping the boy's rights as ruler). Caterina orchestrated a revenge equal to anything Cesare Borgia had visited on his enemies, including the murder of one conspirator's five-year-old child.[18] A chronicle of the period reports how on another occasion she and the duchess of Ferrara laughed and took great pleasure in hearing the story of a man who had been sentenced to burning at the stake for the anal rape of a woman. So entertained were they by this tale that the man was pardoned and absolved.[19] Whether this represents the truth or not, it makes the point that contemporaries were entirely capable of believing and portraying female rulers as no less brutal than men when it came to the treatment of other women.

In the early years of the Italian Wars, with her Forlì fortress situated on a key route between the kingdom of Naples and Milan, Caterina tried to cultivate neutrality, though at times she had no practical choice but to ally with one side or the other in order to ensure the defence of her state and outmanoeuvre the Venetians.[20] It was in such roles, managing logistics, strategy and supply behind the scenes that women were most significant in the Italian Wars and indeed in Europe more widely, though typically the glory in the subsequent write-up went to the battlefield commanders. Caterina's third marriage, in 1497 to Giovanni de' Medici (a member of the family's cadet branch) lasted less than a year before the groom's illness and death, but did produce one child: at first named Ludovico, this boy became a celebrated commander of the Italian Wars and was posthumously nicknamed 'Giovanni delle Bande Nere' (Giovanni of the Black Bands).

The most celebrated events of Caterina's career came in 1499 when the army of Cesare Borgia arrived at Imola. Dispatching her children

to Florence, Caterina prepared to defend herself in the fortress at
Ravaldino. The citizens of Imola capitulated quickly; those of Forlì
wavered, and within a month Cesare's army had taken that city and
besieged Ravaldino. Caterina put up an impressive defence from inside
her fortress – Sanudo praised her 'generous and virile soul' – but was
betrayed by her own side.[21] She was subsequently imprisoned at Rome,
first in the Belvedere then – after an escape attempt – in the Castel
Sant'Angelo which she herself had once commanded. Accused of
trying to poison Pope Alexander VI (an allegation that may be true),
she was put on trial but later released into the custody of the French
army. Nonetheless, Caterina – with the support of her Sforza uncle
Ludovico il Moro – successfully regained possession of her territories
and ruled as regent for her son Ottaviano for thirteen years: in 1503
she wrote to him that he should 'take care with the persons you trust
and who advise you; you must realise that pernicious influences are
everywhere'.[22] She negotiated directly with Machiavelli over Ottaviano's possible entry to Florentine military service.[23] After the fall of
the Borgias she secured Julius II's support for the return of her lost
territories, but was thwarted by local opposition and spent the last
years of her life in Florence, where she died in 1509.

Local opposition – indeed hostility – to women in power was a
problem elsewhere, too, not least in the republics where, in contrast
to the principalities, the role of women was more circumscribed. It
is ironic that the political system with a broader electoral base,
generally perceived as historically progressive in the long term, was
also less inclusive to women. One reason is that when a leading figure
in a republic had to be absent to lead troops, or attend a summit, or
simply visit surrounding towns, there were other elected men who
could stand in his place. Women in these contexts relied instead for
influence on informal networks of power and patronage (which, of
course, were also important to women in the principalities). These
were, however, considerable. In the early fifteenth century, the Medici
had primarily used marriage to consolidate political ties within their
home city, but during their long transition from leading oligarchs to
hereditary rulers of Florence, they adopted a more aristocratic marriage strategy to extend their network across the Italian peninsula and
beyond. Lorenzo 'the Magnificent' married a Roman heiress, Clarice
Orsini; he married his daughter Maddalena into the Cibo family of

Pope Innocent VIII; his eldest son Piero to Alfonsina Orsini, of that family's Neapolitan branch; and a younger son, Giuliano, to a daughter of the duke of Savoy. Another daughter, Lucrezia, married into the Florentine Salviati family but had an important role in managing the household of her son Giovanni, a cardinal. Like Lucrezia Borgia and Isabella d'Este, these women acted as diplomatic links between their birth families and those into which they married. The match between Alfonsina Orsini and Piero de' Medici, for example, was part of Lorenzo's efforts to make peace with Naples after the Pazzi Conspiracy; that of Maddalena and Francesco Cibo helped settle affairs between Florence and the pope. Even the Salviati match helped soothe relations with a family on the other side of the Pazzi affair.

So long as the Medici tried to maintain the rhetoric of republican rule in Florence, too prominent a role for women was problematic, but they could nonetheless act as effective intercessors for clients of their male relatives. The patron–client system was a fundamental element of political and social life: the support of higher-ranking patrons helped those seeking political office, or artistic commissions, or contracts for all sorts of goods and services. The idea of intercession had religious connotations and was linked to the figure of the Virgin Mary, who was believed to be able to intercede with her son Jesus Christ on behalf of penitents. Women of the Medici family received all sorts of requests for intercession on matters ranging from prisoner release to appointments to cathedral chaplaincies to improperly impounded sheep.[24] They also received many petitions from poor women and widows for support,[25] and their charitable activities included the provision of dowries for poor or orphaned girls and the patronage of convents and hospitals. This was not without political benefits: an image of charity and piety was a counterweight to the more negative perceptions that might attach to the Medici's activities as bankers.

Alfonsina Orsini's activities as a patron in the 1510s, however, proved contentious. She had been brought up at the Neapolitan court and – unlike previous Medici brides – had had the opportunity to absorb the norms of an environment which offered relatively more scope to noble women. The mother of Lorenzo, duke of Urbino from 1516 to 1519, she was responsible alongside her son for the completion of the family's villa at Poggio a Caiano, west of Florence, overseeing the work of the architect and taking reports from her son's secretary. During the papacy of Leo X she also had a palace built in Rome. Now known as the Palazzo Medici Lante della Rovere, it stands between Piazza Navona and the Pantheon. In the papal capital, where her Roman Orsini relatives already had two major residences, such a project was possible, even desirable. In Florence, on the other hand, Alfonsina rubbed up contemporaries the wrong way. After the expulsion of her husband Piero de' Medici in 1494, and the exile of the Medici from Florence, it was Alfonsina and her mother Caterina di Sanseverino who successfully lobbied the French to allow Alfonsina to remain in Florence with her children. But she clashed with the republican regime, and hostility to her foreignness and her gender became commonplace in anti-Medicean propaganda, which labelled her involvement in politics unnatural for a woman. Even supporters of the Medici were careful to attribute her interventions to a wife and mother's natural concern for the interests of her husband and children. (This assumption of women's weakness allowed another Medici relative, Lucrezia Salviati to escape the death penalty: her involvement in a pro-Medici conspiracy was written off on account of her sex; as a woman she could scarcely have been exercising independent judgement and must have been led by men. A later history of the same events, however, disagreed, describing her 'prudence' in the affair, a quality typically associated in this period with men.[26])

In the end, it was a marriage alliance that paved the way for the return of the Medici to power: the contentious match of Alfonsina's daughter Clarice with Filippo Strozzi, member of a historically hostile family. The republican regime exiled Strozzi, but Clarice, who as a woman was not affected by the ban, returned to Florence and took a significant role in lobbying for Medici interests. Unimpressed, the regime attempted to confiscate Alfonsina's dowry (an unprecedented step: dowries were normally exempt from the sequestration of exiles' property). But after determined legal action she prevailed against them. In short, the Medici women made the most of their second-class status as women to avoid the sentences of exile or worse that were passed against their male relatives.

After the Medici returned to power in 1512, there were increased opportunities for the women of the family to engage in the sort of patronage that was typical of the ladies of the Italian courts. In the summer of 1515, when her son Lorenzo, duke of Urbino was away at war, Alfonsina acted as de facto regent, an indication of the extent to which the Medici were now behaving as lords of Florence. She issued orders to the city committees dealing with taxation and homeland security, and managed correspondence between her son and the foreign affairs committee on the progress of the military campaign. In a papal brief that autumn, Leo X wrote that 'we have known your prudence and capacity by which the Most High has adorned you above the common condition of your sex'.[27] Others were not so generous. Paolo Giovio, whose assessments of the Medici were generally more friendly, acknowledged her 'manly prudence' but observed that she was 'avaricious and always quarrelling' and over-acquisitive on behalf of her son.[28] Avarice was a vice particularly ascribed in this period to women.

The impact of war on women was not only apparent at the high level of the aristocracy. Guglielmina Schianteschi was the wife of Luigi della Stufa, a supporter of Medici rule in Florence who had been exiled after their son was involved in a plot to assassinate Piero Soderini, *gonfaloniere* of the city. A 1512 letter from Guglielmina gives a sense of their troubles. With Luigi forced to live away, she looked after the family estates. She sold grain, managed debts, lectured her husband on the need to live frugally and budget for fines. 'We will need God to help us all He can,' she wrote. 'Check to see if the supplies, the ten sides of dried meat and other foodstuffs, are on their way.' She feared they had been seized by smugglers. She tried her best to offer suitable hospitality to visiting dignitaries, and advised her husband on childcare. She was worried that the deprivation of wartime might affect their sons' behaviour: 'those who have been in want tend to think more of enjoying themselves than those who have not known hardship'. She was something of a stoic: 'I am never in a good state of mind or body, though I do not want to cry out about this too.' Her letter gives a sense of the psychological burden that wartime and exile placed on individuals.[29] Women at all levels of society had to deal with the absence of their husbands at war, whether they were running a farm, an estate, a business, or simply trying to make ends meet in the absence of a journeyman's income. Some of them no doubt enjoyed the increased independence; for others, however, running household amid wartime shortages and the constant threat of looting was a miserable life.

Chapter Twelve

The Ghetto and the Politics
of Venice

If for some people the wars provided new opportunities for the exercise of power, for others they led to flight and exile. In the aftermath of defeat in the war of 1509, Venice had lost all its mainland territory and numerous refugees sought security in the offshore archipelago of the city itself. Among them were Jews, who benefited from the lifting of a rule that had previously prevented them from long-term residence in Venice. But the legal change was controversial, and once the conflict eased Christian preachers began to call once again for restrictions, suggesting, for example, in 1515, that Jews be required to live on the island of Giudecca. Some advocated outright expulsion.[1]

Jews had been allowed to live in Venice from the late fourteenth century when restrictions on moneylending had been relaxed, and Jewish moneylenders – typically small-scale and more analogous to modern pawnbrokers than to commercial banks – provided modest consumer loans. Christians were prohibited from lending money at interest, which did not stop the establishment of large commercial banks (the hope of profit outweighing potential concerns about salvation). The Christian banks, however, did not provide a general consumer service – for example, to farmers who needed to buy seed in advance of seeing money for their harvest. Beyond that, Jews were excluded from most professions, and as a consequence many found themselves reliant on work in the trade of second-hand goods. They were, moreover, excluded from guilds and from Christian confraternities where social and professional networking took place.

The law also limited Jews to visiting the city rather than living there: stays of more than fifteen days at a time were prohibited (though in practice there were workarounds). Thus the decision in 1516 to establish a specific area in which the Jews of Venice could live – the ghetto – was a compromise between the post-1509 situation of freedom to live anywhere in the city and the pre-1509 situation where Jews were not permitted permanent residence in Venice at all. The Jewish community was able to negotiate a few improvements to the conditions initially proposed, such as extended opening hours of the ghetto gates and permission for Jewish doctors to leave out of hours when required by their patients. On the one hand, therefore, the ghetto allowed Jews to live permanently in the city, though with the exception of a few privileged individuals, they were required to wear identifying yellow hats or badges; on the other hand, once the gates were locked at night the ghetto was an effective prison.[2*]

Expulsions and flight had been a fact of life for Jews on the Italian peninsula for centuries. The one exception was Sicily, which had had a Jewish presence for over a thousand years. In the fourteenth and fifteenth centuries there were perhaps thirty to thirty-five thousand Jews in Sicily, more than on the whole of the rest of the peninsula, where they numbered around twenty-five to thirty thousand out of a total of eight to ten million people. Expulsions and persecutions elsewhere in Europe periodically swelled their numbers: Germans came in the wake of persecutions following the Black Death; French Jews came after the expulsion of 1394. Jews were expelled from a number of Italian cities in the second half of the fifteenth century, including several around Venice: Treviso, Vicenza, Feltre, Cividale del Friuli and Udine. At least some of the Jews who were expelled from Spain in 1492 came to Italy, although the precise numbers are difficult to calculate. Some went to Portugal (where they were initially welcomed) and only later, after the establishment of the Portuguese Inquisition in 1536, did they in turn seek refuge elsewhere. As far as we can tell, the majority of Spanish Jews opted for conversion rather than exile, and there does not seem to have been a particularly large influx of refugees to Italy after 1492.[3]

They arrived, however, to face an increasingly hostile climate. In the 1460s, Italian artist Paolo Uccello, who worked at courts across

---

* The etymology of the word ghetto is disputed. It is sometimes associated with iron-working and the presence of a foundry in a particular area of the city, but other scholars have attributed it to words meaning 'narrow streets'.

the peninsula, painted a series of antisemitic frescoes for the Corpus Domini monastery in Urbino, showing a Jewish merchant desecrating the Christian Host (that is, the bread that in Christian tradition symbolises or indeed literally is the body of Christ). In 1475 the entire Jewish community in the northern city of Trento (Trent) was arrested, and the men put to death, after an accusation of ritual murder: in this and subsequent atrocities the accusers made use of the new technology of printing. Such 'blood libel' accusations were at the heart of the older religious form of antisemitism, central to which were ideas that Jews were agents of the Devil and the killers of Christ (no matter that the Roman authorities had in fact carried out that death sentence). Increasingly, however, Jewishness came to be regarded as innate and therefore able to be inherited, and 'purity of blood' laws spread in Spain.[4] Besides printing, preachers too could whip up hostility: a 1488 sermon by Bernardino da Feltre, a Franciscan, prompted riots in Florence, which had to be put down by the civic authorities; amid concerns for social order Bernardino was expelled from the city.[5] In 1496 the Jews were expelled from the city of Pavia, in the duchy of Milan.[6] In Venice on Good Friday 1509 a preacher declared that 'it was lawful to strip the Jews of all their money and not permit them to live'. For all that the Venetian ghetto was a compromise, the terms of a 1519 debate about Jewish rights among members of the Venetian Council shows how much hostility remained. Jews were 'tak[ing] the bread out of the mouths of Christian secondhand dealers' and engaging in 'tricks' when loaning money. Nonetheless, Council members were prepared to defend them on the basis that Jewish moneylending was necessary to the city. A very similar line of argument was used in relation to prostitution.[7]

Different Italian cities had different approaches to Jewish immigrants. Genoa and Milan largely refused them entry; Florence and Venice eventually allowed them in, though it was hardly a wholehearted welcome.[8] There was persecution under Pope Alexander VI in Rome, primarily (according to a Florentine observer) as a means of extorting money, though perhaps also (on a Venetian account) to win friends in Spain.[9] Jewish migrants had good reason to favour particular locations: for example, those that were well defended (Jews were particularly at risk in wartime because of having cash on hand), with a preference for lordships over republics (because it was easier to win a single prince's favour than a wider vote).[10] Still, there was much debate in Italy about how to resolve the 'problem' of the need for Jewish moneylending, given the interdict on Christian usury. A partial solution was developed by the *Monti di Pietà* (literally, Mounts of Piety), essentially state-run pawnbrokers that provided small consumer loans.* The Lateran Council had been largely favourable to the development of *Monti* and a Rome *Monte* was founded in 1526.[11] There were still, however, limits on the activities of these institutions: their loans could not be used for commercial purposes, nor could depositors be paid interest. In general, however, the role of Jews in moneylending made them vulnerable to accusations of financial exploitation of poor Christians.

A modest number of Jewish intellectuals made successful careers in Italy. Giuda Abarbanel, known as Leone Ebreo (meaning 'Leo the Jew'), was born in Lisbon between 1460 and 1465. His father was a royal treasurer (at a time when such offices might still be held by Jews); when he fell from power, accused of involvement in a conspiracy against the king, Leone followed him into exile in Seville, where he became a physician. In the expulsion of 1492 Leone refused to have his son baptised: the pair were separated and the child subjected to forced baptism, while Leone fled to Naples. There he continued to practise medicine (prominent clients included a Spanish viceroy and Cardinal Raffaele Riario) and took an increasing interest in philosophy. Following the French invasion of 1495 he moved again, to Genoa, where he began his best-known work, the *Dialoghi d'Amore* (Dialogues of Love), which explored the relationships of God, the universe and human beings via the concept of cosmic love. Although some editions of the *Dialoghi* claimed that Leone had converted to Christianity and the author drew on both Christian and pagan philosophers (avoiding, moreover, direct criticism of Christian doctrine), the work was notable for its engagement with Jewish tradition. That said, in Christian intellectual circles it was primarily received as a contribution to courtly literature, allowing readers to overlook that origin in favour of its Platonic and Aristotelian elements; it went through multiple editions and translations and quotations from it may be found in Cervantes' *Don Quixote*.[12]

---

* The Monte dei Paschi di Siena, which traces its roots to 1472, survives as a bank to this day.

Venice was a leading centre for the printing of Hebrew books,[13] and for collaboration between scholars of Hebrew literature and Christian thinkers, not least on account of the interest of Christian humanists in Bible translation. It is no accident that when Henry VIII started to seek opinion on the interpretation of the Old Testament in relation to his divorce, he sent his agents to Venice; they lobbied the Venetian authorities to exempt the Jewish scholar Jacob Mantino from wearing the yellow hat in the hope of his assistance. Such collaboration may have been in the mind of Venetian diplomat (and later cardinal) Gasparo Contarini, when in 1525 he described the Spanish Inquisition as tyrannical in its treatment of converted Jews. His brother Andrea had been arrested in Spain for attempting to import books of scripture annotated by a rabbi, which were banned in Castile.[14] So was Venice 'tolerant'? Certainly the Venetians disliked foreign interference in their affairs, whether Spanish or papal. More prosaically, however, the city valued commerce, whether in the printing business or elsewhere. Ironically, the expulsion of the Jews from Spain had led to a diaspora of families through the Mediterranean port cities, and Venice could benefit from their personal networks in trade.[15]

Like the other maritime cities of Genoa and Pisa, Venice had a long history of trading connections with the Levant. Indeed, it had closer relations with the medieval Byzantine Empire than it had with Rome, and thanks to its role as the departure point for medieval pilgrims (not to mention crusaders) travelling to Jerusalem, it drew travellers from Northern Europe as well as traders from the East.[16] The variety of cultural influences on Venice are apparent in its architecture, which any visitor will quickly note looks decidedly different from much of mainland northern Italy, whether in the curving domes of St Mark's Basilica, the lace-like pink and white of the Palazzo Ducale, or the Byzantine-style church mosaics. During the Fourth Crusade (1202–4) and subsequent Latin Kingdom of Constantinople (1204–1261), many Italian merchants set up shop in Levant ports. They subsequently dealt with the Muslim rulers of the Eastern Mediterranean to maintain these trading relationships, which were considered advantageous on both sides, and expanded their interests to the Mamluk Sultanate of Egypt.[17] Traders might travel overland to Constantinople or via Cyprus to Syria, there to pick up the Silk Roads to China. Another route went to Alexandria in Egypt for goods from the Indian Ocean (originating in Indonesia, Sri Lanka or India). Venice had colonies on the island of Crete and in Acre (a port city now in Israel, near the modern border with Lebanon). Goods traded included wine, oil, fruits, nuts, wheat, beans, sugar; silk, salt, fish, furs, woollen fabrics, metals, red dye, wax, honey, cotton; spices, lapis lazuli and horses. These commercial links had extensive influence on food and clothing in Venice. It is hardly surprising that the Portuguese sought alternative routes to the Eastern markets, nor that they established their Madeira sugar plantations to compete with those of Venice on Crete and Cyprus (and by 1500 were dramatically out-producing their older rival).[18] Like Genoa, Venice also had extensive involvement in the slave trade: it was here that Isabella d'Este's agent came to buy an enslaved African girl.[19] Unlike Genoa, however, Venice's maritime enterprises had a significant degree of state sponsorship. Ships were built in the official Arsenale and merchant galleys sailed in armed convoys. Shipbuilding, along with glassmaking and the supply of timber, became one of Venice's major industries.

To facilitate this trade, Venice had acquired a series of Mediterranean colonies, beginning with Crete, known as Candia (which it held from 1204 to 1669); then Corfu (1396–1797); and Cyprus (1489–1571), where a Venetian noblewoman, Caterina Cornaro had ruled as queen from 1474 to 1489 following the deaths of her husband and infant son, before being forced out in favour of rule by a Venetian governor. Venice had further holdings along the Dalmatian coast (now Croatia) as well as a number of other entrepôts and territories, in which many Venetians made careers.[20] In the context of these Mediterranean geopolitics, the idea of facilitating trade by setting up island colonies – as the Spanish were now doing in the New World – seems entirely unexceptional. They also offered a range of different models for imperial and colonial projects around the early modern world, especially on the fringes of other larger empires, from an entrepôt in which merchants were permitted to operate with licence from the sovereign (often with a posted Venetian official such as the *bailo* of Constantinople), to outright annexation.

Venice had finely balanced relations with the Ottoman Empire, on the one hand keen to ensure maintenance of trade, on the other to secure its own colonies against any potential incursions. Of all the Italian states it had the most developed diplomatic exchanges with the

Ottomans, receiving as well as sending ambassadors.[21] Indeed in 1479, it had sent one of its leading artists, Gentile Bellini, to the Ottoman court as a sign of diplomatic favour.[22] Its engagement with Constantinople gives the lie to any suggestion that relations between Christian and Muslim powers in this period were invariably characterised by war.[23] There were, however, significant conflicts, for example, the war of 1499–1502, during which Venice lost several outposts to the Ottomans under Bayezid II, including Modon, Koron and Navarino (all strategically located around the south-western tip of the Peloponnese), plus the colony of Lepanto further to the north. A peace treaty, however, was quickly agreed: Venice was an important trading partner, relying moreover on wheat imports from Ottoman lands, and ongoing conflict was in no one's economic interest.[24]

In light of these losses, it was no surprise that the conquest of its mainland territories in 1509 came as a severe blow to Venice and the very same year saw another defeat, this time at sea. Under Leonardo Loredan, doge from 1501 to 1521, Venice had encouraged the Mamluk rulers of Egypt to challenge the growing influence of the Portuguese in the Indian Ocean.[25] The Mamluks and their allies, however, were defeated in 1509 by the Portuguese at the Battle of Diu off the coast of Gujarat, and except (as we have seen) for recouping some of its losses, Venice then largely withdrew from the land wars in Italy. Within a decade of the Battle of Diu the power balance shifted again when the Ottoman Empire turned on Venice's Mamluk allies.

With its capital in Cairo, the Mamluk Sultanate had existed since 1250 and stretched down both sides of the Red Sea, including among its territories the city of Mecca. It took its name from the word for a category of person in that society: a *mamluk* was a former slave who had been trained in martial arts and who still owed loyalty to his master. Many *mamluks* served in roles at court and in the military, but after a long struggle in the middle of the thirteenth century they succeeded in wielding power directly with the formation of a sultanate by one of their own: Aybak, the founder of the Bahri dynasty. In the later fourteenth century the Bahri regime declined and was replaced by another Mamluk dynasty, the Burji. Mamluk Egypt supplied products including cotton and sugar to Europe via Venice and Genoa, while the port city of Alexandria offered a useful trading post for goods arriving from further east, such as spices and indigo.

The protection of these trade links was important to Venice, so much so that city merchants were prepared to break the ban on selling firearms to non-Christians, supplying guns both to the Mamluks and to the Aqquyunlu (rulers until 1501 of what is now eastern Turkey, Armenia, Azerbaijan and parts of Iraq and Iran).[26] A picture by a follower of Bellini and now in the Louvre depicting Venetian ambassadors attending the Mamluk viceroy in Damascus, probably painted c.1513–16 and showing events from 1510–12, is visual testimony to these connections, but it also shows the trickier elements of such diplomacy. In 1510 the Mamluks had arrested a Cypriot agent who was passing messages between the Shah of Persia and the Venetian consuls in Alexandria and Damascus, and demanded the consuls come to Cairo to explain themselves. (The consul in Damascus, Pietro Zen, was the Shah's second cousin: marriage alliances could extend family links beyond the Christian powers.) In reprisal for this treasonous correspondence – as the Mamluks saw it – they confiscated the goods of the Venetian merchants in Damascus and had their owners locked up. It took a special embassy to obtain their release, and that of the two hapless consuls.[27]

There was further rivalry between the Mamluk and Ottoman Empires, for control of both trade routes and the holy sites of Islam, which had led to war between 1485 and 1491. That had ended in stalemate, but by 1514 the Ottomans had gained in strength thanks to their victory in the east over the Safavid Persians at the Battle of Chaldiran,[28] which freed up troops to complete their conquest of the Mamluks in the west. Traditionally the Ottoman victory over the Mamluks was credited to their better use of firearms, while the Mamluk army stuck to cavalry archers. In this version of events, pressure from traditionalists in the Mamluk Empire (who placed a greater premium on individual combat) had forced the abandonment of experiments with musketeers. However, that view has now been re-evaluated, with evidence suggesting that in fact the Mamluks were beginning to employ both cannon and handguns in the war of 1485– 91, but that they were limited by the fact that their elite units were cavalry (and the handguns of that period were not yet adapted for use on horseback) and that they struggled with access to iron. In other words, as in Italy these were material and technological, rather than cultural issues.[29] The Ottomans had no such difficulties, however: they had adopted firearms and in 1516 they took first the city of Diyarbekir in south-eastern Anatolia (in the battle of Marj Dabiq, 24 August) and then moved south, seizing territory near Gaza in the battle of Yaunis Khan (28 October). Not constrained by European fighting seasons that usually dictated a winter break, the Mamluks attempted to recover, but to no avail, and on 22 January 1517 the forces of the Ottoman Emperor Selim I defeated those of Al-Ashraf Tuman bay II at the Battle of Ridanieh. A sack of Cairo ensued along with many atrocities, the upshot of which was the submission of Cairo and the subsequent capture of Mecca and Medina, which placed the two holy cities of Islam under Ottoman control.

The conquest changed the dynamics of the Eastern Mediterranean. Without a counterweight to impede it, the Ottoman Empire could now focus attention on expansion elsewhere: east towards the Safavid Empire in modern-day Iran and west through Greece and the Balkans into central Europe and along the coast of North Africa. Quite apart from any implications for trade, these victories mattered in Italy because a military contest on the Holy Roman Empire's eastern border would draw imperial resources away from the Italian Wars. On the other hand, an attack from the Safavid dynasty of Iran could draw Ottoman resources away from Europe; that in turn could free up imperial forces. (The same was also true in the North, of course. An English incursion into Continental Europe could likewise draw troops and finance away from Italian conflicts: if England invaded on the side of the Holy Roman Empire, that was trouble for the French, for example.) This Ottoman victory against the Mamluks was, moreover, a headache for Pope Leo X, who besides his family troubles now had to consider how the Christian princes might address it. In 1518 he sponsored a peace initiative, aiming to unify the European powers against the Eastern threat. He dispatched cardinal-legates across Europe to arrange a truce – and there was, for a little while, peace, with the Treaty of London piloted by Cardinal Thomas Wolsey. In the event, however, it proved easier to convince the princes of Europe to discuss a crusade than to persuade them to finance one, and no joint initiative against the Ottomans came to pass.[30]

★

The years immediately following saw the rise of the two princes whose conflict would define Mediterranean warfare in the coming decades, just as Francis I's accession as king of France had prompted new adventures in northern Italy. In 1519, Charles I of Spain was elected Holy Roman Emperor, becoming Charles V. The emperor was chosen by a group of princes (hence some German nobles enjoyed titles like the 'Elector Palatine'), and Francis had also been a candidate in the election (with the backing of Leo X), but Charles prevailed. His rule now extended from southern Spain north to the Netherlands and his influence (thanks to his sister's marriage to the king of Hungary) even further east to the borderlands with the Ottoman Empire. The following year, on the death of Sultan Selim I, 25-year-old Süleyman became Ottoman Emperor. The power shifts of the Mediterranean may be summed up by the fact that during the fifteenth century Lorenzo de' Medici, the Renaissance patron, was graced with the soubriquet 'Magnificent', whereas in the sixteenth that title fell to the Emperor Süleyman. Ruling until 1566, he outlived all his princely rivals.

On his accession to the throne, Süleyman began a project of military expansion through the Balkans, conquering Belgrade from the Hungarians in 1521. The following year, he launched a combined land and sea attack on the island of Rhodes. This was home to the Knights of St John or Knights Hospitaller, a religious order that had traditionally provided hospitality and medical care to Christian pilgrims bound for Jerusalem, not to mention crusaders, although (as Guicciardini observed) 'they were somewhat notorious for the fact that, spending all their days in piracy against the ships of the infidels, they also at times pillaged Christian vessels'.[31] Rhodes was thus an important symbolic target for the Ottomans as well as being strategically significant. Located just off the Anatolian coast, to the Christian powers it offered a potential base for attacks on Ottoman territory, while for the Ottomans its fortress promised useful protection for their Egyptian treasure fleets. The combined forces of Süleyman's 100,000-strong besieging army and 400-ship navy successfully intimidated the Grand Master of Rhodes, Philippe de l'Isle-Adam, into surrendering the island when the sultan made the offer of an honourable departure, and the Knights spent the next seven years in exile.[32]

By 1526 Süleyman's troops had reached Hungary (as we will see below) and the Ottomans were apparently on their way to becoming a central European power. The importance of the Ottomans in European military affairs points to a significant difference in the ways that the Continent's Jews and Muslims were understood by its Christians. While both were members of religious minorities, Muslims had military clout (not only in the Ottoman Empire but also beyond, in India, where the Mughal Empire was founded in the very same year with Babur's conquest of the Delhi Sultanate). Thus while Jews were perceived through a prism of religious hostility (and increasingly through a racialised concept of inferior blood), Muslims were regarded as potential fifth columnists, who might aid the Ottoman foe. Yet fear of and opposition to the Ottoman Turks in Western Christendom did not exist solely on account of their faith: they were demonised in other ways too.

Italian attitudes towards Muslims in general and the Ottoman Empire in particular shifted from the fifteenth to the sixteenth century. Early on, humanist scholars took an interest both in the rise of Islam, and the rise of the empire under its founder Osman (d. 1323/4), emphasising the illegitimacy of Osman's rule. In fact, what most of these writers were worrying about was the failure of their own institutions, not least to protect Constantinople and to continue the crusades, which despite the rhetoric of successive popes were quite clearly no longer a political reality (if indeed they had ever been what they claimed).[33] Increased Italian contact with the Ottoman Empire in the sixteenth century, however, allowed for the production of more accurate accounts of Ottoman politics, institutions and warfare for circulation in the West. There was, unsurprisingly, a demand for quality information that would provide guidance to policy makers, while there was also a market for the more salacious accounts of murderous dynastic intriguing that the Ottoman court produced quite as regularly as its European rivals. These were typically glossed as tales of an exotic other, although the facts are no more outrageous than those of the Borgias, nor of Henry VIII's six wives (though it is no coincidence that both Henry and the Borgias were compared to Turks). For Italians, Ottomans on the one hand might represent the Antichrist and the antithesis of European civilisation, and on the other might provide an impressive example of a well-organised military state, the envy of the oft-divided Christians. Giovio observed that 'especially now in every stratagem and martial endeavour they are always enjoying the marvellous support of the gods and good fortune'.[34] The writer and diplomat Baldassare Castiglione had one character in his 1528 *Book of the Courtier* praise the noblemen of the Ottoman and Persian courts as 'valiant and mannerly', displaying 'in their feats of arms, games and festivals much magnificence, great liberality and elegance'.[35] Machiavelli did not have a great deal to say about the Ottoman Empire, although in *The Prince* he was impressed by the Ottoman decision to colonise Greece, citing it as an example to those princes who sought to hold conquered territories.[36]

That said, Islam posed a significant threat to Christianity's claim to be a universal religion. And for those Christians living around the Mediterranean conversion to Islam was not a choice to be ruled out: research on the Bosnian nobility and the Venetian colonies suggests religious faith was not nearly as unwavering as stereotypes of this historical period would have it. While there was no requirement to convert within the Ottoman Empire (as there was in Spain), it has been estimated that three hundred thousand Christians converted to Islam around the Mediterranean between 1500 and 1600, generally to improve their social or economic situation, and especially (in the case of slaves) because it might lead to manumission or better chances of escape.[37]

Conversion, of course, might go both ways. One of the best-known Muslim travellers to Europe in these years was the man known as Leo Africanus (his birth name was al-Hasan al-Wazzan). Born in Granada, he likely left after the Spanish conquest of 1492 and ended up in Fez (in present-day Morocco). His uncle was a diplomat; the family owned vineyards in the Rif Mountains to the north of Fez and rented a castle outside the city; al-Hasan was accustomed to travelling from his youth and went to Safi on the Atlantic coast of Africa as well as to trading centres such as Timbuktu on the southern edge of the Sahara Desert. In 1518 he was returning to Fez from Cairo when his ship was attacked by Spanish pirates. Evidently keen to impress the pope with their attacks on Muslim vessels, the Spanish presented him as their captive to Leo X, and he was duly imprisoned in the Castel Sant'Angelo.[38]

His family background in diplomacy may have helped ensure his good treatment: he was allowed to borrow Arabic manuscripts from the papal library and it seems that key members of the papal curia quickly saw that his conversion to Christianity might be a propaganda coup (not least in light of the ongoing challenge from Luther). After a period of catechism by senior officials, he was baptised by the pope on 6 January 1520 in a ceremony at St Peter's.[39] Recording the event, the papal master of ceremonies praised his learning.[40] As with many converts of the period, whether al-Hasan/Leo was a sincere Christian or a dissimulator or somewhere in between remains a mystery, but in any case the conversion was hardly a free choice. According to the doctrine of *taqiyya*, Muslims under pressure to convert were permitted to do so and to perform their new religion in public while exercising mental reservation.[41] His writing, however, is sufficiently ambiguous that we will probably never know.[42] Leo Africanus went on to produce translations of Arabic texts for patrons including Alberto Pio da Carpi, a diplomat in imperial service; from the point of view of Christian thinkers it was always useful to know the enemy. He collaborated with Jacob Mantino (the Jewish scholar later consulted over Henry VIII's divorce) and assisted with corrections on a translation of the Koran into Latin.[43] It was his *Book of the Cosmography and Geography of Africa*, however, completed in 1526, that made his name, although it was not published until 1550.[44] For European readers this book provided an understanding of Africa that substantially added to what they could glean from the ancient works of Strabo or Pliny the Elder.

Africa, Leo wrote, was 'one of the three general parts of the world known unto our ancestors'; they had, however, not thoroughly discovered it, thanks to 'huge deserts full of dangerous sands' and the 'long and perilous navigation upon the African coasts'.[45] He described the continent's woods, mountains, deserts, its mighty lakes and rivers which 'with their yearly inundations they do most wonderfully fatten and enrich the soil'.[46] He divided the inhabitants of Africa into five nations, some of whom were idol-worshippers while others fell into the more familiar categories for his readers of Muslims, Christians and Jews. He included detail of diets, of trade, of the customs of inhabitants, as well as observations on the Portuguese merchants who had set up their trading post on the west coast. In notes to the first English edition, Richard Hakluyt, secretary of state to Elizabeth I and James I and a leading promoter of colonisation projects, described it as 'the very best, the most particular and methodical [history] that ever was written, or at least that hath come to light, concerning the countries, peoples and affairs of Africa'.[47]

In short, within a generation of Columbus' first voyage, there was a substantial expansion of European knowledge of – and engagement with – lands not only to the west, but to the east and south as well. Venetian ties to the Ottoman Empire, however, aroused suspicion, not least as the rulers of Christian Europe competed to demonstrate their religious orthodoxy.

Chapter Thirteen

The Battle for the Church

While Pope Leo X may have been able to boast of his Muslim convert, he had trouble on other fronts, not least from the university town of Wittenberg, in southern Germany. The catalyst for the events of 1517 was something that was, in fact, quite routine in the Catholic Church of the time. Albrecht of Brandenburg had borrowed heavily to finance the cost of his promotion to the archbishopric of Mainz, which not incidentally made him a prince-elector of the Holy Roman Empire. This cost took the form of 'annates', a payment equivalent to the first year's revenues from any benefice, which had to be paid to Rome by new appointees to church offices. A younger son of a noble family, Albrecht had accumulated a number of other rich benefices already, being exempted by the pope from rules that should have prevented him from doing so. As archbishop, he had been responsible for the publication in his territories of a papal bull granting indulgences to those who donated to the project to renovate St Peter's. But suspicions were aroused that the archbishop was taking the money for himself. Moreover, he had delegated the right to sell indulgences to a preacher called Johann Tetzel, whose rousing efforts to convince the population of southern Germany to stump up cash prompted Martin Luther's anger, and led, in October 1517, to the first step in what would spiral into a crisis for the papacy: the publication of his 'Ninety-Five Theses or Disputation on the Power of Indulgences'. Guicciardini later acknowledged that while Luther quickly became 'too immoderate in his opposition to the popes' the initial cause was just: Leo X, 'easygoing by nature', had been rather relaxed about issuing the right to sell indulgences (including to his sister Maddalena), and 'it was known all over Germany' that the money was 'destined to satisfy a woman's greed' rather than be properly directed to the papal treasury.[1]

Luther's ideas were not all new, and might never have had the grip they gained was it not for, on the one side, Luther's personal grasp of the new technology of printing and its potential for propagand- ising and, on the other, the political failures of the Church leaders. In the first three decades after 1517, 3.1 million copies of Luther's works were printed. At first, the papal court thought Luther simply another heretic. They were accustomed to heretics: twenty years before they had dealt quite effectively with Girolamo Savonarola, and Pope Leo X's response to Luther was measured. A series of theolo- gians examined Luther's writings, on paper and then in person. Given the importance of indulgences to Church finances, Leo could not afford to compromise too far, and Luther faced a series of investiga- tions with increasingly higher stakes. The first came from members of his own order, the Augustinian Hermits. This was in April 1518, and came down very much in Luther's favour.[2] Six months later he made the journey south-east to Augsburg, where delegates had assembled for a meeting of the Imperial Diet (the highest represen- tative assembly of the Holy Roman Empire). There he encountered Tommaso de Vio, Cardinal Cajetan, a papal legate originally from the kingdom of Naples who had been dispatched to the emperor in the effort to sue for peace among the Christians after the Ottoman defeat of the Mamluks. Cajetan interrogated Luther over the course of three days. A member of the Dominicans – the same order as Tetzel, whose indulgence sales Luther had so criticised – he was a hostile questioner and, moreover, a backer of papal primacy. He asked that Luther be handed over to face trial for heresy in Rome, but he did not arrest him, creating a loophole that enabled Luther to leave Augsburg under the protection of Frederick the Wise, the elector of Saxony.[3] Frederick's attitude towards Luther remains mys- terious (he seems to have been a devout Catholic) but he was an imperial elector, which gave him a vote on who would succeed the Emperor Maximilian, and the emperor was unwell. An imperial election could not be far away, and so Frederick was a man to be charmed and cajoled by the potential successors and their backers, not challenged on his curious decisions. Diplomatic efforts to resolve the Luther situation took place instead in early 1519 but they proved fruitless. By this time Luther's work was already being translated into Italian.[4]

It was July 1519 when the next round of hearings took place. Now, however, the political situation had changed on two fronts. First, Leo was facing a renewed family crisis. Despite the pope's efforts to see off opposition in Rome, his plans had been thwarted when the last remaining male heir in the main line of the Medici, Lorenzo, duke of Urbino died in spring 1519, leaving the family with only two illegitimate boys (both under ten) and a baby daughter (Catherine, the future queen of France), and an extremely challenging situation so far as holding power in Florence was concerned. One need only recall the troubles that minor heirs had caused the Sforza in Milan at the end of the last century, and in the case of the Medici the available heirs were not even legitimate. Alessandro, the younger of the two Medici bastards, had not been publicly acknowledged before this point: his mother, most likely a housemaid, was variously described as 'a slave', 'Moorish', and 'half-Negro', which did not make him an obvious candidate for high political office.[5] The pope's attention, therefore, was back on family matters and not on managing strategies for Church reform that might have avoided further conflict. Second, the election for Holy Roman Emperor had seen Charles V triumph, and no one had any further interest in conciliating the elector Frederick.[6] His protection was no longer quite such a guarantee of Luther's safety.

Thus in July 1519 the stakes were particularly high for Luther when he disputed with Johann Eck, professor of theology at Ingolstadt. Eck was an impressive debater and provoked Luther into ever more explicit opposition to the pope and, more troublesome still, into support for the teachings of Czech theologian Jan Hus, which so far as the Church was concerned was heresy.[7] (Hus had been burnt at the stake in 1415; his views anticipated many Lutheran tenets.) Luther, however, did not back down, becoming ever firmer in his views. If he was to be labelled a Hussite, so were Sts Paul and Augustine. Moreover, almost two years after his initial critique of indulgences, Luther's arguments were now becoming very public – and here the technology of printing came into its own.

In August 1520, Luther wrote in German 'To the Christian Nobility of the German Nation concerning the Reform of the Christian Estate'. The first edition had four thousand copies: it went to reprints. The trial now switched to the court of Christian public opinion. The theological faculty at Cologne declared his theses heretical in late August 1519, as did that of Louvain three months later, though that verdict was not published until February 1520. Luther was not called to these hearings, nor to his heresy trial in Rome, which concluded in May 1520. The cardinals heard its verdict in their regular meeting or consistory on 1 June, and two weeks later Luther was threatened with excommunication in a papal bull. Published on 24 July, the bull was pinned up at St Peter's and at the Cancelleria.[8]

These were traditional locations for the publication of papal decrees but they symbolise something of the frustration of reformers with Rome: the magnificent rebuilding project for which the contentious indulgences were sold in the first place, and the grand palace of the papal vice-chancellor. Built in the new, fashionable classicising style to house the single most powerful official in the government of the Papal States, the Cancelleria was now occupied by the pope's cousin, Cardinal Giulio de' Medici (who was also responsible for drafting the bulls). It was September before the excommunication bull was published in Germany, and Luther did not relent. The following month he published a treatise in Latin, 'On the Babylonian Captivity of the Church', which was also translated into German, and the next month followed up with 'On the Freedom of the Christian', accompanied by an open letter to the pope.

Having begun with an extensive attack on indulgences, Luther now began to flesh out his revised theology, moving towards what would become the three tenets of Protestantism: justification through faith alone ('good works' on earth were not required for salvation), 'sola scriptura' (the Bible alone was the source of Christian knowledge), and the priesthood of all believers (priests enjoyed no special status or hierarchy). On the basis of scripture, Luther rejected all but three of the traditional seven sacraments of the Church. Holy Communion, baptism and penance remained; ordination of priests, confirmation and the last rites were excluded; marriage had a more ambiguous status, not formally a sacrament but nonetheless enjoying God's protection.[9]

The question now was the attitude of the new Emperor Charles V. Currently freed from responsibilities in Italy thanks to the hiatus in the wars, he was crowned German king on 23 October 1520 in the cathedral at the spa town of Aachen, located in the borderlands with France and the traditional site for the ceremony. Charles was not, as yet, crowned emperor (a task that would fall to the pope) but Leo opted to grant him the title of Emperor-Elect, a concession surely aimed at winning Charles' support in what was a challenging situation for both the papacy and the Medici. While titles might seem a trivial matter today, they were an important tool for the papacy in honouring secular princes: the king of France used the title 'Most Christian King' thanks to a papal grant, and the king of England would soon become 'Defender of the Faith' on the same basis. Besides the title, Leo had dispatched two envoys to the coronation and the Imperial Diet that followed at Worms on the Rhine, the better to make his case, though they do not seem to have done a very good job of conveying back to the pope the weight of the threat that Luther posed.[10] Whether complacent or distracted, Leo was simultaneously managing an equally tricky piece of diplomacy in Florence, where after the death of Duke Lorenzo his cousin Cardinal Giulio de' Medici was trying to maintain the Medici party in power. Bear in mind that this was the pope who, thirty years before, had been advised by his father that while not neglecting ecclesiastical affairs he should take care of his family interests. And Rome had, it must be remembered, seen off the threat of councils before: the medieval popes had survived wide-ranging conflict over their power with medieval monarchs, not to mention the embarrassing episode of three popes at once as the Avignon Schism had come to a close. There must have seemed little reason to think the Church would not survive this.

By the time the Diet of Worms opened on 27 January 1521 Leo had formally declared Luther a heretic.[11] While there was no danger of the traditionally pious Charles V showing sympathy to Luther,[12] there were political considerations to bear in mind. The princes of Germany had elected Charles, but that did not mean he could dictate to them. He was obliged to follow the imperial constitution, and he needed to be sensitive to the public hostility to Rome that had provided Luther with a receptive audience. What followed was a contest over authority and legal priority of the sort that had taxed the Church for centuries. Luther's protector Frederick the Wise played a constitutional card, insisting that imperial law trumped that of Rome, and Luther was assured safe passage to appear at Worms.

Luther himself, meanwhile, had shown no respect of papal authority. In December 1520 he had burnt not only the papal bull, but also books of canon law.[13] On the other hand, when it came to the imperial hearings, he emphasised that he had no wish for social disorder. He was quite distinct here from Savonarola, who had combined his religious views with extensive demands for political reform: Luther, in contrast, respected imperial authority.[14] The whole business frustrated those reformers working within the framework of the Catholic Church. Erasmus insisted he had nothing to do with Luther, that he had not read much of Luther's work and that he took from what he had read those parts that were valuable and left the rest. 'I am neither', Erasmus wrote, 'his inspiration nor his patron, neither his advocate nor his judge.' Erasmus was a fierce critic, however, of those who denounced Luther in excessive terms, who, he claimed, only encouraged more people to buy and read Luther's books.[15] For Luther, meanwhile, it was enough that he continued to enjoy Duke Frederick's protection from arrest; his following grew in Germany and beyond. Leo, whose health had never been good, died on 1 December 1521; he was forty-five.

On Leo's death, the cardinals were divided on who should succeed him. His cousin Cardinal Giulio de' Medici was a likely candidate, but replacing one Medici pope with another was not a popular choice. As often in such situations, with the Spanish and French parties deadlocked, the cardinals settled on a compromise. Prompted by Giulio de' Medici (who had domestic Florentine concerns about a possible attack on Siena in January 1522 and no appetite for extended discussions) they chose a candidate who was not even at the conclave. This was Adriaan Floriszoon Boeyens (1459–1523), a distinguished theologian and former professor at the University of Leuven, who had become a tutor to the future Emperor Charles V in around 1509.[16] Boeyens had also enjoyed a role as political adviser and diplomat; on Charles' initiative, he had been made a cardinal in 1517, and as Inquisitor General of Castile and León played a leading part in Spanish Church affairs during the first years of Luther's challenge. In that capacity he worked on reform of the Church in America (its first diocese, that of Santo Domingo, had been established in 1511) as well as dealing with the ongoing issue of Jewish and Muslim converts whose sincerity was suspect; he opposed attempts to ban anonymous witnesses to the Aragonese Inquisition and reappointed abusive inquisitors whom his predecessor had sacked. In short, he was no naive innocent in either politics or religion (he had been governor of Castile during a major rebellion) and not unlike the Medici he had had his hands in the till himself (to pay Flemish courtiers from Inquisition funds).

After a long delay to prepare for his voyage from the Low Countries, Boeyens did not arrive in Rome until August 1522, just as Sultan Süleyman was conquering Rhodes. One dissatisfied Roman had put up a sign at the Vatican, declaring the palace 'to rent',[17] while another unenthused member of the city's literati observed that he arrived 'together with the plague'.[18] Cardinal Giulio de' Medici, meanwhile, had to deal with the consequences of being out of papal power. He conceded the duchy of Urbino to the previous incumbents, the della Rovere relatives of Pope Julius II, who had secured the backing of the duke of Ferrara, the cardinal choosing to cut a deal rather than risk Francesco Maria della Rovere, a former commander of the papal armies and a formidable opponent (not to mention murderer of Cardinal Alidosi) giving his support to rivals of the Medici in Florence.[19]

Pope Adrian VI (the name taken by Boeyens) is famed for his piety and asceticism, and he found the world of the papal court difficult (his cardinals found him difficult, too, though the reform-minded Gian Matteo Giberti – of whom more below – praised his virtues).[20] It would have been hard for anyone to live up to the lavish style of Leo X's papacy, shot through as it was with an emphasis on magnificence that gave the pope a sheen quite as impressive as that of any secular prince. On arriving in Rome, the new pope used his first consistory to announce a blunt attack on the corruption of the papal court, demanding an end to excessive lifestyles and lascivious living. While Adrian conceded none of Luther's theological objections, he quickly embarked on reforms to the papal curia, aiming to address complaints, for example over simony (the sale of church offices) and nepotism. Such reforms had, of course, been proposed before, but events in Germany now made them more pressing. He was not afraid to criticise his predecessors in public, including in a statement sent to the Imperial Diet of January 1523, which blamed the Lutheran 'persecution' of the Church on 'the sins of the priests and the prelates' and accepted that there had been 'abuses in spiritual matters' and 'violations of the commandments' in Rome.²¹ Some reform-minded Italian humanists welcomed Adrian's efforts. One, Zaccaria Ferreri, advised him to 'purge Rome' as a means to cleanse the world. Rome was a symbol of the whole of Christianity: even the seating plan of the papal chapel was thought to reflect that of God and the twenty-four elders in heaven.²²

Adrian had little choice when it came to economy: Leo's extravagant spending, not to mention the long-term cost of the wars – now heading for their fourth decade after a new offensive over Milan – had left the papal budget in tatters. He reversed a fifteenth-century policy that had allowed curia members to dispose of property in their wills as they wished, confiscating it instead in what was effectively an inheritance tax, which while useful for papal finances put a damper on property development by anyone liable to be hit. These economies, however, also made him highly unpopular with Roman bankers – who had been used to making profitable loans to an indebted papacy – not to mention the artists, architects and builders who depended on curial patronage.²³

The most famous story told about Adrian recounts his disapproval of the *Laocöon* sculpture, which he is said to have described as 'idols of the ancients'. On the other hand, however, he did permit some Venetian envoys into the Vatican sculpture garden to view the collection, and he is known to have given at least one ancient artwork – a marble relief of *Persephone in Hades* – as a gift.²⁴ His poor reputation is due in large part to the subsequent assessment of art historian Giorgio Vasari, who labelled him a 'barbarian' who 'took no delight in pictures, sculptures, or in any other good thing'. The sympathies of Vasari, an artist himself, lay firmly with the sculptors and painters who found themselves out of work in Rome thanks to Adrian's cutbacks:

> during his pontificate all the arts and talents were so crushed down that if the governance of the Apostolic See had remained long in his hands, that fate would have come upon Rome that fell upon her on another occasion, when all the statues saved from the destruction of the Goths [...] were condemned to be burned.²⁵

In fact, despite the brevity of Adrian's pontificate a number of artworks were produced for him, including new vestments for papal rituals, two portraits by Jan van Scorel and one by Sebastiano del Piombo (all now lost) and a fourth attributed to Jörg Breu, now in Hanover, showing the pope in full pearl-trimmed pontificals and gleaming tiara, looking anything but ascetic, especially when compared to Raphael's far more modest portrait of Pope Julius II. Adrian had Raphael's tapestries for the Sistine Chapel retrieved from the pawnbroker in time for his coronation, and there is evidence that he employed the artist Giovanni da Udine and possibly also Antonio da Sangallo. His pontificate saw important Roman commissions from Northern Europeans too, including an altarpiece funded by the Fugger bank for the German national church in Rome, Santa Maria dell'Anima.[26]

However, even for a politician as experienced as Adrian, tackling the vested interests at the papal curia was bound to be a challenge, and having never been a resident in Rome he simply did not have the networks of support in the city that might have helped him in that endeavour. Nor, in the end, did he have the time. He died in September 1523 and was buried in Santa Maria dell'Anima in a tomb adorned with allegorical figures representing the three theological virtues – faith, hope and charity – and the four cardinal virtues: prudence, justice, fortitude and temperance. These latter four were perceived as virtues of civic leaders and advisers and give the lie to the idea that Adrian was solely to be remembered for his religious or theological contribution.[27] It is fascinating to reflect on the counterfactual possibilities had Adrian – with all his connections to imperial politics – survived to lead reform in the Church of Rome in the years immediately following the rise of Luther.

That task, however, fell instead to Giulio de' Medici – cousin of Adrian's predecessor Leo X – who on his election in November 1523 took the name Clement VII. Clement, who had been appointed cardinal in 1513, was the son of Giuliano de' Medici (the murdered brother of Lorenzo the Magnificent). He had held the rich office of vice-chancellor of the Church during his cousin's reign, the same office that had seen Rodrigo Borgia into the papacy some years earlier. Clement's priority, like Leo's before him, was family, and his papacy was dominated by scheming to secure Medici rule in Florence, in the interests of which (and also, to some extent in the interests of the papacy) he played off the Holy Roman Empire and the French.

In 1524 he dispatched the elder of his nephews, Ippolito (now legitimised), to live in the city, with a view to the 13-year-old taking on the mantle of family representative as soon as he was of an age to do so. The pope's reputation was made – or rather unmade – by Francesco Guicciardini. Clement, wrote Guicciardini, was characterised by 'a kind of irresolution and perplexity, which was natural to him'; he would have been a man of the 'greatest capacity if his timidity had not often corrupted his power of judgement'.²⁸ This is, as we will see, both true and unfair to Clement. Sometimes delay was his best political option; moreover, he was a member of the Medici family first and foremost, and judged from that point of view he was more successful than he is often painted.²⁹

For all his preoccupations, Clement did correspond with reformers, including Erasmus, whom he paid two hundred florins for some writings in 1524; the pope went on to defend Erasmus from critics of his orthodoxy. He supported the reform experiments of Gian Matteo Giberti, bishop of Verona, in that diocese: these aimed to address the poor quality and lax living of the clergy and in fact built on reforms already promoted by Clement when he was a cardinal at the Florentine Synod of 1517.³⁰ There is debate among scholars about Giberti's significance in longer-term Catholic reform, but there is no doubt that some of his initiatives did anticipate those developed during the Council of Trent (1545–63). They include the use of a confessional box, poor relief, the encouragement of philanthropy and attempts to improve the quality of preaching.³¹ Without overplaying the religious reforms of Clement's reign, they were certainly present, and they went on with the pope's support, not despite his opposition.³²

Moreover, his election, and with it the prospect of revived patronage, was certainly welcomed by Rome's artists. Clement was a patron with a track record: he had commissioned work from Raphael, Sebastiano del Piombo, Baccio Bandinelli, Giovanni da Udine, Giulio Romano and Michelangelo, who reported that 'everyone is rejoicing'.³³ His interests were not restricted to the visual arts: he was described within living memory as an 'expert musician', 'one of the best musicians alive in Italy', who did much to revive the papal choir; he was praised for his own voice, which was 'sonorous, clear and intelligible'. The first printed reference to a madrigal is to be found in Clementine Rome, and it seems likely that he was also a patron of secular music, though the documentation for this is poorer.[34] So far as support for literary endeavours was concerned, Clement did not live up to the hopes of Rome's writers (and as they mused on his rule they arguably took their revenge).[35] It was in the visual arts that the Medici popes left their most important legacy.

Chapter Fourteen

The High Renaissance

The same popes whose financial strategies would so anger reformers were also the patrons of some of the greatest art of their age, attracting to Rome among others Leonardo da Vinci, Raphael and Michelangelo. Raphael (Raffaello Sanzio) was a generation younger than Leonardo, but their careers coincided at the court of Leo X. There, Raphael painted a celebrated triple portrait of the pope with his relatives Cardinal Giulio de' Medici and Luigi Rossi, all splendour in scarlet, but – in Raphael's characteristic style – still entirely human. The work was dispatched to Florence for the wedding of Duke Lorenzo de' Medici to Madeleine de la Tour d'Auvergne, though Lorenzo, who died within a year of the happy event, did not have much time to appreciate it. It was, moreover, one of Raphael's last works before his own untimely death at the age of thirty-seven.

Raphael had been born in Urbino – the small and highly cultured court centre for which the Medici competed with their della Rovere rivals. His father, Giovanni Santi, was court painter there, but he died in 1494 and the young Raphael had to establish himself independently. He went on to join Perugino's workshop, and in 1504 moved to Florence, where he spent four years developing his work in the city's artistic circles. Presenting himself as a cultured gentleman – no mere artisan – he succeeded in attracting influential patrons, and in 1508 he was invited to Rome where he began to work on the redecoration of apartments for Pope Julius (after Julius' decision to vacate the set occupied by his detested Borgia predecessor). His portrait of Julius captures the features and character of the wizened pope, placing an emphasis on his human frailty: in Vasari's words it was so lifelike as to make those who saw it 'shrink in fear'.[1] The combination of red and white in Julius' garments symbolises Christ's blood on the one hand and his purity on the other.² As we have seen, however, Julius was not above bloody warfare himself. More generally, there had been shifts in the style of religious art compared with that of a century before, not least a greater degree of realism in portrayals of biblical figures. There were fewer haloes, and such as there were tended to be slender and diaphanous rather than the flat gold circlets of earlier years. Leonardo's *Virgin of the Rocks* and indeed his other Virgins could be any mother and child: their humanity is emphasised. (Later, as we will see, this human portrayal would fall into disfavour.)

In the papal apartments project, Raphael was inspired by the grotesque details of art recently discovered in the underground chambers of Nero's Golden House (which were mistaken for caves, hence the name 'grotesque', from the Italian *grottesca* meaning 'cave-like'). These had come to light around 1480 when a young Roman fell into a cleft in the Esquiline Hill, and they quickly became an attraction for artists. At the time, no one knew that the Golden House (Domus Aurea), which lies buried to one side of the Roman Forum, was the ancient residence of the Emperor Nero (r. AD 54–68). It was entirely covered over, so that when anyone climbed down into it, they saw only the barrel-vaulted ceilings and a metre or so of wall below at the top of a room. It was an easy assumption that these were not, in fact, ceilings, but caves and cave paintings. Vasari describes Raphael's visit, along with one of his collaborators, Giovanni da Udine. They had gone to the church of San Pietro in Vincoli, where excavations were taking place in the hope of uncovering antique statues. There:

> Certain rooms were discovered, completely buried under the ground, which were full of little grotesques, small figures, and scenes, with other ornaments of stucco in low-relief. Whereupon, Giovanni going with Raffaello, who was taken to see them, they were struck with amazement, both the one and the other, at the freshness, beauty, and excellence of those works, for it appeared to them an extraordinary thing that they had been preserved for so long a time; but it was no great marvel, for they had not been open or exposed to the air, which is wont in time, through the changes of the seasons, to consume all things. These grotesques – which were called grotesques from their having been discovered in the underground grottoes – executed with so much design, with fantasies so varied and so bizarre, with their

delicate ornaments of stucco divided by various fields of colour, and
with their little scenes so pleasing and beautiful, entered so deeply into
the heart and mind of Giovanni, that, having devoted himself to the
study of them, he was not content to draw and copy them merely
once or twice; and he succeeded in executing them with facility and
grace, lacking nothing save a knowledge of the method of making the
stucco on which the grotesques were wrought.[3]

After Julius' death in 1513, his successor Pope Leo X continued the
apartment project. It included Raphael's most celebrated work (and
one that fell largely outside the traditions of Christian art), the *School
of Athens*. The sequence of rooms also incorporated more traditional
biblical stories, including that of Heliodorus, whose attempt to steal
the treasure of the Temple of Jerusalem was foiled by divine intervention. Other frescoes had more modern parallels, among them the
depiction of the Battle of Ostia in 849 (this has also been attributed
to Raphael's pupil Giulio Romano), which featured figures copied
from Trajan's Column (completed AD 113) in its portrayal of captured,
half-naked 'Saracens' forced to bow to a pope clad in finery, who
distinctly resembled Leo X.[4] It was a victory that Leo, who in 1518
campaigned (unsuccessfully) for a crusade against the Turks himself,
hoped to emulate. Also notable among the details of the Vatican
apartments are the New World plants and birds that feature in the
loggia frescoes: they include Caribbean hummingbirds and American
quails; for Leo X's 1515 entry into Florence the della Robbia workshop
produced a terracotta of *Adam and Eve* which transported the Garden
of Eden to the Americas, showing the pair in a field of maize, and
with a parrot in the tree behind them.[5] The pope was not the only
one to be fascinated by New World commodities: Agostino Chigi,
one of Rome's super-rich, had maize grown on his Roman property
and details of the plant featured in frescoes he commissioned for his
own loggia at the Villa Farnesina.[6]

For all that these artists are often treated as individual stars, they
did not work in a vacuum in relation either to the wider world or
to one another. Raphael's early work shows the influence of Perugino,
while his 1515–16 portrait of Baldassare Castiglione has hints of Leonardo's style in what the Louvre describes as a 'subtle homage to the
Mona Lisa'.[7] Raphael was entrusted with numerous responsibilities at

the papal court. He designed tapestries showing the lives of Sts Peter and Paul to hang in the Sistine Chapel beneath Michelangelo's ceiling and the stories of Moses and Christ painted by Perugino, Botticelli, Cosimo Rosselli and Domenico Ghirlandaio in the frieze.* After the death of Donato Bramante in 1514 Raphael took over the rebuilding project at St Peter's. The following year he became commissioner for antiquities, a post designed to protect parts of Rome's ancient heritage, though it seems to have had little success in the face of acquisitive collecting by members of the papal court.[8] He designed the villa on Monte Mario now known as 'Villa Madama' (after its later occupant Margaret of Parma), which drew inspiration from ancient models.[9] Never completed, it was nonetheless the first villa to be built outside the centre of Rome on the classical model. The work involved in these large architectural projects is beautifully summed up in the painting *Building of a Palace* (c.1515–20) by fellow artist Piero di Cosimo. Made for the Florentine guild of stonemasons and carpenters, it gives a rare sense of the workers, tools and machinery required for construction.

Following Raphael's untimely death on Good Friday 1520 (a date that attracted much comment for its symbolism), members of his workshop continued to keep the Roman art world lively. Raphael alone could not possibly have done the quantity of work necessary to sustain his numerous offices and commissions and, as was standard in the period, he led a team of artists. For architectural projects his deputy was Antonio da Sangallo the Younger, while the resident sculptor in the workshop was one Lorenzetto; Marcantonio Raimondi and Il Baviera worked on engravings; Giovanni da Udine contributed on antiquarian designs especially for stucco; another of the workshop's members was Giulio Romano. They are shown together in a stucco by Giovanni da Udine on the loggia of Pope Leo X. These days 'workshop' is most commonly used to designate a painting not sufficiently the work of the master to qualify as, say, an autograph Raphael

---

* Further sets of tapestries were produced from Raphael's designs for multiple European courts. Henry VIII's set ended up in a German museum and is presumed to have been destroyed during the Second World War; a copy produced for Charles I of England is in the French royal collection; the cartoons themselves are in the Victoria and Albert Museum.

or Leonardo. In historical context, however, the workshop was vital to artistic production: members would paint backgrounds or sketch in figures, leaving the master to complete the final details. Indeed, there was sufficient trust in the skills of Raphael's workshop that after his death they quickly secured the outstanding commissions for the Vatican apartments, but the members subsequently fell out in what – according to the lively but probably embellished account of Benvenuto Cellini – came close to a murderous rivalry. Moreover, in an important sense Raphael was also the last of his time. To manage a full range of artistic enterprises – in architecture, antiquities, history-painting and portraiture – was increasingly difficult as competition among artists grew.[10]

Michelangelo completed work on the Sistine Chapel ceiling in 1512, the physical strain of which had, as he lamented in a poem, left him with a goitre and 'bending like a Syrian bow'.[11] His last commissions connected to Pope Julius II were elements of the pope's tomb in San Pietro in Vincoli. It featured a statue of Moses (still in situ) and two figures of prisoners (now in the Louvre). The latter were renamed 'slaves' in the nineteenth century, but that allusion is not present in the original documentation and Vasari claimed that the figures – which draw on ancient statue types – referred rather to Julius' subjection of rebellious provinces.[12]

Following Julius' death, Michelangelo went to work on a new facade for the church of San Lorenzo in Florence, a commission from Pope Leo X to honour his home city and family. However, the project was cancelled in 1520 (in the aftermath of the death of Duke Lorenzo de' Medici) and Michelangelo subsequently worked on a more modest if no less beautiful project: a funerary chapel for the Medici. Featuring reclining figures representing *Night* and *Day*, this would eventually incorporate the tombs of the two short-lived hopes for the Medici dynasty: Lorenzo and his cousin Giuliano, who had died in 1516. Michelangelo also designed parts of the adjoining Laurentian library, but Leo evidently found the artist difficult, commenting that 'he is terrible, as you see: one can't deal with him'; another prominent figure of the Roman art scene, Sebastiano del Piombo, told Michelangelo in a letter that 'you frighten everyone, even popes'.[13] He had a vicious rivalry with Raphael, and his conflicts with other artists were notorious, one famously culminating in assault, when Pietro

Torrigiano, envious of Michelangelo's talent and the honour he consequently received,

> struck Michelangelo so hard on the nose with his fist, that he broke it, insomuch that Michelangelo had his nose flattened for the rest of his life. This matter becoming known to Lorenzo, he was so enraged that Torrigiano, if he had not fled from Florence, would have suffered some heavy punishment.[14]

Indeed, during the 1510s, Raphael was acclaimed as a 'divine genius' and the majority of contemporaries rated him higher than Michelangelo for the easy and apparently uncontrived style of his painting; Raphael also enjoyed the good favour of influential courtiers.[15] Just as important to Renaissance artists as their workshop was their patron, with whom a fruitful relationship could make a substantial, even dramatic difference, to artistic and architectural outputs. The mediator in the relationship between Leo and Michelangelo appears to have been Leo's cousin Giulio de' Medici, the future Pope Clement VII.[16] Clement took a careful interest in Michelangelo's work in Florence, and had a striking ability to read drawings rather than relying on the more traditional approach of requiring the artist to send a wooden model.[17] Like Machiavelli, Michelangelo was politically hostile to the Medici's increasingly authoritarian rule in Florence, but his relationship with Clement seems to have been sufficient to overcome his qualms.

While the prospects of Medici patronage fuelled the interest of many artists in projects between Florence and Rome, Venice was producing work in a rather different tradition. These were the last years of Giovanni Bellini. Bellini, his father Jacopo and brother Gentile, not to mention brother-in-law Andrea Mantegna, were a group of artists working in and around the lagoon city who had a dramatic influence on successors. Mantegna is most associated with the court of Mantua, where his most famous work is the illusionistic *Camera degli Sposi* (1465–74). He had a long career there and later worked on projects for Isabella d'Este. The Bellini, however, remained in Venice where their pupils included Giorgione and Tiziano Vecellio, known as Titian. Venetian art of this period developed with a distinct style and is particularly noted for its vibrant use of colour. Vasari praised Giorgione's 'images so soft, so harmonious, and so carefully shaded off into the shadows' and his skill at reproducing the 'freshness of living flesh'.[18]

Giorgione was, however, to be surpassed by his much longer-lived pupil Titian. Born into a well-off family, Titian joined Giorgione's workshop following his apprenticeship and later worked on frescoes for the Scuola del Santo in Padua (his first surviving documented work). He painted a wide range of subjects, including a battle scene for the Palazzo Ducale (the Venetians, like the Florentines, liked to commemorate military prowess in their seat of government, but this painting was lost in the fires of 1577). His early portraits include *A Man with a Quilted Sleeve*, showing a Venetian patrician: his ability to flatter his subjects while nonetheless creating a believable figure was no doubt a central attraction.[19] With *Sacred and Profane Love* Titian introduced to Venetian painting an unconventional approach to commemorating a marriage. The title – documented only in 1693 – is misleading, and the enigmatic work more likely shows in its pastoral setting a bride alongside the goddess Venus.[20] In 1516–18 he painted an *Assumption of the Virgin* for the church of Santa Maria dei Frari, notable for the expressive movement of its figures;[21] he was equally at home with classical subjects and contributed three key works to adorn the study of Duke Alfonso d'Este in Ferrara (the 'gunner duke' and husband of Lucrezia Borgia). These were the *Worship of Venus*, *Bacchus and Ariadne* and *The Andrians*, painted over several years in the 1520s, again featuring striking combinations of colour and movement in imaginative treatment of classical scenes.[22] Unlike Michelangelo, Titian was neither a sculptor nor an architect; moreover, although he later travelled to Rome and swept up a series of international commissions, at this stage of his career his work developed rather separately from that of the artists on the Rome–Florence axis.

In contrast, his Venetian contemporary Sebastiano del Piombo (1485–1547), made a grand career as a portraitist and was one of the rare artists to bridge the schools of Venice and Rome. He had a background as a musician prior to becoming a pupil of Giovanni Bellini and perhaps also Giorgione (who is notoriously hard to attribute and whose works have often been reattributed to either Sebastiano or Titian). In his early years Sebastiano painted a number of religious paintings and altarpieces; he met Agostino Chigi when the latter was on a mission to Venice in 1511 and accompanied him to Rome. There he worked on a range of further religious subjects including a *Pietà* (now in Viterbo) in collaboration with Michelangelo, with whom he worked extensively: the painting, according to Vasari, garnered him 'very great credit'.[23] Michelangelo evidently saw Sebastiano as a useful bulwark against the rivalry of Raphael, whom Sebastiano offensively labelled a 'prince of the synagogue'.[24] (Raphael was not, in fact, Jewish.) Sebastiano's career has often been viewed through the distorting lens of his relationship with Michelangelo, but it can tell us much about the impact of the changing political climate on the Roman art world. After Raphael's death in 1520, Sebastiano became Rome's leading painter, and hoped he might acquire some of the outstanding commissions for work in the Vatican.[25]

Leonardo had left Florence by 1508 for Milan where, now in his mid fifties, he produced many of his anatomical drawings, building on his youthful studies of the human body as an artist's apprentice. By this point his fame gave him a wider choice of both patrons and projects. During these years he became a friend and collaborator of the mathematician Luca Pacioli (1446/8–1517); mathematics as a discipline had been given new impetus by the French invasions and the development of artillery, which required the calculation of trajectories.[26] From 1513 to 1516, he worked in Rome for the newly elected Pope Leo X, during which time he produced works including a mechanical lion that performed for Francis I at the king's entry into Lyons in July 1515.[27]

Francis, already victorious in warfare after his defeat of the Swiss at Marignano earlier in the year, saw an opportunity to stake his claim as a patron of art. No aspect of princely life was free from one-upmanship, and the king convinced Leonardo to relocate to the French court, offering him a pension of 2,000 gold *écus* (an extremely generous sum, that put him on a par with the poorer end of the cardinalate). Leonardo was given the manor house of Clos Lucé, near the town of Amboise on the River Loire (about a hundred and forty miles south-west of Paris) where Francis had a castle. In a *Discourse on Architecture* Benvenuto Cellini described Francis as 'enamoured to the very highest degree of Leonardo's supreme qualities' and claimed that in his presence the king had 'said that he did not believe that a man had ever been born in the world who knew as much as Leonardo, not only of sculpture, painting and architecture, but also that he was a very great philosopher'.[28] Cellini was prone to embellishment but in this case he reflected wider views.

At Clos Lucé, Leonardo may have worked on ideas for the château of Chambord, which includes a fascinating double-spiral staircase, though the project was not begun until after his death. So far as painting is concerned, he does not seem to have been particularly productive during his years in France, despite Francis' enthusiasm for a St Anne.[29] He did, however, produce more notes and drawings, and in these later years Leonardo became intrigued by the idea of a great flood that might destroy the earth. He wrote extensively about it and made a series of drawings of a deluge wreaking havoc on the world. He was, perhaps, preoccupied with his own mortality, but may also have been influenced by contemporary millenarianism – the idea that the world was soon to end. In one set of apocalyptic scenes, Leonardo drew fire bursting from a thundercloud, a fortress collapsing into an abyss and the dead rising from their graves.[30]

Leonardo also continued to rework other pieces – he was by no means a prolific painter and a part of our subsequent fascination with him is due to the small number of surviving paintings: only about twenty have firm attributions. In 1517, Cardinal Luigi d'Aragona visited the French court with his entourage, and the travel journal of his secretary Antonio de Beatis gives a glimpse into how contemporaries saw the great man (the 'Florentine woman' he mentions is Mona Lisa):

Our master went with the rest of us to one of the suburbs to see Messer Leonardo Vinci of Florence, an old man of more than seventy, the most outstanding painter of our day. He showed the Cardinal three pictures, one of a certain Florentine woman portrayed from life at the request of the late Magnificent Giuliano de' Medici, another of the young St John the Baptist as a young man, and one of the Madonna and Child set in the lap of St Anne. All three works are quite perfect [...] And although Messer Leonardo cannot colour with his former softness, yet he can still draw and teach. This gentleman has written on anatomy in a manner never yet attempted by anyone else: quite exhaustively, with painted illustrations not only of the limbs but of the muscles, tendons, veins, joints, intestines, and every other feature of the human body, both male and female. We saw this with our own eyes, and indeed he informed us that he has dissected more than thirty corpses, including males and females of all ages. He has also written (or so he said) innumerable volumes, all in the vernacular, on hydraulics, on various machines and on other subjects, which, if published, will be useful and most delightful books.[31]

The secretary's account here sums up the breadth of Leonardo's legacy – ranging from projects in mathematics and engineering, noted down in books full of his famous mirror writing, to experiments with optics, motion and force, to anatomy and physiology, memorialised in his drawing of the *Vitruvian Man* – as well as his ability to bring together numerous themes, often on the same piece of paper, listing questions to investigate and ideas to pursue invariably with an intense sense of curiosity, and all this emerging from someone who emphasised his lack of traditional learning (though he certainly made an effort to acquire it).[32]

It would be a mistake to regard Leonardo as original on all points. In studying musculature he followed the advice of Leon Battista Alberti, who in the fifteenth century wrote treatises on painting and architecture, while the artist Antonio del Pollaiuolo had preceded him in removing the skin from corpses. Yet despite the precedents of artist-engineers, Leonardo's variety is still astonishingly impressive. His drawings include designs for elements of building sites, for textile manufacture, for cloth of gold; he drew a screw-press for oil and a grindstone, labour-saving devices for agriculture. His work, moreover, highlights the interrelationships between his different interests: the flow of water, for example, and the flow of hair. Art and science are intrinsically linked: what Leonardo depicts in his paintings follows the laws of anatomy and optics. His experimental techniques, however, mean some of his work, most notably the *Last Supper*, has not survived as well as it might. Already by 1517 the *Last Supper* was beginning to deteriorate, 'whether because of the dampness of the wall or because of some other oversight, I do not know', wrote Antonio de Beatis in his travel journal.[33]

When Leonardo died in 1519, he left his artworks and papers to his pupil Count Francesco Melzi. Somehow, the count did not receive them all, because another of Leonardo's companions, Gian Giacomo Caprotti (known as Salaì, a nickname derived from the name of a literary demon), ended up with about a dozen, including the *Mona*

Lisa and several others that are now in the Louvre. There is no satis-
factory explanation for how these paintings came into the possession
of Salaì, to whom Leonardo's will left property and not art; nonetheless, they did. The art historian Giorgio Vasari, who was a child at
the time of Leonardo's death, recounts a romantic tale of the artist
dying in the King Francis' arms. It is more myth than fact (the king
was elsewhere that day),[34] but it gives a sense of how much the artist
was valued by his patrons. It gives a sense too of the multiple means
through which the kings of Europe communicated power, and that
their competition was not just over territory but also on the battlefield
of culture.

Chapter Fifteen

From Pavia to Mohács

After the hiatus that followed the French victory at Marignano, the subsequent peace treaties and the imperial election, the Italian Wars resumed in earnest in 1521. Late in the year the Spanish captured Milan and installed Francesco Sforza (second son of Ludovico and brother of Massimiliano) as duke: he held the city until his death in 1535. In response, the French laid siege, enduring horrific winter snows and consequent shortages of supplies, leading to deaths from cold among both the men (already exhausted from a long campaign) and the horses, mules and oxen that served them.[1]

The next decisive moment in the Italian Wars came at the Battle of Bicocca (just outside Milan) on 27 April 1522, when the imperial commander Prospero Colonna (a member of the Roman baronial family who had also served at the battles of Cerignola and Garigliano) successfully exploited the discontent of Swiss mercenaries in the service of the French. Colonna had avoided engaging, which left the unpaid Swiss – who were hoping for a swift battle and consequent booty – frustrated at their masters. The Swiss refused to wait longer, which left the French commanders with little choice but to fight on enemy territory. The imperial side once again gained from the superior use of pike and shot, with a force that combined Spanish units with landsknechts, deploying earthworks (as they had done at Cerignola twenty years before) as well as artillery and arquebus fire, and imposing losses of perhaps three thousand men.[2] Bicocca proved a watershed: in its aftermath, armies increasingly sought to avoid pitched battles unless they could be absolutely sure of their advantage. This in turn had an impact on the ability to secure mercenaries: it was far easier to contract troops for a specific campaign that was expected to culminate in a decisive encounter (with all the associated prospects for booty) than to hire men for a long, unspecified period of manoeuvres, skirmishing and special operations. The obvious beneficiaries of this new style of warfare were the Spanish, who relied less on mercenaries, favouring instead their own national units.[3]

Francis had already been looking to an Italian expedition in 1522–3, not least to emphasise his own role as a defender of Italian liberty against both imperial tyranny and the menace of the Swiss.[4] The Spanish, however, followed up the victory at Bicocca with a second near Romagnano, attacking the French while they were trying to withdraw across the river Sesia in April 1524, and effectively driving them out of Italy, though not for long.[5] Perhaps overconfident, in autumn that year the imperial army tried and failed to invade Provence, then retreated into Lombardy, the French at their heels. The French now retook Milan, where plague had struck and many people had abandoned the city. Forced to retreat, the imperial commanders left a garrison of about 6,000 men at Pavia, about twenty-five miles south of Milan. Most were German landsknechts but there were also some hundreds of Spanish cavalry and infantry. Pavia did not have the modern *trace italienne* fortifications,[6] and as his troops laid siege Francis I might well have expected an easy victory.

Contemporary reports differed on the size of the French army. The watchful authorities in Venice received news that the French had over 25,000 infantry and 2,400 lances, though another observer, their key official in nearby Brescia, put the total higher, at 27,000.[7] Early in the siege some of the mercenary troops in imperial service wavered. Those of Giovanni 'delle Bande Nere' (son of Caterina Riario Sforza) quit to join the French.[8] Holed up in the city, both locals and Spanish endured a bitter siege. 'It seemed,' wrote an anonymous diarist, 'that the sky might fall, and all the world come to ruin, because outside St Augustine's Gate they [the French] had placed much more artillery, among it two large cannon.' This writer also noted the importance of civilian labour in these wars. Overnight, in between bombardments, the townspeople mucked in to repair the damage to the city walls – soldiers, priests, friars, women, citizens and gentlemen all working together. The landsknechts, he wrote, might have been paladins, they fought with such ferocity.[9]

The key to surviving a siege were supplies. Inside, the Pavese, landsknechts and Spanish were running out of gunpowder. But so were the French. Those within the walls made provisions to see out the siege, building temporary horse-powered mills to replace the water-mills outside the city that had been destroyed, thus ensuring there was always bread for sale. They had two months' supply of wine, three of grain and six of cheese. In the absence of beef some people turned to eating donkey and horse-meat, although the wealthier citizens managed to eat very well indeed: one report of a banquet held for three hundred guests on 8 December describes a mixture of courses ranging from marzipans to veal, beef, pork, capons, venison, duck, thrushes (considered a delicacy), plus cherries for dessert.[10] While this no doubt boosted the morale of those invited, it was also a form of deception: those within the siege could predict that reports of the luxury would seep out to the French and convey the impression of plentiful supplies.[11] The biggest shortage was of wood for heating (and for necessary repairs to the defences). Houses were partially dismantled for timber, 'a great cruelty to see'.[12] Heavy rains, meanwhile, put paid to a French plan to divert the River Ticino, which provided a natural defence for Pavia, located at the Ticino's confluence with the River Po. (The potential for schemes such as this explains the military interest in Leonardo's plans for diverting waterways.) Moreover, the rains threatened the French camp, bringing with them as they did the threat of the Po flooding.[13]

Within the city, a near-mutiny by the landsknechts was only resolved by contributions from the Pavese and by melting down the church plate and the university's gold maces.[14] Help, however, was on its way. The Spanish had dispatched troops to relieve the siege, and on Christmas night a spy arrived in the city, with over forty letters from senior figures on the Spanish side, including the duke of Milan, the viceroy of Naples, the duke of Bourbon and the marquis of Pescara, promising that by 12 January at the latest they would put an end to the siege. It was a welcome Christmas present for those inside, who compared their situation to that of souls in Limbo awaiting their liberation by their Lord Jesus Christ.[15]

Nor was it a comfortable time for either the besieging French or the Spanish waiting nearby for an opportunity to fight. When rain wasn't threatening floods, the encamped soldiers had to endure frost; the roads along which supplies arrived were sometimes rendered barely navigable by mud.[16] So far as the top commanders were concerned, life was rather better: they had the wherewithal to avoid shortages and while they waited for battle had plenty of opportunities to entertain themselves with hunting and fine food.[17] At the end of the year, the visit to the camp outside Pavia of Chiara Visconti, a well-known beauty related to the old ruling family of Milan,[18] provided an opportunity for celebrations. Lodged in the house of Fernando Francesco d'Avalos, marquis of Pescara, she was greeted with 'great honour and great banquets' by both Pescara and his fellow commander Charles de Lannoy, viceroy of Naples, and on her departure was accompanied by a thousand well-ordered Spanish infantry, looking like the goddess Venus, no less; the army 'full of sighs'.[19]

On 2 January, bad news arrived in Pavia: the duke of Ferrara had sent the French supplies of gunpowder.[20] With fewer allies in northern Italy, the imperial troops had more trouble obtaining supplies and the conflict wore on. On 12 January, however, two Spaniards made it into the siege with 3,000 ducats and news of the army's approach. While the pope had made a secret alliance with the king of France, including the promise of safe passage to Naples through papal territory, the Venetians were now backing the Spanish, and late in January it looked as if the French might retreat. An inventory of city supplies showed just two weeks' worth of wine remaining, two months' of wheat, and no meat bar the occasional chicken or peacock and the donkey- and horse-meat. It was not unknown, in the sieges of these wars, for people to turn to eating mice, cats and dogs.[21] Most of the city's spare cash and textiles had been used to pay the soldiers. But to their relief, the French, it seemed, were heading off to meet the imperial army, which on 28 January had seized a strategically important castle on the river Lambro, with reports of over 2,000 casualties.

The action now turned away from the besieged city towards the surrounding countryside, where the reinforcements lit fires and fired shots at night to signal their location to those inside. It would, however, be several more weeks, with supplies dwindling inside the city, before help came. Spies brought regular news of events, and used distraction to sneak gunpowder in. On the night of 8 February the Spanish staged a skirmish on one side of the city in an effort to get fifty light horse, each with 100 pounds of powder, into Pavia.[22] Late the following evening, a Frenchman named Saint-Germain, one of the king's gentlemen, was captured by the Spanish. A correspondent of Cardinal Salviati, who provided news from the camp, picks up the story: 'As he was taken a cry went up that he was Signor Giovanni [Giovanni 'delle Bande Nere', who had defected to French service]; at this the whole camp rose crying "Victory, death to the traitor!" and ran towards the prisoner.' The unfortunate Saint-Germain died of fright.[23]

On 18 February, perhaps two thousand people of Pavia – primarily the poor, women, children, camp-followers and artisans – left the city for its orchards to gather fodder and wood. For much of the siege they had been allowed to do so without interference from the troops. That day, however, Giovanni de' Medici, seeking revenge for a defeat of his troops some days earlier, suddenly appeared with a force of three hundred cavalry and two thousand infantry. According to the Pavese diarist there were at least thirty casualties on the Pavese side: only seven of them soldiers, the remainder women, children and poor old men. It was 'more to Medici's shame than his honour', the diarist observed, but the Pavese had the last laugh: Giovanni was shot in the leg as he was retreating and had to retire from battle to recover from his injuries; many of his troops subsequently left the field. He died the following year, after another gunshot wound to his lower leg.[24]

The Spanish now stepped up their attacks on the French camp. The marquis of Pescara (whom Giovio judged had no rivals when it came to military prowess)[25] led an assault on the French vanguard, with reports that his troops had killed a thousand of their Swiss mercenaries, and taken several dozen prisoner. The final battle came on 24 February. Overnight, Pescara had marched his troops into position, fording the stream that divided the Spanish and French camps, to set them up on a foggy battlefield as a major threat to the French left flank. As so often before in these wars, superior Spanish arquebus fire combined with smart tactics confounded the French, who were not helped by their own errors. Francis I, who had arrived to take personal command, contrived at one point to lead a cavalry charge across the line of fire of his own cannon. The Swiss mercenaries proved reluctant to engage, and the remaining landsknechts in the French service were rapidly defeated by their counterparts on the imperial side. Estimates of the dead vary wildly, but all agree that the losses were much higher on the French side (ranging from 4,000 to 17,000, with one Low Countries account claiming 50,000 losses) than on the imperial (four hundred to 4,000 dead). Perhaps about a fifth of the men involved lost their lives.[26] Every one of these deaths has its own story and consequences, but the single most spectacular humiliation was that of the king of France, who was captured by imperial troops. The tone of delight in Charles de Lannoy's letter reporting the events is unmistakable: the victory all the finer for having fallen on the emperor's birthday.[27] Francis was dispatched to his enemy's capital, Madrid, where he remained a prisoner. Nor was it good news for his ally Clement VII, whose support for Francis now left him on the losing side – and a badly losing side at that. As Venetian diarist Sanudo observed, no one expected the news of Francis' capture: that, however, was Fortune for you.[28]

There were, inevitably, recriminations. Blaise de Monluc, a French commander who went on to write a set of *Commentaries* on his military career, had observed the previous year that the French army was notably short of arquebusiers, relying (in his unit at least) on Spanish deserters. He was hardly enthusiastic, however, about the weapon's adoption. 'Would to God,' he wrote,

> that this unhappy weapon had never been devised [...] and that so many brave and valiant men had never died by the hands of those who are often cowards and shirkers, who would never dare look in the eye those who from afar they topple with their wretched bullets. But these are the devil's work, to make us kill one another.[29]

In fact in terms of tactics Pavia is not the watershed that it is sometimes labelled: the battles of Cerignola and Bicocca have better claims to that title. That said, its symbolic value – in terms of Francis' capture and the defeat of the traditional cavalry of the king of France by modern Spanish firearms – cannot be overestimated.[30] It was an enormous blow to Francis I's honour. Guicciardini was scathing about Francis' conduct ahead of the battle, noting that he passed 'most of his time in leisure and empty pleasures, not taking any notice of business or serious planning'.[31] Charles V, the victor, chose to commemorate it with a massive panoramic series of seven tapestries to a design by Bernhard van Orley (now in the Capodimonte Gallery in Naples) recording his triumph.[32] The French, on the other hand, despite the wretched defeat, were able at least to claim the mantle of chivalry in their tales of the battle: the king had risked his life on the battlefield; he had killed men with his own hands. Only thanks to the dishonourable new firearms had the Spanish triumphed.[33]

The French also turned to a new alliance. During Francis' absence in northern Italy he had left his mother, Louise of Savoy, to act as regent. Faced with the prospect of English invasion from the north to take advantage of the crisis following Pavia, Louise needed allies. There was one very obvious person with an interest in doing down the Holy Roman Empire, and that was the Emperor Süleyman. This was of course contentious. Christian princes were supposed to stick together against the infidel and only a few years earlier Pope Leo had been sending legates to the European monarchs to lobby for a new crusade; but politics trumped such religious qualms. If a Franco-Ottoman alliance was what it took to ward off the expansion of the Holy Roman Empire, Louise was ready to make one, and she duly dispatched envoys to make the difficult journey to Constantinople.[34]

The theatre of European conflict thus temporarily shifted away from Italy. In a separate development, Germany had seen a major peasants' uprising in 1524–5, inspired in part by Lutheran (and more radical) religious ideas. It had been put down by the summer of 1525, the peasants unable to match the well-resourced response of the nobility and its troops; Luther himself had disowned the 'robbing and murdering horde of peasants'. In Italy, for now, the affair was observed rather at a distance. There had been incidents of popular heresy before, not least that of the Czech Hussites, and the conflicts on Italian soil no doubt seemed rather closer to home; Pope Clement VII's political priorities were firmly with the consolidation of the next generation of the Medici in Florence. Still, the German conflict stood as a reminder that both religious and social grievances could prompt war.

Meanwhile, Francis' sister Marguerite played a significant role in the diplomacy around the king's imprisonment; she spent three months near him in Madrid but failed to extract concessions from Charles and had to make a dramatic dash for the border when her three-month safe-conduct came close to expiring and Charles threatened her with arrest. On 14 January 1526, however, Francis and Charles concluded the Treaty of Madrid, ensuring the French king's release. Francis agreed to renounce all his claims in Italy, Flanders and

Artois, as well as surrendering Burgundy to Charles. The treaty was, frankly, not worth the paper it was written on, and within a couple of months Francis would disown it, claiming (quite reasonably) that he had signed it under duress.

For all his victories, the Holy Roman Emperor now found himself isolated, as England and France made a rare alliance and the Ottoman Emperor pushed west. Süleyman, capitalising on the victory in Belgrade back in 1521, which allowed him to use Serbian territory as the base for his invasion, now faced the troops of King Louis II Jagiellon of Hungary at the Battle of Mohács on 29 August 1526. The Ottomans, enjoying superiority in both numbers and firepower, benefited from a disciplined core of Janissary troops (an elite infantry corps enslaved from among the Sultan's Christian subjects and trained from boyhood in soldiery), about half of them arquebusiers, who like the Spanish pike-and-shot units held together against their opponents. The news of a 'rout and great massacre' gradually filtered through to the Italian cities. At first King Louis' fate was unclear, but eight days after the battle the papal legate in Hungary reported that there was still no news of him, and if he lived there surely would have been.[35] The Hungarian defeat led, over the course of several years, to the partition of Hungary and an ever-closer threat to the imperial heartlands of Austria.

This was one of the most significant battles of central European history, and the culmination of a century in which the Western European powers had failed to mount a collective military response to Turkish expansion. A combination of disputes between the Western rulers, complacency that Hungary could look after itself and fear of a formidable enemy meant they simply had not acted.[36] Louis, it turned out, had died fleeing the battlefield, which meant an end to the Jagiellon dynasty that had ruled Hungary since 1440. He had been married to Mary of Austria, younger sister of Charles V, in a double alliance that also saw Charles' brother Ferdinand wed Louis' elder sister Anna. With Louis' death the claim to Hungary fell to the Habsburgs. They would not secure it without a challenge.

Hungary had a tradition of elective kingship, and a section of the nobility of Hungary were unhappy at the prospect of joining the Habsburg Empire. Over a decade of civil war ensued, with the nobility divided between supporters of the Habsburg claim and those who

preferred a more distant Ottoman overlord – again an indication that
for all the importance of religion to daily life in this period, sometimes
politics might lead one to prefer an alliance with non-Christian rulers.
Amid this dissatisfaction, János Szapolyai, a wealthy magnate with
wide experience in government, rose to prominence with the backing
of the lesser nobility and gentry (the higher ranks allied with the
Habsburgs) and in November 1526 had himself proclaimed king, a
claim that the Habsburgs vigorously disputed. War followed, then
after drawn-out diplomatic negotiations the parties eventually made
peace and Hungary was effectively partitioned, with one part under
Ottoman dominance and the other ruled by Habsburgs. Szapolyai
ruled the former; he was long portrayed as an Ottoman puppet but
his historical reputation has improved in recent years and he has
enjoyed a more positive assessment as a resister of Habsburg expansion. Among his staff was one Ludovico Gritti, an illegitimate son of
the doge of Venice, who had made a career as a jewel and wine
merchant in Constantinople. Entering Hungarian service in 1527, Gritti
rose rapidly, becoming first treasurer and then governor of Hungary,
second only to the king. There is some speculation that he may have
converted to Islam, but he himself asserted his Christianity, and it is
hard to see how he could have been accepted in Szapolyai's service if
the Hungarians had not been convinced. There were rumours that
he hoped to succeed Szapolyai as king outright; whether they were
true is an open question: Gritti was killed at the siege of Medgyes
(Mediaş) in 1534, before any such plan could come to fruition.[37] Still,
his case illustrates the extent of Italian political networks in this international world of trade, warfare and diplomacy.

Thus, by the autumn of 1526, the Holy Roman Empire faced a
confident and victorious Ottoman Empire in the east. Charles V had
troubles in the west, too. The Italian states looked askance at the
Spanish victory at Pavia, and feared the further rise of the emperor.
So uneasy were they, in fact, that in May that year, the Papacy, Venice,
France, Florence and Milan had united in a league against Charles.
The next few years would prove crucial in the Italian Wars.

Chapter Sixteen

Wars of Words

As the Italian Wars played out, numerous players exploited the media revolution that had come with the rise of print, as did religious reformers. Moveable-type printing had been brought to Italy in the 1460s by two German migrants, Conrad Sweynheym and Arnold Pannartz, who established themselves in Rome by 1467. The monastery of Subiaco, about forty miles east and predominantly a centre for German monks, established a press in the same decade. Venice followed in 1469; in the course of the 1470s so did the other major cities, and by the end of the century Italy had more presses than either Germany or France. The technology had its origins elsewhere (so far as Europe was concerned, in Germany, though moveable type had been used in China for several centuries) but the Italian cities had advantages when it came to its exploitation: capital, substantial literate urban populations providing writers and readers, the necessary paper supplies and established distribution networks. Prior to 1501 Italy was probably producing about forty-five per cent of European books, and the dominant centre for that production was Venice. There printers built on techniques already established for the mass production of manuscripts, though printing had the advantage of being rather less labour-intensive than manuscript publication, which required numerous copyists. (That said, manuscript culture continued to be extremely lively and was by no means replaced by print; indeed, some luxury print editions were made to resemble illuminated manuscripts.[1]) The importance of printing lay in its ability to facilitate wide discussion of the same text, creating a literary culture across Europe, in which learned men (and a smaller number of women) could share and discuss texts on the same topic.

Literacy was far higher in Italian cities than in most of Europe. As well as practical reasons for reading (to be able to understand letters and contracts and laws) there was the prospect of moral improvement and access to reading for pleasure. Across the continent about five per cent of people could read and write, and even in Italy there were significant regional variations, but in Florence in 1480 28 per cent of boys aged six to fourteen were in school, and others were likely home-educated. Many more acquired some functional literacy: an estimate for Florence in 1427 puts the adult male literacy rate at between 69 and 83 per cent, while in 1520s Rome all but a handful of customers who frequented a grocer called Maddalena managed to record their own purchases in her account book. There is, of course, a significant difference between signing a receipt for three bags of flour and reading or writing a sophisticated text, but on the other hand books could be read out loud by a single literate person in a group, so their contents reached a wider audience than just those with the skills to read for themselves. More people could read than write: writing tidily with a quill was a tricky business, and even people who might have mastered it for themselves would instead dictate to a trained secretary or scribe, or to a better-skilled friend or colleague. Women's literacy in the cities may have approached that of men, and mothers were often responsible for teaching their children to read: girls who learned did so in the home or sometimes in convents.[2] However, girls' education tended to be focused on the skills of literacy and numeracy required for household management and they did not receive the full curriculum intended for boys who might enter public life (the few exceptions to this were the women who might be called upon to rule a state). Though there were some town- and university-sponsored schools, most were independent, while the wealthiest families could afford private tutoring. Schools were not religious institutions, though some teachers were clerics. There were a few experiments with free education for poor boys but these were limited, and only a modest number of girls and boys from artisan backgrounds went to school.[3] Italy was home to Europe's oldest university, that of Bologna, founded in 1088, while the universities of Padua and Naples were both founded in the thirteenth century. These early universities trained students for careers in the Church, but also increasingly for roles in government, civil law and medicine.

This was the background against which the most famous of Italy's printers, Aldo Manuzio, established his press in Venice in the late fifteenth century. A humanist by training, he himself wrote a Latin grammar, and his press ensured the distribution of the Greek classics, drawing on the expertise of the Greek community in Venice as well as that of Italian scholars.[4] He published more modern works too: the poetry of Dante and Petrarch as well as the contemporary Erasmus of Rotterdam. Early print runs were small, perhaps a few hundred copies; the exceptions were well-known texts such as Dante's *Commedia* which got a run of 1,200 in 1481, and of course the Bible. A notably large early print run was an edition of the Latin poets Catullus, Tibullus and Propertius of around three thousand copies; by the sixteenth century a typical run hovered around the thousand mark. There were no guarantees in the printing business: it took some time to see a return on the initial investment, and many firms failed. Funding from private backers, whether individuals or religious institutions, could offset to some extent the worst market fluctuations, although state patronage was limited. There were, however, some state commissions and printers might be granted 'privileges', giving them an exclusive right to print a particular text in a particular territory.[5]

Printer/publishers sometimes ran their own bookshops, but they also distributed more widely through shops owned by others, or agents selling on commission in other cities. Chapmen sold small pamphlets in the street, from trays or baskets hanging around their necks; street performers would recite poems before offering copies for sale.[6] Not all writers, however, were keen to go into print. Some might prefer to circulate contentious views on politics to a limited circle of friends; writers for the theatre might regard their scripts as strictly for performance, not for publication; women (as we will see below) had particular questions of reputation and decorum to consider. Baldassare Castiglione thought the courtier 'should be skilled in writing both verse and prose', but that he should be circumspect about showing his work to an audience larger than just one trusted friend.[7] There were significant variations in the approaches of leading writers. Of prominent Florentines, the fifteenth-century philosopher Marsilio Ficino published work within his lifetime. On the other hand, Machiavelli's now best-known works (*The Prince* and the *Discourses on Livy*) were only issued after his death, though some of his writings (his verse chronicles of Florentine history, *Decennali*, along with his play *La Mandragola* and his *Art of War*) were printed earlier. Other works were circulated in manuscript, still reaching a significant readership.[8] Francesco Guicciardini did not publish any of his work in his lifetime.

While the famous names might have been circumspect, there was plenty of information circulating, not to mention cultural output engaged with current affairs. Italians learned about the progress of the wars thanks to new technology, which enabled reports of battles or sacks to circulate. Little books – *libelli*, from which we get the word 'libel' – were widely sold in city piazzas, and all sides of the Italian Wars made best use of their potential as propaganda. Indeed, the need for news about the wars or the latest diplomatic initiative drove demand for this cheap print.[9] Poetry about the invasion of 1494 and the discoveries in America went to print, and there was plenty of more dubious news too, reports of soldiers turning into pigs, or strange portents.[10] Pasquinades – the vicious satirical poems anonymously pinned to the statue of Pasquino in Rome – were in demand all over Europe. An English diplomat in Italy sent one to Henry VIII's chief minister Thomas Cromwell for his entertainment in 1532, observing that Cromwell would be familiar with the statue.[11] On a more practical level, print enabled the wide circulation of the mathematician Luca Pacioli's work on accountancy. This provided merchants with a detailed explanation of double-entry bookkeeping, setting out a process for managing petty cash as well as a daybook and a formal ledger: a model for accounting that is still in use today.[12]

Printing also offered opportunities for religious minorities: the first complete edition of the Babylonian Talmud, the principal source for Jewish law and theology, was published between 1520 and 1523.[13] Savonarola, meanwhile, was one of the first Christian reformers to make wide-ranging use of print, writing for a broad audience in Italian rather than Latin.[14] Luther's exploitation of print did not come from nowhere. Indeed, the popes had already set a fine example. As we have seen, printed imagery had played an important role in Julius II's campaign to consolidate his rule in the Papal States. Yet its power also prompted attempts at control, as we have seen with the decrees of the Lateran Council. State licences (or 'privileges') were required in order to issue a work, although given the divided politics of Italy it was relatively easy to circumvent some types of censorship by printing contentious works in a different state. Printing meant changes for the Italian language, too. It was in the sixteenth century that Florentine (Tuscan) firmly became the 'official' variant of Italian used in written work.[15]

One genre that developed especially in this period was that of history. Much of what we know about the Italian Wars was initially framed by historians who recorded and commemorated the conflicts, high-lighting achievements on the one hand and failures on the other. The invasion of 1494 sparked changes in the ways that history was written. There were no professional historians at the time, and history wasn't nearly as popular as other genres of writing, such as poetry. Yet there were, nonetheless, reasons to write it: family or civic tradition, patri-otism or *campanilismo* (the 'allegiance to the bell-tower' of Italian towns and cities). Two careers popular with humanists – teacher and secretary – might provide a basis for history writing, and the ability to write well was important to a secretary's humanist (and therefore professional) reputation. Yet what was valued in historical writing was not so much expertise in assessing or analysing the facts of the past but elegance as a writer. The point of these histories was to provide not only the facts of what had happened, but also to persuade the reader of the particular lessons that should be drawn from them, whether they were moral or political.[16] The historians of the sixteenth century might draw on models from the classics: ancient Greece and Rome offered a variety of examples for histories and historical biog-raphies in the works of men like Livy, Plutarch, Thucydides and Suetonius. They might also be influenced by the chronicle tradition: produced in many medieval Italian cities, chronicles recounted key events, from visits by foreign dignitaries to deaths of leading citizens, plague and pestilence, or natural disasters. Though some chronicle-writing continued, after 1500 histories increasingly engaged with the question of the foreign invasions, acquiring a sense of contemporary urgency even when they were not formally concerned with contem-porary topics.[17]

This played out differently in the different Italian states. In Florence, Machiavelli's *Florentine Histories* conveyed the drama and bloodiness of war, while for Francesco Guicciardini and others history shifted from being a source of moral lessons (as it had been for the classically inspired fifteenth-century humanists) to something more cautious, prudent or pragmatic. That reflected the reality that states which had once enjoyed liberty now had to find political strategies – and corresponding histories – that accommodated the European power politics playing out in Italy.[18] In Rome, perhaps not surprisingly, God had a more prominent role in history, and writers did not (or not so much) follow the Florentines in their fascination with the elusive *fortuna*. The court of Rome did, however, produce the important collection of biographies by Paolo Giovio, *Notable Men and Women of Our Time*, written in the late 1520s,[19] and the biographical art history of Giorgio Vasari, the *Lives of the Artists*, published in 1550.

These years further saw the production of one of the most influential works of European poetry, Ludovico Ariosto's *Orlando furioso*, published in a partial version in 1516, with the full forty-six canto poem brought out complete in 1532. Described in Giovio's *Notable Men and Women* as 'a work of painstaking composition and adorned with all refinement, charm, and elegance',[20] it was a sequel to an earlier poem, *Orlando innamorato* (Orlando in Love), by Matteo Maria Boiardo. The *Furioso* is a chivalric romance set in the context of a war between Christians and Saracens, but also in a fantastical world featuring orcs and a trip to the Moon. The Orlando of the title, one of Charlemagne's paladins, is in love with a pagan princess, Angelica: his fury is roused when she elopes with a Saracen knight. In another key plot, Bradamante, a Christian woman warrior, is in love with the Saracen Ruggiero. (This pair are presented as the ancestors of Ariosto's patrons, the Este of Ferrara.) So popular was the work – and not only in Italy – that a third poet, Francesco Berni, embarked on a project of revising Boiardo's original *Orlando innamorato*. Like the histories, these poems can well be read as responses to the wars that had been the backdrop to much of their authors' adult lives.[21] For all that his setting was fantastical, Ariosto thought guns were a 'foul and pestilent discovery': unchivalrous weapons through which 'no more shall gallantry, no more shall valour prove their prowess'.[22]

The single most striking development in the literature of these years was the rise of women writers. That Giovio wrote about 'notable women' is no coincidence. The early sixteenth century – and particularly the 1530s and 1540s – were a lively time for women's writing in Italy. The question of how far women were involved in 'the Renaissance' (in the cultural sense) has long taxed scholars. Exceptions like Isabella d'Este aside, the general consensus for some time seemed to be that 'the Renaissance' was by and large the business of elite men. Only one woman, Properzia de' Rossi, a sculptor active in Bologna, got her own chapter in Vasari's *Lives of the Artists* (which also had to accommodate his comments on Plautilla Nelli and Sofonisba Anguissola as well as a brief mention of the much lesser-known Madonna Lucrezia). Yet the question has now shifted not so much to whether women had a Renaissance but when and in which fields, and scholars have pointed to literature as one key field for women's participation.[23]

Printing certainly enhanced the possibilities, although the debate on women's role in society – known as the *querelle des femmes* – encompasses works by women writers that precede the arrival of that technology, going back for example to the author Christine de Pizan (1364–1430), member of a Venetian family in French royal service, and her book *The City of Ladies*. Among the earliest to be printed, however, were the letters of St Catherine of Siena (1347–1380), which were published first in 1492 and subsequently in an Aldine edition (the name given to volumes from the prestigious Venetian printing house of Aldo Manuzio): women were an important audience for devotional books.[24] Women's reading, however, prompted quite some anxiety. Even the Old Testament was not all safe; 'vain and carnal' topics were to be avoided, as was anything that concerned 'sexual desire, gluttony or other sensuality'. A well-advised young lady would stick to the Office of Our Lady, the Psalms and a treatise on 'the glory of wives', according to the recommendations of a Carthusian monk in a treatise published in 1471. She should steer clear of Latin poets, not to mention Boccaccio's *Decameron* (completed in 1353 and one of the celebrated texts of late medieval Italian vernacular writing, its author himself had thought his tales, which feature numerous extramarital affairs, not to mention sex with nuns and monks, unsuitable for women). That said, some editions of Boccaccio were dedicated to women,[25] and in the Italian court societies of the later fifteenth and early sixteenth century so were a significant percentage of vernacular song-books.[26] This was in contrast to the situation in the republic of

Florence, where women's literary production was far more limited, a reflection of the relative marginalisation of women in the city's power structures and associated social circles by comparison to women's position in princely courts.[27]

Laura Cereta (1469–1499), whose writing on the Turks we have already encountered, was an earlier precedent. The daughter of a lawyer in the northern town of Brescia, Cereta had been educated by nuns, and is said to have given public lectures. Her collected letters circulated in manuscript copies rather than print, but they were written to be read by others, covering topics ranging from friendship to the ancient philosopher Epicurus, to marriage and education for women. Although they began with the work of Boccaccio – Cereta had clearly ignored the injunction to stay away – they were highly original and indeed highly critical of the institution of marriage that Cereta (married at fifteen but widowed after eighteen months) observed in the present day. She argued for women's right to education; indeed, for the right to education of all human beings. Just as there was a 'republic of letters', she argued, there was a 'republic of women'. It was a radical view for its time, and Cereta was caustic on the question of wives' dependence on their husbands, and on those women who preferred an easy life to challenging the prevailing norms.[28] Cereta's widowhood was important to her career. The few women to benefit from a humanist education faced a dilemma that one scholar has described as 'thwarted ambitions': on the one hand such study might widen their intellectual horizons, but on the other once they married they were expected to step into a more conventional role. Nuns might enjoy some intellectual autonomy, but their work was expected to be compatible with religious life, which ruled out much secular literature.[29]

Cassandra Fedele was another prominent woman writer of the later fifteenth century. Born in Venice in 1465, Fedele likewise counted a lawyer among her relatives, though her family were not part of the patriciate. In the later 1480s and 1490s she was part of a humanist circle at the University of Padua; she gave public orations, and was courted by royalty and nobility, including the king and queen of Spain. A possible move to the Spanish court was thwarted by the outbreak of war. Fedele conceived of her writing as 'manly work', and repeatedly stressed her inferiority as a woman. She 'blushed' at the insistence of a fellow philosopher that she should deliver a public oration, 'ever mindful that I am a member of the female sex and that my intellect is small'. This did not prevent her from citing Pompey, Plato, Philip of Macedonia and Aristotle. 'And when,' she concluded,

> I meditate on the idea of marching forth in life with the lowly and execrable weapons of the little woman – the needle and the distaff – even if the study of literature offers women no rewards or honours, I believe women must nonetheless pursue and embrace such studies alone for the pleasure and enjoyment they contain.

This oration hints at her view, expressed elsewhere, that scholarship and marriage were not compatible; she did, however, marry in 1499, after which little of her writing survives. It is possible that by this stage she was no longer able to trade on a reputation for youth and beauty that had sustained her earlier career: even in the fifteenth century the appearance of a woman in the public eye was expected to conform to certain expectations. In 1556, at the age of ninety-one, she gave a rare public oration for the visit to Venice of Bona Sforza, queen of Poland (daughter of Gian Galeazzo Sforza, the young duke of Milan whose demand to rule his home city had been the catalyst for the Italian Wars). In it Fedele expressed admiration for Bona's 'singular prudence in ruling your people during peacetime and the fortitude of your admirable mind amid the winds of war'.[30]

The early years of the sixteenth century saw a number of treatises in defence of women, though the most prominent were by men. In the 1520s Galeazzo Flavio Capra wrote on the 'Excellence and Dignity of Women' (*Della eccellentia e dignità delle donne*, 1525), while Cornelius Agrippa wrote a treatise on the 'Nobility and Pre-eminence of the Feminine Sex' (*De nobilitate et praecellentia foeminei sexus*, 1529) which got a translation from Latin into the more widely read Italian in 1549. Cardinal Pompeo Colonna wrote an *Apology for Women* around 1529 ('apology for' here means 'defence of'). The men were not to maintain their monopoly, however. Several women rose to prominence in the literary world of later Renaissance Italy. Among them was Cardinal Colonna's cousin, Vittoria. The wife of Fernando Francesco d'Avalos, marquis of Pescara and commander at Pavia, Colonna became a celebrated poet and lady of letters, corresponding with Michelangelo and

Baldassare Castiglione among others, especially after she was widowed. (The marquis died in late 1525, perhaps owing to the ongoing impact of wounds sustained in warfare.) Colonna was the daughter of another *condottiere*, Fabrizio, famed for his role at the Battle of Bicocca, and of Agnese di Montefeltro, a member of the old ruling family of Urbino. Prior to her marriage she had spent time at the court of her fiancé's aunt, Costanza d'Avalos, whose palace enjoyed a fine location on the island of Ischia in the Bay of Naples. Costanza was noted both for her 'beauty and refinement' and for her skill as a political administrator, and enabled Colonna to meet prominent intellectuals from the Neapolitan court; she subsequently based herself in Rome, where she was likewise part of literary circles.[31] In his *Notable Men and Women*, Paolo Giovio wrote that 'not only has Vittoria raised herself marvellously beyond womanly capacity, but she has equalled the most widely esteemed and wisest men'. That said, his assessment of Vittoria's virtues also included praise for her household management, and an extensive section on her physical appearance, including a detailed paragraph about her 'most delicate cleavage' and breasts 'swelling with heavenly nectar'.[32] Colonna was also the subject of less subtle sexist comment, including an obscene pasquinade that suggested in extremely crude terms ('grasping cunt' is among its choicer expressions) that her interest in religion was prompted by her inability to attract a lover (or, as the writer put it, 'find a pestle to grind her mortar').[33]

During her widowhood Colonna spent extended periods living in convents and engaged extensively with religious reform. As the wife of a prominent commander, however, she would have been accustomed to living apart from her husband for extended periods even before his death, and one poem, written after the capture of her husband and father at the Battle of Ravenna, gives a striking account of a long-distance wartime relationship. While it did her husband no harm to pursue 'dubious campaigns', she was left fearful and suffering at his absence, and wishing for peace so that he might return.[34] On his death she wrote this sonnet:

> O when the tender breeze and my sweet light
> Made beautiful the day and pure and clear
> The air, by paths secure in daring flight
> I sought to raise myself on wings from here.

The glory disappeared, and early ways
Perforce I then abandoned and am sore
Troubled, for through dark skies and soldering maze
A friendly, guiding flame doth shine once more.
Lost is the vigour that my wings did raise,
And the desire, that hope despiseth, grown
Helpless, in vain, in vain doth lift its gaze;
I tarry here below for, mortal pain
Defeating I still life but loveless, lone
The while thought soareth where my Sun doth reign.[35]

Colonna – like many writers of noble birth – preferred to circulate her poetry in manuscript, but it was published unofficially in pirate editions, which proved important in establishing her as a role model for other female poets, as did praise for her in works such as Ariosto's *Orlando furioso*, which cast her not only as great poet and virtuous widow but as a new Artemis.[36] Ironically, she herself was responsible for the pirating of Castiglione's *Courtier*. The first volume of Colonna's poems was published in 1538 with her *Rime spirituali* (Spiritual Verse) following in 1546. She was a groundbreaking poet on several levels: the first woman to achieve such fame for vernacular writing, a significant contributor to the development of the sonnet form (she was noted both for her stylistic ability and her decorum), and perhaps most importantly as a trailblazer for later women writers.[37]

Despite her evident individual significance, Colonna all too often remains a side note in the life of Michelangelo. Though best known as a sculptor and painter, Michelangelo was also a writer of poetry. The pair had an extended correspondence during which Colonna sent Michelangelo sonnets and he sent her drawings. Michelangelo wrote in 1551 that he had 'a little parchment book she gave me about ten years ago, in which there are a hundred and three sonnets, excluding those she sent me from Viterbo on paper, which are forty; these I had bound in the same little book and lent it at that time to many persons, so that they are all in print'.[38] This poem gives a flavour of his sonnets to Colonna:

> I cannot not fall short in wit and art
> Of her who takes my life,

Her help being so excessive
That far more from less grace we realise.
Then does my soul depart,
As when a too great brightness hurts the eyes,
And, far above me, rise
To my impossible; it has not drawn
Me with it to my high and tranquil mistress,
To let me match her least gift; I must learn
What I can do will lead me to her worthless.
She, with abounding graces,
Strews them and sets us with some flame alight;
The too much burns less warmly than the slight.[39]

Nor was Michelangelo the only prominent artist to be connected with Colonna. In 1531 she was the recipient of a painting of Mary Magdalene by Titian, commissioned by Federico Gonzaga (marquis of Mantua from 1519 and later duke), and the subject of high praise from both Gonzaga and his mother Isabella d'Este.[40] One scholar has highlighted the commonalities between the eroticism of Titian's paintings on this theme and that of Colonna's spiritual poetry.[41]

Second only to Colonna in terms of the extent of work published is Veronica Gambara, another noblewoman married to a *condottiere*, in her case to the lord of Correggio, a small state located in Emilia-Romagna which she went on to rule after his death in 1518.[42] Gambara's brother Uberto, a prominent churchman, became papal governor of Bologna. Like Colonna, Gambara's status as an aristocrat and a widow gave her space to write, though she began publishing while still married. Giovio thought she had gone 'beyond her sex' in composing 'with great eloquence'.[43] Early on she wrote love poems and lyrics: her madrigal 'Or passata è la speranza' ('Now hope has gone') was published in 1505, a breakthrough for women's writing in popular music.[44] After a hiatus in the circulation of her poetry from 1518 to 1529, she subsequently wrote a series of sonnets in praise of Charles V's empire, exhorting him and Francis I to conquer their 'disdain and ancient hatred' and make peace, the better to give flight to the 'impious and unjust' Turk'.[45]

Aside from the noblewomen, another significant social group of women who made literary careers were courtesans. Somewhat freed from the constraints that ruled public writing indecorous, Tullia d'Aragona (1501~05–1556) was a prominent early representative of this trend. Perhaps the daughter of Cardinal Luigi d'Aragona (whom we saw visiting Leonardo da Vinci at the French court), her Roman salon attracted a lively set, among them the Florentine Filippo Strozzi, who had married Clarice de' Medici in 1508, a controversial match because the Medici were still in exile at the time. Tullia became Filippo's mistress (probably a few years before Clarice's death in 1528); he was imprisoned in 1537 and a few years later she appears to have married, which would have brought a degree of respectability. While on the one hand d'Aragona's role as courtesan initially brought her into contact with high circles of the curia, on the other it limited her ability to be entirely respected as a writer. She was twice accused of infringing laws which required prostitutes to wear a yellow veil and not to wear certain luxury items of clothing. In both cases she obtained exemptions: in Siena because she was married and led a 'most honest life' and in Florence, after lobbying, on account of her 'rare knowledge of poetry and philosophy'. She drew on this double experience as both courtesan and lady of letters to write her *Dialogue on the Infinity of Love*, which was published in 1547, as were her poems; the former was dedicated to the duke of Florence, the latter to the duchess. In this last decade of her life (after the death of Vittoria Colonna) she was one of Italy's most prominent female writers. Her decision to publish her own poems together with the responses of others to them was a particular innovation in the period.[46]

Other women played roles as patrons and hostesses, like Argentina Pallavicino (wife of Guido Rangoni, a prominent *condottiere*), whose home became something of a salon. Pallavicino, a poet, also took an interest in botany; she was a prominent feature of the Venetian cultural scene, with connections to well-known figures including Cardinal Pietro Bembo and the satirist Pietro Aretino, and was the dedicatee of the latter's *Il Marescalco*.[47] By 1559, Lodovico Domenichi, an editor already committed to promoting work by women, could bring together poems by no less than fifty-three authors for a groundbreaking edition of *Rime diverse d'alcune nobilissime et virtuosissime donne* (Various Poems by some Most Noble and Virtuous Ladies). Never before in Europe had a collection exclusively of women's writing been published, and Domenichi's selection brought to light not only the wealth of their work, but the engagement of these poets with one another. In one poem, Veronica Gambara addresses Vittoria Colonna: 'I would like, Lady, to be able to praise you / As much as I revere, love and adore you.' Colonna's response is more subtle, acknowledging Gambara by echoing her words rather than her effusive affection.[48] In short, the later years of the Italian Wars proved to be a period in which women found it possible to disseminate all sorts of literary work in ways they had not done in the past. Long absences and early deaths of husbands in the wartime context, religious change and the associated questioning of belief were all factors in the ways this writing developed.

Chapter Seventeen

The Invention of Pornography

Printing opened up other new business opportunities, of which two former members of Raphael's workshop took advantage. In 1524, Marcantonio Raimondi produced an edition of erotic engravings based on work by the artist Giulio Romano. *I Modi* (variously translated as *The Ways*, *The Positions* and the *Sixteen Pleasures*) showed couples in sixteen different sexual positions. Only one of the pairings was a church-approved 'missionary' style: the rest would all have been regarded as sinful, particularly the one with the woman on top.[1] It was banned by Pope Clement VII, by now under serious pressure as the Lutherans attacked church immorality, and the copies destroyed – though not all of them. At least one must have survived because in 1550 a rough set of woodcuts derived from the original was published (it survives today in a private collection). Later a classier version was issued under the title *The Loves of the Gods*, the classical allusion providing a gloss of acceptability that Raimondi's portrayal of mere mortals lacked.

The artist responsible for the drawings, Giulio Romano, had been an apprentice to Raphael and had worked on many of the master's key projects of the 1510s and 1520s including the Vatican apartments, where he acquired considerable experience as a project manager. According to one rumour he initially sketched the *Modi* positions on the wall of the Hall of Constantine in annoyance at a late payment, but this seems to be an urban myth. Raimondi – as one might expect from his background in Raphael's prestigious workshop – was the best engraver in Rome, if not in Italy. Their fates in this affair, however, were initially rather different. While Raimondi was jailed, Romano had already left for Mantua to work on the Palazzo Te, and it is possible that following Raphael's death Romano had left the drawings with his colleagues as a saleable asset. There is some question about who was involved in obtaining his release but it may have been Ippolito de' Medici (he was about thirteen at the time, which would have made for an amusing teenage encounter with his uncle Clement). More likely, behind the bail-out was the satirist Pietro Aretino, who explained in a letter what happened next:

> After I arranged for Pope Clement to release Marcantonio of Bologna, who was in prison for having engraved on copper the 'Sixteen Positions', I desired to see those figures which had driven Giberti and his followers to cry out that the virtuoso [Raimondi] should be crucified. On seeing them I was seized by the same spirit that had moved Giulio Romano to draw them. And since ancient and modern poets and sculptors are wont to divert their minds sometimes by writing or chiselling something lascivious such as the marble satyr in Palazzo Chigi attempting to rape a little boy, I tossed off the sonnets which are to be seen beneath [the figures]. With all due respect to hypocrites, I dedicate these lustful pieces to you, heedless of fake prudishness and asinine prejudices that forbid the eyes to gaze at the things they most delight to see.[2]

The Giberti mentioned here is Gian Matteo Giberti, the prominent religious reformer of the 1520s curia, and the conflict between the pair sums up some of the complexities of social attitudes in sixteenth-century Italy. In the factional atmosphere of the wartime curia, the pair were on different sides: Aretino of broadly imperial sympathies and Giberti pro-French.[3] The sonnet affair was the backdrop against which in 1525 Giberti ordered Aretino's assassination, but the attempt failed and the poet spent a year away at war, fighting alongside Giovanni 'delle Bande Nere' (when the *condottiere* died late in 1526, Aretino was at his deathbed).[4] Yet Aretino also wrote poems lauding Giberti and Pope Clement:[5] for now at least Italy offered space (if not always legal space) for a man to play both the reformer and the libertine. That was especially true for the period between Luther's challenge to the Church and the beginning of a formal response with the opening of the Council of Trent in 1545. For this generation – whose adult lives were dominated by the war, and whose basic beliefs were now facing turmoil – these might well be decades of experiment.

One interpretation of Aretino's sonnets for *I Modi* suggests that they (if not the original images) refer to specific sex workers – leading courtesans of the Medici papal court – and their specialities. Two of the named women are listed in the 1526 census of Rome. Another sonnet describes the *condottiere* Ercole Rangoni having sex with Angela Greca, a courtesan whom he later married (to much satirical comment): the lines are a foul-mouthed play on the conventional classical affair between Mars, god of war, and Venus, goddess of beauty. Francis I also makes an indirect appearance, when an enthused lover proves too busy fucking to help save the king of France from his captivity following Pavia.

Aretino is one of the most fascinating figures of the mid-century Italian literary world. Despite his humble birth (he was the son of a cobbler) he achieved high patronage. His prose was often scurrilous and he was famously nicknamed by fellow author Ariosto the 'scourge of princes'. After the scandal of the *Modi* he relocated to Venice, and his patrons included Federico Gonzaga, marquis and later duke of Mantua, son of Isabella d'Este. In the 1530s he worked, among other projects, on a continuation of Ariosto's *Orlando furioso*, and on a play, *Il Marescalco*, the tale of a stable-master whose lord announces that he will find his servant a bride, only for the whole affair to be revealed as a prank when the 'bride' turns out to be a pageboy, Carlo.[6] In some parts of Italy, as we have seen, same-sex relationships were widespread; the joke depends on the fact that of course such a wedding could never happen in practice. Moreover, sex between men was most often a time-limited practice, to be set aside after marriage; it was not always set aside, of course, and when affairs did continue they were most socially acceptable when they involved an older/higher-status active partner and a younger/lower-status passive one.[7] (That said, the historical records reflect what was monitored and/or denounced, and people who contrived to carry on contented relationships behind closed doors do not feature.)

Aretino's play, however, made fun of his patron Federico's own marital aspirations, and Federico's relations with Aretino were tense, not least after the latter published a vicious spoof horoscope for various prominent figures, including Clement VII, leading the pope to make a diplomatic protest.[8] At the marquis' suggestion, Aretino left Mantua and subsequently turned to more popular works, seizing the opportunities that the Venetian printing industry presented.[9] It was in Venice that Aretino published his *Sei Giornate* (Six Days, for the time period over which they are set), dialogues between a courtesan and her daughter, in two parts, the first issued in 1534 and the second in 1536. In part inspired by the second-century writer Lucian these 'whorish dialogues' (as the author called them) involve first Nanna and Antonia discussing the opportunities available to women (to be a wife, a whore or a nun) and second the advice given by Nanna to her daughter Pippa when she is planning to join her mother's trade.

While the publication of *I Modi* was considered scandalous, and Aretino's satire on the popes quite beyond the pale, there was no such controversy around Giulio Romano's erotic frescoes for the Palazzo Te in Mantua, which survive to this day. This suburban palace was built probably between 1527 and 1534 and was praised by contemporary critics.[10] Designed for summer entertaining, its rooms run in sequence around a courtyard and include both more private rooms for Duke Federico of Mantua and spaces intended for public occasions, although Renaissance people did not make such sharp distinctions between types of space as those later developed for royal apartments (nor indeed those of the present day). Important guests might well be invited to visit the most 'private' rooms in a sequence, such as small treasure-filled studies off bedrooms.

In the words of Benvenuto Cellini, the Palazzo Te was a 'marvellous enterprise on a large scale'.[11] Set around a central courtyard, among the more striking rooms is that of Cupid and Psyche. Vasari praised the 'admirable skill and ingenuity' with which Giulio Romano executed the work, using foreshortening to create figures that appeared realistic when viewed from below, the whole sequence showing that the artist was 'versatile, rich and copiously endowed with powers of invention and craftsmanship'.[12] A series of frescoes tell the story of the mortal Psyche's effort to obtain the approval of Cupid's jealous mother Venus for their marriage. The sequence has sometimes been interpreted as a reference to Isabella d'Este's disapproval of her son's affair with Isabella Boschetti (whom at one point he considered marrying), but this is not universally accepted. It remains an open question, too, whether the most sexually explicit fresco, that of Jupiter and Olympias, is intended to depict the couple.[13] Either way, it is clear that the palace had an important role in constructing Federico's princely identity. When in 1530 Charles V came to Mantua on his way to his coronation, he stopped to grant Federico the title of duke of Mantua and was entertained in the Palazzo Te. The Room of Cupid and Psyche is specifically mentioned in an account of his visit as the location for 'diverse conversations' with Federico, Alfonso d'Este (the duke of Ferrara), and other Italian princes.[14] Works of art, even or perhaps especially sexy ones, were intended to be conversation points, and according to a contemporary report by the duke's cousin Luigi (who had been a hostage at the imperial court), the emperor was extremely impressed by what he saw, even though the work was still in progress.[15]

As well as the sexuality of the classical art, it was to have references to warfare, including a series of statues of well-known *condottieri*. Duke Federico became captain general of the imperial troops in Italy, so this emphasis is not surprising. Indeed, Castiglione's *Courtier* had noted the ancient practice of erecting statues of 'famous captains and other outstanding men' in public places, 'both to honour the great and to inspire others to work to achieve the same glory through worthy emulation'.[16] The single most brilliant room of the palace, however, was the Hall of the Giants: it features an immersive *trompe l'oeil* fresco running round all four walls and showing the ancient gods in the ceiling defeating the Titans, who are collapsing down the walls.

Let no one ever imagine [wrote Vasari] seeing a work from the brush that is more horrible or frightening or more realistic than this one. And anyone who enters that room and sees the windows, doors and other such details all distorted and almost on the verge of crashing down, as well as the mountains and buildings collapsing, can only fear that everything is toppling down upon him, especially when he sees all the gods in that heaven running this way and that in flight.[17]

Not only was this superb artistic innovation, it was one of the few Renaissance artworks to give a visceral sense of the disorienting experience of battle.

Erotic art was by no means restricted to the princely court, nor to a select number of artists. Leonardo da Vinci was very capable of down-to-earth vulgarity and his work includes a number of erotic sketches, as well as a punning list of variations on the Italian word 'cazzo' (prick).[18] The townhouse of an upwardly mobile merchant might contain paintings of nudes (the Old Testament stories of Bath-sheba or Susanna, spotted in their baths by a future husband in the first case and predatory voyeurs in the second, were popular subjects, as we saw in Lucrezia Borgia's apartments).[19] Cardinal Bernardo Dovizi di Bibbiena had Raphael decorate his Vatican steam-room with erotic frescoes, among them an image of Venus spied on by a satyr. Baths more generally were widely perceived as a space for erotic activity. Francesco Gonzaga, husband of Isabella d'Este, received from his friend Floriano Dolfo (a priest) a lurid account of sexual activity at the Apennine spa town of Porretta, including pornographic descrip-tions of the count of Porretta seducing a nun and antisemitic comment on the sex lives of Jewish women. Francesco, whose sexual reputation was notorious (and extended to sex with young boys as well as women), evidently welcomed this type of correspondence.[20]

More generally, this period saw a shift in attitudes towards the artistic portrayal of women, which fits into a wider context of artistic change relating to the nude in particular. The revived interest in clas-sical sculpture (whose nudes reflected social practice in ancient Greece) prompted debate among Renaissance thinkers, living as they did in a society with no equivalent practice of public nudity and in which the body was often seen as shameful. They developed a new framework, compatible with their Christian society, for understanding the nude, and the painting of nudes became a test of an artist's skill in creating an ideal. Initially these were primarily images of men but from the early sixteenth century the artistic trend melded with new ideas about women excelling in beauty, in turn relating to courtesan culture and to the literary debates about women's role in society. While in the fifteenth century it had been widely accepted that men could be beautiful, this became an increasingly feminised characteristic,[21] and was the context for numerous portrayals of aristocratic mistresses. Around 1523, Titian painted Laura Dianti, lover of the duke of Ferrara; Leonardo's *Lady with an Ermine* is a portrait of Cecilia Gallerani, mis-tress of the duke of Milan.

Given that marriages between high-ranking spouses were typically arranged for dynastic reasons rather than for affection between partners, wives were sometimes content with these arrangements.

The world of the mistress followed particular patterns. Mistresses of aristocratic men were quite often the wives of courtiers; the relationship was understood and agreed by both parties; the woman's children might be recognised; financial or social benefits for the family might follow, as was the case for Isabella Boschetti in Mantua.[22] Prior to the Counter-Reformation, when Catholicism reasserted itself with more stringent attitudes on moral questions, there were fewer barriers to the promotion of illegitimate children and a number of important Italians of this period were born to parents who were not married (or not married to each other, at least).[23] However, restrictions became more common: as Venice moved into the sixteenth century, in line with the general shift towards a more closed aristocratic ruling caste, it imposed more and more restrictions on the political participation of men born illegitimate.[24]

Aristocratic men did not, of course, restrict their affairs to mistresses. Female servants were vulnerable to sexual advances from their master and his relatives; enslaved women, who could not quit their posts, even more so. Both Charles V and Lorenzo de' Medici, duke of Urbino, had children with servants. Children of higher-ranking mothers were more likely to be acknowledged and legitimised than those of lower-status women (the children of Charles and Lorenzo, who went on to be duchess and duke of Florence, were exceptions). Laura Dianti's portrait is testimony to the presence of enslaved people at the Renaissance courts: she is shown with her hand on the shoulder of an African boy. Looking up, he holds a pair of gloves, and he wears a striped costume – a style associated with slavery and the 'Orient'. As we saw above, Isabella d'Este was a documented purchaser of an enslaved African girl; the young Ippolito de' Medici likewise had a 'Moorish' page and sought to obtain the services of African drummers and dancers for his court; Ippolito's younger cousin Alessandro, illegitimate son of Duke Lorenzo de' Medici, was said to be the son of an enslaved and/or African woman.[25]

That said, even well-off courtesans could be subject to horrific violence. Angela del Moro, known as 'La Zaffetta', is a case in point. She is the subject of a poem, Il trentuno della Zaffetta (The Thirty-One of La Zaffetta), the title of which alludes to gang-rape by thirty-one men (a ritual punishment for courtesans). Angela may have been the model for Titian's Venus of Urbino, painted in 1538 for Francesco Maria della Rovere, duke of Urbino. It is not possible to be sure, because the woman in the painting is not named in any of the sources, where the painting was first titled simply 'the nude woman'. Experts have long argued over whether it represents the goddess or a courtesan or was commissioned to celebrate the owner's marriage. It shows a woman reclining on a couch with long fair hair and fair skin (the ideal complexion); in the background is a domestic scene with a woman and girl looking into a chest; there is a little dog on the couch, which may represent fidelity. The ambiguity of the woman's hand at her pudenda is notable: is this a gesture of modesty or masturbation?[26] In art appreciation today the sexiness of Renaissance art is often ignored in favour of a polite connoisseurship but in light of the wider evidence for sexual cultures of the period this is clearly misleading. Moreover, for all that *I Modi* can be read as an entertaining contribution to a bawdy and libertine culture, the sole surviving sixteenth-century edition, probably a counterfeit, was bound with a group of misogynistic texts, including the poem describing Angela del Moro's rape.[27]

Thus visual representations of sex and sexuality were connected to a broader and thriving sex industry in sixteenth-century Italy. Courtesans like Imperia, a mistress to cardinals and diplomats, were familiar faces in elite Roman social circles; camp followers were a fact of military life. Aretino satirised this world in his *Six Days*, and across Europe, in the centuries to come, numerous authors of erotica would hide behind the pseudonym of 'l'Aretin', a disreputable Italian export, perhaps, but undoubtedly a popular one. The experiences of the people working in the sex industry were many and varied. For the historian, one of the frustrations of this topic is that we hear far more about it from male observers than from the women (and indeed the men) who participated. Only a few courtesans wrote about their lives, and they were the wealthy exceptions. Much like today's sex industry, social rank was a great determinant of experience: the affluent courtesan providing conversation and company alongside sexual services to one man or a small group of regular clients lived a very different life to her street-working counterpart. Still, it was not always an easy one and the writer and courtesan Veronica Franco warned off girls from entering the profession. On the other hand, it afforded women a degree of autonomy in their personal lives that was rarely permitted to wives.

Lower down the social scale, prostitutes were indebted and exploited, subject to persecution and violence, and in many cases prostitution was a response to straitened financial circumstances such as dowry inflation rather than a preferred career choice.[28] Motivations might be coercion, financial incentive, a combination of both, or indeed one leading to the other.[29] A Venetian law of 1542 documented the exploitative relationship of procuresses who hired clothing to prostitutes, thereby putting them in debt, and then required them to work the debt off.[30] Some cities had particular circumstances, such as Rome, a city with a large population of men who were not permitted to marry. William Thomas, a Protestant who visited the city in 1547, gave a description. The Romans' ordinary pastime, he wrote,

is to disguise themselves, to go laugh at the courtesans' houses, and in the shroving time to ride masking about with them; which is the occasion that Rome wanteth no jolie dames, specially the street called Julia [the Via Giulia, named after Pope Julius II], which is more than half a mile long, fair builded on both sides, in manner inhabited with none other but courtesans, some worth 10 and some worth 20,000 crowns, more or less, as their reputation is. And many times you shall see a courtesan ride into the country with ten or twelve horses waiting on her. Briefly, by report Rome is not without 40,000 harlots, maintained for the most part by the clergy and their followers. So that the Romans themselves suffer their wives to go seldom abroad, either to church or other place, and some of them scarcely to look out at a lattice window; whereof their proverb saith, *In Roma vale piu la puttana che la moglie romana*: that is to say, 'In Rome the harlot hath a better life than she that is a Roman's wife.' In their apparel they are as gorgeous as may be and have in their going such a solemn pace as I never saw. In con-clusion, to live in Rome is more costly than in any other place, but he that hath money may have there what him liketh.[31]

Francisco Delicado's 1528 play *La Lozana Andaluza* portrays some of this world through the life of the title character, a Spanish immigrant who used her 'great insight and diabolical cunning' to work out how much money she could make from wealthy men. Another character jokes that 'most of the city is a brothel', which explains why they called it 'Rome, the Harlot'.[32]

Some cities licensed brothels, notably Venice, a city whose large temporary population of migrant seafarers generated a demand for short-term sexual partners. Prostitution was a big industry in Venice, to the point of being something of a visitor attraction. This was not without political problems. A Senate decree of 1543 declared there were 'excessive numbers of harlots in this our city'.[33] That said, the definition of 'harlot' (or 'whore') was wide-ranging. It covered any unmarried woman who had sexual relations or dealings with one or more men – or indeed a married woman separated from her husband who did likewise.[34] The elite courtesans could become rich indeed; the most famous of their number, like Veronica Franco, mixed in highly cultured and aristocratic circles. Some cities passed sumptuary laws to ban them from wearing luxury dress or required prostitutes to wear an identifying hat or badge, very much in the manner of Jews: the two groups were regarded similarly as providing a socially useful but stigmatised service (sex on the one hand, moneylending on the other); as we have seen, elite members of both groups were able to obtain exemptions from these regulations.[35] There was a constant tension between local secular authorities, who thought a regulated sex industry was an asset to their city, and the Church, for which (from an institutional point of view, at least) upholding moral standards was more important.

As the regulations suggest, the Venetian authorities fretted about the potential for confusion between courtesans and respectable women. It is certainly true that the Venetian courtesan of the sixteenth century fashioned herself as an aristocrat. *La tariffa delle puttane di Venegia*, a 1535 poem advising visitors on the availability and prices of Venetian prostitutes, includes references to prostitutes wearing silk and velvet.[36] These were – after cloth of gold – the most prestigious and sumptuous fabrics available to the Venetians.[37] In Aretino's *Sei Giornate*, Nanna's mother dresses her in 'a purple satin gown, neat and simple, without sleeves' when she first decides to put her daughter on the market. Later on in her career, Nanna cons a client into giving her a green silk dress.[38] The inventory of Julia Lombardo, a courtesan in Venice in the first half of the sixteenth century, provides a wealth of detail about the clothing such a woman might own. Chests in a little study off the main bedroom of Julia's house (itself an example of mimicking aristocratic architecture) contained fifteen pairs of shoes and as many as sixty-four chemises. This was more than many patrician brides would have in their trousseau: a more usual number was between twelve and twenty-four.[39] Franco herself was accused of breaking sumptuary laws by wearing 'pearls, golden bracelets and other jewels'. One of Franco's wills included a request to her commissaries to recover from a man whom she claimed was the father of her son 'a string of fifty-one pearls with a value of one hundred ducats, a dress of pale yellow satin with silver and gold inlays, and a crimson bodice'.[40] Contemporary descriptions of courtesans' houses reinforce the impression of luxury. One 1520s *novella* described the fine tapesteries and velvet chairs in the room of a Venetian courtesan: these all helped make sure wealthy clients felt at home.[41]

In Rome, as Aretino's characters point out, visitors 'usually wanted to visit not only the antiquities but also the modernities, that is, the ladies'.[42] There the fact that the papal court was (officially at least) an all-male business made considerable social space for courtesans. An earlier description, from around 1506, of a courtesan's house in Rome is given in a *novella* by Matteo Bandello:

> a salon, a chamber and a small chamber, all so grandly furnished that in them one saw nothing but velvets and brocades, and on the floor there were the finest carpets. In the small chamber [...] the walls were covered with hangings of cloth of gold, embroidered all over and falling in rich folds. Above the hangings there was a cornice decorated with gold and ultramarine [...] On the cornice stood most beautiful vases of various precious materials – alabastrine, porphyry, serpentine and a thousand other kinds. Around about the room were many chests and coffers, richly carved and inlaid, and all of the greatest value.[43]

These rooms were the settings for interactions both pleasurable and traumatic. Celia Romana, probably a Roman courtesan, wrote a series of letters to her lover which were published in 1562: one described how she missed him amid the 'delightful festivities' of Carnival season; 'I am sure,' she wrote, 'that spending time with your companions and other gentlemen is enjoyable to you; however, I rejoice at your well-being and sorrow at my own misfortune, living as I do most of the time in pain and worry.'[44] Even love affairs that (so far as we can tell) were going well tend to be narrated in terms of longing and torment.

Camilla Pisana, one of Filippo Strozzi's mistresses, had much blunter complaints to make in a letter to Strozzi's brother-in-law: Strozzi, she lamented, expected her to sleep with his friends, and had made her an 'object of public contempt'.[45] While Veronica Franco was at one point wealthy enough to break sumptuary laws, by her mid thirties she was suffering significant financial problems and a poetic attack on her suggested that even if she were to pawn all her furniture in the ghetto she would still be too poor to take the ferryboat.[46] Indeed, she went on to write very critically about the realities of a courtesan's life; in a letter first published in 1580, she was keen to persuade a mother not to make her daughter a courtesan:

> Supposing fortune were to be favourable and benevolent to you in everything, this kind of life always results in misery. It leads to such wretchedness, going against the grain of human feeling, forcing both body and mind to such servitude that it is frightening only to think of it. To give oneself as prey to so many men, with the risk of being stripped, robbed or killed, that in one single day everything you have acquired over so much time may be taken from you, with so many other perils of injuries and horrible contagious disease; to drink with another's mouth, sleep with another's eyes, move according to another's desires, always running the clear risk of shipwreck of one's faculties and life, what could be a greater misery?[47]

Aretino's dialogues, on the other hand, suggest that there may have been some more space for women's agency, however limited. The possible readings of the *Sei Giornate* are varied: the text is at once a misogynistic attack on women's greed and immorality, a cheerfully bawdy erotic satire, and an entertaining account of what women must do to get by. Through various scams, for example, Nanna convinces her clients that she is in desperate need of new and better-quality furniture. In one episode she sells all her furnishings to a Jew – and persuades her admirers to replace them.[48] In another she pretends to have decided to lead a moral life: 'The first thing I did was take down the hangings in my room; then I took out the bed and table, donned a skimpy gray woolen dress, removed my necklaces, rings, headdresses, and all other finery.' Having pretended to get religion and then to be talked out of it, Nanna extracts a fully furnished house from her grateful clients.[49] Aretino's work parodied more serious texts of the period such as Pietro Bembo's *Gli Asolani* (a dialogue on love) and Castiglione's *Book of the Courtier*. Like any satire, however, it had a serious political undertone too. After all, Nanna observed, some people 'urge me to set her [Nanna's daughter Pippa] up right off as a courtesan. "This world is rotten anyway," they say, "and even if it becomes a proper one, by making her a courtesan you'll also be making her a lady."'[50] With considerable pragmatism, she advises Pippa: 'But above all study deceit and flattery [...] for these are the embroideries that adorn the gown of the woman who knows how to get by.'[51] There is a clear echo there of *The Prince* and indeed of the wider discussions of the need for compromise and practical solutions in diplomacy, focused on one's own interest, that characterise these middle years of the Italian Wars.[52] Nanna had other practical advice too: to impress a man Pippa should encourage him to speak of his military exploits, whether at the Siege of Florence or the Sack of Rome.[53]

For all that courtesan culture – and that of its less elevated cousins – was widely tolerated in Rome and Venice, when wartime atrocities did break out, they were sometimes seen as just deserts for decadence. That was the case in the Sack of Rome that took place in 1527, a turning point in the wars and – as many would have it – the moment of rupture between Renaissance Rome and the Counter-Reformation city it became.[54]

Chapter Eighteen

The Sack of Rome

After the Battle of Pavia in 1525, Pope Clement VII had begun to be seriously concerned about the rise of imperial power on the Italian peninsula. No longer was he maintaining a balance between two great European rulers: with Francis an imperial prisoner, Charles V had the upper hand. In response, Clement allied himself with Venice and on 22 May 1526 the League of Cognac – consisting of the Papacy, Venice, France, Florence and Milan – was formed in an effort to stop Charles' further progress.

The League was a pragmatic and ultimately fragile alliance. Given that Clement was a Medici, it was perhaps unsurprising that Florence, with its pro-Medici ruling council, would support the League. The army of the League, however, was mainly Venetian and its commander was Francesco Maria della Rovere – an old opponent of the Medici who had benefited from the death of Lorenzo de' Medici to regain his family's duchy of Urbino. Moreover, siding too firmly with one of the European rulers was a gamble, particularly for the pope, alienating as it did old Roman families that had traditionally supported the Empire. Among them were the Colonna (relatives of Vittoria), who in September 1526 led a rebellion in Rome against the pope. Though the rising was put down, it was at the price of Clement offering up hostages from among his own Medici in-laws, including the Strozzi (which did not endear him to them in the longer term, a risky strategy when the Medici still lacked an adult male heir). Moreover, Clement opted not to pardon the Colonna for the uprising, which further roused resentment in Rome. The League was therefore vulnerable to division, and in fact Clement himself came to a bilateral truce with Charles de Lannoy, viceroy of Naples in March 1527, to the frustration of his supposed allies. But it quickly transpired that the viceroy's promises could not be relied upon. In April 1527, as imperial troops advanced south, their commander Charles de Bourbon (who had been a prominent figure at the Battle of Pavia) made a point of allying both with the Colonna and – well aware of Clement's concern for his home city – with exiled Florentine rivals of the Medici. For all the concerns about his loyalty, della Rovere did help suppress a brief uprising in Florence on 26 April, known as the Friday rebellion.[1] But having been thwarted in their effort to seize Florence, imperial troops now continued their march towards Rome. Abandoning heavy equipment to increase their pace, it was barely a week before they reached the outskirts of the city.

The Sack of Rome of 1527 was remembered by many present as God's vengeance on a corrupt city and failing papacy. On the night before, 5 May, 'the Capitoline bell rang all night and all through the day calling the Romans to arms'; the Romans promised 'just like the sons of Mars' to defend the city.[2] Late that evening, to the north of Rome, Charles, duke of Bourbon, stood to address his troops. An account of his speech was given by Luigi Guicciardini, a Florentine politician, in his history of the sack. This should not be read as literal eyewitness testimony but rather as a means of conveying moral lessons for his readers. 'My dearest lords and fellow soldiers,' Guicciardini's Bourbon began, 'if I didn't have proof through long experience of your courage and strength, and if I didn't know how easily Rome can be taken, I would address you differently right now.' He spoke of their suffering and hunger and of the impossibility of turning back, but also of the weakness of the opposition inside the city: only three thousand men, 'mere recruits at that, and unaccustomed to wounds and death.' He was well aware of the ultimate attraction of Rome: its 'inestimable wealth of gold and silver'. There were no 'just and virtuous men' in the city. 'Nowadays,' he told his troops, 'they are immersed in lustful and effeminate pastimes, and totally committed to amassing silver and gold with fraud, pillage, and cruelty, under the banner of Christian piety.' He had other promises too:

Among the Spaniards in this army are some who have seen a New World, which is already entirely obedient to our invincible Majesty, Caesar. Once Rome is taken, as I hope she will be, only a little remains to complete his conquest of the Western Hemisphere. And when I begin to imagine this in future, I seem to see all of you shining in golden armour, all lords and princes of conquered lands that you have received in gift from our most liberal emperor. For of this universal triumph and of the imminent conquest of Rome, our infallible prophet, Martin Luther, has spoken many times.[3]

Imperial conquest, dominance of the West, and religious reform: in these few lines, Bourbon (or Guicciardini's version of him, at least) captured something of the moment. A cynical appeal? Perhaps. Bourbon had ample reason to resent Francis I and his allies. He had formerly been in French service, a contributor to the victory at Marignano, but Francis, wary of Bourbon's power, had subsequently evicted him from the governorship of Milan, attempted to confiscate Bourbon land and – after Bourbon allied with England and the Empire to retrieve it and partition France – had him declared a traitor. Pavia (where Bourbon had been among the imperial commanders) must have seemed delicious revenge. Bourbon would have had more prosaic reasons for a rousing speech too: his troops had not been paid. Four hundred thousand ducats were outstanding: a small fortune, which from the commanders' point of view was most easily secured by allowing a sack.[4]

On 6 May, mutinous imperial troops stormed and looted the city. Bourbon, however, did not live to see what happened: he was shot and killed in the fighting. Clement VII fled along the secret corridor from the Vatican to the Castel Sant'Angelo, his fortress on the Tiber, where he holed up under siege with home comforts including a steam bath and a well in the courtyard for water supplies. He would not easily be starved out, and besides, the imprisonment of the pope was bound to be an embarrassment for the emperor, albeit a convenient one. (It was also, as it turned out, a momentous problem for the king of England. A few months earlier, Henry VIII had begun the inquiries that would lead to his decision to set aside his wife Katherine of Aragon, Charles' aunt. As the sack played out in Rome, Henry's chief minister, Cardinal Wolsey, was holding secret hearings into the validity of the royal marriage. News of the sack and of the pope's imprisonment brought that to a crashing halt.)

Isabella d'Este, marchioness of Mantua, who was visiting Rome, opened up her palazzo to those fleeing the chaos. She was relatively protected from it herself because the youngest of her three sons, Ferrante Gonzaga, was an imperial commander, and although the Este had not always been friendly to Charles V, on this occasion they could be grateful for Don Ferrante's imperial service (he had gone to Charles' court as a child, a 'hostage' for the conduct of his brother Federico and as was typical in that scenario he had been well treated and brought up with the royal children.) The Dutch cardinal Willem van Enckevoirt also offered sanctuary, but though he paid a ransom to the attackers, that did not entirely prevent looting.[5] Spanish cardinals were left alone for a while, but soon they too were forced to pay up.[6] The Florentine politician Luigi Guicciardini, goldsmith Benvenuto Cellini and young Dutch seminarian Cornelius de Fine looked on, and later wrote their recollections. Cellini's account is especially swash-buckling: taking charge of the artillery at the Castel Sant'Angelo, he personally 'slaughtered a great number of the enemy', claiming at one point to have so precisely aimed his falconet (a type of light cannon) at a Spanish soldier that the ball hit the man's sword and 'cut him in two'. On another occasion, by shooting five guns at once, he 'killed more than thirty men at one go', and was further responsible for the death of the prince of Orange.[7] Even the notorious exag-gerator Cellini, however, could not write a version of the sack in which his heroics saved the city, and others give a far less blithe account of events. German landsknechts scrawled 'Luther' on the frescoes of the papal palace. The looters began by seizing what they could – gold, silver, any valuables they could lay their hands on – but once that was done, amid the lawlessness they switched to hostage-taking, using torture to extract promises of ransom. 'Some,' Cornelius de Fine wrote, 'were being hung by their testicles, others tortured by fire under their feet, and still others suffered various other tor-ments.'[8]

Cornelius, a young man well connected in curia circles, had first travelled to Rome in 1511 when he was a student at the University of Leuven. He witnessed the sack and described it in his *Ephemerides Historicae*. He blamed the papal court and in his history wrote critically about Clement's financial policy and his apparently arbitrary demands for taxes. The war had certainly entailed high costs for the papacy and – if Cornelius is to be believed – had alienated both laymen and clerics. In his view, there was only one person to blame for the sack, and that was the pope. In contrast, Marcello Alberini, a member of the local aristocracy, blamed the inadequate military preparation of the locals. Cornelius disagreed, pointing to their efforts in fortifying the city and to their bravery in defending it.[9] Erasmus of Rotterdam observed that the attack went beyond a local atrocity, because Rome was 'not only the fortress of the Christian religion and the kindly mother of literary talent, but the tranquil home of the Muses, and indeed the common mother of all peoples'.[10] Several authors close to Clement, among them the Guicciardini brothers Francesco and Luigi and the reformer Gian Matteo Giberti, pointed the finger at Francesco Maria della Rovere, the duke of Urbino. After all, he had been an opponent of the Medici in the tussle for that city and on that basis alone was hardly trustworthy. (Though it was, perhaps, Clement's fault for trusting him in the first place.) On the other hand, della Rovere was technically in Venetian service, which meant he was to follow Venetian orders: historians have disagreed on how far this excuses his failure to prevent Bourbon's army from reaching Rome.[11] After the limited success of the Colonna rebellion the previous year, many citizens of Rome were complacent about the possibility of a sack, or relaxed about the impact should imperial troops arrive: having the emperor in charge might prove a refreshing change from the pope. Central assistance with the provision of defences was lacklustre. Many of the more capable soldiers had taken posts in the private service of wealthy families and some cardinals had over a hundred guards at their palaces.[12]

The worst of the sack, inevitably, fell on the those with neither international leverage nor cash to pay private security. One notary in Rome, who with his wife Maria had been imprisoned by Spanish soldiers, had to pay a ransom of a hundred ducats to secure his freedom: this was more than double the annual pay of a typical skilled worker. He lost everything he owned, and subsequently left Rome, travelling first the twenty miles east to Tivoli and then to Palestrina, only to face further tragedy when the town was hit by plague and Maria died.[13] Elijah Levita, a Jewish author, wrote that 'it was a time of great distress, for there was no covering in the frost, no bread or fuel in the house, my wife was nursing her young ones and was about to be confined.' Thieves had, moreover, stolen all his books.[14] Leo Africanus seems to have left Rome immediately after the sack and five years later was apparently living in Tunis; we do not know the extent to which he suffered from the fighting.[15] Moreover, while soldiers temporarily gained from their looting, they remained vulnerable to the subsequent shortages of bread and wine in Rome. They had already endured a forced march south; a month after the sack, commanders were seriously concerned about the prospect of death from hunger and disease. Plague had been a persistent issue in Rome: thousands of people had abandoned the city since it had struck in 1522, and instances continued. The price of bread was soaring and money was urgently needed. Those Roman families who had contrived to hold on to their wealth amid the chaos found considerable profit in lending to their less fortunate counterparts.[16] Amid it all, however, there were occasional moments of conscience: stories that echo those told about the sack of Prato fifteen years before. Concerned for the welfare of his soul, Antonio de Zamora, a Spanish bishop, handed back a brocade vestment and silverware that had been stolen by soldiers to the canons of St Peter's; an imperial soldier who stole a Netherlandish triptych from the chapel of the papal apartments later repented and donated it to the Augustinians in Cagliari (Sardinia), where it remains to this day.[17]

After a month's siege, Clement VII settled with the Spanish, but the price was his effective house arrest in the Castel Sant'Angelo, where he remained until December 1527. He had already made provisions for exile, choosing as his base the hilltop city of Orvieto about seventy-five miles north of Rome. Perched atop high cliffs, and only accessible by a steep and winding track, Orvieto was highly defensible, and Clement asked local officials to ensure it was prepared with fortifications and artillery, despite the fact that the papacy was in no situation to guarantee funds. The best-known element of the Orvieto defences – though still incomplete at this point – was the *Pozzo di San Patrizio* (St Patrick's Well), an engineering masterpiece designed by Antonio Sangallo the Younger. The well, which is forty-three feet in diameter, had a double helix passageway built into its walls, allowing pack-mules to descend to collect water and ascend again without passing one another en route.[18] Military innovation in architecture was by no means restricted to the *trace italienne*.

In Rome the situation remained perilous as conditions in the city itself deteriorated badly. There was no effective government, and serious shortages of food and water; as feared, plague hit the city within weeks. The landsknechts ran their own campaign to force the pope to come up with their pay, at one point parading hostages in chains and threatening to hang them.[19] Clement sold off church property, mortgaged every asset he could, and eventually secured a loan, at an interest rate of 25 per cent, from the Grimaldi bank in Genoa and a Catalonian merchant (incidentally just the sort of people to be benefiting at this time from New World wealth). Despite effectively bankrupting the papacy, the pope still did not raise enough to pay the full 400,000 ducat ransom to which he had agreed.[20] The precise details of Clement's escape/departure from Rome were left murky at the time, a piece of diplomacy that allowed everyone involved to save face, and the emperor to avoid the ongoing impression that his troops were detaining the vicar of Christ (not a good look, given his claim to be Holy and Roman). However, it does seem that the 'escape' was sufficiently well organised that advance notice of the pope's arrival could be sent to Orvieto, where conditions for the papal court were hardly luxurious. The tiny town struggled to accommodate the curia numbers, and visiting diplomats were caustic about the poor furnishings and shortages, not to mention the 'riff-raff' surrounding the pope.[21] At least they might console themselves with the dramatic frescoes of Luca Signorelli in the cathedral's San Brizio Chapel: painted at the turn of the century, they showed the events of the Apocalypse, beginning with the preaching of the Antichrist and ending with a Last Judgment that inspired Michelangelo.[22]

Clement was no doubt in need of consolation, for rivals of the Medici in Florence had taken the opportunity afforded by the Sack of Rome to seize power for themselves. They took advantage of dissension within the Medici family (not least Clement's treatment of his cousin Clarice's husband Filippo Strozzi, who had been left as a hostage in the aftermath of the 1526 Colonna sack of Rome). They expelled Clement's 16-year-old nephew Ippolito, who had been slated to take over as the family's chief representative once he came of age. Ippolito fled along with his cousin Alessandro (who had been living outside Florence at the family villa in Poggio a Caiano). Alessandro's half-sister Catherine de' Medici, at eight years old, remained in Florence, an effective hostage of her family's opponents.

★

There is no doubt that the events of May 1527 were a profound psychological shock, but by April 1528, matters were looking more positive for the pope and his allies in the League of Cognac. A Franco-Genoese naval force wiped out the Spanish at the battle of Capo d'Orso or Amalfi, the commander Filippino Doria firing his guns at point-blank range. The engagement, however, left high casualties on the French side too, with perhaps five hundred Franco-Genoese soldiers killed to seven hundred Spanish. (Precise casualty numbers among the enslaved oarsmen were not recorded, an indication of their status among the crew.[23]) Moreover, the League failed to capitalise on the victory and any hope that the political situation might swing back was dashed when later in the summer the Spanish routed the French at Naples. So far as the land war was concerned, the cost came as much from illness as from fighting, though it may have been exacerbated by the decision of the French commander to try to divert the city's water supply, an intervention that created the sort of marshy environment that we now know (though he did not) suits disease-bearing insects. In any case something resembling typhus and dysentery tore through the camp, to the point that accusations began to fly that the Spanish had poisoned the water, and not only the Spanish but their Moors and Jews in particular.[24] The commander himself – Odet de Foix, viscount of Lautrec – succumbed on 15 August, which left the army to straggle home.

Clement, meanwhile, had judged it safe enough to relocate from Orvieto to the more commodious spa town of Viterbo, where he arrived in June 1528, but he returned to Rome that autumn. Any hopes he might have had of further succour from the French vanished in the spring of 1529, when Francis began to cavil at the cost of the conflict and sent only a small force to Italy. Andrea Doria of Genoa, whose naval contract with the French was coming to an end, switched sides and opted for imperial service instead; thus protected by Doria's galleys from Ottoman attack Charles himself decided to travel to Italy for his formal imperial coronation.[25]

First, however, he had to make peace, and he did so with two treaties. The Treaty of Barcelona was concluded by pope and emperor on 16 July 1529, with considerable benefits to Charles on the financial front. Clement played a poor hand well, though, and ever conscious of his family interests extracted a promise of Charles' support in restoring the Medici to Florence. Charles – sincere in his piety – was embarrassed by the Sack of Rome and despite clearly being the stronger player had to be cautious not to force too many visible concessions from the pope. His mind, moreover, was concentrated by the prospect of an Ottoman invasion on the Empire's eastern front.

Charles' deal with Francis took more careful diplomacy – indeed so much care was required that the whole business had to be entrusted to women.[26] Known as the 'Ladies' Peace', the Treaty of Cambrai was negotiated by Francis' mother Louise of Savoy and Charles' aunt Margaret of Austria who were, arguably, less constrained by such tedious masculine notions as honour in settling the younger men's affairs (the men, in contrast, might feel bound to resort to combat). Moreover, their involvement allowed the principals a degree of 'deniability' should the women have to make awkward concessions. Francis could claim that he had not agreed to his mother's terms and – in the words of the French proverb – 'throw the cat at her legs', that is, put the blame on her. He had, in fact, done precisely this in order to repudiate the terms of his 1526 release from captivity, and Charles was quite aware of the possibility he might do so again, commenting in March 1529 that 'women's wishes are not at all to be trusted'. But in any case, with Henry VIII out of contention as a potential neutral arbitrator in light of his divorce proceedings, there was really no alternative.

In fact, the ladies were very well qualified. Both Margaret of Austria and Louise of Savoy had substantial prior experience in government and diplomacy. Following the death of her brother Philip the Fair in 1506, Margaret had taken a substantial role in caring for his children, including her nephew Charles, the future emperor. Praised by Giovio for her 'moderation, temperance, equanimity and prudence',[27] she had acted as regent in the Low Countries for Charles during his minority, and later, during his extended absences in Spain, had been involved in arranging the League of Cambrai (1508) and had intervened in Charles' marriage negotiations (1515). She had held meetings with Cardinal Wolsey not only during the negotiations for the League of Cambrai, but again in 1513, 1520 and 1521 and had played an active part in Charles' campaign to be elected Holy Roman Emperor. In 1525, it was proposed that she might take charge of the 9-year-old Princess Mary of England, who was at the time engaged to Charles V. In a report of 1525, the Venetian diplomat Gasparo Contarini described her as a 'wise woman'. Louise of Savoy had likewise served as regent and numerous reports testify to her involvement in diplomatic business. A Venetian ambassador to France noted that she was 'a most wise lady, and the king her son has great reverence towards her.'[28] Giovio admired her 'steadfastness, courage, enthusiasm, and discernment of a manly and unbroken spirit' in the aftermath of Francis' capture.[29] Others took a different view: a nuncio of the duke of Bourbon apparently sought to dissuade the widowed Queen Eleanor of Portugal from marrying Francis not only because he had the French pox but because her future mother-in-law was 'an imperious woman'.[30]*

After preliminary talks between their representatives, and subsequent amendments to the draft text, Louise's proposed treaty was sufficiently well advanced to be put to Charles late in 1528. The emperor had some doubts, but by the middle of May 1529 he had provided Margaret with full negotiating powers, and the meeting between the ladies went ahead in July of that year. Though the details had been thrashed out in advance between France and the Empire, the interests of the Italian states and England also had to be taken into account, which drew out the process for almost a month. But on 5 August, with a grand ceremony at the city's cathedral, the ladies swore their oaths and the Treaty of Cambrai was finally agreed, providing for 'firm and perpetual peace between the Emperor and King'. There were pageants, garden parties and bonfires to celebrate, but the fact remained that Francis was the loser: among other concessions he had to pay a hefty ransom to Charles, to withdraw his army from Italy and discharge his mercenaries, and to concede to the emperor Milan and the Piedmontese town of Asti as well as the remaining French-held territories in Naples.[31] Charles, on the other hand, could move on to plans for his coronation.

From Charles' point of view, the temporary peace in Italy was welcome indeed. In 1529, the Emperor Süleyman made his most audacious move yet on the Holy Roman Empire's eastern front. Emboldened by his success at Mohács three years before (and with encouragement

---

* Eleanor was not deterred and married Francis, who had already secured heirs with his first wife Claude of Brittany in 1530.

from Venice), Süleyman launched a campaign in support of János
Szapolyai in Hungary, and in May that year extended his efforts with
a plan to capture Vienna. His army – numbering over a hundred
thousand troops – advanced through the Balkans. Unusually wet
weather, however, hampered their march, forcing the abandonment
of key pieces of artillery, and exacerbating illness in the ranks. Nonetheless, they captured Buda (held by German troops on behalf of King
Ferdinand) on 8 September, and then moved on towards Vienna, where
the siege began late in the month. It was not a success: the Ottoman
army struggled – quite literally – to keep its powder dry, and the city
had prepared well with plentiful food supplies as well as good artillery
and well-fortified walls. Foiled by effective fire from inside the city,
after three weeks Süleyman tried an assault, but to no avail, and the
campaign ended in defeat, the troops forced into a miserable and
deadly march home, assailed by snow, which left thousands dead.[32]
Yet for all the relief felt in the empire at the Ottoman retreat, the fact
they had reached Vienna at all was evidence that Süleyman was a rival
to be reckoned with.

Chapter Nineteen

Courtiers and the Art of Power in Italy and Beyond

The hiatus in the Italian Wars that followed the Sack of Rome provided the opportunity for Baldassare Castiglione, secretary and diplomat, to publish his *Book of the Courtier*. Castiglione had apparently not been keen to go into print but a copy had leaked from an enthusiastic Vittoria Colonna who – so Castiglione explained – had 'contrary to her promise, had a large part of it written out'.[1] The text was passed on to others in Naples, and rather than run the risk that they would pirate the work, in 1528 Castiglione opted for a print edition himself. *The Courtier*, with its tales of artful dissimulation and debates on proper conduct at court, became a best-seller across Europe, with a hundred editions by the end of the century. It was translated into Spanish in 1534, into French three years later, and into Latin, English and German in the 1560s. We know that in England Thomas Cromwell had a copy because in 1530 Edmund Bonner, a cleric and diplomat, asked if he might borrow it. Castiglione's players had sharp observations on the manners of French and Spanish courtiers. (The French 'recognise only the nobility of arms and think nothing of all the rest', while the Spanish tended to arrogance.[2]) This was an international text, formed in the international context of the Italian Wars, and indeed, amended by the author himself over time in response to changing diplomatic and political pressures.[3]

The Courtier was a kind of guide to operating at court, a story about the role of aristocratic men (mostly but not exclusively men) in advising their prince. One edition was dedicated to 'gentlewomen', which suggests they were at least part of the intended readership.[4] Castiglione's courtiers were advised to cultivate an impression of nonchalance (the closest word we have to the Italian *sprezzatura*), to conceal their skill and effort behind a facade of ease and grace. Set in 1507, the text consists of a series of conversations, held over four evenings in the ducal palace of Urbino in the aftermath of Pope Julius II's first campaign against Bologna. It features a number of real-life figures, including Pietro Bembo (correspondent of Lucrezia Borgia and future cardinal), Bernardo Dovizi (he of the saucy steam-room), Elisabetta Gonzaga, duchess of Urbino (sister of Francesco Gonzaga and sister-in-law of Isabella d'Este), and her companion Emilia Pia, not to mention Giuliano de' Medici, duke of Nemours, whose death in 1516 had caused such a headache for his family. Their discussions ranged from what made the perfect courtier, through language, literature, beauty, what to wear, how to love, tyranny, prudence, and the fabric of the universe. It is not surprising that scholars of literature and history have found so many ways to read it: one can focus on the politics, on its literary observations, on its debates about nobility, or on its commentary on the role of women in society.

The dialogue structure – a popular one in the period – makes it hard to discern where exactly Castiglione stood on many of the questions his characters debate, and the text is deliberately ambiguous, but its author had all the qualifications to know the typical viewpoints. Castiglione was born into the world of the court. His mother was distantly related to the Gonzaga family of Mantua, for whom he carried out diplomatic missions. In his twenties he moved to Urbino, where he wrote plays, poetry and letters; he had a brief role in Julius II's expedition against Venice. He was painted by Raphael in about 1515, a portrait that evokes the spirit of the ideal courtier – luxuriously but subtly dressed; at once intimately engaged with the viewer and properly reserved – which Castiglione captured in his writing.[5] This Urbino was the same beautiful city that had so long been a site of struggle between the princes of Italy; by the time The Courtier was published it was back in della Rovere hands. One theory of The Courtier argues that it is useful advice for diplomats (along the lines of other texts published in the period on the office of ambassador). Castiglione himself had gone to England on behalf of Duke Guidobaldo da Montefeltro to collect the Order of the Garter, England's highest chivalric honour, to which the duke had been appointed by Henry VII; as we have seen, Guidobaldo was not the first of his family to receive that honour, and the garter and its motto feature in the architecture of Urbino's ducal palace; these early links to England may in part account for the popularity of *The Courtier* at the court of Henry's granddaughter, Queen Elizabeth I.[6]

Traditionally, *The Courtier* was perceived as a last gasp of a dying cultural world – the elegant world of the Renaissance, where no one had anything much better to do than sit around in castles disputing the morals and mores of society. It was nostalgia, a work for a lost golden age, and it was held up in opposition to Machiavelli's *The Prince*, with its 'modern' and pragmatic attitude. More recently, however, historians have begun to take courts more seriously as seats of power. Nests of intriguing vipers they may be, but their ritual and ceremony was not mere frivolity or excess. Given the growing importance of foreign kings and emperors in Italy, navigating court politics was no matter of theory but a useful skill – indeed in some circumstances it was the only way to exercise any influence on political affairs. Civic service was a task Renaissance Italians took seriously (humanists had long debated the importance of an active life in politics as against a contemplative life). As a consequence, being a good courtier made you better able to influence your prince.[7] Of course, more republican-minded thinkers might have preferred not to advise tyrants at all, but that was where much of the office-holding class of Italy found itself after thirty-odd years of war.

Indeed, the elegance of Castiglione's court – and the demand for *sprezzatura* from its personnel – glosses over some extremely foul play in real-life Urbino. Castiglione himself was secretary to Duke Francesco Maria della Rovere, the man responsible for the brutal murder of Cardinal Alidosi among the recriminations over the 1511 rebellion in Bologna. The duke, moreover, also murdered a lover of his sister Maria and had her manservant killed for facilitating their relationship. He had one of his wife's ladies put to death for carrying messages between his son Guidobaldo and a young woman, in an incident sufficiently well known to attract the attention of Queen Marguerite of Navarre.[8] Castiglione, ever the diplomat, called Francesco Maria a 'rare, outstanding and talented ruler', but the structure of his book is such that within a few pages the reader arrives at a discussion of poorly advised princes, who 'become drunk with the power they wield',[9] and how the courtier might deal with them. The ill-fated Cardinal Alidosi, on the other hand, was made a joke of for his

persecuting ways: by the time *The Courtier* gained wide circulation it
must have read as quite a dark comedy to those in the know.[10]

In the nineteenth and early twentieth centuries historians of Renaissance Italy often assumed that the republics represented the dynamic
aspect of the peninsula's history, and wrote off the courts as tyrannical:
republican Florence was the most splendidly modern of them all;
Venice, likewise, was an innovator. There is certainly something to
be said for the particular role of mercantile patronage in artistic developments in Florence, but as we have seen throughout this book, the
idea that the republics alone were the engine of social or cultural
development makes for a very one-sided picture of Italy: 'half a Renaissance', as one scholar bluntly put it.[11]

Besides ruling their own territorial holdings, the smaller court societies of the Italian peninsula played important roles in the military
and cultural activity of this period, with the former enabling the latter.
Not for nothing does one of Castiglione's characters observe that 'the
first and true profession of the courtier must be that of arms', and
that this courtier-soldier should 'stand out from the rest as enterprising,
bold, and loyal to whomever he serves'.[12] Many of the rulers of Italy's
small states were prominent *condottieri*, military commanders who
took contracts with the larger realms. Castiglione's employer Francesco
Maria della Rovere, duke of Urbino, was captain general first for the
Papal States under Julius II, and later (after the accession of the Medici
popes and the dispute over his home state) for Venice. He was an
attractive option as a *condottiere* precisely because he could rely on
raising troops from his own lands. Francesco Gonzaga, marquis of
Mantua also served both the Venetians and the papacy, but the shifting
dynamics of these wars are illustrated by the fact that his son Ferrante,
as we have seen, went outside Italy for his contracts, entering the
service of the Holy Roman Emperor. The credit these princelings
could obtain from their landholdings enabled them to finance warfare
even if they had to wait for payment from the contracting state.[13] In
turn, their wartime incomes enabled them to support spectacular
artistic endeavours. This was a peculiar feature of the Italian economy.
In Northern Europe the cash that might have been paid to *condottieri*
remained in the hands of a far more unified nobility, and patronage
took place in a more limited range of centres, hence elsewhere there

are no simple equivalents to the city states of Urbino, Ferrara or Mantua.[14] However, some of the smallest states struggled to survive, particularly when accidents of inheritance left them without an obvious ruler. After the death of the marquis of Monferrato in 1533, its territories were incorporated into the duchy of Mantua (though Monferrato was resurrected as a duchy in 1574 when this proved convenient for the emperor). The duchy of Camerino likewise suffered from the absence of a suitable heir, and was reincorporated into the Papal States before becoming part of the duchy of Parma.

When they did thrive, though, these small courts were a vital source of patronage – and indeed offered opportunities for advancement for individual artists away from the more competitive environment that pervaded larger centres. In Ferrara, Alfonso I d'Este (husband of Lucrezia Borgia) had a *Camerino dei Baccanali* (Little Room of the Bacchanals) painted by artists including Titian and Bellini. The spectacular, brightly coloured works – now divided among galleries on both sides of the Atlantic – adapted tales from classical myth, and the small study was intended to provide a place for the duke to relax away from his duties. As we have seen, Titian was the major contributor, with three scenes; Giovanni Bellini painted a *Feast of the Gods* and Dosso Dossi (the court artist who also portrayed Alfonso d'Este with his cannon) a *Bacchanal with Vulcan*. Raphael had drafted a *Triumph of Bacchus* for the scheme too, but died before it could be executed.[15] As Vasari observed of Titian's work for the Este, 'in truth, the gifts of those who toil as a result of their brilliance have great strength when they are nurtured by the generosity of princes'.[16] The court of Mantua not only provided patronage to Giulio Romano and Pietro Aretino; its lords had done the same, earlier, for Andrea Mantegna. Titian painted Duke Francesco Maria della Rovere in 1536–8, a portrait that underlines the duke's military might, showing him in dark armour, holding a baton signifying his service to Venice, while in the background the batons of Florence and the papacy refer to his former commands and an oak branch stands in for the name of the della Rovere family.[17] Francesco Maria's son, the future Duke Guidobaldo II, owned Titian's celebrated *Venus of Urbino*.[18]

For many humanists, a position at court offered a reliable income in return for a set of duties that allowed enough spare time to pursue their literary interests. The role of secretary, which required an ability to draft letters in a style appropriate to any recipient (and when writing to a non-Italian speaker to do so in Latin) often suited their skills. Mario Equicola was one such man: perhaps an illegitimate relative of the marquis of Pescara (Vittoria Colonna's husband), after a peripatetic early career he eventually joined the court of Isabella d'Este. His major works include histories of both the Gonzaga and Este families, as well as a *De Mulieribus* (*On Women*), commissioned by Margherita Cantelmo, a close friend of Isabella. The last of these represented a youthful break from the traditions of the Roman academy in which he had been educated (and in which women were not involved), in favour of a study of a topic more germane to his employment in Mantua: the court lady. Indeed, Equicola makes a case in favour of equality between men and women that a rival author, Agostino Strozzi, commissioned by Cantelmo to write on the same topic, did not. If not quite modern feminism (his ladies are expected to be decorative and classically pro-portioned), it was quite distinctive in its acceptance of women in the political sphere, both past and present.[19] Equicola went on to act as a diplomatic agent in France for the duke of Ferrara, again a fairly typical role for an aspiring man of letters, which enabled him to make contact with literary circles in Paris; he courted several potential patrons before finally, in 1508, obtaining direct employment with Isabella d'Este, primarily as a Latin tutor and translator; for all her accomplishments, Isabella struggled with that language. Equicola proved a vocal advocate for Isabella in her rivalry with Lucrezia Borgia.[20] (The career of Lucrezia's daughter Suor Leonora d'Este, meanwhile, points to another important space for artistic endeavour: the convent. Leonora, who became an abbess at the age of just eighteen, was highly respected for her musical abilities and may have been a composer.[21])

Just as Italian *condottieri* were in international demand, so were Italian artists, writers and scholars, and *The Courtier* proved a model with particular international appeal, focused as it was on the court, a pol-itical structure common across the continent (unlike, say, the Italian republican models of government). As we saw, Castiglione's text had significant circulation abroad, not just directly through translations but by inspiring others, such as Sir Thomas Elyot's *The Book of the Governor*, published in 1531; Elyot may have received a copy of *The*

Courtier from Thomas Cromwell. Books were not the only source of Italian influence overseas. The Italians in London in the first half of the sixteenth century illustrate the range of ways this culture was transmitted. Some of them, like Bardi and Cavalcanti and their associates, were primarily there to do business. They ran a company that imported all manner of things, from weapons to textiles, as well as facilitating art commissions. With close links to the Medici (and therefore also to the papal court) they also acted sometimes as informal diplomatic representatives for that family. As well as for trade and diplomacy, English courtiers also looked to Italians for the latest art. Pietro Torrigiani, for example, sculpted Henry VII's tomb in Westminster Abbey; Giovanni da Maiano produced works for the Field of Cloth of Gold summit between the kings of England and France in 1520 as well as external decorations for Cardinal Wolsey's Hampton Court, where his terracotta roundels depicting the heads of ancient emperors survive to this day.[22]

Italian culture also spread via the university system. The University of Padua attracted numerous overseas students (Henry VIII's physician Thomas Linacre, for example, had studied there); so did other institutions, including Bologna. Thirteen of the thirty-one clerics employed in Henry's diplomatic service were educated overseas: among them was the king's Latin secretary, Pietro Vanni (often Anglicised as Peter Vannes), who came from Lucca.[23] An important *History of England* was written by Polydore Vergil, a scholar of Urbino, who came to England by way of his service to Cardinal Adriano Castellesi. Castellesi held the bishopric of Bath and Wells but (as was standard practice) rather than administer it himself he sent a deputy: this was Vergil, who brought with him to England a tradition of Renaissance historical writing.[24] Paolo Emili did much the same in France.[25] Italian military expertise was exported too. A whole series of military architects worked for the Habsburgs in their efforts to improve defences in the borderlands with the Ottoman Empire; others went to the Low Countries and to Poland.[26]

Marriage alliances between Italian noblewomen and European rulers were a further important route for cultural transmission. Italian fashions, for example, were introduced to Poland by Bona Sforza, the Milanese bride of Sigismund I the Old, king of Poland and grand duke of Lithuania (she was queen from 1518 to 1548). Bona was the only surviving child of Gian Galeazzo Sforza, the unfortunate ruler of Milan, but even as her family's fortunes in that city dwindled, she carved out a significant role for herself as a political advocate (if not always a successful one) abroad. Her daughter Catherine Jagiellon, as queen of Sweden, was likewise involved in diplomacy, attempting a rapprochement between her Lutheran husband and the Catholic Church.[27] The most celebrated Italian bride of this period was Catherine de' Medici, who in 1533 married Henri, duke of Orléans. He was the second son of Francis I, but when in 1536 Henri's elder brother died he found himself heir to the throne. Catherine became one of the most powerful women in Europe as queen and then queen mother and regent of France.

Even before that marriage, however, there was a substantial Italian presence at the French court, including (according to a 1523 list) musicians, doctors, diplomats, squires and the king's fool. Francis I even solicited details of Italian fashion from Isabella d'Este so that the ladies of his own court could keep up.[28] Following Leonardo da Vinci, several Italian artists, prominent among them Benvenuto Cellini, Rosso Fiorentino (Giovanni Battista di Jacopo) and Francesco Primaticcio, made successful careers at the court of France.

Yet while Francis might compete on the fashion front, or by importing Italian artists, he could not compete with the emperor when it came to power in Italy. In December 1529 Charles V arrived in Bologna for his coronation as Holy Roman Emperor, an event that would symbolise his triumph over Francis in the latest of the Italian Wars. One of the most important pieces of royal ceremony in the sixteenth century, it has been much pored over and much discussed, and was vital to Charles' authority.

Back in Germany Protestantism was gaining ground. In October 1529, Martin Luther, with fellow reformers Philip Melanchthon and Justus Jonas, had drawn up and presented the Articles of Schwabach, a statement of key tenets of faith; they had significant support from city councils and princes, and there was even a scheme by the Lutheran princes to recognise an alternative candidate to Charles' brother Ferdinand as 'King of the Romans' (a junior title implying emperor-designate).[29] It was in the midst of this pressure from below that Charles' coronation took place. While ceremony can easily seem frivolous – the window-dressing, frills and furbelows of power – the early modern state needed its theatre: this was a way of communicating Charles' power to the everyday watchers, not just in the location itself (though plenty of locals came to watch the show) but across Europe, thanks to multiple pamphlets and engravings like that of Nicolaus Hogenberg, whose festival book was published in The Hague in about 1532.[30*]

Imperial coronations were traditionally held in Rome, though the last emperor to be crowned there had been Frederick III, in 1452, an event of which no one involved in the 1530 equivalent can have had much recollection. Even the eldest of Italy's statesmen, Andrea Doria of Genoa, would not be born for another fourteen years. In the aftermath of the Sack of Rome, however, there were understandable anxieties about holding the ceremony in its traditional location: memories of the 1527 sack were still raw, and a large entourage of Spanish courtiers, not to mention the Imperial bodyguard, were hardly likely to be welcomed by the citizens. St Peter's, meanwhile, was half-derelict. A relatively modest coronation in Bologna, second city of the Papal States, therefore seemed a reasonable compromise on all fronts and the cathedral of San Petronio was duly decked out so as to duplicate the altars of St Peter's that normally played a role in the coronation ceremony.

In advance of the coronation there was an extended period of talks between Clement and Charles. In the Treaty of Barcelona the latter had promised to help restore the Medici to power in Florence; Charles hoped this might be done through diplomacy rather than a military offensive, but the attitudes of both Clement and the more radical republicans in Florence proved too hard-line to make this possible. Three weeks before the coronation, talks between the two sides broke down.[31] This was the fractious environment in which Clement's advisors made their preparations for the great event itself, due to be held on 24 February, which was both Charles' birthday and by happy coincidence the fifth anniversary of the imperial victory at Pavia. The complex power struggles that surrounded the coronation would find expression within the ceremony itself. Since Pope Julius II had

* Hogenberg was active in Mechelen, where Charles' aunt Margaret had presided over a lively court and where his sister Mary of Hungary and illegitimate daughter Margaret were now resident.

succeeded in asserting his power over Bologna, the city had gradually adjusted to a political regime that combined representation of the local elite families with a papal governor. To begin with, then, Clement VII's staff were careful to ensure that in the coronation ceremonies sufficient recognition was granted to the Bolognese citizens, who were given, for example, the honour of carrying the Eucharist in the papal procession. As usual at such occasions, the representatives of other states argued over precedence, and the papal master of ceremonies, Biagio Martinelli, was left to negotiate between members of the imperial and papal courts. When a Hungarian ambassador tried to claim precedence over the English, citing the order of precedence at the imperial court, Martinelli was sent by the pope to show him the decisions of earlier papal ceremonialists, which put the English first.[32] The ambassadors of Mantua and Monferrato also squabbled, the Mantuan envoy asserting his pre-eminence with reference to a precedent set at the court of the Emperor Frederick in the previous century. Martinelli insisted that in the presence of the pope, the rites of the Apostolic See were definitive, and when the French ambassador intervened on Mantua's behalf, Martinelli replied that 'as the old saying goes, when in Rome do as the Romans do'; he then described the French king as a lower-ranking layman. The ambassador was duly put in his place, and stalked off in a huff.[33]

The French might well sulk, for the coronation procession afforded high honour to Charles' allies. The marquis of Monferrato carried the sceptre: this was Bonifacio Paleologo, a distant relative of the last Christian ruler of Constantinople, with all the symbolism that connection brought. Despite his role in the League of Cognac, the duke of Urbino, Francesco Maria della Rovere, evidently now in Charles' favour, bore the sword. The German states were represented by the Count Palatine Philip, who carried the orb, while the duke of Savoy, whose territories around Turin bordered with France, brought the crown. Other participants in the procession highlighted in Hogenberg's engravings included Henry, count of Nassau (another of the German lords and Charles' chamberlain), bishops, ambassadors, and a Burgundian herald generously scattering coins to the assembled crowds. Most striking of all, however, is Hogenberg's depiction of the end of the procession, where he showed not the ceremony but a static display of imperial troops and war machines: cavalry first, then German and

Spanish infantry, with Antonio de Leyva, prince of Ascoli and captain general of the imperial forces, gesturing not towards pope and emperor but towards his cannon.

Finally, Hogenberg showed a riotous street scene (it is probably not a coincidence that the war machines stand between ordered procession and disorderly crowd). A fountain filled with red and white wine incorporated imagery of the imperial eagle watching over two lions, the wine running from their mouths to the people, who look to have been drinking for some time. The crowd is enjoying a spit-roasted ox, ceremonially stuffed with various smaller animals, and as bread is thrown to them, they gather it up and even fight over it. It is quite plausible that such fights happened. The cities of Italy had suffered badly in the years of war. Grain prices had soared and free bread probably was something one would seize. For all its ceremonial value, between the lines of Hogenberg's engraving is a darker story of conflict.

Besides the work of Hogenberg and other, more ephemeral printed pamphlets, the imperial court now became a prime source of commissions for Italian artists. Titian got an introduction to Charles through connections in Mantua (where he was working on a portrait of Duke Federico Gonzaga); he went on to paint the emperor a few years after the coronation, when Charles made a second visit to Bologna.[34] The same year, Titian was issued with a patent of nobility by Charles, becoming Knight of the Golden Spur, Count of the Lateran Palace and Count Palatine: it cited his 'extraordinary faith and respect towards us and the Holy Roman Empire' and labelled him the 'Apelles of this century' after the greatest painter of classical times.[35]

Another artist, Sebastiano del Piombo, also took full advantage of the new political climate in Italy to pursue Spanish patronage. Sebastiano had been part of Michelangelo's circle, but the pair fell out and he became a sought-after portraitist, whose subjects included Pope Clement himself, as well as the Genoese admiral Andrea Doria. Doria's portrait showed him grey-bearded in sober black, pointing down to an antique naval relief; it marked the occasion of Doria's alliance with Clement in the League of Cognac as well as hinting at ideas of a revived ancient maritime empire.[36] Another portrait shows a woman who may be Vittoria Colonna or another literary figure of the period, one hand pointing to an open book on a table covered with a Turkish carpet, the other at her bodice, her eyes turned confidently toward the viewer. Sebastiano was a technical innovator, pioneering the practice of painting on lead. His religious paintings, very much suited to Spanish taste, provided an example for later, Counter-Reformation artists (although he himself seems to have approached them opportunistically, rather than from any great personal devotion). Already in his early career his patrons had primarily been members of the Ghibelline or imperial party at the papal court, among them the Spanish diplomat Don Jerónimo de Vich. He subsequently worked for Don Gonzalo Diez, a canon of the grand cathedral at Burgos, for which he painted a Madonna. Moreover, Ferrante Gonzaga (the son of Isabella d'Este) commissioned Sebastiano to produce a *Pietà* for Francesco de los Cobos, chief minister of Charles V. Another Spanish ambassador, the count of Cifuentes, commissioned a *Christ Carrying the Cross* from Sebastiano. In short, for an ambitious artist in need of patrons the new political climate pointed to new opportunities, and perhaps new necessities.[37]

There were, however, important continuities too. What connects these multiple commissions is the world of the court so brilliantly evoked by Castiglione's book: a world where rulers competed in arts and letters and where ceremony mattered. Yet for all that Castiglione emphasised the importance of culture, he also reminded readers that the courtier's first profession was that of arms. In this world, no one was immune from the fortunes of war.

Chapter Twenty

The Empire at War

Charles' coronation over, Pope Clement VII's attention turned to Charles' commitment to return the Medici to power in Florence. It was not altogether clear to Clement that the emperor would prioritise this campaign. There was also talk about the future of Milan (where Francesco II Sforza had been installed as duke in 1521 with Charles' support, but had subsequently switched sides) and of recapturing from Charles lands disputed by the Papal States and Venice, but Clement's concerns were closer to home. The lesson of the Borgia papacy, and Cesare's campaigns, was that family territories needed to be thoroughly secured before a pope's death, and Clement had been seriously ill in the spring of 1529 – to the point that, thinking himself on his deathbed, he had made the eldest of the Medici nephews, Ippolito, a cardinal, hoping that way to secure at least the family's power in the Church. (Much to Ippolito's frustration this left the younger of the nephews, Alessandro, in line to rule Florence and their rivalry played out to murderous consequences over the next seven years.)

In Florence itself, Michelangelo had left aside his work on the Medici Chapel in San Lorenzo, as well as a new commission for a companion piece to his *David* for the new government (this *Hercules and Cacus* was eventually produced by Baccio Bandinelli). In January 1529 Michelangelo was appointed to the 'Nine of the Militia', a city committee with responsibility for improving defences. This was far from his first experience of military matters: early in the century he had worked with Machiavelli on a project to divert the Arno during the Florentine conflict with Pisa.[1] Michelangelo drew up a series of plans for earthworks at the city gates, but clashed with Niccolò Capponi, the *gonfaloniere*, over the need for fortifications on the high ground at San Miniato, key to defending the city from the south.[2] Capponi was ejected from his post in April, and Michelangelo was subsequently promoted to the role of governor general and procurator of the for- tifications and walls of Florence, developing works already in progress to designs by Antonio da Sangallo the Younger.[3]

Having spent a part of the summer in Ferrara while work went on without him, Michelangelo left Florence altogether in 1529,

> without saying a word to any of my friends and in great confusion [after someone] came out from the gate of San Niccolo where I was at the bastions and spoke in my ear that I shouldn't stay there any longer if I wanted to save my life; and he came with me to my house and dined there, and brought me horses, and never left me until I was out of Florence, showing me that it was my best course. Whether it was God or the Devil I don't know.

Looking back on the episode later in life, when the historian Giambat- tista Busini (a republican sympathiser) was interviewing eyewitnesses to the regime change, Michelangelo cited as his reason for leaving concerns about the *condottiere* Baglione Malatesta. Malatesta indeed later turned out to be a traitor, and Michelangelo's comment may be a product of hindsight, but it did not take a great deal of political nous in the autumn of 1529 to fear that the republican regime might be entering its final months.[4]

What became the last great siege of the Italian Wars began in October 1529. Florence lies in a basin either side of the River Arno, and its defenders had secured the high hill to the south, location of the church and monastery of San Miniato, newly fortified under Michelangelo's supervision. Around fifteen thousand troops defended the city, the balance shifting over the course of the siege from two- thirds mercenaries to two-thirds militiamen.[5] The elder of them must have recalled the Sack of Prato seventeen years before, and the younger recalled the tales of it. There was, moreover, still an attachment to the idea of Florence's ancient liberties that sustained the citizens through appalling hardship, an ideological commitment that neither Charles nor Clement perhaps appreciated. (Even today, the siege has an influential afterlife: an annual game of football is played to mark the anniversary of the time the besieged men went ahead with their traditional match.) What would turn out to be months of siege began with exchanges of artillery fire: those inside mounted a cannon on the top of the city bell-tower and shot out, while the Spanish concentrated their fire on the strategic location of San Miniato.[6] Inside the walls, the citizens endured shortages of food and fears that their water supply might be poisoned and of attack from the surrounding troops. For a while they managed to smuggle goods into the city, and as so often in these circumstances it was the most socially marginalised who suffered most greatly. The men inside discussed sending women and children out of the city, though there was resistance, from fear that the women might be attacked by imperial troops on their flight to safety. Eventually the decision was taken to send only 'prostitutes', for while the honour of respectable women was to be preserved, to the Florentine authorities it did not matter much whether sex workers were raped or not.

From Charles' point of view, losing was not an option. He had his own challenges to contend with in Germany, where he needed to secure support in the Imperial Diet for election of his brother Ferdinand as King of the Romans against the prospect of the Lutherans finding their own candidate. Defeat by Florence would have put a significant dent in his own authority in free imperial cities such as Augsburg, where in June 1530 they had agreed the 'Augsburg Confession', outlining the key tenets of the Lutheran faith. In the end, it was a slow squeezing of supply routes that proved decisive in the campaign for Florence. Bribes pulled away some of Florence's key mercenary commanders (perhaps vindicating Machiavelli's view that mercenaries might cause the 'ruin of Italy'); meanwhile, economic sanctions from the Papal States on merchants dealing with the republic made supply too much of a risk. When a relief force was defeated at the beginning of August 1530 the republic finally agreed to come to terms, accepting a government of Medici loyalists. Opponents of the regime were exiled, and their most prominent leader, Raffaelo Girolami, died a suspicious death in jail. Only thanks to a strong personal relationship with his patron Clement VII did Michelangelo survive reprisals against republican supporters, an outcome arguably due to Clement's personal desire to see the chapel and library at San Lorenzo finished.[7]

The following year, Alessandro de' Medici became the city's de facto lord; he was betrothed to the emperor's illegitimate daughter Margaret (later known as Margaret of Parma) and in 1532 granted the title of duke. Michelangelo chose to supervise the San Lorenzo project at a distance rather than return to the city. Despite the family rivalry that saw Duke Alessandro dead within seven years, the Medici established a stable regime, perhaps because enough of their citizens had accepted that now there was no beating the Spanish in Italy, and that some semblance of Florentine liberty under one of their own – redefined as liberty in the face of foreign domination – was better than continuing with a republic that would constantly be under threat from the predations of barbarian invaders.[8] And so far as the Habsburgs were concerned with allies now in Milan, Genoa and Florence, they could prevent a repeat of any French descent through Italy that would threaten Naples.[9]

The end of the 1520s saw a severe economic crisis in Italy, the consequence of a series of poor harvests that led the cost of basic commodities to soar. These were exacerbated – indeed sometimes caused – by 'scorched earth' policies, and by the absence of key workers to harvest and plant crops. Between 1524 and 1528 the price of grain in Rome almost tripled, from 18 *giulii* to 52 or more. Two English ambassadors, Sir Nicholas Carew and Richard Sampson, who travelled to Italy in 1529 for the emperor's coronation, described 'desolate' country around Pavia; villages reduced to only 'five or six miserable persons'. There were 'neither vines ordered and kept, nor corn sowed in all that way, nor persons to gather the grapes that groweth upon the vines, but the vines growth wild'. In Pavia itself there were 'children crying about the streets for bread, and yea dying for hunger'. When they finally met Pope Clement VII, he told them of destruction elsewhere from 'war, famine and pestilence', and the ambassadors reported that it would be 'many years' before Italy 'shall be any thing well restored, for want of people'.[10] In larger cities, including Rome itself, efforts were made to mitigate the famine through state intervention, but there was only so much that could be done in the absence of good harvests, and in Rome serious shortages recurred through 1528–33, 1538–39, 1545, 1550 and 1556–58.[11]

The shortages are hardly surprising in light of the vast sums that were diverted towards the cost of military campaigns through the period. Estimates for Charles V's army give some sense of the levels of expenditure involved. These place the cost of the Pavia campaign at 943,046 Spanish ducats, out of a total of almost 1.7 million ducats remitted to Italy between 1522 and 1528. This was hardly popular in Spain, but Charles had income from other sources too: his aunt Margaret of Austria negotiated with bankers in Antwerp to provide funding for troops. And Charles enjoyed a significant advantage over his rivals: the wealth that was coming in from the New World. In the early years of European colonisation, silver mining had become central to the exploitation of Mexico and Peru. Charles' income from taxes on silver rose sevenfold between the 1520s and 1540s, from around 39,000 ducats a year to 282,000, an income stream that provided useful security for the bank loans necessary to cover the crown's persistent budget deficit.[12] Indeed, for the next two centuries the need to finance military enterprises across Europe would be, for the Habsburgs, justification for their pursuit of this wealth.[13] It is hardly surprising that, almost fifty years behind the Spanish, the French decided it was time to get in on the colonial act. On 15 January 1541, Francis I granted Jean-François de Roberval a commission to settle 'New France': what we now know as Canada.[14]

For individual Italians, the Spanish colonies were also an opportunity. Genoese bankers – who were important financiers of the early colonial projects – had by now become a significant force in the Spanish finance system. Between 1520 and 1525 they lent Charles V a total of 312,550 ducats (outspending their German counterparts, who lent 288,071). That changed in the subsequent decade, when the Fugger and Welser bankers outspent the Genoese by some way: 2.3 million ducats to the Genoese 1.5 million in 1526–32, and 1.1 million to the Genoese 697,000 in 1533–36; nonetheless, these were hardly trivial sums.[15] The Genoese were particularly involved in the transfer of finance in and out of those Italian states now dominated by the Spanish – Naples and Milan – and by the end of the sixteenth century some of these merchants had dispensed altogether with trade in goods in favour of offering exclusively financial services.[16]

Other Italians found the New World hospitable in different ways. Luca Giraldi, a Florentine republican, most likely found his way to Lisbon after the return of the Medici to power in 1512: he was certainly there three years later, liaising with leading Florentine bankers including the Bardi and Cavalcanti. He rose, via the Madeira sugar trade and a voyage to India, to become naturalised as a Portuguese nobleman. His son went into diplomatic service and became governor of the Portuguese colony of Bahia in Brazil.[17] Another Italian, Giovanni Paoli of Brescia, was responsible for establishing the Americas' first printing press, in Tenochtitlán in Mexico.[18] Meanwhile, wealthy Europeans began to collect artefacts from the New World. At a summit meeting in Bologna in 1533, Charles V was presented with gifts from the 'New Indies' by a Dominican friar, including coverlets made from parrot feathers.[19] Images of the Americas featured at the wedding of Cosimo de' Medici to Eleonora di Toledo in 1539, and by 1545 one might spot the image of a turkey in a tapestry at the Medici court.[20] In short, the process of colonisation impinged not only directly on European finances, where expropriated wealth facilitated Spanish military projects in Europe, but also more broadly on European culture.

The rise of Spanish power in Italy was far from universally welcomed, as Eleonora's father Don Pietro di (or Pedro de) Toledo discovered when he took up his appointment as viceroy of Naples in 1532. Don Pietro, a distant relative of Spanish royalty, became responsible for a city where the memory of the French siege remained strong. Moreover, he had to manage the tense relationships with the local barons, who had rarely been enthusiastic in their allegiance to whoever happened to be overlord. But he did so with considerable dexterity, founded on a policy of 'divide and rule', and in addition ran an elegant and cultured court.

Don Pietro's major preoccupation was in fact elsewhere: the protection of Neapolitan territories from attack by the Ottomans. There were repeated incursions, not only in Puglia, the vulnerable heel of Italy (including in July 1538 a highly symbolic assault on Otranto) but on the islands of Capri and Ischia in the Bay of Naples. These were raids in which local residents were captured and enslaved, so Don Pietro oversaw a programme of coastal fortifications which, if nothing else, ensured that residents were given adequate time to hide in advance of an attack.[21]

For others, Spanish power here meant further opportunity: Genoese merchants took advantage of their existing links with Spain to establish themselves in the South, some rising to senior court and military positions in Naples or Palermo. In the second half of the sixteenth century many of them bought up titles and estates, becoming landed gentry as well as securing bishoprics and other ecclesiastical benefices.[22] On the other hand, there was considerable resentment among Neapolitans of both Spaniards and other immigrants to Naples (the city's population grew fourfold in the first half of the sixteenth century, largely a consequence of migration from the countryside, which suffered from famines and economic depression). In 1547, when the Spanish attempted to introduce the Inquisition to the city, the locals rebelled: three thousand troops were sent to put down the rising, in which two hundred and fifty rebels died, though not without 'cruelly cutting to pieces' eighteen of the Spanish.[23]

In Rome Spain's ambassadors found themselves dealing with the long legacy of the sack and wider resentment of Spanish power in Italy.[24] Italians had long regarded themselves as rather superior to their Iberian neighbours. Vincenzo Querini, who had spent three months on embassy in Spain in 1506, wrote that the Spanish were 'ugly in body, both men and women, and all full of jealousy', while his secretary thought the nation was 'rustic and discourteous'.[25] Now, however, attitudes were hardened by direct observation. As one observer of the Sack of Rome had noted: 'the Germans were bad, the Italians worse, and the Spanish worst of all'.[26] Venice was scarcely more friendly. Andrea Navagero, a Venetian ambassador in Spain from 1524 to 1528, wrote an account of his travels that was quite unfavourable to the Spanish, especially so far as their supposed piety was concerned. Far from properly converting the Moors of Granada, he claimed they had made them 'half Christians' only by force, leaving them

> so little instructed in the matters of our Faith [...] that in secret they are either Moors as before, or have no faith at all. They are very much enemies of the Spanish, by whom they are still not very well treated.

The Christians themselves, he added, were 'not very industrious' and preferred adventure in the wars or the Indies as a means of enriching themselves over the traditional work of farming.[27] As we will see, through the 1540s and 1550s the Spanish struggled to rein in a pope determined on his own course. For all their victories, they had hardly won friends.

★

266THE BEAUTY AND THE TERROR

Having established his arc of influence across Italy, Charles turned his attention to North Africa. Taking advantage of Süleyman's absence on campaign in Persia, he invaded in the summer of 1535, seizing first the fortress of La Goletta, then the city of Tunis. Leo Africanus, who seems to have left Rome immediately after the sack of 1527, may have been there when Charles' troops invaded; perhaps his writings even informed the briefings on the city of Tunis that the scholar Paolo Giovio drew up for the imperial commanders.[28] Tunis had been left largely defenceless after the Ottoman admiral Khair ad-Din Barbarossa had decided not to stand and fight, instead making his escape: the imperial army proceeded to a ferocious sack, breaking down doors and windows, killing civilians, destroying books and manuscripts in the mosques and seizing all the riches they could lay their hands on. They took the Muslim men, women and children of the city captive and sold them as slaves, forcibly separating families in the process: in all perhaps ten thousand people were enslaved.[29] Despite subsequent Spanish losses on the islands of Majorca and Minorca (where Barbarossa likewise sacked a town and seized captives), Charles framed his African conquest as a considerable victory and after wintering in Naples followed it up with a spectacular triumphal procession in Rome, after the fashion of an ancient conqueror. The Forum was tidied up so that he could better see the antiquities during his visit.[30] The emperor styled himself as a new Augustus, the peacemaker of Italy; observers might have noted that just as Augustus' peace had been achieved through force, so had been Charles'.

By now, French interests were confined to northern Italy: the descent of 1494 was a faint memory. As their rivals pulled back, Spanish power on the Italian peninsula increased, and so did Italian Hispanophobia. But it was not all good news for Charles. Once the French had decided not to pursue their claim to Naples, they were able to concentrate their efforts in one place, and in February 1536 – in the hope of retaking Milan after the death of Francesco II Sforza – they invaded Savoy and Piedmont, seizing several towns and the city of Turin. Charles responded quickly, forcing a French retreat from all but Turin by July. He then, however, stretched his troops too far when he launched an invasion of Provence. The French responded with a scorched-earth policy. Shortages of provisions and men (at one point Charles had to write to his wife Isabella, regent of Spain, asking her to send four thousand extra troops), along with effective French defences that prevented imperial troops from reaching their target, the port of Marseilles, forced a retreat.[31]

Meanwhile, in a crucial development for Mediterranean geopolitics, France and the Ottoman Empire formalised their alliance. In 1535, Francis I proposed to Süleyman a joint attack on Sicily and Sardinia. Süleyman demurred but later that year the two powers signed a treaty that ensured a harbour for the Ottoman fleet off Marseilles and French trading rights in the Ottoman Empire. Two short truces between France and the Holy Roman Empire followed in 1537, and with Charles V facing not only France's new ally in the Mediterranean but also trouble with his own Protestant princes, in 1538 Francis and Charles concluded a ten-year truce, the Truce of Nice, leaving France with the city of Turin and some surrounding territory.[32]

The Franco-Ottoman alliance had the further impact of beginning to cut out Venice as the Ottomans' principal western trading partner.[33] Venice had played only a limited role in the wars on the Italian peninsula after its defeat at Agnadello in 1509 and the consequent loss of much of its mainland territory. It had responded with a series of defensive measures, almost doubling the size of its fleet of galleys (from twenty-seven to fifty) by the end of 1536.[34] There were improvements to fortification across its territories and the establishment of a militia (and later, from 1545, the use of convict galleys).[35] That, however, was expensive, and over the course of the sixteenth century the level of taxation in Venice was effectively doubled. This was the backdrop to the Ottoman–Venetian war of 1537–40.

This war began with an Ottoman attack on the Venetian colony of Corfu, withdrawing after a few weeks.[36] Venice now threw in its lot with the papacy, which was also concerned at Süleyman's incursion, and with the Empire, forming a new Holy League against the Ottomans.[37] This did not, however, prevent significant Ottoman gains in the Aegean, where they captured from Venice the islands of Andros, Naxos, Paros and Santorini, as well as Venetian settlements on the Peloponnese. (The perennial difficulties of mercenary warfare arose again when it was alleged that the Genoese admiral Andrea Doria, who now commanded the Holy League fleet, having switched to imperial service some ten years before, was trying to cut a deal with the Ottomans to keep Chios for the Genoese.[38]) The Ottomans went on to victory against a navy commanded by Andrea Doria at the Battle of Preveza in 1538, and in the 1539 Siege of Castelnuovo (present-day Herceg Novi in Montenegro), though in the latter case not without heavy losses.

Just as military equipment and tactics had gradually changed in the land wars, so they had at sea. The design of ships was altered to allow for heavier cannon, which had to sit on a gun deck closer to the waterline than their lighter counterparts, or risk capsizing.[39] That said, modern tactics did not always function as well as one might like. Sir Roger Ascham, who like many English writers of the period enjoyed a dig at the Spanish, observed in a 1545 treatise on the virtues of archery that the Spanish defeat at Castelnuovo (translated here to 'Newcastle') had been down to over-reliance on firearms:

> Shooting [archery] is the chief thing, wherewith God suffereth the Turk to punish our naughty living withal [...] the might of their shooting is well known of the Spaniards, which at the town called Newcastle in Illirica, were quite slain up, of the Turks' arrows: when the Spaniards had no use of their guns, by reason of the rain.[40]

In October 1540 Venice concluded a treaty with the sultan, conceding two fortresses in the Peloponnese; the truce between France and the Empire, moreover, continued to hold. When in the 1540s some Italian churchmen demanded a crusade against the heretic Henry VIII (who by that point had broken with Rome in order to divorce Katherine of Aragon), the agents of the Holy Roman Emperor pointed out that there was a far more serious threat to Western Europe: the Turks.[41]

In mainland Italy the internal rivalries of the Medici family came to a head in 1537, when Alessandro de' Medici, duke of Florence, was murdered by his distant cousin Lorenzino (his old rival Ippolito having been poisoned in 1535). Lorenzino, however, did not succeed in his stated aim of ending the tyranny of the ducal regime; nor did the exiled opponents of the Medici after they were defeated with the backing of imperial troops at the Battle of Montemurlo in the summer of 1537. That victory confirmed the accession to power of Cosimo de' Medici (1519–1574), a member of the cadet branch of the family, who had succeeded Alessandro as duke. Cosimo was the son of Giovanni 'delle Bande Nere', who had been prominent at the Battle of Pavia; his other distinguished ancestors included on his mother's side Lorenzo the Magnificent and on his father's Caterina Riario Sforza. Cosimo, who went on to acquire a considerable reputation as a soldier, tried and failed to marry his cousin Alessandro's widow Margaret, illegitimate daughter of Charles V; he had to settle instead for Eleonora di Toledo, daughter of the viceroy of Naples. Their wedding was a celebration of the Medici dynasty; so too was the decorative scheme for their apartments, executed under Vasari's supervision, which survives in Florence's Palazzo Vecchio to this day.

The peace with France, meanwhile, allowed Charles V to make a grand entry into Milan, which was notable for its decorations featuring his conquests in the New World. On one triumphal arch, the emperor was shown on horseback, his mount crushing three Native Americans beneath its hooves, with a legend reading: 'Our age will be more rich and perfect / With the New World discovered and vanquished.'[42] Peace with Francis also enabled Charles to refocus on North Africa, but his attempt to capture Algiers failed despite a large naval force, when rain once again ruined the Spanish powder.

The peace did not, however, last for long. War broke out again in 1542, while Francis' sometime ally, the Ottoman Admiral Khair ad-Din Barbarossa, went on in 1544 to mount a series of incursions on the coast of Naples on his way to retirement in Constantinople, where he wrote his memoirs and died in 1546.[43] Francis, meanwhile, invaded Piedmont and in 1544 the French defeated the imperial army at the Battle of Ceresole (north-west of Turin, in the borderlands of Savoy and France). France's attention, however, was then diverted by an Anglo-imperial invasion of northern France (if Francis could ally with the Ottomans, Charles could certainly ally with the excommunicated Henry VIII, whose break with Rome was looking increasingly long-term). With much of the Italian peninsula now tied to Spanish interests, the theatre of war was shifting elsewhere.

Chapter Twenty-One

Weapons of War

Among the major developments of these wars was the rise of handguns.[1] Already important at the start of the century, the significance of guns in warfare gradually increased, with knock-on consequences for civilian life. By the end of 1530 two imperial captains general had died from gunshot wounds,[2] and the prevalence of such weapons was prompting regulations on civilian ownership. Like printing, small gunpowder weapons had come to Italy thanks to migrants from Germany: they had been invented 'in our time', wrote Pius II, who noted that no armour could withstand them.[3] Despite the trouble rain could cause, small arms had been decisive not only at the famous Battle of Pavia but earlier, too, at Cerignola and Bicocca.

Unlike heavy artillery, which in this period was manufactured by states in their own foundries, handguns were produced in large quantities by private companies. In Italy, this production happened to be concentrated heavily in one place: Gardone Val Trompia, near Brescia in the Italian Lakes area, the location both then and now of the Beretta company. The reasoning for that choice of location was straightforward and connected to environmental factors: easy access to iron mines, to water and to wood. Elsewhere in Europe, too, arms production centres boomed: Tours, Malines, Liège, Málaga and Milan all saw the benefit. It was Brescia, however (a city for the most part under Venetian rule) that stood out. Obliged to supply its overlords in Venice first, Brescia was given permission in 1542 to export a further 7,800 guns elsewhere.[4]

The first archive reference to Beretta is to be found rather earlier, however, in 1526, when Bartolomeo Beretta sold 185 gun barrels to the Venetian state for the sum of 296 ducats.[5] That means each barrel cost about a month's wages for an unskilled labourer. The barrels

Beretta supplied were for a type of gun called an arquebus. (As noted above, those who were charged with their use in battle, arquebusiers, were expected to supply their own weapon, although they received a pay premium to cover it.) The barrel alone, of course, did not make a gun: it required a lock (to light the powder) and a stock (the wooden frame) too, hence the phrase 'lock, stock and barrel'. In military contexts, the arquebus was most often fired with a matchlock. This was a mechanism that brought a long, slow-burning cord – the match – into contact with the gunpowder. For the gun to work, the match had to be kept alight, which given that the user was probably also carrying a flask full of gunpowder on his person, could be a pretty hazardous business. An alternative mechanism, known as the wheel lock, was developed around the turn of the fifteenth to the sixteenth century. This worked rather like a wind-up clock (in fact clockmakers were known for producing these locks on the side). The wheel was wound with a spanner, and when the trigger was pulled the wheel spun against a hard stone to produce a spark to light the powder, dispensing with the need for a lighted match. There was a long-running argument between historians about whether Leonardo da Vinci came up with the wheel lock design first (one appears in his 'Codex Atlanticus') or whether it was invented in Germany and Leonardo simply drew an example of a technology he had seen in use. This is unlikely ever to be settled but one plausible explanation is that Giulio Tedesco – which means Julius the German – a craftsman who worked with Leonardo in the 1490s, took the design back to southern Germany, and perhaps refined it further himself. It was certainly in Germany that the manufacture of wheel locks initially took off early in the sixteenth century. Experimental archaeology conducted in the 1980s suggested that perhaps Leonardo took the key steps in working out the 'expeditious manufacture of the lock' with Giulio, who worked for him from 1493 to 1499 at the latest.[6]

Wheel locks were often temperamental and (elite Spanish units apart) they never became a widespread substitute for matchlocks on the battlefield. They came into their own, however, because they were developed in smaller and smaller varieties: what we now would call a pistol, which could be primed and loaded in advance, then concealed beneath a cloak, pulled out and fired quickly. In short, it was the perfect weapon for all manner of skulduggery, such as the 1569 shooting of Cardinal Carlo Borromeo by a disaffected friar. In that case the cardinal was miraculously protected by his embroidered cope and survived to see the plotters put to death,[7] but unless you were a future saint these were dangerous weapons. Nonetheless, there was considerable interest in them. One of the first recorded people to buy a wheel lock gun – in 1507 – was Cardinal Ippolito d'Este, younger brother of Alfonso, the 'gunner duke' of Ferrara. Realising the risks of the new weapons, Ferrara banned wheel locks in 1522, and the Habsburgs got there even earlier, with a gun control law in 1517.[8] On the other hand, rulers, among them Henry VIII of England, also saw that these weapons had potential. In 1537, Sir Peter Mewtas, a gentleman of the king's privy chamber, was apparently sent to Italy to assassinate one of Henry's leading Catholic opponents, Cardinal Reginald Pole. His mission failed, but the weapon of choice had been a handgun.[9]

Yet while guns were winning battles – indeed, Charles V gave credit to 'the fuses of my Spanish arquebusiers' – Europeans were ambivalent about gunpowder weapons.[10] These attitudes went back beyond the handgun, to the cannon of the fourteenth century. As we have seen, Francesco Guicciardini thought artillery more diabolical than human.[11] In his life of the marquis of Pescara, Giovio lamented the loss of the cavalry's virtue, describing the new style of fighting as 'marvellous and cruel'; in a biography of Paolo Vitelli, a *condottiere* in Florentine service, he noted Vitelli's practice of plucking out the eyes of arque-busiers, and cutting off their hands, 'mainly on account of their dishonourable killing of noble knights from a distance'.[12] The poet Ariosto was one of many Italian writers who claimed that gunpowder was actually a German invention, which to readers with a knowledge of classical literature carried an association of 'barbarian'. Some said the man who developed it was an alchemist, while later Protestant writers liked to emphasise that he was a Catholic monk, one Berthold Schwarz, and the image of a crazed German alchemist monk acci-dentally producing the devil's black powder became a staple of popular culture. The English playwright Ben Jonson was only one writer to play on the figure of the friar 'who from the Divels-Arse did Guns beget'. The Germans, however, were not invariably to blame. Another theory blamed the Chinese, and it is now generally accepted that gunpowder was developed in China well before it made its way to

Europe. Other people liked to link it to the Moorish rulers of southern Spain. Of course, to European Christians both the Chinese and the Moors were infidels, and if one thought gunpowder weapons were the Devil's work then blaming the infidels for them was logical enough.[13]

Devil's work or not, Christian rulers were very happy to get their hands on this new technology, and in 1546 Niccolò Tartaglia of Brescia published a compilation of advice on the use of guns and ammunition.[14] By this time the rulers of Italy were buying guns in serious quantities for military use. That same year, Pier Luigi Farnese, son of Pope Paul III and commander of the papal armies, concluded a contract to purchase 4,000 arquebuses.[15] In 1550 the militiamen of the Florentine dominion alone (excluding Pistoia and Florence, and excluding soldiers currently in action) included 6,463 arquebusiers.[16] On 16 December 1551, Cosimo de' Medici wrote to his secretary Pier Francesco Riccio, expressing satisfaction with Battista di Chino of Brescia's agreement to provide Florence with an annual supply of nine hundred arquebuses and one hundred muskets (a larger firearm).[17] In short, by these late stages of the Italian Wars, there were very simply a lot of guns about, in production and in the hands of the militia, and they began to pose serious social problems. An indication of the scale of this growth in prevalence can be gleaned from the records of the Medici household: in 1492, the inventory of Lorenzo the Magnificent's possessions included five steel arquebuses, but the 1538/9 inventory of Duke Cosimo de' Medici's wardrobe, a couple of years after his accession to power, lists a total of ninety-one firearms, an eighteen-fold increase on the holdings of forty years before.[18] The memoirs of the artist Benvenuto Cellini, written 1558–63 but reflecting on his earlier life, are notable for the number of references to gun ownership. Cellini recalled hunting with guns in the 1530s and described gun use in Rome as early as the 1520s, when his brother Cecchino (who was there as a soldier in the service of the Medici family) and his friends got into a fight with the police in which Cecchino was shot in the leg, later dying of his injuries.[19] That said, even as guns became more readily available, knives and daggers remained the most commonly used weapons in violence across Europe. It was a similar story on the battlefield, where for a long time soldiers stuck to the old-style matchlock, which was simple to operate, and cheap.

The rise of guns prompted changes in medical practice, as surgeons tried to establish how best to treat gunshot wounds. Alessandro Benedetti had recorded in his account of Charles VIII's campaign during the first years of these Italian Wars, how he had assessed an injury to the count of Pitigliano, asking him 'whether he had fallen unconscious, or vomited, or spat out blood, and whether urine and stools were bloody'. Along with 'excellent surgeons' from Pavia and Milan, he saw off a 'quack' who promised a cure from drinking 'medicated water'.[20] Knowledge of how to treat such injuries became essential and the main surgical manual of its time, Giovanni da Vigo's *Practica copiosa in arte chirurgica*, published in 1514, featured a chapter on the treatment of gunshot wounds. It recommended cauterisation with boiling oil, followed by the application of melted butter to the wound; it should then be bandaged with a mixture of turpentine, oil of roses and egg yolks. Giovanni's method, however, left out a crucial element: the painstaking removal of all fragments of shot. During the 1536 siege of Turin, when oil for cauterisation ran short, another surgeon, Ambroise Paré, abandoned cauterisation in favour of the methodical removal of all fragments and the simple application of the turpentine mixture, in the process discovering that this older method worked better. Quite why Giovanni had abandoned fifteenth-century practice in the first place remains unclear: one suggestion is that amid battlefield chaos, cauterisation was simply quicker and easier.[21]

Gun control laws, meanwhile, were extended to much of the Italian peninsula. Duke Cosimo de' Medici banned wheel lock guns in his Tuscan territories in 1547, and there is some evidence for the enforcement of this edict. The Medici wardrobe records of the 1560s include various examples of confiscated weapons: 'One small wheel lock arquebus, which they say was found in the baggage of some Germans [...] Two big wheel lock arquebuses, which they say were left in Calcione [a village near Arezzo] by certain bandits.'[22] Yet for all that states kept banning wheel locks, they also allowed repeated exemptions. In 1551 Ferrara exempted travellers in transit at the discretion of local officials, and in 1560 allowed soldiers to carry defensive weapons (though not wheel locks) by day.[23] Furthermore, there was considerable diplomatic activity on behalf of well-connected citizens who infringed bans on firearms. When in 1540 a young French student was arrested in Florence for possession of an arquebus, Bonifacio Ferrero, Cardinal d'Ivrea, wrote from Bologna to Cosimo de' Medici asking for clemency and attesting to the young man's good character.[24] It seems that there may have been a repeat incident, because the student was re-arrested in Pisa in 1545, this time obtaining the support of Cardinal Benedetto Accolti to lobby Cosimo for his release.[25] Travellers could of course avoid such problems by obtaining permission in advance to carry weapons that were otherwise banned. In 1559, Cosimo wrote to the viceroy of Sicily requesting that the Florentine merchant Giovanni Caccini and his servants, who were travelling there, be permitted to carry wheel locks, in light of the risk of robbery by 'ill-living persons'.[26]

Moreover, the Italian princes also had an interest in facilitating arms exports. In the early part of the sixteenth century, Italian weapons and expertise played a significant role in the development of a domestic English gun industry. In 1512 one Peter Corsi, an Italian, was paid by the English Crown for 420 handguns; Henry VIII was intrigued by Venetian gunners and requested a demonstration of shooting in 1518 when the Venetian fleet lay off Southampton.[27] The Bardi and Cavalcanti company was responsible for the import of handguns and arquebuses to England in the same decade; Bardi and Cavalcanti had a close relationship to the Medici rulers of Florence, and it is at least possible that there was an element of regime patronage there too. The two surviving guns from Henry VIII's collection, now in the Royal Armouries, are dated late 1530s or early 1540s, and are both of Brescian production.

In Italy, meanwhile, German firearms seem to have been highly valued. South Germany was the earliest centre for firearms production, and the technology was transmitted to Italy by German masters before the domestic industry became established. Alessandro de' Medici, duke of Florence from 1532 to 1537, gave new German guns to the lord of Monterotondo, father of one of his courtiers, and his chief minister Cardinal Innocenzo Cibo. The timing of the latter gift suggests the gun may have come from someone in the entourage of his fiancée, Margaret of Austria (better known by her later name, Margaret of Parma), who had recently visited Florence. The gun may even have come from Margaret herself: her aunt Anna, archduchess of Austria, hunted with a firearm in the 1520s.[28]

Cellini wrote admiringly about Alessandro's armoury in his memoirs, and the luxury weapons found at court could be highly ornate, like the miniature double- and triple-barrelled pistols in the collection of Charles V. Cosimo de' Medici, Alessandro's successor, who owed his rule to Charles's patronage, had some spectacular gilded presentation guns, described in records as 'bellissimo': most beautiful. One came in 1551, from Don Diego Hurtado de Mendoza, Spanish governor of Siena.[29] The designs on weapons of this period are eye-opening. Some guns – predictably – were adorned with scenes of hunters on horseback, hounds by their sides, chasing deer across the side of the weapon. Others appealed to God's protection, with religious imagery, which was also common on armour of the day. Others still featured erotic scenes. Their elegant stocks might be made of cherrywood, inlaid with ivory, with powder flasks to match. As guns were used in hunting as well as warfare, they might be regarded as a courtly or leisurely gift as well as a strictly military one, an example being the boar-spear with two small arquebuses attached that Cosimo received from the incoming commander of the German Ducal Guard in 1566 (these novelty weapons survive in surprising numbers).[30] This distinction, however, should not be taken too far: writers in the period, including Machiavelli, regarded hunting as useful preparation for warfare, in terms of the need for hunters to understand terrain and endure long days in the saddle. The fancy inlaid guns were not, probably, Cosimo's most practical weapons, because he also had four wheel lock handguns made in the German style which he took with him when he travelled,[31] not to mention a much larger supply of guns for his courtiers and guards. Cosimo's predecessor, after all, had been assassinated and while that incident had not involved a gun, the prospect of attack probably loomed larger in Cosimo's mind than it did for most rulers.

Guns were traditionally accorded a central role in the stories of European empire-building, particularly in the New World, but it is now accepted that the picture is more complex. Guns gave advantages in European warfare, because they could pierce the armour that protected soldiers from arrow wounds, and could be used with less training than a bow. Beyond western European powers, the Russians under Ivan the Terrible had musketeers by 1550,[32] but it was mainly the Ottoman

Empire which made use of firepower. Elsewhere, Leo Africanus recorded a handgun among diplomatic gifts presented to the king of Gaoga (in central Sudan) by an early sixteenth-century Egyptian traveller;[33] later in West Africa, European traders exchanged guns for slaves: this was one part of the world where firearms did take root effectively, not least because of their usefulness for infantry in forest territory.[34] But where opponents did not typically wear armour, as was the case for the Mamluk Empire and in China, for example, and where the use of bows was a skill routinely acquired for hunting, there was simply not the same motive to switch to gunpowder.[35] Italian reports on the New World repeatedly emphasised the absence of weapons among the people they encountered. 'On one island,' wrote Allegretto Allegretti, a prominent office-holder in Siena, 'there are men who eat other men from a nearby island, and they are great enemies to each other and do not have any type of weapons.' A Venetian writer observed that, lacking iron, these 'timid' people 'use for weapons the tips of reeds on top of sticks'.[36]

Michele da Cuneo, who went with Columbus to Jamaica in search of gold, recorded how Columbus' party 'equipped the[ir] boats with shields, crossbows and bombards'.[37] Firearms, however, had a modest role in the combination of factors that enabled the Spanish conquests: quite as important was the ability of the conquistadors to build alliances with the people they encountered.[38] This was, of course, a familiar strategy to anyone who knew how the Italian Wars had run: via alliances between small forces and large to the benefit of both. In the New World context the position of the conquistadors was often analogous to that of the small Italian states such as Ferrara, who maintained their position by offering high-quality military forces and innovative technology to larger powers. The 1521 victory of Spanish troops at Tenochtitlán, for example, had depended on an alliance with Aztec tributaries and indigenous rivals including the Tlaxcalán.[39]

That was not, however, the way Europeans told themselves the story at the time. In 1580, the French writer Michel de Montaigne, a critic of the 'trickery and sleight-of-hand' used in colonisation, observed that

the lightning flashes of our cannons, the thundering of harquebuses [would have been] able to confuse the mind of Caesar himself in his day if they had surprised him when he was as ignorant of them as [the peoples of the New World] were.[40]

Montaigne was far from the first critic. Italian writers – who had no enthusiasm for the rise of Spanish power on their own peninsula – made hay with tales of Spanish cruelty in the Indies, among them Girolamo Benzoni, a Milanese historian whose *History of the New World* was published in Venice in 1565.[41] The trouble with all this disavowing of Spanish misconduct, of course, was that plenty of Italians were making money from it: Genoese bankers, Florentine merchants, individual sailors and adventurers. Machiavelli, in *The Prince*, had been an advocate of colonisation as a means to securing new territory. It was preferable to dispatching and maintaining troops, which was expensive. But in their propaganda war against the Spanish colonisers, the image of conquistadors wielding ungodly guns became another weapon in the armoury of Spain's adversaries.

Chapter Twenty-Two

The Council of Trent

From 1544 onwards, the principal theatre of war had shifted away from central Italy: to the northern borderlands with France on the one hand, and to the Mediterranean on the other. Within Rome, therefore, political attention could turn (finally, some might say) to Church reform.

Clement VII had died in 1534, and his successor Alessandro Farnese took the name Pope Paul III. Paul had obtained his promotion to the cardinalate in 1493, thanks to his sister Giulia's affair with Pope Alexander VI, a circumstance that led to his nickname 'the petticoat cardinal'. A member of an old Roman family (and the first Roman pope since the death of Martin V in 1431) Paul was a broadly welcome choice in the city. He was already sixty-six when he was elected in a conclave lasting just two days and many of the cardinals did not expect him to survive more than a few years.[1] (Guicciardini claims that the rumours of ill health were put about by Paul himself, 'with considerable skill'.[2]) In fact he enjoyed better health than his Medici contemporaries (he was slightly older than Leo and Clement, with whom he had been educated in Florence) and went on to reign for over fifteen years.

Early in his papacy Paul was confronted by the threat of Ottoman invasion when the sultan's fleet anchored briefly in the Tiber estuary, and just as the Venetians had carried out a programme of fortifications (and the dukes of Florence had built themselves a fortress outside the city) he began planning extensive works to Rome's defences. Convincing the citizens to bear the cost, however, was another matter, and with the exception of a single bastion at Porta Ardeatina the scheme was never completed.[3]

Like the Medici and Borgia popes before him, Paul had dynastic ambitions, not least to establish his son Pier Luigi Farnese in a state of his own. On his election, Paul promptly promoted two of his teenage grandsons to the cardinalate, and went on to secure the marriage of another (Ottavio Farnese) to the emperor's illegitimate daughter Margaret, recent widow of Alessandro de' Medici.[4] But while Paul was a subtler politician than Clement, he was no less ruthless. Those who got in his way quickly ended up dead (as in the case of Cardinal Ippolito de' Medici, a murky affair in which Paul at best turned a blind eye to the plot) or in the dungeons of Castel Sant'Angelo (as in the case of Cardinal Benedetto Accolti, deservedly tried for abuse of power but bailed out after a year by Charles V).

Paul was not solely concerned with family interests but also made a point of promoting serious theologians and diplomats. Pietro Bembo (whom we met as a character in *The Courtier*) and the noted scholar Jacopo Sadoleto also joined the College of Cardinals; other promotions included long-serving diplomats Jean du Bellay (of France), Gasparo Contarini (of Venice) and David Beaton (of Scotland, but in French service) as well as Nikolaus von Schönberg, a close confidant of the Emperor. Paul's appointment of two English cardinals was particularly contentious: these were the exiled Reginald Pole and the not-exiled John Fisher, who was executed shortly afterwards, his promotion having made it impossible for Henry VIII to ignore Fisher's refusal to swear the Oath of Supremacy that recognised Henry as head of the Church of England in preference to the pope. Four hundred years on in 1935, Fisher and his fellow dissident Thomas More were canonised.

The beginning of Paul's reign coincided with the rise of one of the Catholic Church's most influential institutions: the Society of Jesus. The Jesuits were not the only new religious order to be established in sixteenth-century Italy: they were preceded by lesser-known orders including the Theatines (established in 1524 under Clement VII), a small and aristocratic order that included among its members the future Pope Paul IV.[5] The Jesuits were, however, by far the most significant.

Though the order's status in the Church was controversial at first, Jesuit missionaries became vital to its expansion overseas. The order was founded by Ignatius Loyola (1491–1556), a Spanish-Basque theologian who had grown up in the aftermath of the Spanish *Reconquista* of Granada, not to mention the New World conquests. He had spent time at war, and subsequent accounts date his religious vocation to his convalescence from a serious cannonball injury to his leg acquired at a battle with the French during the war for Navarre in 1521 (which left him with a permanent limp).[6] Loyola went on to make a pilgrimage to Jerusalem, during preparations for which he drew up the key elements of the *Spiritual Exercises* that became central to Jesuit life: this set of meditations and prayers seeks to help Christians better understand God's will. However, Loyola's plans to stay in the Holy Land permanently were frustrated and he returned instead to Spain before attending university in Paris. In 1537 he and a group of companions found themselves in Venice, where they were planning a further journey to the Holy Land, but the Ottoman–Venetian war put paid to any plans to sail east. The aftermath of conflict on the Italian peninsula, however, provided plenty of opportunities for the social welfare work to which the companions were now committed. (In October 1537 they adopted the name Compañía de Jesús meaning company or Society of Jesus, which has a notable military resonance.) In this postwar environment the charitable efforts of the Jesuits quickly received praise. Among their work was service at the *Incurabili* hospital at Venice, which treated victims of syphilis, and such roles became a distinguishing feature of the order to the extent that in time novices were expected to spend a month in hospital work as part of their training.[7] They preached in cities including Venice, Ferrara, Bologna, Siena and Padua; Vittoria Colonna was among their early hosts at Ferrara, while they also acquired the goodwill of Cardinal Gasparo Contarini.[8] The Jesuits subsequently sought papal patronage, which coincided nicely with the early efforts of Paul III to promote spiritual renewal in Rome.

On 27 September 1540, Paul issued a bull establishing the order and Loyola went on to work on developing its *Constitutions*, a process that took some six years. Like the Dominicans and Franciscans, the Jesuits were a mendicant order, relying for their income on alms; they were also a 'regular' order, meaning that they followed a rule concerning the conduct of their everyday life. Unusually for a religious order Jesuits took a vow of obedience to the pope; they were exempted from episcopal authority, meaning they did not need permits to preach in a given diocese. They were granted the church of Santa Maria della Strada in Rome, and their numbers rapidly increased, reaching a thousand within fifteen years and five times that by the end of the century.[9] The year 1551 saw the foundation of the Roman College, described by its first rector as a 'grand ornament' of Rome.[10] Among their prominent recruits was Francisco Borgia, duke of Gandia and grandson of Pope Alexander VI. Also a grandson of Ferdinand the Catholic, king of Aragon, this Borgia was perhaps the most respectable of his family; joining the order after the death of his wife in 1546, he became its general in 1565.[11] As we will see, as Catholicism expanded with the European empires, Jesuit missionaries took a central role.

A small group of Italian Christians, in contrast, were moving closer to Protestantism.[12] There had long been a dissenting Italian church, which survives to this day: that of the Waldensians, who called themselves the Brothers, Poor of Christ or Poor of Lyons. The name Waldensians was given to them by opponents, and is derived from the name of their founder, a man named Vaudès, who was probably a merchant of Lyons and decided late in the twelfth century to embrace a life of poverty. As well as poverty, the early Waldensians advocated close attention to scripture and preaching: the latter was contentious because preaching was supposed to be the preserve of clerics, although they did initially gain papal authorisation. However, their preaching (including preaching by women) gradually drew them into conflict with the Church authorities. They were excommunicated early in the thirteenth century and subsequently went into hiding.

Largely a peasant movement, whose members lived in southern France and Savoy and Lombardy, they were able to operate a clandestine countryside church by means of a group of preachers who travelled throughout these territories to visit the faithful. These men lived a life of poverty and asceticism that had much in common with the Catholic mendicant orders. On the other hand, while their doctrine was by no means a straightforward precursor to Luther's thought, it had similarities with later Protestant ideas. Waldensians criticised the holding of secular offices, for example, and were sceptical of the cult of the Virgin Mary and about saints. Like Protestants they criticised the idea of Purgatory, which they said was the invention of the Antichrist (Purgatory, in which the dead spent time to purge themselves of sin, is not mentioned explicitly in the Bible). The Waldensians were subject to periodic persecutions and crusades, including one in the Alpine valleys in the late 1480s.

The rise of Protestantism, however, brought fundamental change to the Waldensian Church. They accepted Luther's ideas about the priesthood of all believers and the idea of scripture as sole authority, while rejecting the idea that salvation might be achieved through faith alone. They went on to obtain copies of Protestant books and in 1530 met reformers in Basel and Strasbourg, subsequently changing their doctrine quite radically to align it with the new thinking. They published a French vernacular Bible in 1535 at Neuchâtel. Funded by the Waldensians, it was not in their traditional language (the *langue d'oc* of southern France), and reflected the Swiss tendency within Reformation thought most commonly associated with John Calvin, a particularly austere variety of Protestantism that emphasised there was nothing people could do to win or lose salvation, since their fate was predestined. Contact with the mainstream Reformation changed Waldensian life substantially, if not quickly. Over the course of a generation, the practices that had enabled them to live secretly, such as marrying in Catholic churches, or commissioning Masses for the dead, were set aside, and by the 1560s the group was largely indistinguishable from other Protestants.

Meanwhile, through the 1530s and 1540s, Catholic reformers debated how far they might support Lutheran ideas. Like Protestants, the reform group known as the *spirituali* were interested in the centrality of Christ's sacrifice for human salvation, and in the idea that by sacrificing his son God had saved (at least some of) humankind without any further action being necessary. Their theology was grounded in reading of the Bible, and they were concerned that its message be properly preached. Justification by faith, the related idea that salvation depended on faith in God and not on an individual's good works, was a doctrine that had a perfectly proper theological basis within Catholicism, dating back to St Augustine of Hippo (AD 354–430) but Cardinal Gasparo Contarini – who along with the Spanish reformer Juan de Valdés and Cardinal Pole was one of the key *spirituali* – was anxious that those hearing of it should not suddenly assume that good works could be abandoned. In fact, there was a relatively relaxed attitude towards religious discussion and debate within elite circles, provided that it did not upset the social order. Learned men (and indeed sometimes women) could read heretical books, and discuss their content:

apart from anything else, as lords or city office-holders they had a legitimate reason to be informed about the prevailing heresies. In contrast, a local artisan caught with the same texts had no such excuse. In Mantua, the court – and specifically Cardinal Ercole Gonzaga, son of Isabella d'Este – played host in 1538 to Bernardino Ochino, a radical preacher. Indeed, the Cardinal appears to have protected Ochino when the latter decided to flee to Germany rather than answer a papal summons to Rome to justify his beliefs.[13] Ochino had also preached in Venice where in 1543 the single most important book for the evangelicals, *Il Beneficio di Giesù Christo Crocifisso* (The Benefit of Jesus Christ Crucified), was published and widely read.[14] He spent much of his later life as a religious refugee, seeking sanctuary first in England then later in Poland and Moravia.

Cardinal Gonzaga also liaised with his cousin Ercole d'Este, the duke of Ferrara (Lucrezia Borgia's son), about how to handle the request of his wife Renée of France for the attendance of a Protestant preacher at court. Renée, the daughter of Louis XII and Anne of Brittany, was attracted to the new religion. Her religious beliefs apparently crystallised after a 1540 visit by John Calvin, then an up-and-coming Strasbourg reformer; she began to shelter religious refugees and offer them financial support.[15] Her conduct, however, attracted papal censure; her husband refused to allow her contact with her children and in 1554 she was briefly imprisoned for heresy, though she was freed after she recanted. It rapidly became clear, however, that this was merely a concession to obtain her release, because from 1560, following her husband's death, Renée retired to France and lived openly as a Protestant.

Another evangelical, Pier Paolo Vergerio, bishop of Capodistria and a former papal nuncio, also found support from Cardinal Gonzaga, who protected him from the inquisitions of both Venice and Rome, allowing him to stay at a monastery near the city of Mantua and asking his agent in Rome to lobby the pope in Vergerio's favour. The pair's relationship became increasingly tense, and broke down altogether when a local priest declared that Vergerio had encouraged him to read a range of books by leading Protestant thinkers. It was one thing for the cardinal and his friends to be informed of these 'heresies', quite another for a guest to encourage the lower ranks.[16] Vergerio was subsequently tried for heresy, but he converted to

Protestantism, abandoned Italy in favour of Geneva and in the 1550s embarked on a project to create a Lutheran Church in Poland and Lithuania.[17] Gonzaga was also among the prominent supporters of Cardinal Giovanni Morone, accused of heresy under Paul III's successor.

On the other hand, there was also ample support in Italy for a more traditional papal approach and for continuity rather than change. There was no shortage of pomp and ceremony at the court of Paul III, which after all had hosted Charles V's spectacular triumphal entry following his victory at Tunis. Paul encouraged public processions, including for Carnival, and the glories of the papal city came to the fore as the Church turned towards a Counter-Reformation. Moreover, the style of the *spirituali* preachers tended to be ambiguous (for reasons of self-protection) and in fact far less bluntly challenging to the church hierarchy than, say, Savonarola had been. Unlike the Protestant preachers of the German States and Central Europe, at no point did the *spirituali* prompt listeners to direct action against the institutions of the Roman Catholic Church.[18]

The rather contradictory nature of Paul III's court is summed up in the travel account of William Thomas, a Welshman, who visited Rome in late 1547 at the start of the reign of Edward VI. In the decade after England's break with Rome, Thomas would have seen the substantial social change that followed its Dissolution of the Monasteries, though not yet any major theological shifts within the Church of England: those were about to come. Thomas wrote a detailed account of his travels that shows both the continuing criticism of papal luxury levelled by reformers of all stripes but also how Italian culture – even as viewed by someone from a hostile religious point of view – could prove attractive. Thomas himself was executed for his part in Wyatt's rebellion of 1554, a rising prompted by opposition to Queen Mary's marriage to Philip of Spain: he was, in other words, not a disinterested observer.

Of the ground contained within the walls [of the city of Rome, he wrote,] scarcely the third part is now inhabited, and that not where the beauty of Rome hath been but for the most part on the plain to the waterside and in the Vatican, because since the Bishops began to reign every man hath coveted to build as near the court as might be. Nevertheless, those streets and buildings that are there at this time are so fair that I think no city doth excel it, by reason they have had the beautifullest things of the antiquities before rehearsed to garnish their houses withal, specially the Bishop, his cardinals, prelates and other members of his church, who have all at their commandment.[19]

Thomas watched the festivities as cardinals arrived for Mass at St Peter's on Christmas Day 1547. Paul III was presiding, and Thomas rather disapproved of the luxury of the proceedings.[20] For all that the pope was committed to reform he had not abandoned the splendours of his predecessor's courts, of which Thomas' account gives a good impression.

A thorough programme of religious reform, however, could only be enacted by a council, the progress of which was both shaped and delayed by war. Councils (as we have seen) brought together an international group of church dignitaries, diplomatic representatives and expert theologians to address doctrinal debates and wider issues of church reform. There were often tensions over whether pope or council should have the final say. The most recent had been the Lateran Council of 1512–17; in the century prior to that there had been just two, plus a quickly abandoned third, and many debates about the extent of their power besides. Clement VII had – in principle at least – conceded the need for a new council but Clement was above all a political pope and his priority was the security of the Papal States and his family's rule in Florence. With Paul III's accession supporters of a council found hope, but in the first years of his papacy he struggled to make one happen. Early on, he commissioned a report on reform of the church from a committee of cardinals, including Gasparo Contarini, Gian Pietro Carafa (a future pope himself) and Reginald Pole,[21] but reform was not straightforward on either the domestic or the international stage. On the domestic front, the papal civil service feared that the generous benefits they obtained from the current system of patronage and office-holding might disappear in the face of a tough reform package.[22] These were substantial vested interests; many curialists had ties to city families and were in a position to make life extremely difficult for a reforming pope.

Paul tried for a council in 1536 – to be held either in Mantua or Vicenza – but was stymied by the opposition of the Protestant princes. Luther, who had initially supported a council, was now sceptical about the prospect, in part because of papal claims to superiority over any council decisions, in part on the theological grounds that the word of God as expressed in the Bible should be the ultimate authority.[23] A further effort was put on hold in 1538 when peace negotiations between the Empire and France for the Truce of Nice took precedence. In fact, both Charles and Francis had their own reasons for avoiding a council. Charles feared it might precipitate conflict with the Lutheran princes of the Holy Roman Empire, who in 1531 had formed the Schmalkaldic League in order to resist any attempt to force them to return to Catholicism. Facing the French on one front and the Ottomans on the other, he had no desire to add a third. Francis was concerned that if a council ruled firmly against the Lutheran princes then they would no longer be tenable military allies. The Lutherans themselves took the view that attending a council would inevitably lead to their being condemned as heretics, prompting the Catholic powers to pursue them, and were consequently refusing to participate.[24]

The council nearly opened at Trent in 1542, but was delayed when Francis I again declared war on Charles,[25] and once again the emperor could not risk alienating the Protestant princes, who were entirely capable of allying with the French against him. Despite the French king's enthusiasm for persecution of reformers in his own realm, Francis had every interest in sustaining religious division in his rival's. Only after Charles and Francis had settled their differences in 1544 with the Treaty of Crespi, and Charles had commenced a war against the Schmalkaldic League – which he went on to win with victory at the Battle of Mühlberg in 1547 – could the council begin. Even as it did, the military competition between Spain and France spilled over into a diplomatic dispute over precedence: the Spanish won for the duration of the Council, but in 1564 (twenty years is not a long time in papal diplomacy) Pope Pius IV ruled in France's favour.[26]

Thus the Council of Trent finally opened on 13 December 1545, almost thirty years on from the publication of Luther's 'Ninety-Five Theses'. Luther himself died the following year, in February 1546; Paul – now seventy-seven – did not attend. After opening arguments about precisely who should be entitled to vote, it settled on a formula for its discussions, which would focus on the reformers' doctrinal errors, rather than the reforms themselves. There were awkward questions about whether this council might challenge the pope. And the decision to begin with doctrine, rather than measures for church reform, was itself contentious: surely if the Church addressed its own problems first (Charles V's preferred approach) then it would be better placed to combat the challenges of others. The row was settled by a decision to address the two in parallel, but this displeased Paul III, which held up discussions until he was talked round.

Eventually the substantive debates got under way, addressing issues ranging from original sin to the propriety of Bible translation and the question of apostolic tradition as a source of Christ's message. Criticised for making rather little progress, the council then moved on to reform, dealing with questions of clerical education and preaching. A proposal to require bishops to preach on Sundays was grounded in an assumption that they would be present in their diocese to do so, but in an age where absentee bishops were common, this proved controversial. Moreover, the demands for reform entailed demands for money, which prompted contention throughout the council. By the summer of 1546 the members were able to move on to the complex issue of justification by faith, which they resolved with remarkable success, acknowledging the importance of faith without entirely abandoning the significance of free will. They subsequently addressed the problem of bishops holding multiple dioceses (known as pluralism), before returning to doctrine to discuss the sacraments. (The Catholic Church recognised seven sacraments, that is, rites in which God's grace was enacted in the world: baptism, confirmation, the Eucharist or Holy Communion, penance, the anointing of the sick or last rites, ordination, and marriage; Protestant reformers disputed whether these were all properly sacraments, and there was firm agreement only on baptism and communion.)

In March 1547, however, fears of plague led to a decision to move the council to Bologna. This was practical – it was within easy travelling distance and the city had the facilities to accommodate the meeting – but it was politically awkward. Charles V and Paul III had fallen out. This was in part a consequence of the deaths in 1547 of both Francis I and Henry VIII, which had left Charles as the senior ruler in Europe; on top of which he was prevailing in his war against the Protestants, and Paul worried at the prospect of an emperor so unchallenged by any other Christian prince. To Charles' fury, the pope refused financial support for his campaign against the Lutherans, and the emperor was further angered when the council voted to leave the agreed venue of Trent in favour of the second city of the Papal States. The pope, in turn, became convinced of the emperor's involvement in the murder of his son, Pier Luigi Farnese. Amid hectic diplomacy, discussions at Bologna were adjourned and in September 1549 called off entirely. More than thirty years on from Luther's initial challenge to the Church, there was still no firm decision on a response. Once again, politics had got in the way.

Chapter Twenty-Three

Art, Science and Reform

The shifting religious climate in Italy had important consequences for its art and literature. Besides the flurry of women's writing in the 1530s and 1540s, these decades saw experiments in visual art, as painters and sculptors worked out how best to accommodate changing religious attitudes. In the first few years after Luther's Theses, reformers had attacked church art in an outbreak of iconoclasm, destroying images which, they argued, were idols. It was by no means the first phase of iconoclasm in the history of Christianity: the concept first arose in eighth-century Byzantium, following the rise of Islam, which tended to be far stricter about the restrictions on worship of graven images shared by the three Abrahamic religions. The initial Protestant argument was (to a large extent) resolved not by an absolute opposition to religious images but by their removal from churches into private settings where they might legitimately be appreciated.[1]

Iconoclasm, however, had limited impact in Italy where, as we have seen, the influence of Protestantism was rather distinct from its northern counterpart. On the other hand, in the two decades before the Council of Trent, influential figures in Italian culture did debate the growing distinction between sacred and profane art. Already in the 1520s there had been criticism from reformers of the extent of classical (that is, pagan, non-Christian) elements in religious art and poetry. Members of the circle of the Veronese bishop and reformer Gian Matteo Giberti were among those who objected, as was Erasmus (though Erasmus' complaints about curial practice seemed to be based on a certain amount of misinformation). Others complained about religious art on social welfare grounds, arguing that money should be directed not to church ornament but to poor relief,[2] an argument that had considerable force in the context of wartime scarcity.

Over time – and particularly after the Council of Trent's conclusion in 1563 – the prevailing style shifted and in particular more dignified and heavenly portrayals of religious figures were preferred over sensual styles emphasising their human qualities. This is not to say that such portrayals disappeared entirely, but even when such elements remained there were compromises. Titian's 1565 Mary Magdalene, for example, while still conveying a sense of human emotion, would be more decorously covered than his bare-breasted version of 1531.[3] Though there was a long Franciscan tradition within Catholicism of stressing Christ's humanity, in the Counter-Reformation context this had become increasingly contentious. While Catholics and Protestants (a handful of radicals excepted) agreed that Christ was both God and man, preachers and artists could choose to emphasise either his divinity or his humanity. In art, for example, Christ's godly nature could be signified by the inclusion of an obvious halo (as we saw above, in works such as Leonardo's *Virgin of the Rocks* such imagery was all but abandoned). Echoes of these debates pervade the art of the mid sixteenth century: in 1543, for example, Titian portrayed Aretino (who had written a study of *The Humanity of Christ* in 1535–8) as Pontius Pilate in a painting that, like Aretino's own work, emphasised Christ's humanity. A further clue to Titian's sympathy for reformist thinking lies in the fact that he gave lodgings to a refugee from the Brescian Inquisition, Andrea di Ugoni; in 1565, after Andrea was questioned, recanted and released by the Venetian Inquisition, he returned to Titian's house.[4] Other artists whose support for reform made them vulnerable at this time included Michelangelo, who painted his *Last Judgment* between 1535 and 1541, and the poet Vittoria Colonna, who were among the group known as the *spirituali*. The Inquisition took an interest in Colonna's affairs, and began gathering evidence against her, but her death in 1547 saved her from any formal trial.[5]

Another was Bronzino (Agnolo di Cosimo), who came to prominence as court painter to Cosimo de' Medici. He engaged with a different strand of *spirituali* thought in his art – the emphasis on humanity's redemption through the sacrifice of Christ – painting an extraordinary *Christ Crucified* for a Florentine family, the Panciatichi, who would also be accused of heresy for their radical beliefs. Though of Florentine lineage, Bartolomeo Panciatichi had been born in 1507

17. The poet Laura Battiferri is portrayed here by the Florentine court artist Bronzino in the manner of Dante or Petrarch.

18. The most explicit scene of Giulio Romano's scheme for Palazzo Te shows *Olympias Seduced by Jupiter*.

BORBONE OCCISO, ROMANA IN MOENIA MILES
CAESAREVS RVIT, ET MISERANDAM DIRIPIT VRBEM. 1527.

19. This engraving
of the *Sack of Rome*
shows the death of
the commander
Charles de Bourbon
in the foreground,
while the city burns
behind him.

20. Raphael's
portrait of Baldassare
Castiglione shares
the subtle and elegant
style of its subject's
Book of the Courtier.

21. Titian's equestrian portrait of Charles V at the Battle of Mühlberg is an early portrayal of a European ruler with a handgun.

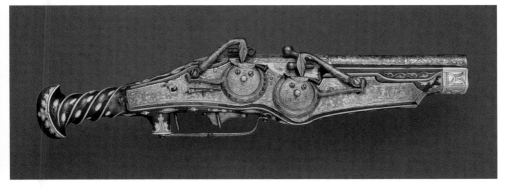

22. Designed by Peter Peck in the 1540s, this early double-barrelled wheel lock pistol features Charles' motto 'Plus Ultra' (More Beyond).

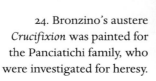

23. Michelangelo's celebrated fresco for the Sistine Chapel prompted controversy even before it was completed.

24. Bronzino's austere *Crucifixion* was painted for the Panciatichi family, who were investigated for heresy.

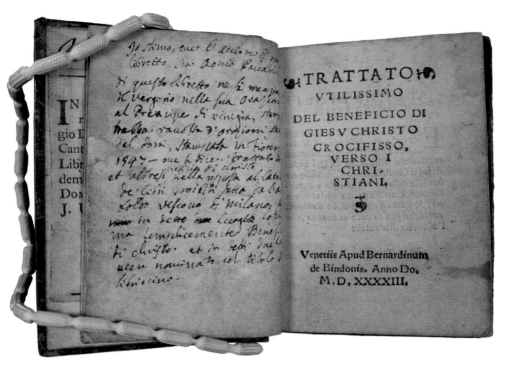

25. Published in 1543, *The Benefit of Christ Crucified* was the single most important book for the evangelicals of Italy.

26. Titian's 1543 *Ecce Homo* includes a portrait of Pietro Aretino as Pontius Pilate.

27. Sofonisba Anguissola's
remarkable painting shows
her teacher Bernardino
Campi painting a portrait
of Anguissola herself.

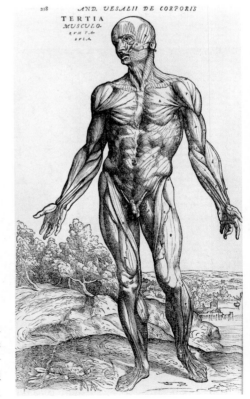

28. Jan Stefan van
Kalkar's illustrations
for Vesalius' anatomy
book were influenced
by classical statuary.

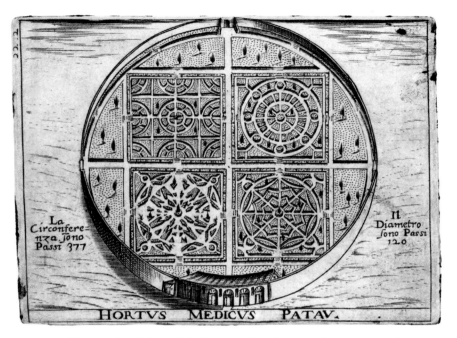

29. The circular design of the botanical garden at Padua represented
the world surrounded by an ocean.

30. Titian's portrayal of the mythological flaying of Marsyas may allude
to the real-life flaying of Marc'Antonio Bragadin after the fall of Famagusta.

31. The Christian victory at the Battle of Lepanto became a popular subject in Counter-Reformation art like this painting by Veronese.

32. Firearms, the compass and printing are celebrated alongside Columbus and Vespucci in the frontispiece to 'New Inventions of Modern Times'.

in the French city of Lyons, becoming a page to Francis I before moving to Florence in his thirties. Here he capitalised on his French connection to become an envoy to the Francis' court for Duke Cosimo I. Panciatichi knew Bronzino through the Accademia degli Umidi (later the Accademia Fiorentina), an intellectual salon for erudite citizens which they had both joined as poets. Panciatichi was in contact with religious reformers in Lyons, and corresponded with Aretino about the French translation of the latter's *Humanity of Christ*. Such connections were increasingly risky, and in 1552, as the campaign against the *spirituali* picked up, he and his wife Lucrezia were put on trial, accused of being Lutherans and owning Lutheran books. Panciatichi's elite connections, however, saved him from a public recantation. Cosimo de' Medici intervened in the trial and he and Lucrezia were acquitted.[6] The Panciatichi *Crucifixion* looked so unlike other works of the period – still, austere, only the figure of Christ on the cross against the background of a cold, grey classically inspired niche – that for a very long time it was not attributed to Bronzino: that came about only after restoration in 2005.

The idea of reflection on Christ's sacrifice – from which humanity might gain salvation – was in fact central to reform thinking. Michelangelo sent Vittoria Colonna a drawing of *Christ on the Cross*, which she hoped to share with the entourage of Cardinal Ercole Gonzaga who had an interest in spiritual reform.[7] In a sonnet Michelangelo meditated on the crucified Christ:

> The thorns and nails, the left and the right palm,
> Your face, benign, humble, and filled with pity
> Pledge that for great repentance there is mercy
> To the sad soul give hope You will redeem.[8]

Colonna's own spiritual poetry seems to have been inspired by her reading of the *Benefit of Christ Crucified*, the same evangelical text that got the Panciatichi family into so much trouble in Florence. In 1543 Rinaldo Corso, a scholar from Correggio, published a commentary on Colonna's work, which itself was quite unprecedented for a living poet, let alone a female one, and gives an indication of her significance. He linked it to the preaching of Bernardino Ochino, but in later editions this and other references to evangelical trends were cut.[9]

Moreover, in a sculpture known as the *Deposition* (or the Florentine *Pietà*), Michelangelo included alongside figures of Christ, the Virgin Mary and Mary Magdalene a self-portrait as Nicodemus, a biblical figure associated at this time with religious dissidence. In the Gospel of John, Nicodemus visits Jesus at night to hear his teachings; he subsequently tells the Sanhendrin (assembly of rabbis) that a person must be heard before he is judged, and – the scene most often depicted in art – he assists with the embalming of Jesus' body before burial. In the sixteenth century, the word 'Nicodemite' came to mean a person who concealed his religious beliefs. Sometimes it was a term of abuse, but for those who did dissent from the religious orthodoxy, secrecy might be a matter of life or death. In 1555 Michelangelo mutilated the sculpture, an episode that has prompted much speculation: one scholar has suggested it may indicate Michelangelo's concern about an association with a figure increasingly linked to Protestant sympathies.[10]

Following his departure from Florence in 1529, Michelangelo had focused on work in Rome including St Peter's. After the initial concerns about the state of the basilica which had prompted renovation plans under Julius II, there had been further work under Leo X, but after his death in 1521 progress had slowed. Sketches by Maarten van Heemskerck, an artist from the Netherlands who visited Italy between 1532 and 1536, show what appears to be an abandoned building site. The project got under way again only once Rome had recovered somewhat from the 1527 sack, and in 1538 the works were sufficiently active that a wall was built to divide the functioning part of the old basilica from the building site of the new one.[11]

During the papacy of Paul III Michelangelo also worked on designs for the Campidoglio piazza, a central element in urban renewal, suiting the pope's ambitions for Rome to be a major court centre.* Between 1536 and 1541 Michelangelo also worked on the *Last Judgment* for the Sistine Chapel. Vasari claimed that here the artist 'surpassed even himself', but others were not so sure: the elaborate fresco was the subject of a satirical poem, noting that the figure of St Catherine was

---

* Paul's interest in city redevelopment also encompassed major improvements to his family palace: this Palazzo Farnese is now the French embassy.

'naked as nature made her', while other saints were 'showing their arses to Don Paulino', a reference to Pope Paul III.[12]

Despite Michelangelo's personal absence from Florence, his artistic legacy at the San Lorenzo complex became an inspiration for numerous ducal architectural projects including the creation of new apartments at the Palazzo Vecchio (city hall) after the Medici relocated there from their private family palace. Begun in 1555 and decorated to a scheme by Giorgio Vasari, the apartments emphasise the family's dynastic history, incorporating a range of classical elements; 'pagan' art had far from disappeared in the palaces of Italy's nobility. Meanwhile, Michelangelo himself was producing overtly republican work for opponents of the Medici, including a *Brutus* for presentation to Cardinal Ridolfi, depicting the assassin of Julius Caesar: a symbol of opposition to tyranny. He presented sculptures of prisoners originally intended for Julius II's tomb (representing subjected provinces and now known as the *Slaves*) to another leader of the anti-Medici party, Filippo Strozzi.[13] (Strozzi himself joined the rebellion against Cosimo de' Medici's rule in 1537; he was imprisoned and died, famously leaving an apparent suicide note calling for Florentine liberty, in 1538.) Art was used to argue for reform in politics as much as in religion at this time.

And it was also used, of course, to debate about art itself. Bronzino produced vivid and stylish portraits of the Medici and their household, including the Duke Cosimo himself, alternately nude as Orpheus – a striking break from tradition – and more conventionally in armour; his wife Eleonora di Toledo in rich, fashionable dress (but also later in life clearly suffering from illness); and Morgante, the court dwarf, whose double-sided nude portrait shows him both before and after a hunt. These portraits, naturally, were designed to underline the grandeur of the ruling family but in the case of Morgante's portrait, Bronzino was making a contribution to a debate of the late 1540s between a group of leading artists – Michelangelo, Pontormo, Cellini and Bronzino – over the merits of painting and sculpture. Whereas in writing, Bronzino made the case for sculpture, here the double-sided nature of the portrait added a new element to the debate when it illustrated that painting, unlike sculpture, could also show the passage of time.[14]

★

The leading portraitist of these years was, however, undoubtedly Titian, whose 1543 depiction of Pope Paul III shows the pope bearded and a little stooped, but still sharp-eyed, light and shadow falling across the folds of his red velvet vestments. Titian also painted a series of portraits of Charles V and his courtiers, a number of which have a military theme. The *Allocution of Alfonso d'Avalos*, for example, painted in 1540–41, showed the commander settling a mutiny of his troops. Later in the decade, Titian went on to show the emperor on horseback, commemorating his victory against the Schmalkaldic League at the Battle of Mühlberg. Charles is shown in the garb of the Spanish light cavalry, a wheel lock firearm at his hip: it is the first portrait to show a European monarch armed with a gun. As Vasari observed, one of Titian's assets in his career was his ability to engage with patrons (rather like Raphael):

> Many princes, men of letters and gentlemen of his time who went to Venice visited him at his house, because beyond his excellence in art, he was gentlemanly, attractive, and with the most polite manners and manner. He has had rivals in Venice, but not of great talent, so that he has easily triumphed over them with excellence in art, and knowledge of how to act and be agreeable to gentlemen.[15]

Vasari, however, had not always been so favourable to the artist. His decision to include Michelangelo in the first edition of the *Lives of the Artists*, published in 1550, and not Titian (Michelangelo was the only living artist included), prompted the Venetian author Ludovico Dolce to mount a defence of his compatriot in particular and Venetian artistic style in general, which favoured what was known in Italian as *colorito* (the creation of form through colour, light and style) rather than Michelangelo's preferred *disegno* with its focus on line and drawing. In the second edition of the *Lives*, published in 1568, Vasari continued to insist on the pre-eminence of *disegno*, but added a life of Titian, in which he conceded the beauty of the artist's later works.

The 1550s also saw the start of the career for one of the first named women artists since Properzia de' Rossi to make a substantial career for herself. Sofonisba Anguissola was the daughter of a nobleman from Cremona, near Milan. Educated from the age of about fourteen

in the house of a local painter, Bernardino Campi, she was encouraged
by Michelangelo who (on Anguissola's father's account) showed her
'honourable and thoughtful affection', writing to her more than once
and praising her work.[16] Her best-known painting is her *Lucia, Minerva,
and Europa Anguissola Playing Chess* (1555), a portrait of her sisters,
significant for the laughing smile of the girl in the middle and the
wider image of domestic warmth and informality that was a novelty
in portraiture of this period.[17] She also painted a striking self-portrait
in the form of *Bernardino Campi Painting Sofonisba Anguissola* (1559). It
shows the artist's image emerging on the canvas of another painting,
perhaps a tribute to Campi, who had been her teacher, but one in
which her larger figure surpasses him.[18] In 1559 she was invited to the
court of Philip II in Madrid where she became an attendant to the
Infanta (Princess) Isabella Clara Eugenia and a lady-in-waiting to Philip's third wife, Elisabeth of Valois. Among her subjects was Alessandro
Farnese, grandson of Pope Paul III, whose portrait she painted about
1560, a sumptuous portrayal of the fifteen-year-old in a pearl-studded
cap and fur-lined cloak, one hand on the hilt of his sword.

For Vasari, writing in 1566, still relatively early in her career, Anguissola had

> laboured at the difficulties of design with greater study and better grace
> than any other woman of our time, and she has not only succeeded
> in drawing, colouring, and copying from nature, and in making excellent
> copies of works by other hands, but has also executed by herself alone
> some very choice and beautiful works of painting.[19]

She married a Sicilian, Fabrizio de Moncada, and was widowed around
1579; her second husband was Orazio Lomellino, a Genoese nobleman,
and she spent the later part of her career in Genoa. Living well into
the seventeenth century, she was able to meet the next generation of
European painters, among them Anthony van Dyck (1599–1641), whose
pen-and-ink sketch and subsequent portrait show her still lively in her
nineties.[20] Anguissola not only illustrates the importance of Spanish
patronage in Italian artistic careers, but also provides a link between
this last generation of Renaissance artists and those more usually
categorised as baroque.

*

Vasari's *Lives of the Artists*, the founding text of western art history, was just one of the literary innovations in mid-century Italy. Between 1538 and 1557 Pietro Aretino (he of the *I Modi* sonnets, also known as *The Sixteen Pleasures*) pioneered a new genre of book for the printing industry: editions of his letters. The first volume went through twelve reprints in its first two years. Aretino was infamously labelled the 'scourge of princes' but his letters – in Italian rather than the less accessible Latin – cheerfully addressed people of every rank on a whole variety of subjects. He did Michelangelo no favours when the pair fell out and Aretino decided to denounce the artist as inferior to Raphael, imply that he was improperly close to his young male friends, and hint that the religious orthodoxy of the *Last Judgement* was suspect.[21] The second of those observations, at least, was very plausible, in light of Michelangelo's passionate sonnets to Cecchino Bracchi and Tommaso Cavalieri. In one of them he played on Cavalieri's name (cavalier or knight) to suggest that he, Michelangelo, naked and alone, was prisoner of an armed (or armoured) knight.[22] The combined accusation of immorality and heresy was dangerous indeed, however, and Michelangelo responded with a highly sarcastic letter in which he pronounced it a shame that he was too late to put Aretino's suggestions for the *Last Judgment* into practice and urging the satirist not to change his mind about travelling from his home in Venice to Rome, where Michelangelo continued to be based.[23]

Aretino was also a religious writer, and in the 1540s produced (surprisingly, perhaps, to those of us who might expect a sharp contrast between the pornographer and the religious commentator) a series of saints' lives. His later works have been described as 'prudent nicodemism' (meaning that he concealed his precise religious beliefs) and while it is impossible to say what he thought about spirituality there is reason to think that like Contarini, Michelangelo and Colonna he too was sympathetic to the idea of justification by faith that had become inextricably associated with Protestantism. He corresponded not only with Colonna, but with the heretic Vergerio.[24]

And if the shifting religious context had an impact on writers, so too did the wars. It was not all to the good. The cost of warfare absorbed money that patrons might otherwise have spent on artistic endeavours. In 1548 Paolo Giovio observed to Cosimo de' Medici, duke of Florence, that 'these most turbulent times have castrated patrons, and hence crippled the right hand of authors'.[25] However, the new possibilities for marketing their work in print gave authors options outside the traditional patronage system, though it simultaneously created pressure to deliver what the purchasing public might want.[26] Those like Aretino, however, who cultivated controversy or catered to new and suspect religious tastes, did so at considerable risk.

Elsewhere in the world of knowledge, the 1540s saw a series of significant developments in science, ranging from anatomy to botany. Just as the intellectual climate between Luther and Trent was relatively hospitable to debate on reform and to women's writing, so it proved favourable to scientific investigation. A key centre here was Padua, a town close to Venice, famous for the frescoes by Giotto (c.1267–1337) in its Capella degli Scrovegni but also important for its historic university, founded in 1222, which attracted students from across Europe. In 1543, Andreas Vesalius, a professor at Padua, published the defining text of Renaissance anatomy, the *De Humani Corpis Fabrica* (On the Fabric of the Human Body). Born in Flanders, and grandson of the court physician to the Emperor Maximilian, Vesalius trained at several European universities before completing his doctorate at Padua in 1537, where he was immediately appointed professor of surgery and anatomy. Vesalius' methods paved the way for the future development of anatomy. He emphasised the importance of human dissection, through which he was able to revise many mistaken claims of the ancient physician Galen (AD c.129–c.200~216) regarding the human body, including on the structure of the skeleton and the heart. (Though Galen's work was a millennium and a half old it still dominated much medical training.) To illustrate his work Vesalius employed among others Jan Stefan van Kalkar, a student of Titian, who produced drawings inspired by classical statuary to illustrate the new scientific findings.[27]

Padua was also the site for the world's first university botanical garden, founded just two years later in 1545. Established by the Venetian authorities, its designer is unknown but Andrea Moroni, an architect from Bergamo, played a role. The development of the garden followed a growing interest in plants and, in particular, efforts to revise and correct classical works such as Pliny's *Natural History*. There was increasing emphasis on the observation of botanical specimens, in part prompted by European interest in the plants they found overseas. Maize, for example, had been imported from the New World before 1500,[28] and from 1530 onwards such plants began to be recorded in updated editions of the books known as *herbaria*, which for the first time began to incorporate not just drawings but pressed and dried samples. This was the context for the opening of the Padua garden, which with its circular design was intended to represent the world surrounded by an ocean.

Not to be outdone, the Tuscans established a botanical garden in Pisa the same year, and in 1548 members of the Medici court were presented with a crop of tomatoes from one of their country estates (though it was believed that they were harmful to eat).[29] There were gradual experiments with the new seeds and fruits, notably with maize-growing, where there was some competition between the Tuscan nobility, as well as attempts to classify the new plants. The trend for botanical gardens spread across Europe, with an example in Leiden dating from 1577.[30] Thus the plants of the New World were slowly adopted into the Old, a development that in the longer term made for dramatic changes to the European diet, to the point that it is impossible now to imagine Italian cuisine without the tomato.

There was no shortage of connections between the Italian world of arts and science and the growing European empires in the New World. Pietro Aretino's secretary, for example, travelled to Paraguay.[31] Matteo Pérez de Alesio, a pupil of Michelangelo who contributed to the frescoes of the Sistine Chapel and Villa d'Este, spent the second half of his life in Peru. There he became court painter to the Spanish viceroy, a member of the powerful Hurtado de Mendoza family.[32] Out of these connections came in the 1550s the beginning of a series of major publications on the New World, and Italian printers played a significant role in circulating them, not least because the Spanish and Portuguese authorities were keen to keep the details of their discoveries a secret, and placed restrictions on their publication.

Venetian printers had no such problem. In 1556 Francisco López de Gómara's *La Historia generale delle Indie Occidentali* (The General History of the West Indies), banned in Spain for its failure to toe the official line on the legal and theological justifications for conquest, was published in Venice. It was widely criticised even in Spain for glorifying Cortés (the author's main aim), but went through twelve editions between 1555 and 1576.[33] Giovanni Battista Ramusio, a geographer from Treviso, began the publication of his *Delle navigationi e viaggi* (On the Navigations and Voyages) in 1550 with a volume on 'Africa and the Orient'. Two further volumes – one on the New World, one on Central Asia – followed in 1556 and 1559.[34] A fourth, possibly intended to cover South America, was never published. These included about thirty plates based on information received from Gonzalo Fernández de Oviedo, the official chronicler of the Indies on behalf of the Spanish Crown. It went through multiple reprints and circulated well beyond Italy including to Northern Europe, becoming a model for subsequent travel and geographical compendia, including Richard Hakluyt's *Principal Navigations* (the second edition of which came out in three volumes from 1598 to 1600). Hakluyt followed Ramusio's model (without the images) but took a much more propagandistic line, with a clear political objective to praise English prowess in exploration.

Both Ramusio's and Hakluyt's books were surpassed – from a publication point of view if not an informational one – by the work of Theodor de Bry, a Low Countries engraver whose thirteen volumes of *Voyages*, published between 1590 and 1634, featured illustrations of numerous travel accounts collected from a range of earlier sources.[35] There were also some rather more dubious characters about the whole publishing enterprise. In 1558, Nicolò Zen (a Venetian patrician and subject of a portrait by Titian) claimed the Venetians had discovered an island called Frislanda as well as reaching the New World prior to Columbus. The veracity of his claim has long been debated, but its interest lies primarily in its Venetian patriotism and insistence that Zen's home city, and not any other Italian state, was a real source of expertise on the Americas.[36]

Given the significance of conversion to Christianity as a justification for colonisation projects, the popes were inevitably drawn into the debates. Individual explorers might dream of El Dorado, but the mission of saving souls provided the ideology that could win public support for their adventures. Across the world, the Church began to evangelise: a Franciscan province was established on Hispaniola in 1505;

the global reach of Christianity was emphasised when in 1533 Clement VII received an embassy from the king of Ethiopia (a country with an ancient Christian tradition) who pledged obedience to the pope.[37] In 1541 the first Jesuit mission, led by the future saint Francis Xavier, departed for Goa on the south-western coast of India, where the Portuguese had established a trading post. Supported by King John III of Portugal, the mission was firmly a Portuguese enterprise and there is some suggestion that Pope Paul III – who preferred to have the Jesuits working on social projects in Italy – may have been rather lukewarm. From the point of view of the missionaries, their project enjoyed considerable success: by 1556 the Jesuit College in Goa had recruited over a hundred students. This came, however, at considerable cost to the existing residents of Goa: Xavier obtained authorisation from the Portuguese Crown to impose tough restrictions on the practice of Hinduism in Goa, including a ban enforced by searches of private property for 'infidel' statues.[38] The Jesuits tried to reach China in 1552: these were the first steps in making the Catholic Church a global power, and both Francis Xavier and Ignatius Loyola were canonised in 1622. This is not to say that the Church or the missionaries simply accepted the process of empire-building. Xavier could be a harsh critic of colonial administrators and was not afraid to raise his concerns with the king. This contradiction between missionaries' conviction of their own religion's incontrovertible truth and their criticism of colonial projects lies at the heart of much imperial history.

The Church's attitude towards enslavement is a case in point. As we have seen, canon law prohibited enslavement of indigenous Americans (albeit leaving some loopholes). In 1537, Paul III intervened to reinforce this, with a bull setting out that the Amerindians should enjoy both their liberty and their property and emphasising that they were fully 'human'.[39] From the point of view of Charles V, however (who had a tense relationship with Paul), this was unwarranted interference in Spanish affairs, and Charles made his own legislation in the form of the New Laws of 1542 which banned the enslavement of indigenous people under any circumstances. These were partly suspended in the Americas but were successfully used by indigenous people in Spain to plead their freedom in court. A decade later, a watered-down version of the laws was applied but in such a way as to leave considerable space for forced labour.[40] In practice, however, many Spanish colonists ignored the rules; moreover, they were never extended to Africans, whose enslavement was even justified on the basis that it might relieve the Indians. There were occasional words of condemnation from Catholic clergy, but the general attitude is summed up by the fact that the most important Jesuit college in Africa was founded by a slave-trader.[41] In other words, the reform movements of the period cannot be separated from the wider process of colonisation and empire-building, which influenced too the world of scientific investigation and in the longer term even the everyday diet.

Chapter Twenty-Four

The Peace of Cateau-Cambrésis

It is testament to Paul III's determination that he contrived to combine effective action on religious reform with the promotion of his family, the Farnese, as hereditary aristocracy: a feat that had eluded every previous sixteenth-century pope. As a young cleric, Paul had fathered at least three children – Pier Luigi, Costanza and Ranuccio – and he had not neglected their dynastic interests since: Costanza was married to a member of the Sforza family of Milan, while Pier Luigi married Gerolama Orsini of the Roman baronial family. And as noted previously, early in his papacy Paul secured the marriage of his grandson, fourteen-year-old Ottavio, to Charles V's illegitimate daughter Margaret, widow of the assassinated ruler of Florence, Alessandro de' Medici. This was a frustration for the Medici (Alessandro's successor Cosimo had hoped to keep Margaret for himself) and for Margaret, too, who did not welcome the match and avoided consummating the marriage, resulting in a very public scandal. While satirical writers had a field day, a possible reason for Margaret's reluctance to entertain a pregnancy was that she had already miscarried during her first marriage, in 1536, when she was fourteen.[1] Continuing Clement's strategy of marrying relatives into both France and the Empire, Paul arranged for another grandson, Orazio Farnese, to wed Diane of France, an illegitimate daughter of Henri II, in 1543; having already promoted two relatives to the cardinalate following his election, he added a third, his grandson Ranuccio, in 1545.[2]

So far as the Farnese were concerned, however, the scandal around Ottavio and Margaret was the least of it. There was far worse around the conduct of his father, Pier Luigi. Born in 1503, Pier Luigi had embarked on a military career while still in his teens, fighting at Parma and Perugia in the 1520s and with imperial troops during the Sack of

Rome (when, however, he ensured his own men protected the Farnese family palace). He subsequently tried to make himself the lord of Castro, a town near Viterbo, only to be faced with excommunication by Pope Clement VII, who reasonably objected to this attempt to usurp papal territory. Pier Luigi continued in imperial military service, while also attempting to secure his own territories north of Rome. Following the election of his father to the papacy he undertook both diplomatic and military roles and in 1537 he became *gonfaloniere* of the Church (the most senior military position), and finally secured Castro for himself, becoming its duke. That same year, however, a major scandal erupted when Pier Luigi was accused of raping the 24-year-old bishop of Fano, Cosimo Gheri, who died a few days after the attack.

According to the report of Florentine historian Benedetto Varchi, a contemporary, Gheri was far from Pier Luigi's only victim: the latter had been 'going about through the lands of the Church raping any lads he liked the look of'. His father had already warned him off such behaviour two years before (when Pier Luigi had been on a diplomatic mission to the imperial court). William Thomas may have been alluding to this culture when he commented of Farnese Rome, 'And lightly there is none of them without three or four pages trimmed like young princes, for what purpose I would be loath to tell.'[3] An anonymous satirist was less coy, claiming that Pier Luigi liked to watch his pages bugger one another, and the author of a pasquinade on the Fano affair noted that Pier Luigi's reward had been promotion to captain general of the papal armies.[4] Three years on, Pier Luigi attacked another young man, who escaped only by jumping from a window.[5]

Pier Luigi was not the only prominent commander of these years to be accused of rape or domestic violence. Francesco Gonzaga's sexual interest in boys was tolerated and even encouraged by certain of his courtiers at Mantua.[6] Francesco Maria della Rovere, duke of Urbino, was responsible for both political and domestic killings. There was a great deal of impunity when it came to sexual and domestic violence during the Italian Wars – both for the commanders and, during sacks, for their men. Occasionally charges were brought: as a teenager Giovanni 'delle Bande Nere' was expelled from Florence for involvement in the rape of another teenage boy,[7] and as we will see, the nephews of Pope Paul IV were convicted of rape and murder, but in that case only after their father's successor decided a prosecution was in his interests. For all that rape might result in public scandal, especially when the victim was socially prominent, it did not necessarily have consequences for the perpetrator.

The allegations against Pier Luigi, for example, did not prevent the pope making him duke of Parma and Piacenza, which he became in 1546. Paul had already added a series of territories to his family's holdings (some but not all of which had historically been Farnese land). In addition to Castro these included the towns of Ronciglione, Bisenzio and Nepi to the north of Rome. The architect Antonio da Sangallo was hired to oversee not only the building of a papal fortress at Ancona and the Rocca Paolina in Perugia, but for work on the family properties, too. In fact, the creation of the new Parma and Piacenza duchy was achieved via the sale of papal lands to members of the Farnese family, who were obliged to pay 9,000 ducats a year back to the papacy. That in turn more or less guaranteed high taxes, and quickly roused resentment in the two cities. Local nobles took advantage of Charles V's expansionist project around Milan (which was now in Habsburg hands) and in particular of the city governor, Ferrante Gonzaga (son of Duke Francesco and Isabella d'Este), who ruled on Charles' behalf, to rouse imperial opposition to the new duke. While Pier Luigi sought to consolidate his position by the marriage of his daughter to the duke of Urbino (and more literally by a major fortifications project), Ferrante convinced Charles to back a conspiracy against him, which culminated in Pier Luigi's murder by stabbing in 1547; his body was hung from the window of his palace in Piacenza. As one might imagine, the satirists made hay with the affair: on the death of Paul III in 1549 one pasquinade described Pier Luigi astride a goat, 'catamites innumerable' about him, welcoming his father to Hell. It quickly got a translation into English, predictably appealing to anti-papal Protestant tastes.[8]

Paul was, to say the least, unimpressed by Ferrante's expedition and by the subsequent seizure of the duchy for the Habsburgs. He insisted on the installation of his grandson Ottavio as duke of Parma against rival claimants, although it was only after Paul's death that Ottavio succeeded in 1551 in securing his rule, one of the many localised conflicts that characterised these later stages of the Italian Wars. The

Farnese had thus succeeded where the Borgias had failed in making a state for themselves off the back of the papacy. It is testament to the writing of history by the winners that the Borgias are famously remembered for their murderous and nepotistic conduct, while outside Italy at least the Farnese have a far lower profile. Anti-Spanish sentiment is undoubtedly a factor here, as well as the fact that Paul III's reputation was burnished somewhat by his positive role in calling the Council of Trent. Moreover, had Alexander VI lived a few more years, he might well have helped his son Cesare consolidate his rule in the Romagna in much the same way Paul later managed. The Farnese held the duchy until the extinction of their line in 1731, testimony to what a determined pope could do for his family.

Meanwhile, as we have seen, there had been substantial changes in the ruling houses of Europe. Francis I died in 1547 and was succeeded by his son Henri II, who was married to an Italian, Catherine de' Medici, the first of two Medici queens of France. Catherine and he had been married in 1533, when she was fourteen; she was just short of her twenty-eighth birthday when she became queen. Her marriage to Henri had not been the easiest of relationships: he was enamoured of a much older woman, Diane de Poitiers, who continued to exercise considerable power at court following his marriage; but such were the realities of court life and mistress and queen maintained an uneasy alliance.[9] Her most important function as princess, of course, was to produce children, which she eventually did (a total of ten offspring though not without some difficulty); she went on to play a central role in European politics when her husband died young and she came to act as regent for her sons, just as Louise of Savoy had acted as regent for Francis. Unlike Louise, however, Catherine had another problem: she was not perceived as sufficiently royal by the French, who derided the Medici for their mercantile origins, and would be stigmatised for this, against which she resolutely defended herself. In fact she had a tense relationship with the Medici dukes: many of the family's exiled opponents found refuge at her court,[10] among them her cousin Piero Strozzi, who became a commander in the French service.

Under Henri, the French expanded their control in northern Italy, fomenting trouble for the Empire both through their Ottoman alliance, which now attacked imperial fortresses across the Mediterranean, and their support for the Protestant princes of the Schmalkaldic League. Charles V's victory over them at the Battle of Mühlberg did not mean he had won that war. In 1552 a coordinated attack by Henri II and Maurice of Saxony took him by surprise, and he was eventually forced into retreat.[11]

The climactic event of the Italian wars was, however, the struggle for – and siege of – Siena.[12] The republic was a long-standing rival of Florence; it was also legally a part of the Holy Roman Empire, and technically the emperor was its overlord.[13] The power struggles in Italy had, inevitably, had an impact on factional politics within the city throughout the 1520s, and following the end of the siege of Florence in 1530, with Spanish hegemony established in Tuscany, the Sienese were effectively forced to accept the authority of an imperial minister over their troops.[14] The presence of a Spanish commissioner and garrison in Siena was not, however, popular and in 1545 an uprising saw the Spanish expelled from the city along with members of the ruling council who had worked with them. Cosimo de' Medici contrived to mediate sufficiently to avoid major reprisals and to secure the return of a Spanish garrison to Siena, but further attempts at diplomacy failed and there was a second uprising in 1547, after which Cosimo once again brokered a deal for their return: imperial backing for the restoration of the Medici back in 1530 was certainly paying off.

Cosimo was, however, a more careful diplomat than Charles' official representative in Siena, Diego Hurtado di Mendoza, a 'proud man of great cunning'[15] who arrived in 1548 and promptly decided that half the members of the city's ruling councils should be personally appointed by himself. He further alienated the population through the imposition of strict arms control and by the announcement that Charles would be following the example of the Florentine dukes by building a new fortress. The Fortezza da Basso (as it is now known) in Florence, constructed in the early years of the duchy, was widely perceived as a symbol of tyranny, which any competent diplomat of the period would have known. But unlike the Florentine fortress, which had been built quickly and efficiently (and by the use of forced labour), the Sienese project was far from complete when the city rebelled once again in July 1552. With an Ottoman attack on Naples distracting Spanish attention, the timing was fortunate. In the space of just over a week, the citizens of Siena forced the Spanish to retreat to their half-finished fortifications – which the Sienese subsequently destroyed. Cosimo de' Medici sent ambassadors to protest at the detention of two Florentine captains and their troops who had fought on the Spanish side, and they were permitted to depart along with the Spanish. Citing the proverb that 'when your enemy wishes to leave, make him a golden bridge', the Sienese authorities found them a hundred packhorses and mules to carry their bags. Not everyone agreed with that approach: some of the citizens would rather have cut them to pieces, but they were restrained.[16] The Spanish were replaced as defenders of the city by an army under a local patrician, Enea Piccolomini and a French commander, Louis de Lansac (later replaced as French representative by Cardinal Ippolito d'Este, son of Lucrezia Borgia). Once again Cosimo de' Medici tried to act as honest broker, presenting a deal in which neither Spanish nor French troops would enter Siena and it would remain a free imperial city on the German model. The French, however, opted to capitalise on their victory and moved their soldiers into Sienese territory. From their point of view, an independent, friendly Siena would provide a bulwark against imperial power in northern Italy. The stage was set for war.

In January 1553 the Spanish made a first attempt to attack with a landing at the Tuscan port of Livorno. This imperial army was commanded by Pietro di (or Pedro Álvarez de) Toledo, viceroy of Naples and father of Eleonora di Toledo, the duchess of Florence, while another, under the command of Garzia di (Garcia de) Toledo, Eleonora's brother, marched up from Naples. Cosimo offered limited support to the enterprise but it faltered when the viceroy died. Cosimo now capitalised on the situation (and the recall of the incompetent Mendoza to Spain) to make a deal in his own interests. In November 1553 he secretly agreed to recapture Siena on Charles V's behalf. This was, in part, motivated by rivalry within the Medici family: Cosimo's second cousin Piero Strozzi (who thanks to Queen Catherine de' Medici had French backing) was hoping to use Siena as a base to overthrow Cosimo's regime. His father Filippo had tried the same tactic at the Battle of Montemurlo in 1537, but had been captured and died in prison the following year, most likely by suicide. A renewed challenge from this faction of the family was intolerable for the duke, who now prepared to take on the challenge.

The Siege of Siena was to endure for months with Blaise de Monluc in command of the city while Piero Strozzi managed the French army on the outside. It was particularly notable for the role of women in preparing the defences: divided into three groups, one led by Signora Forteguerra, one by Signora Piccolomini and one by Signora Livia Fausta, they took responsibility for improvements and repairs to the city walls, and to this day one of the bastions is known as the *fortino delle donne*: the little fort of the women. They were, wrote Monluc, 'deserving of eternal praise'.[17] After Strozzi's defeat by a Florentine–imperial army at the Battle of Marciano in August 1554, the Florentines were able to turn their attention to the siege, and made an attempt to starve out the Sienese. It took another eight months – during which time, in order to reduce demand on food supplies, Monluc first released the landsknechts and then in February 1555 another 4,400 'useless mouths', of whom about half died within a week of leaving the city, unable to find anything to eat but grass and plants. Inside, by April supplies of bread were running desperately short; what little food remained was being hoarded and traded at extortionate prices. On 21 April the city decided to surrender: Monluc declined to do so publicly, and left before the formal capitulation. The chronicler Alessandro Sozzini described the immense relief when at last food was brought into the piazza, and wine that had been sold just a few days before for 33 soldi now went for three, while eggs that had cost 21 soldi the pair now cost just two.[18] Siena was incorporated into the territories of Duke Cosimo de' Medici, whose wider claim to Tuscany gained papal recognition in 1569 when Cosimo was awarded the title of grand duke. Once again, imperial wealth had helped an Italian state see off opposition: Cosimo's victory was testimony to Spanish power in Italy.

From 1554, suffering badly from gout, Charles V began the process of abdicating, effectively splitting his empires apart. It would be another two and a half centuries before any other European ruler contrived a personal empire to match it. Charles' brother Ferdinand took power in the German states and Austria, while Charles' son Philip II became king of Spain – and of its growing empire. Philip also took charge of the Emperor's Italian interests in Milan, Sicily and Naples; he had, moreover, married the new queen of England, Mary I, and for a while there were hopes of reviving England as a Catholic power. Charles himself made his home at the monastery of Yuste in Extremadura where he lived until his death in September 1558.

The final conflict in the Franco-imperial war took place not in Italy but around Flanders in the north, where in 1557 imperial troops defeated the French at the Battle of St Quentin.[19] With both sides war-weary (and the expense of conflict taking a considerable toll), there was little appetite to continue. The French poet Joachim du Bellay, who worked as a secretary in the Roman household of his cousin, a cardinal, wrote of the atmosphere in the city:

> The air's corrupt; the god of war is normal here
> And so is hunger, pain and fear […]
> You see no one but soldiers, the helmets on their heads
> You hear nothing but drums and it seems a tempest
> And every day Rome expects another sack.[20]

Nerves were apparent on the other side too. A Venetian diplomatic report of 1559 suggested Spain was spending ten million ducats a year on warfare: even allowing for some exaggeration (and for inflation), compare this to the 2.73 million spent in Naples over *ten years* at the start of the wars.[21] Naples in particular was subject to exorbitant taxation to cover the cost of the long-running wars, which had been funded by loans secured against future tax income.

> Nor can one imagine any method of extracting money from the people, that is not in use in this kingdom. The subjects, for the most part, are broke and desperate, and many take to the streets, having no other way to live, which breeds more thieves and outlaws than there are in the whole of the rest of Italy.

Moreover, instead of spending sensibly on defence procurement, the viceroy was in the habit of throwing up fortresses and appointing friends to run them, but failing to equip them adequately, leaving them open to easy occupation by an enemy.[22]

This was the backdrop against which Philip and Henri began talks in 1558; on 3 April 1559 they signed the Peace of Cateau-Cambrésis. This was a complex peace treaty that drew in many European partners, and it was sealed with a deal involving two marriages: that of Henri's sister Marguerite to the duke of Savoy and that of either Philip II or his son Don Carlos to Henri's eldest daughter Elisabeth. So far as Italy was concerned, however, the fate of many of the contested territories had already been settled by battle. There were a handful of outstanding challenges for the negotiators to address: the return of the fief of Monferrato to Mantua; the French claim to sovereignty over Saluzzo (in western Piedmont); the ancient French claims to Milan and Burgundy (which were both left in limbo). The French agreed to restore the island of Corsica to Genoa and to make various restitutions in Tuscany and Sienese territory to the duke of Florence. All in all, though, the settlements in Italy left Spain the dominant power.[23]

Sixty-five years after the French descent into Italy, the French Crown's hopes on the peninsula had largely been thwarted. It had lost Piedmont, the region of northern Italy centred on Turin, which was strategically vital for invasions from the north. Saluzzo, where the dukes of Savoy reserved their claim, was a modest consolation prize by comparison. The loss of Corsica, meanwhile, left France dependent on its Ottoman allies for any major Mediterranean campaign. Spain, on the other hand, had emerged victorious. In the course of these six and a half decades it had secured first Naples, Sicily and Sardinia, then ensured the establishment of allies in Tuscany (both Florence and Siena) as well as Corsica and Genoa; such was the power of the Spanish Empire. Taken together, Spain now controlled a swathe of the Western Mediterranean coast, which would soon provide a basis for a serious challenge to their naval rivals: the Ottomans.

Over time, and especially following the rise of Spanish power in Italy, more and more Italians came into imperial service directly, not merely through the *condotta* system. By the 1540s, Charles V's council included several Italians, and some attempted to salvage pride with the assertion that the Spanish needed the guidance of Italian captains and really couldn't manage without them. Lorenzo Contarini, a Venetian ambassador to the court of Charles' brother Ferdinand in 1548, attacked the 'common opinion' that Spanish troops were bold and Spanish commanders expert. In fact, they were not 'as valorous as they thought themselves', and very few Spanish captains were judged competent to command troops at high level: the duke of Alba, captain general of the Emperor, 'knows very little indeed of the business of war, and everyone thinks him quite timid'. Charles had not appointed a single Spaniard to his secret war council, only Italians. And it was commonly claimed that if Spaniards were good soldiers, they were 'mere emulators' of Italians. Contarini concluded:

> In sum, I hold the Spanish to be a useful nation in warfare, but not of that excellence that they themselves would claim; indeed, they are the vainest nation I've ever dealt with, which doesn't blink at telling a thousand lies in praise of itself and to make believe that they do everything alone.[24]

The narrative of Spanish arrogance and Italian superiority would have been familiar to Contarini's listeners: moreover, it persisted. Almost fifty years later, the Piedmontese thinker Giovanni Botero insisted that Spanish infantry fought better under Italian commanders than under one of their own.[25]

Nor was Spain the only option for Italians abroad. As we have seen, Piero Strozzi, a cousin of Catherine de' Medici, went on to serve the French after her husband became heir apparent. Lower down the ranks, plenty of Italians found their humanistic skills as secretaries and diplomats were valued in other countries. Florentine secretaries worked in Poland, Hungary and England, and leveraged their international networks to secure privilege and promotion for family members and friends, and in return to supply news from across Europe and beyond to those at home in Italy.

The Italian peninsula now faced the aftermath of conflict, with all the issues that entailed. Among them was the problem of arms proliferation. This was particularly bad in the area most associated with firearms production, Gardone Val Trompia, site of the Beretta factory, which had become notorious for its gun culture. In 1553, the Venetian Senate heard a formal complaint from its local official there. 'Everyone carries an arquebus,' he wrote, 'and [...] they're not content with one, but even the women carry two, one in their hand and the other in their belt, both wheel-locks, and they're a bad breed, untameable overbearing Lutherans.'[26] Gun proliferation was bad enough but combined with religious radicalism it was deeply worrying.

Sometime around the 1570s, an anonymous author made a proposition for international gun control.[27] He (or less likely she, though we will come to at least one woman who wrote anti-war literature) argued that the abuse of wheel lock handguns had become so bad that

> if the pope, as chief, and then the other princes do not make some prompt provision, life will so badly be corrupted in this matter, that it will become even more difficult, and soon there will be no place nor state with personal security, given that every low herdsman or shepherd you meet in the countryside today has a wheel lock arquebus over his shoulder.

But the problem was that it wouldn't do for just one of the Italian states to ban wheel locks. It would have to be a multilateral deal, because there was no way you would get people living close to the borders to give up their guns if bandits from the next-door state could still get their hands on them. In other words, given the division of the Italian peninsula into different polities, weapons proliferation was a problem that could only be addressed through diplomatic initiative. The author proposed that the princes of Italy should agree not to use large wheel lock arquebuses in warfare at all, and that they should hire only infantry with matchlock weapons 'as a safer weapon'. And he wanted drastic measures: specifically, the introduction of the death penalty for anyone who made or mended wheel locks.

Weapons proliferation was an unsurprising consequence of wars in which guns had been widely distributed to communities for civic defence in times of attack. Records from Ferrara, Florence and the Papal States illustrate just what a wide cross section of society had firearms: in the Florentine siege of 1530 they included two tailors, a barber, a baker, two shoemakers, a dyer, two blacksmiths, a carpenter, an innkeeper, a weaver, a hatter and a miller.[28] It doesn't take a great deal of imagination to see how guns might start to go astray under such a system – most obviously, soldiers who had been issued guns would simply hang on to them. Benvenuto Cellini was one such: he recounted in his autobiography how while passing through Siena he got into an argument with a postmaster who confiscated the stirrups and pillion from Cellini's horse. When the postmaster picked up a halberd, Cellini raised his gun (on his account in self-defence) and (again on his account) it 'went off by itself', the shot ricocheting off a doorway and catching the postmaster in the throat.[29] And as demobilised soldiers, lacking employment, turned to crime, and local barons took advantage of the available manpower to resist attempts from their overlords to enforce social order, banditry also become a major problem in these years, not only in Italy, but across Europe.[30] In November 1578 a Venetian newsletter reported that four members of the Peretti household in the village of Canda, north of Ferrara, had been murdered by a gang dressed as shepherds and armed with wheel lock guns. This was the context for demands (again, not just in Italy but across Europe) that the proliferation of firearms should be addressed.[31]

The anonymous author arguing in favour of gun control had points to make about the inadequacy of guns for self-defence that are remarkably resonant in the twenty-first century: 'One finds with difficulty an example of anyone who has been attacked with an arquebus and even though neither impeded nor injured has nonetheless shot back at the enemy.' A bandit who expects his victim to have a gun will attack in such a way as to prevent him from using it. In the final section of his discussion, the author moved on to the problem of actually carrying out this policy. He argued that the papacy had a degree of moral authority that other princes did not and was therefore well placed to lead, an idea tying into the image cultivated by successive popes that they were maintainers of the balance of power in Italy and indeed beyond. Perhaps more surprisingly, the writer also made the case for tackling firearms manufacturers: 'he who wants to remove a tree,' he commented, 'must not simply cut the branches but set himself to the roots.' As well as the death penalty for makers and menders of wheel locks, he argued for a ban on foreign imports. This was tough rhetoric indeed, and it is striking that the heaviest penalties were to be levied on the arms manufacturers as opposed to people who owned these weapons; indeed he seemed quite sympathetic to their fears of attack. It clearly was not a good thing that every low herdsman or shepherd had an arquebus, but the solution lay not in penalties on those people but – quite remarkably – in coordinated international action against arms producers.

Criticism of militarism came not only from those concerned about public order but also at a more intellectual level. Chiara Matraini, a poet, was among those who made a case for the superiority of the sciences over the military arts. Matraini lived quite an extraordinary life. An orphan, she married at fifteen and had a son three years later, in 1533; her family was involved in an uprising in Lucca in 1534 as a consequence of which some of them were exiled, imprisoned or executed. She was widowed in 1542 while still in her thirties and subsequently ran a salon (and embarked on a very public affair) with a fellow poet, Bartolomeo Graziani, who was married. While Baldassare Castiglione's characters might have opined that the 'first profession' of the courtier was that of arms, Matraini had more complex opinions. The first edition of her work, published in the last year of the Siena War, 1555, had included an oration in praise of the art of war, justifying the use of arms (for defensive purposes at least) as second only to the learning of philosophy (a pursuit of her likely audience of academicians). She noted the role of 'wise and expert captains' in the preservation of states, emphasising the importance of oratory in inspiring their men. One should be cautious about assuming that this represented her own views, rather than what her audience might want to hear, or a set-piece argument; it is notable that in later writing Matraini was more ambivalent about armed conflict. The 1597 edition of her works dropped the oration, and included a letter arguing for the superiority of learning over war. While she was clear that a knowledge of warfare was necessary, she insisted that:

Thus, the finest valiant warriors, worthy of true honour shall be those who, following the best [teachings of the] sciences, will strip themselves of ambition, of hatred, of greed of plunder, worldly vainglory, and all their immoderate affections and desires; they will arm themselves with faith, justice, charity, and all virtuous behaviour and with these most powerful weapons they will overcome their internal and external enemies. Yet, with all this, I believe rarely are men such as these to be found, since if everyone acted this way, one would see only peace, wonderful calm, and a most happy union among men.[32]

Chapter Twenty-Five

The Index and the Inquisition

The year 1559 was significant not only for the formal conclusion of almost seven decades of international conflict on the Italian peninsula, but also for a key development in the Catholic Church's response to its Protestant rivals: the establishment of the Index of Prohibited Books. The Index was not entirely an innovation: there had been plenty of previous efforts to crack down on publications that the Church (and indeed some secular rulers) perceived to be religiously or morally unacceptable, including during the Lateran Council. These included censorship prior to publication as well as the issuing of lists of banned books, and they can be seen in papal bulls of 1487, 1501 and 1515.[1] There had also been efforts to ban obscene illustrations in Treviso and Venice (these were often blacked out rather than the books being destroyed). Political censorship, meanwhile, had been evident in Rome, Florence and Venice during the 1510s and 1520s; Milan took measures against Lutheran books in particular in 1523, and in 1538 it was the Milanese, not the Church, who issued the first Index of Prohibited Books,[2] with Bergamo following suit the next year. The first initiative for a Roman Index, meanwhile, had come with the establishment of the Roman Inquisition in 1542, and alongside pre-publication censorship and listing of banned books there would now also be inspections of imports and bookshops. It was in 1559, though, that the establishment of the principal Index took place, in the same year as the treaty of Cateau-Cambrésis.

It happened amidst a series of short-lived papacies that followed the death of Pope Paul III in 1549. Paul was succeeded first by Giovanni Maria Ciocchi del Monte, who ruled as Pope Julius III. A former papal legate to the Council of Trent, Julius reconvened proceedings in 1551, but moves toward further reform were stymied by continued conflict between the German princes. Julius' principal legacy in Rome was, in fact, not religious reform, but his luxurious Villa Giulia, an elegant mannerist retreat outside the city walls (now Rome's Etruscan Museum) where he spent his time with his adopted nephew Innocenzo. Innocenzo, a servant responsible for the care of Julius' pet monkey, was widely assumed to be his master's lover; this impression was merely confirmed when Julius notoriously made him a cardinal.

Julius died in 1555; his replacement Marcello Cervini degli Spannocchi (Pope Marcellus II) fell ill shortly after his election and died twenty-two days into his papacy. He in turn was succeeded by Gian Pietro Carafa, who took the name Pope Paul IV. Carafa had been cardinal archbishop of Naples and head of the Roman Inquisition. He was not the expected choice, but emerged as the compromise candidate (his advanced age was a relevant factor here). There was no love lost between Carafa and Charles V: the former resented Habsburg claims on his ancestral home, Naples, and as pope ensured that key Habsburg allies were exiled from the city. Charles' compromise with the Lutherans at Augsburg that September, which allowed the princes of Germany freedom to choose the religion of their state, riled the pope yet further. In an echo of Leo X's claims around the 1517 'Cardinals' Conspiracy' Paul IV accused Spanish agents of plotting his assassination, and even went so far as to indict Charles V. He described Charles and his followers as 'Lutherans and half-Jews'.[3] Unfortunately for Paul, Henri II was no enthusiast for war, and the pope had no choice but to compromise with the imperial faction. Even so, on hearing of Charles' death, he 'refused to offer intercessions for his soul'.[4]

Paul was, moreover, an enthusiastic persecutor of Protestants,[5] and took the opportunity to attack old enemies among the *spirituali* (whom he had opposed in the 1530s and 1540s). Cardinal Pole's absence in England enabled him to avoid the worst of it: he had secured the position of papal legate there under Julius III on the basis that the accession of Queen Mary Tudor to the throne brought the prospect of an English return to Roman allegiance. Cardinal Giovanni Morone, however, had no such overseas option, and was arrested and interrogated by the Inquisition: although the commission of cardinals who tried him found no reason to convict, Paul refused to acknowledge Morone's innocence and the cardinal remained in jail until he was cleared by Paul's successor Pius IV. Morone then went on to preside over the Council of Trent, which was not finally concluded until 1563, and in fact came close to winning the papacy himself in the conclave of 1566.

Paul IV's 1559 Index ranged well beyond books sympathetic to Protestantism or other heresies to cover a much wider variety of works. Around five hundred authors were subject to complete bans, among them Aretino[6] and Machiavelli; other well-known texts including the highly popular *Decameron* were permitted only in expurgated editions. There were immediate protests, and Paul's death the same year meant the provisions were never fully enacted; there were nonetheless substantial burnings of Protestant literature in cities including Florence and Venice. It was left to the Council of Trent to provide a definitive list, and the eventual version was not quite so hard-line as Paul's edition, giving more scope for works to be published with cuts, and delegating more decision-making to bishops and local inquisitors (some of whom were more relaxed than others about pursuing offenders). The 1564 Index, for example, ruled acceptable some works by Savonarola and Erasmus of Rotterdam; still, a large volume of popular Italian literature from the first half of the century came to be regarded as suspect. Of the authors discussed in this book, Ariosto, Boiardo, Castiglione, Machiavelli, Aretino and Colonna were all subject to censorship. Too much sex, an overly favourable attitude to duelling, or an emphasis on 'Fortune' rather than God's will could all get an author into trouble. There were inevitable tensions as the Florentines, for example, asserted that there was much to value in Machiavelli's writing, and Christian theologians complained that bans on Jewish religious texts made it impossible for them to do their job. Censorship imposed new costs on publishers: in Venice, the process of obtaining state approval for a text took between one and three months, and the publishers were required to pay the official readers.[7] All this came, moreover, in the context of a wider crackdown on heresy, which involved more systematic spying on religious dissidents and increased use of torture in trials. Italian Protestants were forced to organise themselves more secretly.[8] The relative tolerance of debate that, in elite circles at least, had characterised the 1530s and 1540s was no more.

*

Catholic reform, moreover, was far from positive for Italy's largest non-Christian minority, the Jews. It was a characteristic of the new religious situation that Protestants and Catholics competed to prove their orthodoxy. Both confessions were more serious about priestly education, more concerned for their laity, more active in their moves against heretics and those who would threaten the new religion. Jews provided a common target – just as they had done, in fact, in wartime, especially for Spanish soldiers who had grown up with stories of the 1492 expulsion and ongoing persecution of converted Jews in their home country.[9]

As we have seen, the Lateran Council of 1512–17 had already initiated a softer policy towards the *Monti di Pietà*, through which the state was able to provide modest loans.[10] By 1542 the papacy had permitted the payment of interest to depositors in the *Monti*, which allowed them to become fully fledged banks. That in turn meant the traditional reason for accommodating Jews – to avoid Christians sinning through moneylending – was no longer valid. The Church's desire to avoid any impression of laxity in the face of Protestantism had further negative consequences for the Jews of the Papal States. Despite the appearance of tolerance in his 1523 pamphlet *That Jesus Christ was Born a Jew*, Luther's views were consistently antisemitic. He described Jews as 'disgusting vermin' and recommended that they be expelled from the Holy Roman Empire, or at least that their books and right to worship be suppressed, their synagogues burnt and their houses destroyed. The 1543 publication of his pamphlet *On the Jews and their Lies* provoked anti-Jewish riots in the imperial city of Brunswick.[11]

Erasmus, a fellow reformer but no Protestant, had no time for the Jews either. Criticising Wolfgang Capito, a scholar who favoured Hebrew studies of the Old Testament, he said that he saw the Jews as 'a nation of the most tedious fabrications'. Martin Bucer called the Jews the enemies of Christ and said 'Papist and Jewish belief and religion are thus simply identical', lamenting in 1538 that his patron Philip of Hesse (a Protestant prince) permitted Jews to remain in his territories. The most prominent Lutheran to stand up for the Jews was Andreas Osiander of Nuremberg, who wrote a pamphlet attacking the 'blood-libel' myth; it was published by two Jews in 1540, and Osiander's enemies sought to discredit him by saying he was Jewish himself.[12]

That was the context in which first Paul III and then Paul IV moved against the Jews of Rome, initially with an expulsion in 1541, then, after they were readmitted, with confinement to a ghetto from 1555, a papal bull requiring that:

> In all future times in this city, as in all other cities, holdings and territories belonging to the Roman Church, all Jews should live solely in one and the same location, or if that is not possible, in two or three or as many as are necessary, which are to be contiguous and separated completely from the dwellings of Christians.[13]

In contrast to the Venetian ghetto, the foundation of which in 1516 had been something of a compromise between tolerance on the one hand and demands for the expulsion of the Jewish refugees who had temporarily been allowed sanctuary on the other, the Roman ghetto clearly denoted a hardening of attitudes.[14] The ghetto in Rome lay near the Tiber, in a part of the old quarter of the city that was already the centre of the city's Jewish community, as the 1526 census shows.[15] Paul's bull prohibited the construction of new synagogues and required Jews to wear a blue hat or other identifying marker. It clamped down on exemptions from the latter rule and barred Jews from dining with Christians or becoming their close friends. A number of the provisions targeted moneylending, implicitly accusing Jewish bankers of trying to defraud Christian borrowers, and restricted Jews to just one profession besides moneylending: the trade in second-hand clothing. Jewish physicians were banned from treating Christians (bear in mind that previous popes had themselves had Jewish doctors). Christians were not permitted to be the servants of Jews, nor to be wet nurses to Jewish children.

Paul IV had a track record of hostility to Jews. He had encouraged the public burning of the Talmud in 1553 in the Campo de' Fiori (an event timed to coincide with Jewish New Year); according to a diplomatic report, he had opposed Pius III's decision to let Portuguese *conversos* settle in the papal town of Ancona on the Adriatic coast, saying they should be burnt alive; once established as pope, he carried through on this threat, confiscating property and executing those who did not get away in time. There was some discussion about coordinated international reprisals but no effective action was taken. (Debate

continues as to why.) While there were thirteenth-century precedents
for much of the content of Paul's bull, the evidence is that in the mid
sixteenth century it came (in the words of one historian) as a 'profound
shock to the Jews'.[16] Other states expelled the Jews entirely: Naples in
1541, the Papal States except Rome and Ancona in 1569, Milan in 1597.
Those Jews who remained on the peninsula now lived primarily in
Mantua, Ferrara and Venice and to a more limited extent in Tuscany
and Savoy: indeed, by the 1570s Venice was actively seeking to attract
Jewish and *converso* (former Jews who had converted to Christianity)
merchants.[17] In the cities where Jews were still permitted to live,
ghettoisation followed, including in Florence and Siena in 1571.[18] It was
not until the eighteenth century that we see the first moves to treat Jews
as in any way equal citizens in Christian Europe: the Venetian ghetto
was abolished in 1797 and Jews gained full rights in the city in 1818.[19]

Elsewhere, the shifting social dynamics of sixteenth-century Italy led
to changes in thinking about women's role in society on a number
of levels. In the 1520s we find (male) writers recommending on the
one hand that marriage should be characterised by mutual love and
on the other that it is essentially a matter of public service to ensure
the reproduction of the human race. In the more experimental literary
period of the 1530s and 1540s adultery seems to have been more tolerated, but after Trent, where marriage was debated and reaffirmed
as a sacrament (this arguably in response to the Protestant emphasis
on marriage), there was perhaps more emphasis on loving marriage,
or at least on some degree of affection between the spouses. That
said, not all women were impressed by the realities of later sixteenth-
century marriage: in the dialogues by Moderata Fonte, *Il merito delle
donne* and *La giustizia delle donne* (published posthumously in 1600),
her female characters are highly critical of masculine behaviour. So
far as courtesans were concerned, the Counter-Reformation brought
with it a less lenient attitude towards prostitution, as Catholic authorities sought to establish their reform credentials in the face of Protestant attacks.[20]

On the other hand, as we saw with writers such as Vittoria Colonna,
the climate of reform may have afforded women opportunities to
assert themselves in religious circles, and this was by no means
restricted to literary interventions: in 1547, women in Bologna

succeeded in gaining admission to the confraternity of Santa Maria della Pietà. Confraternities were religious organisations that also had a significant social networking function for the men involved, and women protested at their exclusion. The shrine cared for by this particular group included a popular devotional image of the Virgin Mary; according to the confraternity statutes, 'the Blessed Virgin in this place demonstrated gracious favour as much to one as to the other sex'. The men of the confraternity voted to accept them into membership 'as good mothers and sisters', with one Mona Lucia as their leader; however, this was 'separate but equal' membership of a specific women's company.[21]

The poet Laura Battiferri degli Ammannati was another woman who turned towards religious experssion. Like her fellow writer Tullia d'Aragona she was the illegitimate daughter of a high-ranking Vatican figure; unlike d'Aragona she was acknowledged by her father and probably also educated by him. In 1560, Battiferra, who was portrayed by the Florentine court artist Bronzino in a striking portrait showing her in profile after the typical images of Dante and Petrarch, had begun by publishing sonnets characterised by an experimental style, among them works dedicated to the rulers of Florence and Urbino and the 'unvanquished king' Philip II of Spain.[22] Her second book, however, was quite different. Published the year after the final session of the Council of Trent, it was a translation of the *Seven Penitential Psalms*, reflecting her engagement with Counter-Reformation ideas and her support for the Jesuits.[23] Indeed, over the course of the 1560s, the practice of dedicating a wide range of printed texts to women (for example a volume of Battiferri's poems published in 1560 was dedicated to the duchess of Florence, Eleonora di Toledo[24]) seems to have declined and thereafter dedications to women were more strictly spiritual (at least according to a study of one Venetian press; perhaps reflecting the post-Tridentine climate).[25]

Too dramatic a religious vocation, however, could be just as dangerous for a woman as suspicions of Lutheranism, as Paola Antonia Negri found to her cost. Negri was a popular mystic and 'living saint' whose charismatic convent leadership attracted followers including Isabella of Capua (widow of Ferrante Gonzaga). Her claim to the title of 'divine', however, pushed too far into heresy; she was expelled from Venetian territory in 1551, tried by the Inquisition the following year, and required to enter an enclosed convent, where she remained until she was close to death.[26]

Convents continued to provide a home – sometimes a welcome one, sometimes not – to many women, especially those of higher ranks. This was particularly true in Venice where strict legislation on marriages among the ruling elite led to huge inflation in the level of dowry a woman was expected to bring to her marriage, and as a result many families opted to send daughters to convents instead. It is estimated that in 1581 over half the patrician women in Venice lived in enclosed convents.[27] This was the context within which, in the following century, Arcangela Tarabotti would write a ferocious attack on convent life, suggesting that one in three Venetian nuns lacked vocation.[28] There were clearly examples of this: girls who were forced into convents by physical violence or psychological coercion. On the other hand we know of some of these examples because the women in question (sometimes after several years) successfully petitioned to be released from vows made under duress. The Church was not necessarily unsympathetic to their plight, but equally there could be significant resistance to their leaving.[29]

For all the challenges they faced, however, the women writers of the sixteenth century, along with early female artists such as Anguissola, paved the way for a whole subsequent group of Italian women to come to the fore as writers, singers and artists: among them, the painter Lavinia Fontana, a distinguished portraitist in Bologna and Rome; Isabella Andreini, an actress and singer, whose play *La Mirtilla* (1588) emphasised women's intelligence and agency; and in the seventeenth century Artemisia Gentileschi, known for her dramatic portrayal of *Judith and Holofernes*.[30] If women had a Renaissance it is perhaps here, during the Italian Wars and in the decades that followed, that it is easiest to see.

This is not to say, however, that women of sixteenth-century Italy had escaped oppression: far from it. Violante Carafa, a niece of Pope Paul IV, is a case in point. Accused of having an affair, she was murdered by her husband Giovanni and other male relatives in an honour killing.

The murder of Violante, which took place during the conclave of 1559 to elect Paul's successor, only compounded ill feeling towards the Carafa family, who had become decidedly unpopular in Rome over the course of Paul's papacy, and in particular with the Roman office-holding class. Violence was common during the *sede vacante* (empty chair) period that fell between papacies, and this one was no exception: partly in response to the murder, Paul's family home was sacked and his statue vandalised in an echo of the treatment of Julius II's statue in Bologna half a century earlier. In due course, the conclave elected Giovanni Angelo Medici (from Milan, and only distantly related to the rulers of Florence), who as Pius IV capitalised on Violante's case to launch a prosecution of his predecessor's nephews Giovanni and Carlo (it is fair to say that he was as concerned here with securing his own power as with justice for Violante herself). In 1560–61 Pius IV moved against them, mounting a case based not only on the killings of Violante and her lover, but a string of accusations of murder in both Naples and Rome, along with a massacre at Bettona, a town near Perugia, two charges of rape and one of frequenting prostitutes.[31] While prominent men often enjoyed impunity when it came to such conduct, just sometimes it caught up with them. In a striking assertion of Pius IV's papal power, he secured sufficient support in the College of Cardinals to have both Paul's nephews put to death. Unlike the Farnese, the Carafa family had failed to secure the power they briefly enjoyed.[32]

Pius IV went on to oversee the final session of the Council of Trent. If the literal wars – at least on the Italian peninsula – were over, the battles of ideas were not. It was 1563 before the Council finally ended its deliberations, with a series of conclusions that, while addressing some of the worst abuses (such as absentee clerics and the sale of indulgences), also ensured the division between Catholic and Protestant would remain. Those who had hoped for reconciliation were to be disappointed. Yet there was more in common between reformed Catholic and Protestant than the subsequent wars of religion might suggest. When the Council concluded, its decrees and doctrines promulgated a greater emphasis on education of clergy; a focus on the self and confession: a more individual type of religion; tighter bureaucracy and centralisation of control. The confession box, so familiar to Catholics today, is a product of these debates, though for a long time the new, more individualised idea of religion did not filter out beyond a relatively narrow elite.[33]

There has long been debate among historians as to how best to understand these developments. It was traditional to see this as a 'Counter-Reformation', a reaction to Protestantism. More recently, however, scholars have turned to descriptions including Catholic Reformation or Catholic Renewal to describe the process, emphasising the continuity with earlier trends in Church reform such as (for example) the efforts of Gian Matteo Giberti or even Girolamo Savonarola, or with the conciliar movement of the late fourteenth and early fifteenth centuries, in which councils of the Church sought to resolve the schism that had left it with one pope in Avignon and another in Rome.

In fact, the very proposal for a Council to deal with Church reform – the first since the Lateran Council of 1512–17 – in some ways harked back to this longer tradition of reforming councils. Indeed, there were parallels between the view, endorsed by the Council of Trent, that bishops were primarily spiritual leaders (despite their fulfilling governmental roles, with all the political compromise and potential for corruption that that entailed) and numerous earlier initiatives over the centuries that aimed to shift the Church towards a simpler, less worldly, model, in which the imagined early years of the Apostles were often evoked. Trent endorsed the validity of the seven sacraments which had also been confirmed by the Council of Florence in 1438. Trent was favourable to the idea that Mary had been immaculately conceived (that is, conceived without the original sin that afflicted every other human being), and it endorsed the doctrine of Purgatory: both were points of difference with Protestantism but had been under discussion well before Luther came on the scene.[34] Similarly some historians have rejected the idea that the Jesuits were particularly novel in their work, instead arguing that there were precedents for the worldly type of work they undertook, and that their medieval predecessors – especially the Franciscans and Dominicans – were not characterised by closing themselves off from secular life. Far from it, their preaching (as we have seen) was vitally important to the rise of figures like Savonarola, and it arguably provided a bridge between earlier enclosed monastic orders, with their emphasis on contemplation and prayer, and newer, more evangelical, approaches to Christianity.

The implementation of the Tridentine reforms varied considerably, and depended on the attitude of the bishop or archbishop involved, who had significant autonomy within his own diocese. Some clerics engaged seriously with the process, following the earlier example of Giberti in Verona. Others, particularly in the less wealthy south of the Italian peninsula, were hampered by the lack of resources for clerical education well into the eighteenth century. Indeed, the region around Otranto, the southern town occupied by Turkish invaders almost a century before, fell so far short that the Jesuits saw the need for a mission there in 1573.[35] In Italy itself, however, with the peripheral exception of those Waldensians who had effectively adopted Protestantism, the challenge to Catholicism never really took hold, and the peninsula avoided the religious conflict that was enveloping Northern Europe. From about 1580 the Inquisition focused not so much on trials for heresy but emphasised instead the problems of magic and witchcraft, and in Venice the last death sentence issued to a heretic was in 1588. True, there were individual dissenters, like the miller Menocchio (Domenico Scandella), who was twice tried for heresy and executed at the turn of the sixteenth to the seventeenth century, but his beliefs were so idiosyncratic that they can hardly be called Protestant.[36]

Art was important in Trent's efforts to renew Catholicism, and changing religious ideas prompted changes in what kind of art was considered fashionable. The appropriate style for religious works was now more respectful, more dignified, more heavenly. Mary, for example, was to be transcendent, the queen of the heavens, no longer earthy or pregnant or anything too human. In this new environment, Michelangelo's *Last Judgment* was among the art to attract controversy. Even before the fresco was complete Biagio da Cesena, the papal master of ceremonies, had already declared it 'a most unseemly thing in such a venerable place to have painted so many nudes that so indecently display their shame and that it was not a work for a pope's chapel but rather one for baths or taverns'.[37] Michelangelo had his revenge, painting Biagio's portrait onto the figure of Minos among the devils in Hell, but Biagio had the last laugh when after Michelangelo's death in 1564 it was ruled that the nudes should be painted over. Another to attract criticism was Paolo Veronese, who ran into trouble with the Inquisition in relation to his 1573 *Feast* for the monastery of SS Giovanni e Paolo in Venice, which portrayed Christ and his disciples among a crowd of soldiers and drunkards. To mollify the critics it was retitled *Feast in the House of Levi*, despite its lack of several key figures typically associated with that title.[38]

This is not to say that classically inspired art was abandoned. Far from it: ancient myths continued to be sources for artworks for court settings. The Villa d'Este in Tivoli, outside Rome, is a case in point. Designed by Pirro Ligorio before 1550, though not completed for another decade, it was to be a spectacular residence for Cardinal Ippolito II d'Este, grandson of Alexander VI, son of Lucrezia Borgia and Alfonso d'Este. The villa, famous for the thousands of fountains lining its garden, was built to a fantastical classicising scheme, engaging with the ancient sites of the surrounding landscape. Ligorio, who carried out his own archaeological excavations, was infamously a forger, but he had a genuine interest in antiquities and a more systematic one than the earlier explorers of the Roman grottoes. Another artist who continued to paint classical subjects was Titian, who lived until 1576 and whose works in the later years of his life included the *Death of Actaeon* and the *Flaying of Marsyas*, in an experimental style that has been labelled 'magic impressionism'.[39] He also returned to subjects he had treated earlier in his career: the *Allegory of Prudence* (1550–65) showed the three ages of man in a triple portrait, a theme he had addressed more conventionally fifty years before in his *Three Ages of Man*.

Vasari called Titian's later works 'less skilful',[40] suggesting that the elderly master had lost his touch, but in the 1570s they were to be highly important. For while the land wars in Italy were over, the naval battles for the Mediterranean were not, and Titian turned his hand to memorialising what became an iconic event for the Catholic reformers: the Battle of Lepanto.

Chapter Twenty-Six

The Battle of Lepanto

The land wars in Italy had largely been settled with the peace of 1559. That is not to say that there was no conflict at all beyond that point, but it tended towards lower-level territorial consolidation: the peninsula was no longer the European theatre of war it had been at the beginning of the century. The same could not be said for the Mediterranean, however, where the early 1570s saw a major sea war between Venice and the Ottoman Empire.

As we have seen, under Süleyman the Magnificent the Ottoman Empire had captured Belgrade in 1521, then Rhodes the following year. In 1538 an Ottoman force had also prevailed against the Spanish in the naval battle at Preveza (on the western coast of Greece); Venice had subsequently made peace. In 1560 the Ottomans defeated another Christian alliance at Djerba (an island off the coast of Tunisia). And five years later, in 1565, they laid siege to Malta, where the Knights of St John had relocated following the conquest of Rhodes (they paid tribute for it in the form of a falcon, hence the *Maltese Falcon*).[1] Admittedly that campaign was not such a success: after months of fighting the Ottomans miscalculated, attacked a Italian–Spanish relief force, and lost badly.[2] They made up for it in the next two years, however, winning a series of Italian colonies in the Eastern Mediterranean – Chios, Naxos, Andros and Sifanto (Sífnos)[3] – even if the Genoese 'lords' of Chios, the Giustiniani family, contrived to maintain a significant presence on that island under Ottoman rule, and a Genoese community remained there until the second half of the seventeenth century.[4]

In the autumn of 1566 Süleyman died while on campaign in south-west Hungary. He was succeeded by his son Selim II, two of whose rivals had been murdered on Süleyman's orders while a third had succumbed to a serendipitous (for Selim) case of smallpox. Selim continued his father's expansionist policy and in 1570 launched an invasion of Cyprus, then under Venetian rule. After three weeks the Ottomans succeeded in conquering the town of Nicosia, which lies inland towards the north of the island, and went on to lay siege to Famagusta, on its east coast.[5]

Venice appealed to the other Christian states for help, but it was an easy time for no one. After the untimely death in 1559 of Henri II in a jousting accident, France was briefly ruled by the 15-year-old Francis II; he died eighteen months later and the throne passed to his 10-year-old brother Charles IX. Catherine de' Medici, as adviser to her sons, became a key figure in French politics throughout this period, confronting the religious conflicts that broke out after the massacre of Huguenot (Protestant) worshippers at Vassy in 1562. This was not a political context that favoured intervention in wars elsewhere. The Spanish were likewise dealing with religious resistance in the Netherlands, which in 1568 flared into the first stage of an Eighty Years War that would encompass the formation and secession from Spain of an independent Dutch Republic. Philip II of Spain, however, was eventually persuaded to join the campaign against the Ottomans with the prospect of territorial acquisitions in North Africa to build on the tribute obtained by his father Charles in the 1530s.

The delay in forming an alliance left the Ottomans free to pursue their campaign for Famagusta. The city was well stocked with meat, grain and water from wells, if not with wine; the question for those inside the siege was whether these food supplies would hold out until relief arrived.[6] The propaganda was literally bloody: Hassan Pasha, the Ottoman captain who had seized Nicosia, dispatched to Marc' Antonio Bragadin, governor of Famagusta, a letter declaring that he would have to pay for his city in blood, and to underline his point sent the head of Niccolò Dandolo, commander at Nicosia, too.[7] In January of 1571, Venetian ships under the command of Marco and Marc'Antonio Querini headed to relieve Famagusta. This was early in the season to sail, risking bad weather, but – importantly for events later in the year – it forced the Ottoman navy out into the Mediterranean two months in advance of the usual fighting season. In the process of delivering artillery, gunpowder, cash and a relief force to Famagusta the Venetians contrived to destroy two Ottoman ships and a gun battery. Selim, evidently most unhappy at proceedings, had his representative in Chios beheaded, and sent out orders to assemble reinforcements for a new assault on Cyprus.

Meanwhile, the debates between the Western powers dragged on, and it was not until May 1571, more than six months after the initial occupation of Cyprus, that they finally agreed the terms of their alliance. The Holy League included the Papacy, Spain, Venice, Genoa, Tuscany, Savoy, Urbino, Parma and the Knights of Malta: a rare show of unity for the Italian states, who in a fine piece of crusading rhetoric declared that they aimed to retake not only Cyprus but the Holy Land too. When news of the decision to attack reached the Ottomans, their admiral declared that 'all the Muslim community found it most proper and necessary to find and immediately attack the Infidels' fleet in order to save the honour of our religion and state'.[8] It is worth recalling that some Italian converts to Islam were commanders on the Ottoman side, having made careers in service to the sultans; indeed, the Ottoman system enabled men from modest backgrounds to rise to positions that were largely restricted to noblemen in the countries of their birth.[9]

It was almost a year after the initial Venetian appeal for help that the Christian fleet finally left Sicily for Corfu on the western coast of Greece, and it was too late. The Ottomans had assembled their guns, some confiscated from the captured city of Nicosia, and beginning in May bombarded the walls of Famagusta for more than two months. A large number of civilians had been allowed to leave the city and return to the local villages, leaving those inside to hold out with their remaining food and ammunition. But there was simply not enough gunpowder, and when the Venetian commanders gave the order to reduce the rate of fire the Ottomans knew they had an advantage, which they pursued with a relentless campaign of mining beneath the city walls. By the time the Holy League's navy arrived, the Ottomans had offered terms of surrender, and the Famagustans, on one report down to their last seven barrels of powder, eventually accepted.

The surrender proved far from civil. Bragadin was accused of allowing reprisals against Ottoman prisoners who should have been released, and, moreover, of having food stocks destroyed. The Ottoman general Mustafa Pasha responded by arresting Bragadin and his fellow generals. The latter, along with their soldiers, were slain,

while Bragadin himself was tortured and his ears cut off: having
refused conversion he was flayed alive and his skin, cut into four
pieces and stuffed with straw, was hung on the city towers.[10] Even for
the sixteenth century this was particularly appalling treatment (though
it is worth remembering that Christians were guilty of such atrocities
too: Vasco da Gama's first voyage to the Indian Ocean saw him capture
a group of Arab merchants, cut off their ears and noses, and burn
them alive).[11]

The news of Bragadin's fate concentrated minds among the Holy
League, which had been riven by dissension between so many formerly
warring powers: Habsburg commanders, for example, objected to the
conduct of Sebastiano Venier, commander of the Venetian fleet, in
putting down a mutiny. News of the affair reached the Ottoman
commanders too, who might have been more inclined to celebrate,
but they also had their disputes, not least over the question of where
their fleet should have wintered in 1570–71. On both sides, Famagusta
provided motivation: for the Ottomans a victory to build on; for the
Holy League a defeat to avenge.

The fleets engaged on 7 October 1571 in the Gulf of Patraikos, about
forty nautical miles from Lepanto (now called by its Greek name
Nafpaktos). Assessments of the size of the two forces vary, but it is
generally agreed that the Ottomans had more ships and the Holy
League more guns. On the Christian side there were over two hundred
galleys (of which half were Venetian and the large majority of the
remainder Spanish) and half a dozen of the larger Venetian galeasses
(which could carry heavier cannon).[12] The Ottoman fleet had closer
to three hundred ships. This was, however, to be a sea battle fought
at close quarters, effectively hand to hand, and thus the numbers of
fighting men mattered. The oarsmen of the Venetian galleys were
primarily waged, and available to fight, and to add to their numbers
the enslaved convicts who rowed the Holy League galleys were
unchained and promised their freedom in the event of victory. In a
poem dedicated to the Habsburg commander Don Juan of Austria,
Juan Latino, a former slave who became a professor at the University
of Granada, gave a vivid portrait of a Moorish rower, threatened by
his captain with bloody punishment if he should treacherously help
the Turks, rowing 'poised between death and liberty in the gravest
danger', remembering 'the fields of his sweet fatherland'.[13]

As the two fleets approached, the Venetian galleasses fired a 'tempest of great cannonades', benefiting from a favourable wind that drove the smoke from their fire back against the Turks. In four hours of fighting, there was an 'infinite number of dead and wounded', galleys cut in half, sinking or burning, corpses, discarded barrels and oars floating on the sea.[14] Among the dead was Ali Pasha, commander of Ottoman forces and brother-in-law of Sultan Selim II, whose head was taken for a Spanish trophy, and put up on a pike to demoralise his troops: a later, poetic image had it gruesomely 'oozing with miserable black gore'.[15] From cannonades the battle switched to close combat as each side boarded the other's ships, and between swords, scimitars, maces, knives, bows, guns and grenades, few survived unscathed.[16] One poem on Lepanto described how

> the battered boats drift on the tide, along with torsos of men; here and there, shore birds swoop down on their dismembered bodies and feed on their exposed entrails; far and wide the water reddens with spilled blood.[17]

There was a great deal of luck involved in the Christian victory. That the Ottoman fleet had been at sea quite so long was no doubt a factor. The rain held off until evening, enabling the effective use of firearms, and this gave the Holy League an advantage. So did the favourable wind and the larger numbers of fighting men. Still, the League won only with considerable losses: perhaps 8,000 men dead on their side. Reports in Venice put the number of Ottoman dead at almost double that. By the time Pope Pius V (Antonio Ghislieri, who had been elected in 1566) was notified, the Ottoman death count had been enthusiastically raised to twenty thousand, along with 'a great many prisoners taken' and fifteen thousand Christian slaves freed. Pius celebrated: in letters to Christian rulers he anticipated further victories and enthused at the God-given victory. There were bonfires in Rome, just as there had been almost eighty years before at the news of the Spanish *Reconquista*, the defeat of the Muslim rulers of Granada; there were artillery salvoes too and even plans for 7 October to be made a holiday. Pius would no doubt be gratified to find a Lepanto metro station in twenty-first century Rome, and to discover that today numerous Italian cities have a 'Via Lepanto' or Lepanto Street.

The pope hoped that the campaign for the Holy Land might now proceed, but in vain. He died in 1572: his elaborate tomb in the church of Santa Maria Maggiore includes reliefs showing both the victory at Lepanto and the 1569 defeat of the French Protestants at Moncontour. Dissension between the Christian allies put paid to an effective naval campaign that summer, and the Spanish commander Don Juan of Austria (an illegitimate son of Charles V) opted to focus his attention on Tunis, which he captured in 1573 only to lose it in the face of an Ottoman assault the following year. Meanwhile, Venice made a unilateral peace with the Ottomans, agreeing the surrender of Cyprus, payment of 300,000 ducats in tribute and territorial concessions in Dalmatia.

Lepanto's significance lay less in any great geopolitical advantage for the victors – by the end of the decade, for example, the Ottomans (with French support) had strengthened their control of the North African coast – and more in its symbolism. Both sides saw the outcome as a product of divine intervention. The Turks wondered why God had turned away from them, while in the propaganda of the Counter-Reformation, the triumph at Lepanto was painted as divinely ordained. Pius V ordered new frescoes from Giorgio Vasari, for the Sala Regia, the hall where kings and emperors were received in the Vatican.[18] One of the eventual works showed the preparations for the battle, with improbably neat lines of galleys, while in the foreground allegorical female figures representing the Christian powers were contrasted with the skeletal figure of Death terrifying the enemy. Another showed the chaos of the battle itself, again with an allegorical element of God and the angels in the sky seeing off the enemy demons.[19] The Palazzo Colonna was also adorned with frescoes, and numerous artists took up the subject, among them Titian, Tintoretto and Veronese.

Titian's *Allegory of the Battle of Lepanto* celebrates both the battle (seen in the background) and the birth of Crown Prince Ferdinand of Spain (1571–1578). Acclaimed in Juan Latino's poem on Lepanto as 'a beloved prince granted from heaven for all',[20] the baby is held up by his father to greet the winged figure of Victory, while in the foreground a half-naked Turk appears bound and defeated. Paolo Veronese's treatment of the event (a commission for the church of St

Peter Martyr on the Venetian island of Murano) shows the battle in its lower half while above a series of saints (accompanied by the lion, symbol of Venice and St Mark) invoke the assistance of the Virgin Mary, and an angel casts down flaming arrows against the Turkish fleet. Tintoretto (Jacopo Comin) included a fresco of the battle in his scheme for the Palazzo Ducale in Venice, but it was lost a few years later in a fire. He also produced a portrait of Sebastiano Venier, captain general of the Venetian fleet, showing the battle in the background, an angel overhead. Veronese, too, portrayed Venier in an enormous canvas for the Sala del Collegio, the room of the Palazzo Ducale dedicated to meetings of the ruling council. In it, Venier gives thanks to Christ the Redeemer for the victory, again attended by the symbolic lion along with the figures of Faith and Justice: a spectacular piece of patriotic and religious inspiration for members of Venice's ruling elite. In Spain, there were similar commemorations. Following his move from Italy to Spain, El Greco (Doménikos Theotokópoulos, born in the Venetian colony of Crete) featured Don Juan of Austria, Philip II, the doge of Venice and Pope Pius V, in an *Adoration of the Name of Jesus* for the prestigious royal monastery of El Escorial.

Nor was the art confined to the corridors of power. Numerous more popular poems, pamphlets and engravings were issued, exalting the Venetians and deploring Ottoman misdeeds. 'These noble sons of Romulus,' wrote Giovanni Battista Amalteo in a poem addressed to Sebastiano Venier, 'rush in and fight fiercely through the savages' spears and fire.'[21] In 1572, the victory provided a theme for the annual Venetian Carnival celebrations, which featured the figures of Faith and Victory, the former trampling a Turkish serpent, the latter a Turkish slave.[22] Pope Pius V marked the victory with a new feast for 7 October, that of Our Lady of Victory, later changed to the feast of the Most Holy Rosary, on the grounds that it had been thanks to prayers to Mary that the Christians had prevailed. (Devotion to Mary more broadly was encouraged in this world of Catholic reform.) The 1575 jubilee, an occasion for the issue of special papal indulgences, became an opportunity to celebrate Rome as a global power.[23]

The brutal execution of Marc' Antonio Bragadin, meanwhile, may have inspired Titian's *Flaying of Marsyas*. Painted between 1571 and 1576, it shows the story from Ovid in which the satyr Marsyas is skinned alive for his hubris in challenging the god Apollo.[24] Ovid's description of the mythical scene is both brilliant and horrific:

> The Satyr Marsyas, when he played the flute
> in rivalry against Apollo's lyre, lost that audacious contest and, alas!
> His life was forfeit; for, they had agreed
> the one who lost should be the victor's prey.
> And, as Apollo punished him, he cried,
> 'Ah-h-h! why are you now tearing me apart?
> A flute has not the value of my life!'

> Even as he shrieked out in his agony,
> his living skin was ripped off from his limbs,
> till his whole body was a flaming wound,
> with nerves and veins and viscera exposed.[25]

For Venetian viewers, familiar with the reports from Famagusta, the image must have had a resonance that went far beyond the classics.

Their northern neighbours, meanwhile, were about to face renewed religious war. The year 1572 might have been one of celebration for Venice, but in France the date is remembered for the St Bartholomew's Day massacre, when Huguenot leaders who had gathered in Paris for the wedding of Marguerite de Valois (daughter of Catherine de' Medici and Henri II) to the Protestant king of Navarre were massacred on royal orders in an atrocity that then sparked slaughter, leaving thousands dead. Catherine de' Medici – whose policy of appeasement was unpopular – and her 'Machiavellian' courtiers came to be blamed for the massacre. This is unlikely to be true, but it did much to establish the popular image of the wicked Machiavelli that still prevails today.

If Catherine had trouble in France, so too did Margaret of Parma, wife of Pope Paul III's grandson Ottavio Farnese. She had been governor of the Netherlands since 1559 but repeatedly clashed with her half-brother King Philip II over the approach to religious dissenters. When in 1567 Philip sent an army under the duke of Alba – and gave the duke power to overrule Margaret – she retired to Italy, where she became governor of Abruzzo in the kingdom of Naples. She returned to the Netherlands in 1578, to be coregent with her son Alessandro

Farnese, third duke of Parma, but the experiment failed and she retired again to Italy five years later, where she died in 1586.

For all that Lepanto was a high point for the Catholic powers of Europe, it would in fact be a long time before they fully saw off the military threat of the Ottoman Empire. A century later, in 1683, there would be a second (albeit again unsuccessful) siege of Vienna by the Turks. Meanwhile, there would be ample opportunity to complain of their northern, and especially Protestant, neighbours' alliances, public or secret, with the infidel. In a century when the rhetoric of the crusade had been so frequently deployed to little effect, and when any hard-headed assessment had to concede that the Ottomans had expanded their territory at the expense of both Habsburgs and Venetians, Lepanto offered a rare triumph for a Christian alliance. It was, moreover, a Catholic triumph of which the Catholic powers could boast. They, not the Protestants, had seen off the infidel. It was an image that suited the reformed Rome, sitting as it did at the heart of a newly global Christianity.

Epilogue

From Hard Power to Soft

By the 1570s, Italy had changed and the world had changed around it. Its place at the crossroads of the old trade routes counted for less than it once had because the Western world had a new geography: Antwerp and Amsterdam first, then London, would take advantage of the rise of Atlantic trade, whereas Italy did not have the political structure that would have enabled it to compete with the imperial projects of the large, consolidated European states – though plenty of individual Italians turned those projects to profit. On the other hand, Italy would not suffer the religious wars that convulsed France; the major Italian wars being over, the economy benefited from something approaching peace; and the Mediterranean remained an important trade centre. The decline of Italy was relative, not absolute, and elite Italians remained among the richest people in Europe.[1]

In his 1575 autobiography, Girolamo Cardano, a doctor, mathematician and gambler, identified three technological innovations that had changed his world. They were firearms, the compass and printing. To these he added the discovery of the New World.[2] Similar lists appeared elsewhere: the frontispiece of Jan van der Straet and Philips Galle's *Nova Reperta* ('New Inventions of Modern Times'), shows a map of America celebrating Columbus and Vespucci, along with illustrations of these three technologies among other evidence for scientific progress.[3] In fact, as early as the 1520s, Giovio's *Notable Men and Women* had highlighted firearms and printing alongside Columbus' voyage to the New World as inventions that had 'made this age so renowned for its good fortune'.[4] In these decades, Italian explorers had found territories whose raw materials would be vital to Europe's economic future. They and their Spanish allies had used their experience of Mediterranean colonies and warfare to significant advantage for themselves and their masters, and to the significant detriment of the people whom they enslaved and whose land they appropriated. Italian writers had no qualms about asserting the importance of their contribution. As Piedmontese thinker Giovanni Botero wrote towards the end of the century, 'The Spanish, led by an Italian, have discovered a New World.'[5] But other portrayals of the new technologies sometimes seem more ambiguous. The striking allegorical picture of *Fire* painted by the Milanese artist Giuseppe Arcimboldo in 1566 shows the face of a man constructed from objects that make fire – among them a cannon and handgun – and around his neck the symbol of the Holy Roman Empire's order of chivalry, the Golden Fleece.

The Italian Wars had a long legacy in European warfare, both in a general sense as a practice ground for the tactics and technologies that came to dominate later in the sixteenth and into the seventeenth century, and in a personal sense, as commanders and soldiers moved from Italy on to other wars. On the Italian peninsula itself, meanwhile, the legacy of the wars was, as we have seen, a crisis of banditry and violence, the authorities in disarray over how best to address the availability of guns and to restore public order. The Inquisition, moreover, was making life arduous indeed for prominent scientists: Giordano Bruno was burnt at the stake in 1600 and Galileo put on trial in 1633. Yet if the 'theatre of the world' was no longer the economic powerhouse it had been, it remained a source of wide cultural inspiration. In Northern Europe the Reformation brought some limits to Italian fashions but it is striking that Italian culture and style would manage to transcend religious division in its popularity at the courts of rulers such as Elizabeth I. Italy's association with the classical pagan past meant that some aspects of Renaissance culture could appeal to both Protestants and Catholics. One of St Paul's letters, after all, was written to the Romans: one can hardly write the Roman Empire out of Christianity. In fact, Italy's relative military powerlessness made its cultural legacy peculiarly unproblematic. Tudor students continued to study at Padua, a university notably in the north of Italy, associated with papal rival Venice, and as a consequence less awkward in religious terms for Protestants. Shakespeare set a number of plays in Italy. Indeed, there was what one historian has called a 'late Elizabethan vogue for tourism and for education travel'.[6]

Even as the Italian states struggled to compete with the rising European empires, they managed on a modest scale to consolidate themselves with some degree of independence, often secured by playing off one larger power against another. After the death of the last legitimate heir to the duchy of Ferrara in 1598, it was incorporated into the Papal States: almost a century after Pope Alexander VI had recognised the Este as its rulers in return for his daughter Lucrezia's marriage to Alfonso, Ferrara was firmly papal territory. But many of the great dynasties were entering a long decline. The duchy of Mantua, for example, was troubled throughout the seventeenth century: when the direct line of the ruling family died out in 1627 there followed a disastrous 'War of the Mantuan Succession'. What happened next is testimony to the cultural status of Italian art: amid the crisis King Charles I of England bought a large selection of works from their art collection, which is how Andrea Mantegna's *Triumphs of Caesar* found its way to Hampton Court Palace. Eventually, in 1708, the cadet branch of the Gonzaga family that had succeeded in Mantua was effectively deposed and the duchy fell to Habsburg rule.

In Florence, meanwhile, the Medici dynasty came to an end in 1737. The last of the family, Anna Maria Luisa, the Electress Palatine, endowed the city with the family art collection, securing its status as a jewel-box for the numerous Grand Tourists who came to see the sites of Italy in the eighteenth and nineteenth centuries. In that sense Florence was fortunate: other art collections were sold off and scattered, surviving among the various court collections of Europe and (as European art became fashionable with collectors elsewhere) across the world. Some of the Italian republics – Venice, Lucca, Genoa – were longer-lived. The Lucchese, more cautiously diplomatic when it came to their larger neighbour Florence, contrived to avoid the fate of Siena,[7] while Venice survived until 1797, when it could no longer defend itself against Napoleon. Genoa fell the same year; Lucca lasted only a little longer. Napoleon took the opportunity to acquire (steal) the best of the papal art collections. Some works were returned but many were not, which explains the wealth of Italian art at the Louvre today.

Naples remained under Spanish rule, and became a major European cultural centre attracting leading artists and musicians. At the end of the eighteenth century, in the aftermath of the French Revolution, a republic was established, but was swiftly overturned with the assistance of a British force under Lord Nelson, under whom the leaders of the revolution were executed. Napoleon subsequently invaded but did not hold the city, which returned to the Spanish sphere until the start of Italian unification. It was the Kingdom of the Two Sicilies, in fact, incorporating the kingdom of Naples as well as the island, that provided the basis for Giuseppe Garibaldi's 1860 expedition in pursuit of that unification. Like the Renaissance, the movement for Italian unification quickly acquired a name: the *Risorgimento* or resurgence, the rising (again) of Italy to become a nation. Machiavelli had argued in *The Prince* that Italy should be unified; it had been, of course, in the long-distant Roman past. From 1865, Florence was briefly the new nation's capital, so long as the Papal States held out, but after Bologna voted to join the Kingdom of Italy, and then Rome fell, the pope was left a prisoner in the Vatican. The status of the Vatican remained uncertain until 1929, when it was formally recognised by the Fascist regime. Today, however, Christianity is the world's largest religion, and Roman Catholicism its largest denomination. The Papal States may have been reduced to a tiny enclave, but the global reach of the papacy is greater than ever. Indeed, the election of Francis I points to the legacy of the sixteenth century in the present-day Catholic Church: the child of Italian immigrants to Argentina, he is the first Jesuit pope.

Machiavelli was an important influence elsewhere, too, in the context of debates about how best to organise republics, first in seventeenth-century England and then in eighteenth-century America and France. His works were in the libraries of several of the United States' Founding Fathers; they were discussed by the Genevan philosopher of the Enlightenment, Jean-Jacques Rousseau. Histories of the Italian Renaissance came to have a particular purchase in nineteenth-century America, because the story of how wealthy merchants such as the Medici commissioned the world's greatest art spoke to a new class of person: the bankers and merchant princes of America and beyond. For all that the motivations of these new men were often different from the Catholic piety of their Florentine models, the latter offered a historic and respected template that provided an alternative to claims to the greatness of aristocracy.

It was at the turn of the nineteenth to the twentieth century that the first university courses in Renaissance history were developed. Often these came in a survey of 'Western Civilisation', of which Florence was the cradle.[8] There is a long list of Anglophone literature inspired by Italy from around this time: the work of Henry James, for example, or that of George Eliot who set her 1862 novel *Romola* in Florence at the turn of the fifteenth to the sixteenth century. The British art critic John Ruskin, convinced that art students from all backgrounds should see the best of Italy's culture, brought sketches and drawings of its artworks to the artisans of industrial cities; the villa of Bernard Berenson in the hills outside Florence attracted numerous visitors enthused by his new methods in art history. E. M. Forster, who had taken his own Grand Tour and lectured on Renaissance history at the Working Men's College in London, immortalised Italy's 'pernicious charm' in his 1908 novel *A Room with a View*.

In the Fascist period, the Roman Empire was a more important historical reference point, but Renaissance heritage mattered too. Improvement work was undertaken in key Renaissance cityscapes, such as that of Arezzo, birthplace of Petrarch, which was developed as a focus for tourism; Mussolini himself frequently addressed crowds from Rome's fifteenth-century Palazzo Venezia.[9] A 1930 exhibition of Italian art at the National Gallery in London, featuring works by Botticelli and Titian obtained via strenuous diplomatic effort, was facilitated by Lady Chamberlain, wife of the former British foreign minister and something of a fan of Mussolini; the exhibition made an international statement about both Italian culture and the regime's care for it.[10] Equally, there were ample Renaissance influences in the opposition to fascism. Antonio Gramsci, the leading thinker of the Italian Communist Party, used the metaphor of *The Modern Prince* to describe the revolutionary party. Indeed it is one of Machiavelli's fascinations that one may find him everywhere.

During the Second World War, Renaissance artworks were among those stolen by retreating Nazi troops, and also among those protected by the work of the 'Monuments Men' who coordinated with Allied Forces ahead of the campaign to take Florence. The documentation of sixteenth-century Italy was not so well secured, though: Allied bombing destroyed the archive in Naples. One of the loveliest stories of art protection in the Second World War is told about Piero della Francesca's *Resurrection*. This beautiful fifteenth-century painting shows Christ rising from his tomb as soldiers slumber at his feet, unaware of what is happening. Painted in the 1460s, it was to be found in a monastery in Sansepolcro in southern Tuscany (the town's name means 'Holy Sepulchre' so the painting has particular civic significance) and in an essay published in 1922 was described by the writer Aldous Huxley as 'the greatest picture in the world'.[11] In 2011 Tim Butcher, a BBC journalist, found the diaries of Tony Clarke, the British officer in charge of troops in the area during the war. Clarke had written of his dismay at the destruction of the ancient monastery of Monte Cassino, and told of how rather than risk a repeat of such destruction at Sansepolcro he delayed carrying out his orders to fire on the town. He calculated correctly: its German occupiers surrendered without a shot being fired, and Clarke is remembered with a street name in Sansepolcro.[12] In fact, the flood of 1966 proved a greater threat to Florence's heritage: although over a hundred people died, it is more often remembered internationally for the damage caused to millions of artworks and documents, some of which still have not been fully restored.

Economists today like to complain of the state of the Italian economy – more than once Italy has been labelled the 'sick man of Europe'.[13] Still, Italy remains one of the largest economies in the world, and has been exceptionally good at exporting its past: it sold a history and an image long before 'the brand' was considered crucial to marketing. Half the world's oldest family companies are Italian. Leaving aside the hotels that have been in continuous operation, these firms make bells, wine, glass, jewellery, boats, ceramics and (as we have seen) guns. Then there are the many more modern firms that trade on the reputation of 'made in Italy'. There are fashion houses: Gucci, Prada, Versace, Ferragamo. There are luxury motor brands: Ferrari, Ducati, Alfa Romeo, the last of which uses for its logo the 'biscione' design that was once incorporated in the arms of the Sforza of Milan. In 2019, Emmanuel Macron, president of France, chose the name 'Renaissance' for a liberal-democratic platform in the European Parliament elections.[14]

The modern Grand Tour continues. The museums of Florence are, in one sense, a product of the Renaissance themselves, for at their core lies the collection of the city's rulers, the Medici family. It was in the nineteenth century, however, in the run-up to Italian unification, that a self-conscious process of glorification of the great Italians of the past really picked up pace in Florence's museums. Between 1842 and 1856 the Uffizi Gallery was adorned with a series of statues of these celebrated men. Around the same time, the church of Santa Croce, already a burial place for illustrious local families, became a national and international pantheon of these famous names: its monuments commemorate Galileo, Machiavelli, Michelangelo, Rossini, Dante. Such tombs were described by the Romantic poet Ugo Foscolo, who himself is buried there, as 'urns of the strong, that kindle strong souls to great deeds'.[15] The theme has never gone away. Modern marketing strategists decided to rebrand the city's Science History Museum, reopened in 2010 on the 400th anniversary of Galileo's *Starry Messenger*, as the Museo Galileo. One can see, visiting one museum after another, an emphasis in the interpretation on individual genius, as in the description of the building of Florence's cathedral in the Museo dell'Opera del Duomo, where Brunelleschi's 'architectural genius' takes credit for its dome with no mention of what must have been hundreds of workmen, assistants and the like.

The modern equivalents of the Grand Tour are now no longer the preserve of Europeans. In recent years the fastest growth in tourism to Italy has come from outside the West. The exporting of Italian culture that began in the sixteenth century still sustains the country's economy. Between 2010 and 2017, the number of visitors to Italy from China and Korea tripled. Rising tourism is not without its costs, however: with over 50 million visitors a year, Italy is the fifth-most-visited country in the world. Liberalisation of the housing market has filled many city centres with short-term holiday flats at the expense of tenancies for locals; Venice is beset by controversy over the large cruise ships that bring day-trippers to its lagoon; there are proposals for a tax on day visitors.[16] This is not only tourism, however, but part of a global dynamics of economic power: in 2019, Italy became the first western country to join China's new 'Silk Road' initiative.[17]

As one of the few western powers that – despite Mussolini's efforts – never really succeeded in building a modern empire, Italy has always had a curious role in the world: its importance has been defined by culture and ideas more than by wealth and territory. Indeed, it is a joy to appreciate the art and literature produced in Italy during the Renaissance and I hope that many more people will have the pleasure of visiting the artworks of Florence, or reading the satires of Aretino, or the elegant poetry of Vittoria Colonna. It is hard to imagine that they will stop: as I finished this book in the late spring of 2019, a debate on the authenticity or otherwise of the *Salvator Mundi*, a five-hundred-year-old painting controversially attributed to Leonardo da Vinci, was front page news in Britain.[18] But it is also important to know where that work comes from, how it fits into the wider history of the world, and how even in its own time its interpretation was shaped by men like Giorgio Vasari for future audiences. At the end of the *Art of War*, after a furious critique of the failure of the Italian princes, Machiavelli looked in contrast at the rich cultural life about him and observed that Italy 'seems born to resuscitate dead things'.[19] Yet today the resuscitation of Renaissance culture often leaves out the turmoil and trauma of the society from which it emerged, or else (as in the case of Machiavelli himself) accords it a distorted image of scheming and wickedness. Perhaps it is better to think of this period of history as a Pandora's Box, which even as it released all sorts of evils into the world, also preserved the possibility of hope.

Acknowledgements

This book could not have been written without the input of many colleagues and friends, too numerous to list here, with whom over the years I have had the opportunity to discuss the various themes covered. I am immensely grateful to Sarah Cockram, Caroline Dodds Pennock, Sheryl Reiss and Ellie Woodacre for reading and commenting on the manuscript, to the students of my Special Subject, 'The Borgias and Beyond' for their insights, and to Swansea University for the research leave that allowed me to complete the book. Any errors are, of course, my own. I am indebted to the librarians and archivists not only at Swansea but also at the British Library, the Warburg Institute and the Institute for Historical Research for developing and maintaining the collections that made my research possible. An alumni residency at the British School at Rome in summer 2017 helped me get started on the writing. Further thanks go to my agents Catherine Clarke at Felicity Bryan Associates and Katie Langridge at Knight Hall Agency, to my editors Will Hammond at Bodley Head and Tim Bent at Oxford University Press, to Henry Howard for copy-editing and Stephen Parker for the cover design.

Extracts from translations are reproduced by kind permission of the following: Brepols Publishers for Geoffrey Symcox and Luciano Formisano (eds), *Italian Reports on America, 1493–1522: Accounts by Contemporary Observers* and Geoffrey Symcox (ed.) *Italian Reports on America, 1493–1522: Letters, Dispatches and Papal Bulls*; Oxford University Press for Giorgio Vasari, *Lives of the Artists*, trans. Julia Conaway Bondanella and Peter Bondanella, and for *A Corresponding Renaissance*, trans. Lisa Kaborycha; the Hakluyt Society for *The Travel Journal of Antonio de Beatis*, trans. John Hale; Princeton University Press for

Complete Poems and Selected Letters of Michelangelo, trans. Creighton Gilbert; Italica Press for Luigi Guicciardini, *The Sack of Rome*, trans. James H. McGregor. Every effort has been made to trace copyright holders and to obtain their permission for the use of copyright material. The publisher apologises for any errors or omissions in the above list and would be grateful if notified of any corrections that should be incorporated in future reprints or editions of this book.

Bibliography

NB: date of most recent access of all websites: 4 November 2019.

Primary sources

An Anthology of Italian Poems, 13th–19th Century. 1922. Ed. and trans. Lorna de' Lucchi. New York.

Aretino, Pietro. 1900. *Un pronostico satirico di Pietro Aretino.* Ed. Alessandro Luzio. Bergamo.

———. 1957. *Lettere sull'Arte di Pietro Aretino.* Milan.

———. 1994. *Dialogues.* Trans. Raymond Rosenthal. New York.

Ariosto, Ludovico. 1909–13. *Orlando Furioso.* Ed. Filippo Ermini. 3 vols. Rome.

Ascham, Roger. 1904. *English Works.* Ed. W. A. Wright. Cambridge.

Barbaro, Nicolò. 1969. *Diary of the Siege of Constantinople, 1453.* Trans. J. R. Jones. New York.

Battiferra degli Ammanati, Laura. 2006. *Laura Battiferra and Her Literary Circle: An Anthology.* Ed. Victoria Kirkham. Chicago.

The Battle of Lepanto. 2014. Ed. and trans. Elizabeth R. Wright, Sarah Spence and Andrew Lemons. Cambridge, Mass.

Beatis, Antonio de. 1979 *The Travel Journal of Antonio de Beatis.* Ed. J. R. Hale. Trans. J. R. Hale and J. M. A. Lindon. London.

Benedetti, Alessandro. 1967. *Diaria de bello carolino (Diary of the Caroline War).* Trans. Dorothy M. Schullian. New York.

Benivieni, Antonio. 1528. *De abditis nonnullis ac mirandis morborum et sanationum causis.* Paris.

Botero, Giovanni. 1612. *Relationi.* Venice.

Bracciolini, Poggio. 1984–7. *Lettere.* Ed. Helene Harth. 3 vols. Florence.

Burchard, Johann. 1907–42. *Liber notarum.* Ed. Enrico Celani. 2 vols. Città di Castello.

Cardano, Girolamo. 2002. *The Book of My Life.* Trans. Jean Stoner. New York.

Castiglione, Baldesar. 1967. *The Book of the Courtier.* Trans. George Bull. Harmondsworth.

Cellini, Benvenuto. 1998. *Autobiography*. Trans. George Bull. Harmondsworth.

Cerretani, Bartolomeo. 1993. *Ricordi*. Ed. Giuliana Berti. Florence.

Columbus, Christopher. 1990. *Journal of the First Voyage, 1492*. Ed. and trans. B. W. Ife. Warminster.

Commynes, Philippe de. 1840–47. *Mémoires*. 3 vols. Paris.

———. 1906. *The Memoirs of Philip de Commines*. Ed. and trans. Andrew R. Scobie. 2 vols. London.

Contarini, Giovanni Pietro. 1645. *Historia delle cose successe dal principio della guerra mossa da Selim*. Venice.

Correspondenz des Kaisers Karl V. 1844–5. Ed. K. Lanz. 2 vols. Leipzig.

A Corresponding Renaissance: Letters Written by Italian Women, 1375–1630. 2016. Ed. and trans. Lisa Kaborycha. New York.

Le cronache bresciane inedite dei secoli xv–xix. 1927. Ed. and trans. Paolo Guerrini. Brescia.

Cronache dell'assedio di Pavia. 2012. Ed. Mattia Belloni. Pavia.

Crónicas del Gran Capitán. 1908. Ed. Antonio Rodríguez Villa. Madrid.

D'Aragona, Tullia. 2014. *The Poems and Letters of Tullia d'Aragona and Others*. Ed. and trans. Julia L. Hairston. Toronto.

Decrees of the Ecumenical Councils. 1990. Ed. Norman P. Tanner S. J. 2 vols. London.

Diario anonimo dell'assedio di Pavia (ottobre 1524–febbraio 1525). 2015. Ed. Marco Galandra. Pavia.

Diario Ferrarese. 1738. In *Rerum Italicarum Scriptores* vol. 24, cols 173–408. Milan.

Documenti inediti per la storia delle armi da fuoco italiane. 1869. Ed. Angelo Angelucci. Turin.

Du Bellay, Martin and Guillaume. 1908–19. *Mémoires de Martin et Guillaume Du Bellay*. 4 vols. Paris.

Egidio da Viterbo. 2012. *Orazioni per il Concilio Lateranense V*, ed. F. Troncarelli, G. Troncarelli and M. P. Saci with Antonio Lombardi and Rocco Ronzani. Rome.

Erasmus of Rotterdam. 1974–. *Collected Works*. 89 vols. Toronto.

d'Este, Isabella. 2017. *Selected Letters*. Ed. and trans. Deanna Shemek. Toronto.

Fantaguzzi, Giuliano. 1915. *'Caos': Cronache Cesanati del sec. XV pubblicate ora per la prima volta di su i manoscritti con notizie e note e cura del Dott. Dino Bazzocchi*. Cesena.

Fedele, Cassandra. 2000. *Letters and Orations*. Ed. and trans. Diana Robin. Chicago.

Foscolo, Ugo. 1985. *Poesie e Carmi*. Ed. Francesco Pagliai, Gianfranco Folena and Mario Scotti. Florence.

Gambara, Veronica. 1759. *Rime e lettere*. Ed. Felice Rizzardi. Brescia.

Gilino, Coradino. [*c*.1497/8.] *De Morbo quem Gallico nuncupant*. Ferrara.

———. 1930. *The 'De Morbo Quem Gallicum Nuncupant' (1497) of Coradinus Gilinus*. Ed. Cyril C. Barnard. Leiden.

Giovanni da Empoli. 1846. 'Lettera di Giovanni da Empoli a Leonardo, suo padre.' In *Archivio Storico Italiano*, Appendix, vol. 3.

Giovio, Paolo. 1597. *La vita di Alfonso da Este duca di Ferrara*. Trans. Giovambattista Gelli. Venice.

———. 1931. *Le vite del Gran Capitano e del Marchese di Pescara*. Bari.

———. 1956. *Lettere*. Ed. G. G. Ferrero. Rome.

———. 2006. *Elogi degli uomini illustri*. Ed. Franco Minonzio. Turin.

———. 2013. *Notable Men and Women of Our Times*. Ed. and trans. Kenneth Gouwens. Cambridge, Mass.

Giustinian, Antonio. 1876. *Dispacci*. Ed. P. Villari. 3 vols. Florence.

Guicciardini, Francesco. 1763. *The History of Italy*. Trans. Austin Parke Goddard. 10 vols. London.

———. 1969. *The History of Italy*. Ed. and trans. Sidney Alexander. London.

Guicciardini, Luigi. 1993. *The Sack of Rome*. Ed. and trans. James H. McGregor. New York.

The Illustrations from the Works of Andreas Vesalius of Brussels. 1973. Ed. J. B. deC. M. Saunders and Charles D. O'Malley. New York.

Italian Reports on America, 1493–1522: Letters, Dispatches and Papal Bulls. 2001. Ed. Geoffrey Symcox and Giovanna Rabitti. Trans. Peter D. Diehl. Turnhout.

Italian Reports on America, 1493–1522: Accounts by Contemporary Observers. 2002. Ed. Geoffrey Symcox and Luciano Formisano. Trans. Theodore J. Cachey, Jr. and John C. McLucas. Turnhout.

Landi, Giulio. 1574. *La descrittione de l'isola de la Madera*. Trans. Alemanio Fini. Piacenza.

Leo Africanus. 1896. *The History and Description of Africa*. Ed. Robert Brown. 3 vols. London.

Leonardo da Vinci. 1877. *A Treatise on Painting*. Trans. John Francis Rigaud. London.

———. 2008. *Notebooks*. Selected by Irma Richter. Ed. Thereza Wells. Oxford.

Letters and Papers, Foreign and Domestic, of the Reign of Henry VIII. 1862–1932. Ed. J. S. Brewer, R. H. Brodie and James Gairdner. London.

Levita, Elias. 1867. *The Massoreth Ha-Massoreth*. Ed. and trans. Christian D. Ginsburg. London.

Loise de Rosa. 1971. *Napoli aragonese nei ricordi di Loise de Rosa*. Ed. Antonio Altamura. Naples.

[Lorenzi, Giovanni Battista.] 1870–2. *Leggi e Memorie Venete sulla Prostituzione fino alla Caduta della Repubblica*. Venice.

Lorenzo de' Medici at Home: The Inventory of the Palazzo Medici in 1492. 2013. Ed. and trans. Richard Stapleford. Philadelphia.

Luna, Fabricio. 1536. *Vocabulario de cinquemila vocabuli toschi.* [Naples.]

Luther, Martin. 1857. *Table Talk.* Ed. and trans. William Hazlitt. London.

———. 1914. *D. Martin Luthers Werke*, Ser. 2, vol. 3, *Tischreden aus den dreissiger Jahren.* Weimar.

Machiavelli, Niccolò. 1908. *The Prince.* Trans. W. K. Marriott. London.

———. 1968–82. *Opere.* Ed. Sergio Bertelli. Milan.

———. 1984. *The Prince.* Ed. Peter Bondanella. Trans. Peter Bondanella and Mark Musa. Oxford.

———. 1989. *The Chief Works and Others.* Trans. Allan Gilbert. 3 vols. Durham, NC.

———. 2003. *Art of War.* Ed. and trans. Christopher Lynch. Chicago.

Marguerite of Navarre. 1999. *Heptaméron.* Ed. Renja Salminen. Geneva.

Michelangelo Buonarroti. 1963. *The Letters of Michelangelo.* Ed. and trans. E. H. Ramsden. 2 vols. London.

———. 1965–83. *Il carteggio di Michelangelo.* Ed. P. Barocchi and R. Ristori. 5 vols. Florence.

———. 1980. *Complete Poems and Selected Letters.* Ed. Robert N. Linscott. Trans. Creighton Gilbert. Princeton.

Modesty, Jacopo. 1842. 'Il miserando sacco dato alla terra di Prato dagli spagnoli l'anno 1512'. *Archivio Storico Italiano* 1: 233–51.

Monluc, Blaise de. 1864–72. *Commentaires et lettres de Blaise de Monluc, Maréchal de France.* Ed. Alphonse de Rable. 5 vols. Paris.

Montaigne, Michel de. 1991. *The Essays of Michel de Montaigne.* Ed. and trans. M. A. Screech, 3 vols. London.

Montoiche, Guillaume de. 1881. 'Voyage et Expédition de Charles-Quint au Pays de Tunis, de 1535'. In *Collection des Voyages des Souverains des Pays-Bas, Tome troisième* Ed. [L.-P.] Gachard and [C.] Piot. Brussels, 317–400.

Muffel N. 1999. *Descrizione della città di Roma nel 1452.* Ed. and trans. G. Wiedmann. Bologna.

Navagero, Andrea. 1563. *Il viaggio fatto in Spagna et in Francia.* Venice.

Ovid, *Metamorphoses.* 1922. Trans. Brookes More. Boston. Online at http://www.perseus.tufts.edu/hopper/text?doc=urn:cts:latinLit:phi0959.phi006.perseus-eng1

Pasquinate romane del Cinquecento. 1983. Ed. Valerio Marucci, Antonio Marzo and Angelo Romano. Rome.

Piccolomini, E. S. (Pope Pius II). 1685. *Historia Rerum Friderici Imperatoris.* Ed. J. H. Boecleri. Strasbourg.

———. 1988. *Secret Memoirs of a Renaissance Pope: The Commentaries of Aeneas Sylvius Piccolomini, Pius II.* Ed. Leona C. Gabel. Trans. Florence A. Gragg. London.

Pigafetta, Antonio. 1906. *Magellan's Voyage Around the World.* Ed. James A. Robertson. 2 vols. Cleveland.

The Portuguese in West Africa, 1415–1670: A Documentary History. 2010. Ed. Malyn Newitt. Cambridge.

Primary Sources on Copyright (1450–1900). Ed. L. Bently and M. Kretschmer. http:// copyrighthistory.org

Raphael in Early Modern Sources, 1483–1602. 2003. Ed. John Shearman. 2 vols. New Haven–London.

Relazioni degli ambasciatori veneti al Senato. 1839–55. Ed. Eugenio Albèri. 3 series. Venice.

Romano, Giulio, Marcantonio Raimondi, Pietro Aretino and Count Jean-Fréderic-Maximilien de Waldeck. 1988. *I Modi. The Sixteen Pleasures: An Erotic Album of the Italian Renaissance*. Ed. and trans. Lynne Lawner. London.

Sanuto [Sanudo], Marin. 1738. 'De Bello Gallico'. In *Rerum italicarum scriptores* vol. 24, cols 1–166. Milan.

———. 1883. *La spedizione di Carlo VIII in Italia*. Ed. Rinaldo Fulin. Venice.

———. 1969–70. *Diarii*. Ed. Rinaldo Fulin et al. 58 vols. Bologna.

Savonarola, Girolamo. 1973. *Il primo Savonarola: Poesie e prediche autografe dal codice Borromeo*. Ed. Giulio Cattin. Florence.

———. 2003. *A Guide to Righteous Living and Other Works*. Trans. Konrad Eisenbichler. Toronto.

———. 2006. *Selected Writings of Girolamo Savonarola: Religion and Politics, 1490–1498*. New Haven–London.

The Siege of Constantinople 1453: Seven Contemporary Accounts. 1972. Trans. J. R. Melville Jones. Amsterdam.

Sozzini, Alessandro di Girolamo. 1842. 'Il successo delle rivoluzioni della città di Siena d'imperiale franzese e di franzese imperiale'. *Archivio Storico Italiano* 2: 1, 3–434.

State Papers Published under the Authority of His Majesty's Commission. 1830–52. London.

Street Life in Renaissance Rome. 2013. Ed. Rudolph M. Bell. Boston.

Taegio [Franciscus Taegius/Francesco Tegio]. 1655. *Rotta e prigionia di Francesco Primo Re di Francia*. Pavia.

Tartaglia, Niccolò. 1546. *Quesiti et Inventioni Diverse*. Venice.

Thomas, William. 1549. *The Historie of Italie*. London. *Early English Books Online Text Creation Partnership*, http://name.umdl.umich.edu/A13726. 0001.001

Valeriano Giovanni Pierio. 1620. *De litteratorum infelicitate libri duo*. Venice.

Varthema, Ludovico di. 1863. *The Travels of Ludovico di Varthema*. Ed. John Winter Jones and George Percy Badger. London.

Vasari, Giorgio. 1912–14. *Lives of the Most Eminent Painters, Sculptors and Architects*. Trans. Gaston du C. De Vere. 10 vols. London. Online at https:// ebooks.adelaide.edu.au/v/vasari/giorgio/lives

———. 1991. *The Lives of the Artists*. Trans. Julia Conaway Bondanella and Peter Bondanella. Oxford.

Venice: A Documentary History. 1992. Ed. D. Chambers and B. Pullan. Oxford.

Vergil, Polydore. *Anglia Historia*. Ed. and trans. Dana F. Sutton. Online at
http://www.philological.bham.ac.uk/polverg

Vespasiano da Bisticci. 1926. *The Vespasiano Memoirs: Lives of Illustrious Men
of the XVth Century*. Trans. William George and Emily Waters. London.

*The Voyages of Cadamosto and other Documents on Western Africa in the Second
Half of the Fifteenth Century*. 2017. Ed. and trans. G. R. Crone. London.

Whitcomb, Merrick. 1903. *Source-Book of the Italian Renaissance*, revised ed.
Philadelphia.

Secondary literature

Abulafia, David. Ed. 1995. *The French Descent into Renaissance Italy*. Aldershot.

Ágoston, Gábor. 2005. *Guns for the Sultan: Military Power and the Weapons
Industry in the Ottoman Empire*. Cambridge.

———. 2013. 'War-winning weapons? On the decisiveness of Ottoman
firearms from the Siege of Constantinople (1453) to the Battle of Mohács
(1526)'. *Journal of Turkish Studies* 39: 129–43.

Ait, Ivana. 2005. 'Clement VII and the Sack of Rome as represented in the
Ephemerides Historicae of Cornelius de Fine'. In Gouwens and Reiss, 109–24.

Ambrosini, Federica. 2000. 'Towards a social history of women in Venice:
from the Renaissance to the Enlightenment'. In J. Martin and D. Romano,
Venice Reconsidered: The History and Civilization of an Italian City State.
Baltimore, 420–53.

Aquilecchia, Giovanni. 2000. 'Aretino's *Sei giornate*: Literary parody and social
reality'. In Panizza, 453–62.

Arbel, Benjamin. 2001. 'Jews in International Trade: The Emergence of the
Levantines and Ponentines'. In Davis and Ravid, 71–96.

Arfaioli, Maurizio. 2005. *The Black Bands of Giovanni: Infantry and Diplomacy
during the Italian Wars*. Pisa.

Arnold, Thomas F. 1995. 'Fortifications and the military revolution: The
Gonzaga experience, 1530–1630'. In Rogers, 201–26.

Arrizabalaga, Jon, John Henderson and Roger French. 1997. *The Great Pox:
The French Disease in Renaissance Europe*. New Haven–London.

Audisio, Gabriel. 1999. *The Waldensian Dissent: Persecution and Survival,
c.1170–c.1570*. Cambridge.

Avery, Victoria. 2018. *Michelangelo: Sculptor in Bronze: The Rothschild Bronzes*.
Cambridge.

Azzolini, Monica. 2013. *The Duke and the Stars: Astrology and Politics in Renaissance Milan*. Cambridge, Mass.

Baker, Nicholas Scott. 2013. *The Fruit of Liberty: Political Culture in the Florentine Republic*. Cambridge, Mass.

Baker-Bates, Piers. 2017. *Sebastiano del Piombo and the World of Spanish Rome*.
London.

Baker-Bates, Piers, and Miles Pattenden. Eds. 2014. *The Spanish Presence in Sixteenth-Century Italy: Images of Iberia*. Farnham.

Bamji, Alexandra, Geert H. Janssen and Mary Laven. 2016. *The Ashgate Research Companion to the Counter-Reformation*. London.

Barbieri, Costanza. 2005. 'The competition between Raphael and Michelangelo and Sebastiano's role in it'. In Hall 2005a, 141–64.

Barkan, Leonard. 2011. *Michelangelo: A Life on Paper*. Princeton.

Barzaghi, Antonio. 1980. *Donne o Cortigiane: La Prostituzione a Venezie: Documenti di Costume dal XVI al XVIII secolo*. Verona.

Beinart, Haim. 2002. *The Expulsion of the Jews from Spain*, trans. Jeffrey M. Green. Oxford.

Bejczy, István. 2011. *The Cardinal Virtues in the Middle Ages: A Study in Moral Thought from the Fourth to the Fourteenth Century*. Leiden.

Bellonci, Maria. 2000. *Lucrezia Borgia*. London.

Benner, Erica. 2013. *Machiavelli's Prince: A New Reading*. Oxford.

———. 2017. *Be Like the Fox: Machiavelli's Lifelong Quest for Freedom*. London.

Bentley, Jerry H. 1987. *Politics and Culture in Renaissance Naples*. Princeton.

Bestor, Jane Fair 1996. 'Bastardy and legitimacy in the formation of a Renaissance state in Italy: the Estense succession'. *Comparative Studies in Society and History* 38: 549–85.

Biagioli, Mario. 1989. 'The social status of Italian mathematicians, 1450–1600', *History of Science* 27: 41–95.

Bicheno, Hugh. 2003. *Crescent and Cross: The Battle of Lepanto 1571*. London.

Bireley, Robert. 1999. *The Refashioning of Catholicism, 1450–1700: A Reassessment of the Counter-Reformation*. New York.

Bisaha, Nancy. 2006. *Creating East and West: Renaissance Humanists and the Ottoman Turks*. University Park, Pa.

Black, Christopher. 2000. *Early Modern Italy: A Social History*. London.

———. 2009. *The Italian Inquisition*. New Haven–London.

Black, Robert. 2013. *Machiavelli*. Abingdon.

Blockmans, Wim. 2002. *Emperor Charles V, 1500–1558*. London.

Bonfil, Robert. 1994. *Jewish Life in Renaissance Italy*, trans. Anthony Oldcorn. Berkeley.

Bosker, M., S. Brakman, H. Garretsen, H. de Jong and M. Schramm. 2007. 'The development of cities in Italy, 1300–1861.' Online at http://www.ehs.org.uk/dotAsset/491c2f80-6f0e-42c2-becb-228b23ef47b7.pdf

Bourne, Molly. 2010. 'Mail humour and male sociability: Sexual innuendo in the epistolary domain of Francesco II Gonzaga'. In *Erotic Cultures of Renaissance Italy*, ed. Sara F. Matthews-Grieco. Abingdon, 119–221.

Bowd, Stephen. 2018. *Renaissance Mass Murder: Civilians and Soldiers during the Italian Wars*. Oxford.

Brackett, John K. 2005. 'Race and rulership: Alessandro de' Medici, first Medici duke of Florence, 1529–1537'. In Earle and Lowe, 303–25.

Bradford, Sarah. 2005. *Lucrezia Borgia: Life, Love and Death in Renaissance Italy*. London.

Bratchel, M. E. 1995. *Lucca 1430–1494: The Reconstruction of an Italian City-Republic*. Oxford.

Braudel, Fernand. 1975. *The Mediterranean and the Mediterranean World in the Age of Philip II*, trans. Siân Reynolds. London.

Brege, Brian. 2017. 'Renaissance Florentines in the tropics: Brazil, the Grand Duchy of Tuscany, and the limits of empire'. In Horodowich and Markey, 206–22.

Breisach, Ernst. 1967. *Caterina Sforza: A Renaissance Virago*. Chicago.

Brigden, Susan. 2013. 'Henry VIII and the crusade against England.' In *Henry VIII and the Court: Art, Politics and Performance*, ed. Thomas Betteridge and Suzannah Lipscomb. Farnham, 215–34.

Brooks, Francis. 2001. 'The impact of disease', in Raudzens, 127–65.

Brotton, Jerry. 2003. *The Renaissance Bazaar*. Oxford.

Brugnoli, Maria Vittoria. 1974. 'Il Cavallo', in Reti, 86–109.

Brummett, Palmira Johnson. 1994. *Ottoman Seapower and Levantine Diplomacy in the Age of Discovery*. New York.

Brundin, Abigail. 2002. 'Vittoria Colonna and the poetry of reform'. *Italian Studies* 57: 61–74.

———. 2016. *Vittoria Colonna and the Spiritual Poetics of the Italian Reformation*. London.

Bruscoli, Francesco Guidi. 2012. 'John Cabot and his Italian financiers', *Historical Research* 85: 372–93.

———. 2014. *Bartolomeo Marchionni 'Homem de grossa fazenda' (ca. 1450–1530): Un mercante fiorentino a Lisbona e l'impero portoghese*. Florence.

Buchanan, Iain. 2002. 'The "Battle of Pavia" and the tapestry collection of Don Carlos: New Documentation'. *Burlington Magazine* 144: 345–51.

Buranelli, Francesco. 2008. 'L'appartamento Borgia in Vaticano'. In *Pintoricchio*, ed. Vittoria Garibaldi and Francesco Federico Mancini. Milan, 69–73.

Burke, Jill. 2013. 'Nakedness and other peoples: Rethinking the Italian Renaissance nude'. *Art History* 36: 714–39.

———. 2018. *The Italian Renaissance Nude*. New Haven–London.

Burke, Peter. 1974. *Venice and Amsterdam: A Study of Seventeenth-Century Elites*. London.

———. 1995. *The Fortunes of the Courtier*. Cambridge.

———. 2002. 'Early Modern Venice as a center of information and communication'. In *Venice Reconsidered: The History and Civilisation of an Italian City-State, 1297–1797*, ed. John Martin and Dennis Romano. Baltimore, 389–419.

Byatt, Lucinda M. C. 1988. 'The concept of hospitality in a cardinal's household in Renaissance Rome', *Renaissance Studies* 2: 312–20.

Campbell, Caroline, and Alan Chong. 2005. *Bellini and the East*. London.

Cantagalli, Roberto. 1962. *La guerra di Siena (1552–1559)*. Siena.

Carboni, Stefano. 2007. *Venice and the Islamic World, 828–1797*. New York.

Carlsmith, Christopher. 2010. *A Renaissance Education: Schooling in Bergamo and the Venetian Republic, 1500–1650*. Toronto.

Cartwright, Julia May. 1908. *Baldassare Castiglione: The Perfect Courtier, his Life and Letters*. 2 vols. London.

Chambers, David. 1966. 'The economic predicament of Renaissance cardinals'. In *Studies in Medieval and Renaissance History* 3, ed. William M. Bowsky. Lincoln, 289–313.

Chase, Kenneth. 2003. *Firearms: A Global History to 1700*. Cambridge.

Chastel, André. 1983. *The Sack of Rome, 1527*, trans. Beth Archer. Princeton.

Chen, Andrew. 2018. *Flagellant Confraternities and Italian Art, 1260–1610: Ritual and Experience*. Amsterdam.

Cicogna, Emanuele Antonio. 1855. *Della vita e delle opere di Andrea Navagero*. Venice.

Clayton, Martin. 2018. *Leonardo da Vinci: A Life in Drawing*. London.

Clough, Cecil H. 1967. 'The relations between the English and Urbino courts, 1474–1508'. *Studies in the Renaissance* 14: 202–18

———. 2003. 'Three Gigli of Lucca in England during the fifteenth and early sixteenth centuries: Diversification in a family of mercenary merchants'. *The Ricardian* 13: 121–47.

———. 2005. 'Clement VII and Francesco Maria della Rovere, duke of Urbino'. In Gouwens and Reiss, 75–108.

Cochrane, Eric. 1980. 'The transition from Renaissance to Baroque historiography', *History and Theory* 19: 21–38.

———. 1981. 'The profession of historian in the Italian Renaissance', *Journal of Social History* 15: 51–72.

Cocke, Richard. 2001. *Paolo Veronese*. Aldershot.

Cockram, Sarah. 2016. *Isabella d'Este and Francesco Gonzaga: Power Sharing at the Italian Renaisssance Court*. London.

Comerford, Kathleen M. 2017. *Jesuit Foundations and Medici Power, 1532–1621*. Leiden.

Coniglio, Giuseppe. 1984. *Il viceregno di don Pietro di Toledo (1532–53)*. 2 vols. Naples.

Cook, Weston F. 1994. *The Hundred Years War for Morocco: Gunpowder and the Military Revolution in the Early Modern Muslim World*. Boulder.

Cools, Hans, Catrien Santing and Hans de Valk. Eds. 2010. *Adrian VI: A Dutch Pope in a Roman Context*. Special issue of *Fragmenta: Journal of the Royal Netherlands Institute in Rome* 4.

Cox, Virginia. 2008. *Women's Writing in Italy 1400–1650*. Baltimore.

Creighton, M. 1882. *A History of the Papacy during the Period of the Reformation, Volume II: The Council of Basel to the Papal Restoration, 1418–1464*. London.

Cresti, Carlo, Amelio Fara and Daniela Lamberini. Eds. 1988. *Architecture militare nell'Europa del XVI secolo*, Atti del Convegno di Studi, Firenze, 25–28 novembre 1986. Siena.

Crowley, Roger. 2008. *Empires of the Sea: The Siege of Malta, the Battle of Lepanto, and the Contest for the Center of the World*. New York.

Crummey, Robert O. 1987. *The Formation of Muscovy, 1304–1613*. London.

Cummins, Stephen. 2014. 'Encountering Spain in Early Modern Naples: Language, customs and sociability'. In Baker-Bates and Pattenden, 43–62.

Dall'Aglio, Stefano. 2010. *Savonarola and Savonarolism*. Toronto.

———. 2015. *The Duke's Assassin: Exile and Death of Lorenzino de' Medici*, trans. Donald Weinstein. New Haven–London.

Dalton, Heather, Jukka Salo, Pekka Niemela and Simo Orma. 2018. 'Frederick II of Hohenstaufen's Australasian cockatoo: Symbol of detente between East and West and evidence of the Ayyubids' global reach'. *Parergon* 35: 35–60

Dandelet, Thomas. 2001. *Spanish Rome, 1500–1700*. New Haven–London.

Davidson, Miles H. 1997. *Columbus Then and Now: A Life Re-examined*. Norman, Okla.

Davis, Natalie Zemon. 2008. *Trickster Travels: The Search for Leo Africanus*. London.

Davis, Robert C. 2008. 'The Renaissance goes up in smoke', in *The Renaissance World*, ed. John Jeffries Martin. London, 398–411.

Davis, Robert C., and Benjamin Ravid. Eds. 2001. *The Jews of Early Modern Venice*. Baltimore.

Dean, Trevor, and K. J. P. Lowe. Eds. 1998. *Marriage in Italy, 1300–1650*. Cambridge.

De Jong, Jan L. 2003. 'The painted decoration of the Sala Regia in the Vatican: Intention and reception'. In *Functions and Decorations: Art and Ritual at the Vatican Palace in the Middle Ages and the Renaissance*, ed. T. Weddigen, S. De Blaauw and B. Kempers. Turnhout, 153–68.

———. 2013. *The Power and the Glorification: Papal Pretensions and the Art of Propaganda in the Fifteenth and Sixteenth Centuries*. University Park, Pa.

Delaborde, Henri François. 1888. *L'Expédition de Charles VIII en Italie*. Paris.

Dell'Orto, Giovanni. 2000. 'Pier Luigi Farnese'. In *Who's Who in Gay and Lesbian History*, ed. *Robert Aldrich and Garry Wotherspoon. 2 vols, London, vol. 1, ad vocem; online at http://www.giovannidallorto.com/biografie/farnese/farnese.html*

De Roover, R. 1963. *The Rise and Decline of the Medici Bank, 1397–1494*. Cambridge, Mass.

DeSilva, Jennifer M. 2008. 'Senators or courtiers: Negotiating models for the College of Cardinals under Julius II and Leo X'. *Renaissance Studies* 22: 154–73.

DeVries, Kelly. 1990. 'Military surgical practice and the advent of gunpowder weaponry'. *Canadian Bulletin of Medical History* 7: 131–46.

——. 1999. 'The lack of a Western European military response to the Ottoman invasions of Eastern Europe from Nicopolis (1396) to Mohacs (1526)', *Journal of Military History* 63: 539–59.

Dictionary of Canadian Biography. Toronto, 2003–19. Online at http://www.biographi.ca

Domenici, Davide. 2017. 'Missionary gift records of Mexican objects in early modern Italy'. In Horodowich and Markey, 86–102.

Donati, Claudio. 1995. *L'Idea di nobiltà in Italia secoli XIV–XVIII*, 2nd edition. Rome–Bari.

Donattini, Massimo. 2017. 'Three Bolognese Franciscan missionaries in the New World in the early sixteenth century'. In Horodowich and Markey, 63–85.

Doria, Giorgio. 1986. 'Conoscenza del mercato e sistema informative: il know-how dei mercanti-finanzieri genovesi nei secoli XVI e XVII'. In *La repubblica internazionale del denaro tra XV e XVII secolo*, ed. Aldo De Maddalena and Hermann Kellenbenz. Bologna, 57–121.

Dursteler, Eric. 2006. *Venetians in Constantinople: Nation, Identity and Coexistence in the Early Modern Mediterranean.* Baltimore.

——. Ed. 2013. *A Companion to Venetian History, 1400–1797.* Leiden.

Eamon, William. 2013. 'Science and medicine in Early Modern Venice'. In Dursteler 2013, 701–41.

Earle, T. F., and K. J. P. Lowe. Eds. 2010. *Black Africans in Renaissance Europe.* Cambridge.

Eisenbichler, Konrad. 1999. 'Charles V in Bologna: The self-fashioning of a man and a city'. *Renaissance Studies* 13: 430–39.

——. 2012. *The Sword and the Pen: Women, Politics and Poetry in Sixteenth-Century Siena.* Notre Dame.

Elam, Caroline. 2005. 'Michelangelo and the Clementine architectural style'. In Gouwens and Reiss, 199–225.

Epstein, Stephan R. 2007. 'L'economia italiana nel quadro europeo'. In *Il Rinascimento Italiano e l'Europa*, vol. 4, *Commercio e cultura mercantile*, ed. Franco Franceschini, Richard A. Goldthwaite and Reinhold C. Muller. Vicenza, 3–47.

Epstein, Steven A. 1996. *Genoa and the Genoese, 958–1528.* Chapel Hill, NC.

——. 2009. *An Economic and Social History of Later Medieval Europe.* Cambridge.

Eschrich, Gabriella Scarlatti. 2009. 'Women writing women in Lodovico Domenichi's anthology of 1559', *Quaderni d'italianistica* 30, no. 2: 67–85.

Esposito, Anna, and Manuel Vaquero Pineiro. 2005. 'Rome during the Sack: Chronicles and testimonies from an occupied city'. In Gouwens and Reiss, 125–42.

Ettlinger, Helen S. 1994. 'Visibilis et invisibilis: The mistress in Italian Renaissance court society'. *Renaissance Quarterly* 47: 770–92.

Falciani, Carlo. 2010. 'Bronzino and the Panciatichi', in *Bronzino: Artist and Poet at the Court of the Medici*, ed. Carlo Falciani and Antonio Natali. Florence, 153–73.

Fantoni, Marcello. 1997. 'Un Rinascimento a metà: Le corti italiane nella storiografia anglo-americana'. *Cheiron* 27–28: 403–33.

Fenlon, Iain. 2004. 'Music in Titian's Venice'. In Meilman 2004a, 163–82.

Fernández Álvarez, Manuel. 1979. *España y los españoles en los tiempos modernos*. Salamanca.

Fernández-Armesto, Felipe. 1996. *Columbus*. London.

———. 2007. *Amerigo: The Man who Gave his Name to America*. London.

Ferraro, Joanne M. 2012. *Venice: History of the Floating City*. Cambridge.

Fletcher, Catherine. 2012. *Our Man in Rome: Henry VIII and his Italian Ambassador*. London.

———. 2013a. '"Uno palaço belissimo": Town and country living in Renaissance Bologna', in Miller et al., 19–32.

———. 2013b. 'The altar of St Maurice and the invention of tradition in Saint Peter's,' in McKitterick et al., 371–85.

———. 2015. 'Mere emulators of Italy: The Spanish in Italian diplomatic discourse, 1492–1550'. In Baker-Bates and Pattenden, 11–28.

———. 2016. *The Black Prince of Florence: The Spectacular Life and Treacherous World of Alessandro de' Medici*. London.

———. 2017. 'Murder at the Vatican', *History Today*, 67.10: 56–67.

———. 2018. 'The Ladies' Peace revisited: Gender, counsel and diplomacy'. In Matheson-Pollock et al., 111–13.

Foley, Vernard, Steven Rowley, David F. Cassidy and F. Charles Logan. 1983. 'Leonardo, the wheel lock, and the milling process', *Technology and Culture* 24: 399–427.

Frede, Carlo de. 1982. *L'impresa di Napoli di Carlo VIII: Commento ai primi due libri della Storia d'Italia del Guicciardini*. Naples.

Freedman, Luba. 2004. 'Titian and the Classical heritage'. In Meilman 2004a, 183–202.

Freeman, John F. 1972. 'Louise of Savoy: A case of maternal opportunism'. *Sixteenth Century Journal* 3: 77–98.

Frigo, Daniela. 2000. '"Small states" and diplomacy: Mantua and Modena'. In *Politics and Diplomacy in Early Modern Italy: The Structure of Diplomatic Practice, 1450–1800*, ed. Daniela Frigo. Cambridge, 147–75.

Gaibi, Agostino. 1978. *Armi da fuoco italiane dal Medioevo al Risorgimento*. Busto Arsizio.

Gaisser, Julia Haig. 2005. 'Seeking patronage under the Medici popes: A Tale of Two Humanists'. In Gouwens and Reiss, 293–309.

Garrard, Mary D. 1994. 'Here's looking at me: Sofonisba Anguissola and the problem of the woman artist', *Renaissance Quarterly* 47: 556–622.

Gelli, Jacopo. 1905. *Gli archibugiari milanesi*. Milan.

Gentilcore, David. 2017. 'The impact of New World plants, 1500–1800: The Americas in Italy'. In Horodowich and Markey, 190–205.

Ghirardo, Diane Yvonne. 2008. 'Lucrezia Borgia as entrepreneur.' *Renaissance Quarterly* 61: 53–91.

Ginzburg, Carlo. 1982. *The Cheese and the Worms*, trans. John and Anne Tedeschi. Harmondsworth.

Gleason, Elisabeth G. 1993. *Gasparo Contarini: Venice, Rome and Reform*. Berkeley.

Goffen, Rona. 2002. *Renaissance Rivals: Michelangelo, Leonardo, Raphael, Titian*. New Haven–London.

Goldthwaite, Richard. 1993. *Wealth and the Demand for Art in Italy, 1300–1600*. Baltimore.

Gorse, George L. 2005. 'Augustan Mediterranean iconography and Renaissance hieroglyphics at the court of Clement VII: Sebastiano del Piombo's *Portrait of Andrea Doria*'. In Gouwens and Reiss, 313–37.

Gouwens, Kenneth. 1998. *Remembering the Renaissance: Humanist Narratives of the Sack of Rome*. Leiden.

Gouwens, Kenneth, and Sheryl E. Reiss. Eds. 2005. *The Pontificate of Clement VII: History, Politics, Culture*. Aldershot.

Grafton, Anthony, with April Shelford and Nancy Siraisi. 1992. *New Worlds, Ancient Texts: The Power of Tradition and the Shock of Discovery*. Cambridge, Mass.

Grendler, Paul F. 1978. 'The destruction of Hebrew books in Venice, 1568'. *Proceedings of the American Academy for Jewish Research* 45: 103–30.

———. 1989. *Schooling in Renaissance Italy: Literacy and Learning, 1300–1600*. Baltimore.

———. 2006. *The European Renaissance in American Life*. Westport, Conn.

Groesen, Michiel van. 2008. *The Representations of the Overseas World in the De Bry Collection of Voyages (1590–1634)*. Leiden.

Guerzoni, Guido. 2007. 'The social world of price formation: Prices and consumption in sixteenth-century Ferrara'. In *The Material Renaissance*, ed. Michelle O'Malley and Evelyn Welch. Manchester, 85–105.

Guilmartin, John Francis, Jr. 1974. *Gunpowder and Galleys: Changing Technology and Mediterranean Warfare at Sea in the Sixteenth Century*. Cambridge.

———. 1995. 'The Military Revolution: Origins and first tests abroad', in Rogers, 299–333.

Hairston, Julia L. 2000. 'Skirting the issue: Machiavelli's Caterina Sforza', *Renaissance Quarterly* 53: 687–712.

Hale, John R. 1966. 'Gunpowder and the Renaissance'. In *From the Renaissance to the Counter-Reformation: Essays in Honor of Garrett Mattingly*, ed. C. H. Carter. London, 113–44.

———. 1990. *Artists and Warfare in the Renaissance*. New Haven–London.

Hale, Sheila 2012. *Titian: His Life*. London.

Hall, Bert S. 1997. *Weapons and Warfare in Renaissance Europe*. Baltimore.

Hall, Marcia B. Ed. 2005a. *The Cambridge Companion to Raphael*. Cambridge.

———. 2005b 'Classicism, mannerism, and the relieflike style'. In Hall 2005a, 223–36.

Hallman, Barbara McClung. 2005. 'The "disastrous" pontificate of Clement VII: Disastrous for Giulio de' Medici?'. In Gouwens and Reiss, 29–40.

Harris, Jonathan. 1995. *Greek Emigrés in the West, 1400–1520*. Camberley.

Haskell, Francis. 2000. *The Ephemeral Museum: Old Master Paintings and the Rise of the Art Exhibition*. New Haven–London.

Hayward, John. 1962. *The Art of the Gunmaker*, vol. 1. London.

Hillgarth, J. N. 1996. 'The image of Alexander VI and Cesare Borgia in the sixteenth and seventeenth centuries'. *Journal of the Warburg and Courtauld Institutes* 59: 119–29.

———. 2000. *The Mirror of Spain, 1500–1700: The Formation of a Myth*. Ann Arbor.

Hirst, Michael. 2011. *Michelangelo: The Achievement of Fame, 1475–1534*. New Haven–London.

Hohti, Paula. 2010. 'Domestic space and identity: Artisans, shopkeepers and traders in sixteenth-century Siena'. *Urban History* 37: 372–85.

Hook, Judith. 1979. *Siena: A City and its History*. London.

———. 2004. *The Sack of Rome 1527*. Second edition. Basingstoke.

Hope, Charles. 2003. 'Titian's life and times'. In *Titian*, ed. David Jaffé. London, 11–28.

Horodowich, Elizabeth. 2005. 'Armchair travelers and the Venetian discovery of the New World', *Sixteenth Century Journal*, 36: 1039–62.

———. 2014. 'Venetians in America: Nicolò Zen and the virtual exploration of the New World'. *Renaissance Quarterly* 67: 841–77.

———. 2017. 'Italy and the New World'. In Horodowich and Markey 2017, 19–33.

Horodowich, Elizabeth, and Lia Markey. Eds. 2017. *The New World in Early Modern Italy, 1492–1750*. Cambridge.

Hsia, R. Po-Chia. 2005. *The World of Catholic Renewal 1540–1700*. Cambridge.

Humfrey, Peter. 2007. *Titian*. London.

Huxley, Aldous. 1922. *Along the Road: Notes and Essays of a Tourist*. London.

Hyde, Helen. 2009. *Cardinal Bendinello Sauli and Church Patronage in Sixteenth-Century Italy*. Woodbridge.

Imber, Colin. 2002. *The Ottoman Empire, 1300–1650: The Structure of Power*. Basingstoke.

Inalcik, Halil. 1974. 'Lepanto in the Ottoman documents'. In *Il Mediterraneo nella seconda metà del '500 alla luce di Lepanto*, ed. Gino Benzoni. Florence, 185–92.

Irwin, R. 2004. 'Gunpowder and firearms in the Mamluk Sultanate reconsidered'. In *The Mamluks in Egyptian and Syrian Politics and Society*, ed. Michael Winter and Amalia Levanoni. Leiden, 117–39.

Jaffé, David. 2003. *Titian*. London.

Jaffé, David, and Amanda Bradley. 2003. 'Sacred and Profane Love'. In Jaffé, 92–94.

Joannides, Paul, 'Titian and Michelangelo/Michelangelo and Titian'. In Meilman 2004a, 121–45.

Jones, Evan T. 2008. 'Alwyn Ruddock: "John Cabot and the Discovery of America"', *Historical Research* 81: 224–54.

Jütte, Robert. 1994. *Poverty and Deviance in Early Modern Europe*. Cambridge.

Kamen, Henry. 2014. *The Spanish Inquisition: A Historical Revision*. Fourth edition. New Haven–London.

Katz, Dana E. 2008. *The Jew in the Art of the Italian Renaissance*. University Park, Pa.

Kelly, Joan. 1977. 'Did women have a Renaissance?'. In Renate Bridenthal and Claudia Koonz, eds, *Becoming Visible: Women in European History*. Boston, 137–64.

Kemp, Martin. 1970. 'A drawing for the *Fabrica*; and some thoughts upon the Vesalius Muscle-Men', *Medical History* 14: 277–88.

————. 2006a. *Leonardo da Vinci: Experience, Experiment and Design*. London.

————. 2006b. *Leonardo da Vinci: The Marvellous Works of Nature and Man*. Oxford.

Kemp, Martin, and Giuseppe Pallanti. 2017. *Mona Lisa: The People and the Painting*. Oxford.

Kempers, Bram. 2013. 'Epilogue. A hybrid history: The antique basilica with a modern dome'. In McKitterick et al., 386–403.

Kidwell, Carol. 1991. *Pontano: Poet and Prime Minister*. London.

King, Margaret L. 1976. 'Thwarted Ambitions: Six Learned Women of the Italian Renaissance'. *Soundings* 59: 280–305.

Kinross, [Patrick] Lord. 1977. *The Ottoman Centuries: The Rise and Fall of the Turkish Empire*. New York.

Ki-Zerbo, Joseph, and Djibril Tamsire Niane. Eds. 1997. *The UNESCO General History of Africa IV: Africa from the Twelfth to the Sixteenth Century*, abridged edition. Oxford.

Knecht, R. J. 1996. *Renaissance Warrior and Patron: The Reign of Francis I.* Cambridge.

Kolsky, Stephen. 1991. *Mario Equicola: The Real Courtier.* Geneva.

Kosior, Katarzyna. 2018. 'Bona Sforza and the Realpolitik of queenly counsel in sixteenth-century Poland–Lithuania'. In Matheson-Pollock et al., 15–34.

Kristof, Jane. 1989. 'Michelangelo as Nicodemus: The Florentine Pietà'. *Sixteenth Century Journal* 20: 163–82.

Kruse, J. 1993. 'Hunting, magnificence and the court of Leo X'. *Renaissance Studies* 7: 243–57.

Kuehn, Thomas. 2002. *Illegitimacy in Renaissance Florence.* Ann Arbor.

Kunt, Metin. 1995. 'State and sultan up to the age of Süleyman: Frontier principality to world empire'. In Kunt and Woodhead, 3–29.

Kunt, Metin, and Christine Woodhead. Eds. 1995. *Süleyman the Magnificent and his Age: The Ottoman Empire in the Early Modern World.* London.

La Malfa, Claudia. 2009. *Pintoricchio a Roma: La seduzione dell'antico.* Milan.

Landon, William J. 2013. *Lorenzo di Filippo Strozzi and Niccolò Machiavelli: Patron, Client, and the Pistola fatta per la peste.* Toronto.

Lasansky, Medina. 2004. *The Renaissance Perfected: Architecture, Spectacle and Tourism in Fascist Italy.* University Park, Pa.

Le Gall, Jean-Marie. 2015. *L'honneur perdu de François Ier: Pavie 1525.* Paris.

Lev, Elizabeth. 2012. *The Tigress of Forlì: The Life of Caterina Sforza.* London.

Levin, Michael J. 2002. 'A New World Order: The Spanish campaign for precedence in Early Modern Europe'. *Journal of Early Modern History* 6: 233–64.

———. 2005. *Agents of Empire: Spanish Ambassadors in Sixteenth-Century Italy.* Ithaca, NY.

Lewis, Bernard. 1982. *The Muslim Discovery of Europe.* London.

Liberman, Anatoly. 2009. 'Why don't we know the origin of the word ghetto?', online at https://blog.oup.com/2009/03/ghetto

Lovett, Frank. 2012. 'The path of the courtier: Castiglione, Machiavelli, and the loss of republican liberty'. *Review of Politics* 74: 589–605.

Lowe, Kate. 1993. *Church and Politics in Renaissance Italy: The Life and Career of Cardinal Francesco Soderini (1453–1524).* Cambridge.

———. 2007. '"Representing" Africa: Ambassadors and princes from Christian Africa to Renaissance Italy and Portugal, 1402–1608'. *Transactions of the Royal Historical Society* 17: 101–28.

Lowry, Martin. 1979. *The World of Aldus Manutius: Business and Scholarship in Renaissance Venice.* Oxford.

Lubkin, Gregory. 1994. *A Renaissance Court: Milan under Galeazzo Maria Sforza.* Berkeley.

Luzio, Alessandro and Rodolfo Renier. 1890. 'Delle relazioni di Isabella d'Este Gonzaga con Ludovico e Beatrice Sforza'. *Archivio Storico Lombardo.* 2nd series, 17: 619–74.

Lynn, John A. 1995. 'The *trace italienne* and the growth of armies'. In Rogers, 169–99.

MacCulloch, Diarmaid. 2004. *Reformation: Europe's House Divided, 1490–1700*. London.

———. 2018. *Thomas Cromwell: A Life*. London.

McIver, Katherine. 2006. *Women, Art and Architecture in Northern Italy, 1520–1580: Negotiating Power*. Aldershot.

Mack, Rosamond E. 2002. *Bazaar to Piazza: Islamic Trade and Italian Art, 1300–1600*. Berkeley.

McKitterick, Rosamond, John Osborne, Carol M. Richardson and Joanna Storey. Eds. 2013. *Old Saint Peter's, Rome*. Cambridge.

Maddox, Sara Sturm. 2005. 'Catherine de' Medici and the two lilies'. *Court Historian* 10: 25–36.

Maglaque, Erin. 2018. *Venice's Intimate Empire: Family Life and Scholarship in the Renaissance Mediterranean*. Ithaca.

Maiorini, Maria Grazia. 1992. *Il viceregno di Napoli: Introduzione alla raccolta di documenti curata da Giuseppe Coniglio*. Naples.

Malcolm, Noel. 2019. *Useful Enemies: Islam and the Ottoman Empire in Western Political Thought 1450–1750*. Oxford.

Mallett, Michael. 1971. *The Borgias*. London.

Mallett, Michael, and Christine Shaw. 2012. *The Italian Wars 1494–1559*. Harlow.

Mancini, Francesco Federico. 2007. *Pintoricchio*. Milan.

Manfroni, Camillo. 1897–1902. *Storia della marina italiana*. 3 vols. Livorno.

Markey, Lia. 2016. *Imagining the Americas in Medici Florence*. University Park, Pa.

Martin, John Jeffries. 2004. *Myths of Renaissance Individualism*. Basingstoke.

Martines, Lauro. 2006. *Fire in the City: Savonarola and the Struggle for Renaissance Florence*. New York.

Martínez, Miguel. 2016. *Front Lines: Soldiers' Writing in the Early Modern Hispanic World*. Philadelphia.

Masson, Georgina. 1975. *Courtesans of the Italian Renaissance*. London.

Matheson-Pollock, Helen, Joanne Paul and Catherine Fletcher. Eds. 2018. *Queenship and Counsel in Early Modern Europe*. New York.

Maurer, Maria F. 2016. 'A love that burns: Eroticism, torment and identity at the Palazzo Te.' *Renaissance Studies* 30: 370–88.

Maurette, Pablo. 2019. 'The living envelope: The fascination with skin and its removal'. *Lapham's Quarterly*, 18 March 2019, online at https://www.laphamsquarterly.org/roundtable/living-envelope

Medioli, Francesca. 2000. 'To take or not to take the veil: Selected Italian case histories, the Renaissance and after'. In Panizza, 122–37.

Meilman, Patricia. Ed. 2004a. *The Cambridge Companion to Titian*. Cambridge.

————. 2004b. 'An introduction to Titian: Context and career', in Meilman, 2004a, 1–32.

Menchi, Silvana Seidel. 1994. 'Italy'. In *The Reformation in National Context*, ed. Bob Scribner, Roy Porter and Mikuláš Teich. Cambridge, 181–201.

Meserve, Margaret. 2008, *Empires of Islam in Renaissance Historical Thought*. Cambridge, Mass.

Michelson, Emily. 2013. *The Pulpit and the Press in Reformation Italy*. Cambridge, Mass.

Miller, Stephanie, Elizabeth Carroll Consavari and Erin Campbell. Eds. 2013. *Perspectives on the Early Modern Italian Domestic Interior, 1400–1700*. Farnham.

Milligan, Gerry. 2018. *Moral Combat: Women, Gender and War in Italian Renaissance Literature*. Toronto.

Minnich, Nelson H. 1974. 'The participants at the Fifth Lateran Council', *Archivum Historiae Pontificiae* 12: 157–206, repr. in Nelson H. Minnich. 1993. *The Fifth Lateran Council (1512–17)*. Aldershot.

————. 2001. 'The Last Two Councils of the Catholic Reformation: The Influence of Lateran V on Trent'. In *Early Modern Catholicism: Essays in Honour of John W. O'Malley, S. J.*, ed. Kathleen M. Comerford and Hilmar Pabel. Toronto.

Modigliani, Anna. 1999. 'Taverne e osterie a Roma nel tardo Medioevo: Tipologia, uso degli spazi, arredo e distribuzione nella città.' In *Taverne, locande e stufe a Roma nel Rinascimento*. Rome, 19–42.

Molho, Anthony. 1998. 'The Italian Renaissance: Made in the USA'. In *Imagined Histories: American Historians Interpret the Past*, ed. Anthony Molho and Gordon S. Woods. Princeton, 263–94.

Monaco, M. 1960. 'Il primo debito publico pontificiale: il Monte della fede (1526)'. *Studi Romani* 8: 553–69.

Moore, Jason W. 2009. 'Madeira, sugar, and the conquest of Nature in the "first" sixteenth century: Part I: From "Island of Timber" to Sugar Revolution, 1420–1506'. *Review (Fernand Braudel Centre)* 32: 345–90.

Morin, Marco. 1979–80. 'The origins of the wheellock: A German hypothesis. An alternative to the Italian hypothesis'. *Art, Arms and Armour* 1: 80–99.

Morin, Marco and Robert Held. 1980. *Beretta: The World's Oldest Industrial Dynasty*. Chiasso.

Motta, Uberto. 'Baldassarre Castiglione'. In *Pathways through Literature: Italian Writers*, online at http://www.internetculturale.it/directories/ViaggiNel-Testo/castiglione/eng/index.html

Mullett, Michael. 1999. *The Catholic Reformation*. London.

Mungello, D. E. 2013. *The Great Encounter of China and the West, 1500–1800*, 4th edition. Lanham.

Murphy, Caroline. 2004. *The Pope's Daughter*. London.

Murphy, Paul V. 2007. *Ruling Peacefully: Cardinal Ercole Gonzaga and Patrician Reform in the Sixteenth Century*. Washington DC.

Myers, W. David. 1995. 'Humanism and confession in Northern Europe in the age of Clement VII. In Gouwens and Reiss, 363–83.

Nagel, Alexander. 1995. 'Experiments in art and reform in Italy in the early sixteenth century'. In Gouwens and Reiss, 385–409.

Najemy, John M. 1993. *Between Friends: Discourses of Power and Desire in the Machiavelli and Vettori Letters of 1513–1515*. Princeton.

———. Ed. 2010. *Cambridge Companion to Machiavelli*. Cambridge.

———. 2013. 'Machiavelli and Cesare Borgia: A reconsideration of Chapter 7 of *The Prince*.' *Review of Politics*, supplement, 'Machiavelli's *Prince*', 75: 539–56.

Newton, Stella Mary. 1988. *The Dress of the Venetians, 1495–1525*. Aldershot.

Niiranen, Susanna. 2018. 'Catherine Jagiellon, queen consort of Sweden: Counselling between the Catholic Jagiellons and the Lutheran Vasas'. In Matheson-Pollock et al., 83–110.

O'Malley, John W. 1995. *The First Jesuits*. Cambridge, Mass.

———. 2013. *Trent: What Happened at the Council*. Cambridge, Mass.

Oman, Charles. 1937. *A History of the Art of War in the Sixteenth Century*. London.

Otto, Enrique. 1986. 'Il ruolo dei Genovesi nella Spagna del XV e XVI secolo', in *La repubblica internazionale del denaro tra XV e XVII secolo*, ed. Aldo De Maddalena and Hermann Kellenbenz. Bologna, 17–56.

Pallucchini, Rodolfo. 1969. *Tiziano*. 2 vols. Florence.

Panizza, Letizia. Ed. 2000. *Women in Italian Renaissance Culture and Society*. Oxford.

Papo, Gizella Nemeth, and Adriano Papo. 2002. *Ludovico Gritti: Un principe-mercante del Rinascimento tra Venezia, i Turchi e la corona d'Ungheria*. Venice.

Paredes, Cecilia. 2014. 'The confusion of the battlefield: A new perspective on the tapestries of the Battle of Pavia (c.1525–1531)'. *RIHA Journal* 0102 (28 December 2014), online at https://www.riha-journal.org/articles/2014/2014-oct-dec/paredes-battle-of-pavia

Parker, Geoffrey. 1995. 'The "Military Revolution" – A Myth?'. In Rogers, 37–54.

Parks, George B. 1962. 'The Pier Luigi Farnese scandal: An English report', *Renaissance News* 15: 193–200.

Parrott, David. 1997. 'The role of fortifications in the defence of states: The Farnese and the security of Parma and Piacenza', in *I Farnese: Corti, Guerra e nobiltà in antico regime*, ed. Antonella Bilotto, Piero del Negro and Cesare Mozzarelli. Rome, 509–60.

———. 2012. *The Business of War: Military Enterprise and Military Revolution in Early Modern Europe*. Cambridge.

Partner, Peter. 1960. 'The "budget" of the Roman Church in the Renaissance period'. In *Italian Renaissance Studies*, ed. E. F. Jacob. London, 256–78.

————. 1976. *Renaissance Rome, 1500–1559. A Portrait of a Society*. Berkeley.

————. 1980. 'Papal financial policy in the Renaissance and Counter-Reformation'. *Past and Present* 88: 17–62.

Pastor, Ludwig. 1891–1953. *The History of the Popes from the Close of the Middle Ages*. 40 vols. London.

Pattenden, Miles. 2013. *Pius IV and the Fall of the Carafa: Nepotism and Papal Authority in Counter-Reformation Rome*. Oxford.

Penn, Thomas. 2011. *Winter King: The Dawn of Tudor England*. London.

Pepper, Simon. 1976. 'Planning versus fortification: Sangallo's project for the defence of Rome'. *Architectural Review* 159: 162–9.

————. 1995. 'Castles and cannon in the Naples Campaign of 1494–95', in Abulafia, 263–93.

————. 2006. 'The face of the siege: fortification, tactics and strategy in the early Italian Wars', in Shaw 2006, 33–56.

Pepper, Simon, and Nicholas Adams. 1986. *Firearms and Fortifications: Military Architecture and Siege Warfare in Sixteenth-Century Siena*. Chicago.

Pérez, Joseph. 2007. *History of a Tragedy: The Expulsion of the Jews from Spain*. Trans. Lysa Hochroth. Urbana, Ill.

Perlingieri, Ilya Sandra. 1992. *Sofonisba Anguissola: The First Great Woman Artist of the Renaissance*. New York.

Perry, Mary Elizabeth. 2005. *The Handless Maiden: Moriscos and the Politics of Religion in Early Modern Spain*. Princeton.

Philippides, Marios, and Walter K. Hanak. 2011. *The Siege and the Fall of Constantinople*. Farnham.

Phillips, Mark. 1979. 'Machiavelli, Guicciardini and the tradition of vernacular historiography in Florence'. *American Historical Review* 84: 86–105

Pike, Ruth. 1966. *Enterprise and Adventure: The Genoese in Seville and the Opening of the New World*. Ithaca.

Pisano, Raffaele. 2016. 'Details on the mathematical interplay between Leonardo da Vinci and Luca Pacioli'. *BSHM Bulletin: Journal of the British Society for the History of Mathematics* 31: 104–11.

Pullan, Brian. 1971. *Rich and Poor in Renaissance Venice: The Social Institutions of a Catholic State, to 1620*. Oxford.

Rabitti, Giovanna. 'Vittoria Colonna as role model for Cinquecento women poets'. In Panizza, 478–97.

Raudzens, George. Ed. 2001. *Technology, Disease, and Colonial Conquests, Sixteenth to Eighteenth Centuries: Essays Reappraising the Guns and Germs Theories*. Leiden.

Ravid, Benjamin. 2001. 'The Venetian government and the Jews'. In Davis and Ravid, 3–30.

Rawlinson, Kent. 2017. 'Giovanni da Maiano: On the English career of a Florentine sculptor (*c*.1520–42)'. *Sculpture Journal* 26: 37–51.

Rebecchini, Guido. 2010. *"Un altro Lorenzo": Ippolito de' Medici tra Firenze e Roma (1511–1535)*. Venice.

Reiss, Sheryl E. 2005. 'Adrian VI, Clement VII, and art'. In Gouwens and Reiss, 339–62.

———. 2017. 'Praise, Blame, and History: The Patronage of the Medici Popes at San Lorenzo over Five Centuries'. In *San Lorenzo: A Florentine Church*, ed. Robert W. Gaston and Louis A. Waldman. Cambridge, Mass. 481–503.

———. 2020. 'A Word Portrait of a Medici Maecenas: Giulio de' Medici (Pope Clement VII) as Patron of Art'. In *The Mirror and the Compass – Michelangelo and Sebastiano*, ed. Matthias Wivel. Turnhout.

Reti, Ladislao. Ed. 1974. *The Unknown Leonardo*. London.

Reynolds, Anne. 2005. 'The papal court in exile: Clement VII in Orvieto, 1527–28'. In Gouwens and Reiss, 143–61.

Rice, Louise. 1997. *The Altars and Altarpieces of New St Peter's: Outfitting the Basilica, 1621–1666*. Cambridge.

Richard, John. 2015. 'Siege of Siena, January 1553–April 1555', 6 February 2015, online at http://www.historyofwar.org/articles/siege_siena_1553_5.html

Richards, John F. 1995. *The Mughal Empire*. Cambridge.

Richardson, Brian. 1999. *Printing, Writers and Readers in Renaissance Italy*. Cambridge.

Richardson, Carol M. 2009. *Reclaiming Rome: Cardinals in the Fifteenth Century*. Leiden.

Riverso, Nicla. 2017. '*La Mirtilla*: Shaping a New Role for Women', *MLN (Modern Language Notes)* 132: 21–46.

Roa-de-la-Carrera, Cristián. 2005. *Histories of Infamy: Francisco López de Gómara and the Ethics of Spanish Imperialism*. Boulder, Col.

Robin, Diana. 2000. 'Humanism and feminism in Laura Cereta's public letters'. In Panizza, 368–84.

———. 2012. 'The breasts of Vittoria Colonna'. *California Italian Studies* 3.1, online at https://escholarship.org/uc/item/13f38850

Rocke, Michael. 1996. *Forbidden Friendships: Homosexuality and Male Culture in Renaissance Florence*. Oxford.

Rogers, Clifford J. Ed. 1995. *The Military Revolution Debate*. Boulder, Col.

Romano, Dennis. 1996. *Housecraft and Statecraft: Domestic Service in Renaissance Venice, 1400–1600*. Baltimore.

Roper, Lyndal. 2017. *Martin Luther: Renegade and Prophet*. London.

Rosenthal, Margaret F. 1992. *The Honest Courtesan: Veronica Franco, Citizen and Writer in Sixteenth-Century Venice*. Chicago.

Rospocher, Massimo. 2015. *Il papa guerriero. Giulio II nello spazio pubblico europeo*. Bologna.

Rowland, Ingrid D. 2005. 'The Vatican Stanze', in Hall 2005a, 95–119.

Rubiés, Joan-Pau. 2000. *Travel and Ethnology in the Renaissance: South India through European Eyes, 1250–1625*. Cambridge.

Rubinstein, Nicolai. 1995. *The Palazzo Vecchio, 1298–1532: Government, Architecture and Imagery in the Civil Palace of the Florentine Republic*. Oxford.

Ruggiero, Guido. 1993. *Binding Passions: Tales of Magic, Marriage and Power at the End of the Renaissance*. Oxford.

Runciman, Steven. 1965. *The Fall of Constantinople 1453*. Cambridge.

Russell, Joycelyne G. 1986. *Peacemaking in the Renaissance*. London.

———. 1992. *Diplomats at Work: Three Renaissance Studies*. Stroud.

Salamone, Nadia Cannata. 2000. 'Women and the making of the Italian literary canon'. In Panizza, 498–512.

Salzberg, Rosa. 2014. *Ephemeral City: Cheap Print and Urban Culture in Renaissance Venice*. Manchester.

Sannazzaro, G. B. 1982. *Leonardo a Milano*. Milan.

Santore, Cathy. 1988. 'Julia Lombardo, "Somtuosa Meretrize": A portrait by property'. *Renaissance Quarterly* 41: 44–83.

Scaraffia, Lucetta. 1993. *Rinnegati. Per una storia dell'identità occidentale*. Rome–Bari.

Schilling, Heinz. 2017. *Martin Luther: Rebel in an Age of Upheaval*, trans. Rona Johnston. Oxford.

Schwoerer, Lois. 2016. *Gun Culture in Early Modern England*. Charlottesville.

Seidel, Linda. 1995. *Jan Van Eyck's Arnolfini Portrait: Stories of an Icon*. Cambridge.

Setton, Kenneth M. 1976–78. *The Papacy and the Levant (1204–1571)*. 4 vols. Philadelphia.

Seward, Desmond. 2006. *The Burning of the Vanities: Savonarola and the Borgia Pope*. Stroud.

Shaw, Christine. 1993. *Julius II: The Warrior Pope*. Oxford.

———. Ed. 2006. *Italy and the European Powers: The Impact of War, 1500–1530*. Leiden.

Shemek, Deanna. 2002. 'Aretino's *Marescalco*: Marriage woes and the duke of Mantua'. *Renaissance Studies* 16: 366–80.

Sherer, Idan. 2017. *Warriors for a Living: The Experience of the Spanish Infantry during the Italian Wars, 1494–1559*. Leiden.

Sherr, Richard. 2005. 'Clement VII and the golden age of the Papal Choir'. In Gouwens and Reiss, 227–50.

Sicca, Cinzia Maria. 2002. 'Consumption and trade of art between Italy and England in the first half of the sixteenth century: The London house of the Bardi and Cavalcanti company.' *Renaissance Studies* 16: 163–201.

Sicca, Cinzia Maria, and Louis A. Waldman. Eds. 2012. *The Anglo-Florentine Renaissance: Art for the Early Tudors*. New Haven–London.

Silverblatt, Irene. 2008. 'The Black Legend and global conspiracies: Spain, the Inquisition and the emerging modern world'. In *Rereading the Black Legend: The Discourses of Religious and Racial Difference in the Renaissance*

Empires, ed. Margaret R. Greer, Walter D. Mignolo and Maureen Quilligan. Chicago, 99–116.

Simonetta, Marcello. 2014. *Volpi e Leoni: I Medici, Machiavelli e la rovina d'Italia*. Milan.

Simonsohn, Shlomo. 1982–86. *The Jews in the Duchy of Milan*. 4 vols. Jerusalem.

Siraisi, Nancy. 1990. *Medieval and Early Renaissance Medicine: An Introduction to Knowledge and Practice*. Chicago.

Smith, Robert S. 1989. *Warfare and Diplomacy in Pre-Colonial West Africa*. London.

Soyer, François. 2019. *Medieval Antisemitism?* Leeds.

Soykut, Mustafa. 2011. *Italian Perceptions of the Ottomans: Conflict and Politics through Pontifical and Venetian Sources*. Frankfurt.

Steen, Charles R. 2013. *Margaret of Parma: A Life*. Leiden.

Stein, Stanley J., and Barbara H. Stein. 2000. *Silver, Trade, and War: Spain and America in the Making of Early Modern Europe*. Baltimore.

Stephens, J. N. 1983. *The Fall of the Florentine Republic, 1512–1530*. Oxford.

Stinger, Charles. 2005. 'The place of Clement VII and Clementine Rome in Renaissance history'. In Gouwens and Reiss, 165–84.

Storey, Tessa. 2005. 'Fragments from the "life histories" of jewellery belonging to prostitutes in early-modern Rome'. *Renaissance Studies* 19: 647–57.

———. 2008. *Carnal Commerce in Counter-Reformation Rome*. Cambridge.

Stras, Laurie. 2018. *Women and Music in Sixteenth-Century Ferrara*. Cambridge.

Strathern, Paul. 2009. *The Artist, the Philosopher and the Warrior: The Intersecting Lives of da Vinci, Machiavelli, and Borgia and the World they Shaped*. New York.

Surdich, Francesco. 1991. *Verso il nuovo mondo: la dimensione e la coscienza delle scoperte*. Florence.

Talvacchia, Bette. 1999. *Taking Positions: On the Erotic in Renaissance Culture*. Princeton.

———. 2007. *Raphael*. London.

Taylor, F. L. 1921. *The Art of War in Italy, 1494–1529*. Cambridge.

Terpstra, Nicholas. 1990. 'Women in the brotherhood: Gender, class, and politics in Renaissance Bolognese communities'. *Renaissance and Reformation* 14: 193–212.

———. 2000. Ed. *The Politics of Ritual Kinship: Confraternities and Social Order in Early Modern Italy*. Cambridge.

Thompson, I. A. A. 1995. '"Money, money, and yet more money!" Finance, the fiscal-state, and the military revolution: Spain 1500–1650'. In Rogers, 273–98.

Tomas, Natalie. 2003. *The Medici Women: Gender and Power in Renaissance Florence*. Aldershot.

Tommasino, Pier Mattia. 2015. 'Otranto and the self'. *I Tatti Studies in the Italian Renaissance* 18: 147–55.

Toomaspoeg, Kristjan. 'I Turchi nel Salento. Alcuni riflessioni sulla guerra del 1480–81'. In *Tierra de mezcla. Accoglienza ed integrazione nel Salento dal Medioevo all'Età contemporanea*, ed. Mario Spedicato. Galatina, 47–57.

Tracy, James. 2010. *Emperor Charles V, Impresario of War: Campaign Strategy, International Finance and Domestic Politics*. Cambridge.

Vale, M. G. A. 1974. *Charles VII*. London.

Veltri, Giuseppe. 2004. '*Philo* and *Sophia*: Leone Ebreo's concept of Jewish philosophy'. In *Cultural Intermediaries: Jewish Intellectuals in Early Modern Italy*, ed. David B. Ruderman and Giuseppe Veltri. University Park, Pa, 55–66.

Verheyen, Egon. 1977. *The Palazzo del Te in Mantua: Images of Love and Politics*. Baltimore.

Viggiano, Alfredo. 2013. 'Politics and constitution', in Dursteler 2013, 47–84.

Villari, Pasquale. 1895-7. *Niccolò Machiavelli e i suoi tempi*. Second edition. 3 vols. Milan.

Viroli, Maurizio. 1998. *Machiavelli*. Oxford.

———. 2000. 'Niccolò Machiavelli e Caterina Sforza'. In *Caterina Sforza: Una donna del Cinquecento*, [various authors:] Editrice La Mandragora. Imola, 85–91.

Waddington, Raymond B. 1993. 'Elizabeth I and the Order of the Garter'. *Sixteenth Century Journal* 24: 97–113.

———. 2004. *Aretino's Satyr: Sexuality, Satire and Self-Projection in Sixteenth-Century Literature and Art*. 2nd edition. Toronto.

———. 2006. 'Pietro Aretino, religious writer'. *Renaissance Studies* 20: 277–92.

———. 2009. 'Aretino, Titian, and 'La Humanità di Christo''. In *Forms of Faith in Sixteenth-Century Italy*, ed. A. Brundin and M. Treherne. Aldershot, 171–98.

Wallace, William E. 2005. 'Clement VII and Michelangelo: An anatomy of patronage'. In Gouwens and Reiss, 189–98.

Weinstein, Donald. 2011. *Savonarola: The Rise and Fall of a Renaissance Prophet*. New Haven–London.

Welch, Evelyn. 1995. *Art and Authority in Renaissance Milan*. New Haven–London.

Wellman, Kathleen. 2013. *Queens and Mistresses of Renaissance France*. New Haven–London.

Whistler, Catherine. 2003. *Battle of Pavia*. Oxford.

Wiesner-Hanks, M. E. 2008. 'Do women need the Renaissance?' *Gender and History* 20: 539–57.

Williams, Allyson Burgess. 2013. 'Silk-clad walls and sleeping Cupids'. In Miller et al., 175–90.

Williams, Ann. 1995. 'Mediterranean conflict'. In Kunt and Woodhead, 39–54.

Wills, John E, Jr. 2011. 'Maritime Europe and the Ming'. In *China and Maritime Europe, 1500–1800: Trade, Settlement, Diplomacy and Missions*, ed. John E. Wills, Jr et al. Cambridge, 24–77.

Wilson, Frederick. 2010. *A History of Handguns*. Marlborough.

Wilson, N. G. 1992. *From Byzantium to Italy: Greek Studies in the Italian Renaissance*. London.

Wolk-Simon, Linda. 2005. 'Competition, collaboration and specialisation in the Roman art world, 1520–27'. In Gouwens and Reiss, 253–76.

Woodhouse, J. R. 1978. *Baldesar Castiglione: A Reassessment of The Courtier*. Edinburgh.

Woods-Marsden, Joanna. 2005. 'One artist, two sitters, one role: Raphael's papal portraits'. In Hall 2005a, 120–40.

Woolfson, Jonathan. 1998. *Padua and the Tudors: English Students in Italy, 1485–1603*. Toronto.

Wyatt, Michael. 2005. *The Italian Encounter with Tudor England: A Cultural Politics of Translation*. Cambridge.

Endnotes

These notes are designed primarily to point readers to accessible resources for further study. For that reason I have given references to works in English translation so far as possible. In relation to the Italian Wars I am indebted to the late Michael Mallett and to Christine Shaw, whose book on that subject has been an essential point of reference. I am further grateful to the authors and editors of the *Dizionario biografico degli italiani*, on which I have relied for biographical information, and of the Oxford Bibliographies: Renaissance and Reformation, which I recommend to students seeking further reading on this topic.

NB: date of most recent access of all websites: 5 November 2019.

Abbreviations:

ASF   Archivio di Stato di Firenze
ASV   Archivio di Stato di Venezia
BAV   Biblioteca Apostolica Vaticana
MdP   Archivio Mediceo del Principato

Introduction

1. Burchard, vol. 1, 336–8. • 2. Beinart, 284–90, suggests 200,000; Kamen, 28–9, argues that in fact there were only 80,000 Jews remaining in Spain by 1492, of whom a majority likely opted to convert to Christianity and stay. • 3. Pérez, 2. • 4. Mallett and Shaw, 11. • 5. Translation from Whitcomb, 82–6, online at https://sourcebooks.fordham.edu/source/lorenzomed1.asp • 6. Mallett, 104–10. • 7. Mallett, 112–13. • 8. Columbus, 29. • 9. Fernández-Armesto 1996, 5; Grafton, 74. • 10. Davidson, 75 (Toscanelli); 21–35 (early voyages). • 11. *Italian Reports* 2002, 29. • 12. Molho; Grendler 2006. • 13. Luther 1914, 348.

Chapter One

1. Creighton, 296–9. • 2. Bracciolini, vol. 1, 124. • 3. For further discussion see Fletcher 2013b. • 4. Muffel, 43, 95. • 5. For further discussion of the siege and its contemporary descriptions see Philippides and Hanak. • 6. Barbaro, 9. • 7. Barbaro, 14–23, 24–5. • 8. *Siege of Constantinople*, 3 (an account by the Florentine Giacomo Tebaldi). • 9. Setton, vol. 2, 114–15. • 10. Barbaro, 27–61. • 11. Barbaro, 67. • 12. *Siege of Constantinople* (Tebaldi), 5. • 13. Barbaro, 39. • 14. *Siege of Constantinople* (Angelo Giovanni Lomellino, former podestà of Pera), 132. • 15. Commynes 1906, vol. 2, 90. • 16. Translations from Lewis, 30–31. For background see Harris. • 17. Setton, vol. 2, 140. • 18. Translation from Lewis, 30–31. • 19. Pius II, 31. • 20. Wilson 1992, 86–7. • 21. Harris, 119–29. • 22. Wilson 1992, 55. • 23. Epstein 2007, 3–47. • 24. Vespasiano, 66. • 25. Bentley, 7, 10, 11 • 26. Bentley, 22. • 27. Kidwell. • 28. Bentley, 26. • 29. Loise de Rosa 184, cited in Bentley, 4–5. • 30. Mallett and Shaw, 10. • 31. Commynes 1840–47, vol. 2, 375–6. • 32. Richardson 2009, esp. 143–81. • 33. DeSilva. • 34. On the Sforza see Lubkin. • 35. Guicciardini 1969, 7. • 36. Guicciardini 1969, 4.

Chapter Two

1. Seidel, 79–81, 118. • 2. De Roover, 190; Bratchel, 134. • 3. See the essay by Walter Denny, online at: https://www.metmuseum.org/toah/hd/isca/hd_isca.htm. • 4. Seidel, 95. • 5. Donati, 29–51. • 6. Penn, 25. • 7. Woolfson, 26–27. For more on the artistic exchanges see Sicca and Waldman and for the later period Wyatt. • 8. On the history of the Inquisition see Kamen. • 9. Silverblatt. • 10. *Portuguese in West Africa, 1415–1670*, 7. • 11. The bull *Dum diversas*. • 12. Richards, 5. • 13. Mack; see also *Venice and the Islamic World, 828–1797*; and Brotton. • 14. Ki-Zerbo and Tamsire Niane, 1–4; Lowe 2007, 118. • 15. Benedetti, 143; Sanuto 1883, 527. • 16. Dalton et al. I am grateful to Alex West for advice on the likely Indonesian origin. • 17. Fernández-Armesto 2007, 42. • 18. Crummey, 16–19. • 19. Soykut, 75–6. • 20. Tommasino. • 21. Robin 2000, 372. • 22. For the context to this apocryphal remark see Runciman, 71. • 23. Toomaspoeg.

Chapter Three

1. Brugnoli; Vasari 1912–14, online at https://ebooks.adelaide.edu.au/v/vasari/giorgio/lives/part3.1.html • 2. For a detailed discussion of the documents see Kemp and Pallanti, esp. Ch. 2. Rumours that Caterina was enslaved seem unlikely to be true. • 3. Rocke, 5. • 4. The sketch is now in the Musée Bonnet, Bayonne. • 5. Strathern, 17–18. • 6. Leonardo 2008, 276–7. • 7.

Commynes 1906, vol. 2, 104, 108. • 8. Mallett and Shaw, 10–11. • 9. Epstein 2007, 24–5. • 10. Black 2000, 219. • 11. Guicciardini 1763, vol. 1, 141–2. • 12. Commynes 1906, vol. 2, 93. • 13. Benedetti, 61. • 14. Commynes 1906, vol. 2, 199. • 15. Guilmartin 1995, 306–7. • 16. Delaborde, 519, cited in Mancini, 128. • 17. Benedetti, 71. • 18. Setton, vol. 2, 384, 425. • 19. Guicciardini 1969, 71. • 20. Mallett and Shaw, 26. On Ferrandino and Alfonso see Benedetti, 71. • 21. Luzio and Renier, 622–3; translation from Mallett and Shaw, 26. • 22. Guicciardini 1969, 92–3; Sanuto 1738, col. 20. • 23. Guicciardini 1969, 54. • 24. Benedetti, 89. • 25. Commynes, vol. 2, 201. • 26. Benedetti, 99, 101. • 27. Benedetti, 107. • 28. Sanuto 1738, col. 31. • 29. Benedetti, 105. • 30. Benedetti, 109. • 31. Giovio 2013, 55. • 32. Martinez, 68. • 33. Commynes vol. 2, 204. • 34. Benedetti, p. 75. • 35. Benivieni, fol. 12v. (Translation from Arrizabalaga et al., 20–21.) • 36. Arrizabalaga et al., 45–6; 113, 48, 155. • 37. Arrizabalaga et al., 40–42. • 38. Guicciardini 1969, 44. • 39. Azzolini. • 40. Giovio 2013, 43. • 41. Siraisi, 19–20. • 42. Grafton, 188; Arrizabalaga et al., 34–6. • 43. The complex relationships between wealth and art in Italy are discussed in Goldthwaite. • 44. Richardson 2009, especially 143–81. • 45. Kempers, 388.

Chapter Four

1. On the Borgias the definitive account remains Mallett, on which I largely rely here; for Lucrezia see also Bradford and Bellonci. • 2. Guicciardini 1763, vol. 1, 14. • 3. Mallett, 85–6. • 4. Modigliani, 29. • 5. *Corresponding Renaissance*, 116–17. • 6. Mallett, 139–42. • 7. *Diario Ferrarese*, col. 403; Mallett, 71. • 8. For translations see *Italian Reports* 2001, 31–7. • 9. Online report at https://www.washingtonpost.com/local/vatican-first-known-depiction-of-native-americans-may-be-in-1494-painting/2013/05/10/1157f4ae-b8f2-11e2-aa9e-a02b765ffoea_story.html?noredirect=on&utm_term=.b8ec62e75989. For context on portrayals of indigenous people as naked, Burke 2018, 34–8 and Burke 2013. • 10. Vasari 1991, 250. On Pinturicchio and this fresco sequence see Mancini; La Malfa, 113–41; Buranelli. • 11. La Malfa, 127, 131. • 12. Buranelli, 71–2. • 13. La Malfa, 122–3. • 14. La Malfa, 123. • 15. On Savonarola see Dall'Aglio 2010; Weinstein; Martines. • 16. Savonarola 2003, 35–7. • 17. Savonarola 1973, 210–14. • 18. Vasari 1991, 177. • 19. Grafton, 81. • 20. Weinstein, 79–80. • 21. Seward, 61. • 22. Arrizabalaga et al., 39–44. • 23. Guicciardini 1969, 83. • 24. Seward, 66–7. Weinstein, 95. • 25. Commynes 1906, vol. 2, 287. • 26. Savonarola 2006, 261, 262–3. • 27. Weinstein, 174–6. • 28. Vasari 1991, 228. • 29. Chambers 1996, 302, 309. See also Mallett, 143–4. • 30. Nagel, 404. • 31. With the bull *Execrabilis*. • 32. Mullett, 30 says Savonarola appealed to a Council; Dall'Aglio 2010, 61, says he was just considering it and may have drafted letters to the emperor and the kings of France and Spain to that effect. • 33. Weinstein, 267–76. • 34. Dall'Aglio 2010, 65–6.

Chapter Five

1. Sannazzaro, 42, translation from Welch, 267. • 2. Black 2013, 49. For wider context on Machiavelli, see Najemy 2010. • 3. Clough 1967. • 4. Machiavelli 1968–82, vol. 1, 267–8. Translation from Mallett, 175. • 5. Strathern, 107–8. • 6. Leonardo 1877, 62. • 7. Kemp 2006b, 219–21. • 8. Online at https://www. bl.uk/collection-items/view-of-venice • 9. Machiavelli 1989, vol. 1, 142. • 10. Machiavelli 1989, vol. 1, 169. • 11. Machiavelli 1989, vol. 1, 142. • 12. Giustinian, vol. 1, 150; translation from Mallett, 181. • 13. Guicciardini 1969, 165–6; Giovio 2013, 167. • 14. Strathern, 226–31. • 15. Kemp 2006b, 223. • 16. Castiglione, 97. • 17. Ágoston 2013, 129–30, citing Pepper 1995; see also Pepper 2006. • 18. Chase, 64–5. Lynn, 172–4. See also Pepper and Adams. • 19. Arnold, 222. • 20. Hirst, vol. 1, 59. • 21. Cellini, 18. • 22. Goffen. • 23. Rubinstein, 74–5. • 24. Kemp 2006b, 217. • 25. Vasari 1991, 294. • 26. Kemp and Pallanti, 108–9. • 27. *Voyages of Cadamosto*, 4, 8–10. • 28. Kemp and Pallanti, 35.

Chapter Six

1. Sherer, 182. • 2. Mallett and Shaw, 32–4. • 3. Giovio 2013, 77. • 4. Guicciardini 1969, 72. • 5. Arfaioli, 4. • 6. Bratchel, 211. • 7. For a wider discussion of the myth of individualism, see Martin. • 8. Sherer, 183, 219. • 9. Castiglione, 179. • 10. Giustinian, vol. 1, 490. • 11. Leonardo 2008, 174–5. • 12. Giustinian vol. 2, 40. • 13. Giustinian, vol. 2, 485–7. • 14. Sherer, 49 citing *Crónicas del Gran Capitán*, 519 and 403. • 15. Machiavelli 1968–82, vol. 2, 344. Machiavelli 2003, 21. • 16. Giovio 2013, 65. • 17. Sherer, 23. • 18. Sherer, 17–21. • 19. Paris Bordon, *Portrait of a Man in Armour with Two Pages*. Oil on canvas, 46 × 62 in. Metropolitan Museum of Art, New York. Accession number 1973.311.1. • 20. Sherer, 31, 35, 37. • 21. Sherer, 27. • 22. Parrott 2012, 46–54. • 23. Parrott 2012, 55–70. • 24. Mallett and Shaw, 198–202, 209–11. • 25. Sherer, 36, 40–45. • 26. Mallett and Shaw, 202, 211. • 27. Arfaioli, 8–9. • 28. Black 2000, 218–20. • 29. On the impact of the Black Death see Bosker et al., 8–9; on demography see Black 2000, 21. • 30. Chen. • 31. Terpstra 2000. • 32. Romano 1996, 233–4, 108, 155–63. • 33. https://www.nationalgallery.org.uk/paintings/sandro-botticelli-three-miracles-of-saint-zenobius • 34. Hohti, 384. • 35. Barkan, 82. • 36. Hale 1990, 121. • 37. Arfaioli, 55. • 38. Sherer, 65–8. • 39. Sherer, 78. • 40. Sherer, 59. • 41. Sherer, 92–101. • 42. Thompson, 274.

Chapter Seven

1. Bruscoli 2014, xvii, xix, 81, 84, 85, 90–95, 133. • 2. Bruscoli 2014, 111–22. • 3. Bruscoli 2014, 109–10. • 4. Bruscoli 2014, 150, 168. • 5. Bruscoli 2014, 169. •

6. Bruscoli 2014, 193. • 7. Davidson, 34; Fernández-Armesto 2007, 51. • 8. Davidson, 21–2, 26. • 9. Horodowich 2017, 31. • 10. Fernández-Armesto 2007, 63 • 11. Fernández-Armesto 2007, 14–21, 52–5. • 12. Epstein 1996, 310–11; Davidson, 388. • 13. Fernández-Armesto 2007, 58. • 14. Fernández-Armesto 2007, 163, 167. • 15. *Italian Reports* 2002, 10. • 16. Fernández-Armesto 2007, 67–8, 89. • 17. Fernández-Armesto 2007, 182. • 18. Fernández-Armesto 1996, 127–8. • 19. *Italian Reports* 2002, 9–10. • 20. Pigafetta, vol. 1, 83–5. • 21. Fernández-Armesto 2007, 120–34. • 22. Fernández-Armesto 2007, 188, 190, 195. • 23. Sicca 2002. • 24. Jones; Bruscoli 2012. • 25. See his entry in the *Oxford Dictionary of National Biography*. • 26. Wills, 24–7; Mungello, 16; Giovanni da Empoli, 29–30, 59–60. • 27. Horodowich 2017, 20–21. • 28. Doria, 87. • 29. Otto, 17–32. • 30. Otto, 30. • 31. Guilmartin 1995, 312. • 32. Martínez, 129. • 33. Horodowich and Markey, 1–16. • 34. *Italian Reports* 2002, 28, text 3. • 35. *Italian Reports* 2002, 70. • 36. Braudel, 66. Another explanation suggests the indigenous name was similar. • 37. Guicciardini 1969, 182. • 38. Grafton, 49, 51. • 39. Fernández-Armesto 2007, 22, 74. • 40. Grafton, 45–8. • 41. *Italian Reports* 2002, 34–5. • 42. Grafton, 54. • 43. Varthema, 125–6; translation from Rubiés, 147. • 44. *Italian Reports* 2002, 110. • 45. *Italian Reports* 2002, 95. • 46. *Italian Reports* 2002, 123. • 47. *Italian Reports* 2002, 133. • 48. Markey, 13. See the examples in the Museo Nazionale Preistorico Etnografico 'Luigi Pigorini', Rome (since 2016 part of the Museo delle Civiltà). • 49. Markey, 34. • 50. Gleason, 36–7. • 51. *Relazioni*, ser. 1, vol. 2, 50. • 52. Fletcher 2015, 19. • 53. *Italian Reports* 2002, 95. • 54. Pike, 103–17. • 55. Markey, 38. • 56. Guicciardini 1763, vol. 3, 310–11; Markey, 8. • 57. Markey, 8–9. • 58. *Italian Reports* 2002, 117; see also the introduction, 16. • 59. Landi, 41.

Chapter Eight

1. Hillgarth, 119, 122; Kamen, 402, n. 13 is sceptical about this reading of 'marrano' and argues it may refer instead to a person who 'mars' the Christian faith. • 2. La Malfa, 130. • 3. Hillgarth 1996, 120. • 4. Rospocher, 44–5. • 5. Guicciardini 1969, 172. • 6. Shaw 1993, 219–20. Burchard vol. 2, 487. • 7. Rospocher, 17. • 8. Rospocher, 93–111. • 9. DeSilva. • 10. Kempers. • 11. Hirst, vol. 1, 85–94. • 12. Shaw 1993, 204–7, is sceptical about parallels between Julius and Caesar. • 13. Shaw 1993, 147–8. • 14. Machiavelli 1989, vol. 1, 255 (*Discourses* I. xxvii). • 15. Shaw 1993, 150–53. • 16. Shaw 1993, Ch. 5, especially 157–61. • 17. Shaw 1993, 277–8; Mallett and Shaw, 100–101. • 18. Guicciardini 1763, vol. 5, 299. • 19. Shaw 1993, 300; Hirst, vol. 1, 83 and 106; Avery, 76–9. • 20. Rospocher, 222. • 21. Rospocher, 141–70. • 22. Rospocher, 274, 281–7. • 23. Erasmus 1974–, vol. 27, 168–9. • 24. The attribution is made in the *Collected Works* though it is not universally accepted. See the introduction by Michael J. Heath to his translation in Erasmus 1974–, vol. 27, 156–67. • 25. *Le cronache*

bresciane, vol. 2, 172. For context on this and other sacks see Bowd. • 26.
Sanuto 1969–70, vol. 13, col. 509. • 27. Engraving by Master Na. Dat., in Hale
1990, 141; Giovio 2013, 123. • 28. Guicciardini 1763, vol. 5, 420. • 29. Mallett
and Shaw, 108. • 30. Guicciardini 1763, vol. 5, 430. • 31. Baker, 59–61. • 32.
Maddox, 25. • 33. Baker, 232. • 34. Guicciardini 1969, 261–3, cited in Sherer,
152. • 35. Modesty 237–42; for the news in Florence, Cerretani 278. • 36.
Michelangelo Buonarroti 1980, 210. • 37. Black 2013, 75–9. • 38. Grafton, 87. •
39. Epstein 1996, 273–4. • 40. Giovio 2013, 171. • 41. Epstein 1996, 312–15. • 42.
Bratchel, 293, 159, 134 (citing Vale, 223), 210. • 43. Bratchel, 191–2; see also
Michele Luzzati's entry in the *DBI*. • 44. Clough 2003. • 45. Hook 1979, 161.
• 46. Viggiano 52, 67–8. • 47. Landon, 80; on this period of Machiavelli's life
see also Najemy 1993. • 48. On failed princes see Najemy 2013; on irony see
Benner 2013. • 49. Viroli 1998, 125. • 50. Viroli 1998, 3. • 51. Black 2013, 77. •
52. Black 2013, 97. • 53. Machiavelli 1984, 74, cited in Black 2013, 107. • 54. Black
2013, 130–61. • 55. Machiavelli, 1989, vol. 1, 228 (*Discourses* I. xii.13, translation
from Black 2013, 168.) • 56. Machiavelli, 1989, vol. 1, 255 (*Discourses* I. xxvii.7,
translation from Black 2013, 168). • 57. Black 2013, 166–71.

Chapter Nine

1. Schilling, 80–84. • 2. Luther 1857, numbers 459, 444, 889, 888 and 470; *Street
Life*, 141–6. • 3. Schilling, 84–5. Roper, 62–5. Roper allows for more influence
of the visit to Rome on Luther's later attitudes than does Schilling. • 4. Cited
in Baker-Bates, 15. • 5. Michelangelo Buonarroti 1980, poem no. 10, p. 8; Hirst,
vol. 1, 100–01. • 6. Erasmus, vol. 3, 94. • 7. Chambers 1966, 302, 309. See also
Mallett, 143–4. • 8. For a case study see Guerzoni. • 9. Richardson 2009, 10,
12. • 10. Stinger 2005, 178. • 11. Byatt; Chambers 1966, 297, 299. • 12. Roper,
44. • 13. Grafton, 32. • 14. Mallett, 37. • 15. Stinger 2005, 170; for more detail
see Partner 1960 and 1980. • 16. For the address: Egidio da Viterbo; on the
Council see Minnich 1974 and 2001. • 17. *Decrees*, vol. 1, 615. • 18. Mullett, 8,
15–16. • 19. *Decrees*, vol. 1, 618. • 20. *Decrees*, vol. 1, 632. • 21. *Decrees*, vol. 1,
607. • 22. Creighton, vol. 5, 203–6. BAV, MS Vat. Lat. 12275, fols 3–15. • 23. Tomas,
126–7. • 24. Stephens, 103. • 25. Clough 2005, 90. • 26. On the so-called 'Conspiracy' see Hyde, 131–72; Lowe 1993, 104–13; Simonetta, 161–201. The discussion
here incorporates extracts from Fletcher 2017, a synthesis of this scholarship.

Chapter Ten

1. Sanudo 1969–70, vol. 8, cols 249–50. • 2. Guicciardini 1763, vol. 4, 274–5. •
3. Mallett and Shaw, 92–5. • 4. Mallett and Shaw, 96. • 5. Shaw 1993, 245. • 6.
Mallett and Shaw, 85–115. • 7. Williams 2013. • 8. Ghirardo. • 9. Giovio 1597, 16.
• 10. *Raphael in Early Modern Sources*, vol. 1, 431. • 11. Taylor, 91–2. • 12. Bradford,

Ch. 14. • 13. Guicciardini 1763, vol. 1, 148–9. • 14. Machiavelli 2003, 163. • 15. Arfaioli, 4. • 16. Taylor, 91. • 17. Gilino, fol. 1v, translation from Arrizabalaga et al., 50. [Gilino 1930, 7–8.] • 18. Knecht, 1–18. • 19. Castiglione, 88; Guicciardini 1763, vol. 6, 290. • 20. Castiglione, 312. • 21. Du Bellay, vol. 1, 75. • 22. Sanudo, vol. 21, col. 97. • 23. On the battle see Parrott 2012, 27–9 and Mallett and Shaw, 128–30. • 24. *Correspondenz*, vol. 1, 49. • 25. Mallett and Shaw, 213. • 26. Guicciardini 1763, vol. 1, 151. • 27. Machiavelli 1908, 98, cited in Sherer, 105. • 28. Parker, 38–9; Sherer, 39. • 29. Parrott 2012, 43. • 30. Mallett and Shaw, 203. • 31. Mallett and Shaw, 209. • 32. MacCulloch 2018, 22–53. The Frescobaldi connection, though not the specifics of Cromwell's time at war, is substantiated by a letter of 1533; the remainder of this account comes from a rather romanticised story by Italian writer Matteo Bandello.

Chapter Eleven

1. Cited in Tomas, 14. • 2. Tomas, 14–15. • 3. Black 2000, 108–10. • 4. Dean and Lowe. • 5. McIver, 19–25. • 6. Giovio 2013, 499. • 7. Murphy 2004, 115–18. • 8. Castiglione, 219. • 9. D'Este, 298, no. 412. • 10. Cockram, 162–70. • 11. Shemek, 'Introduction' in D'Este, 16, citing Aretino 1900, 9. • 12. Shemek, 'Introduction', in D'Este, 6. • 13. Frigo. • 14. Kruse, 252. • 15. Fletcher 2012, 132. • 16. Bestor; for a useful survey of the historiography see the introduction to Kuehn. • 17. Hairston 2000. • 18. Lev, 178–83. • 19. Talvacchia 1999, 114–15, citing Fantaguzzi, 255. • 20. Breisach, 153–89. • 21. Sanuto 1738, col. 135. • 22. *Corresponding Renaissance*, letter from Caterina dated at Florence 28 October 1503, written to her son after the death of Pope Alexander VI, 138–40. • 23. Viroli 2000. • 24. Tomas, 53–4. • 25. Tomas, 57. • 26. Tomas, 109–10, citing Niccolò Valori's life of Lorenzo de' Medici. On the question of whether women could be prudent see Bradshaw. • 27. Cited in Tomas, 173. • 28. Cited in Tomas, 179. • 29. *Corresponding Renaissance*, 112–15.

Chapter Twelve

1. For this and what follows: Ravid, 3–30; Bonfil, 32–3. • 2. On the origin of the word 'ghetto' see Liberman. • 3. Bonfil, 20, 60–61. • 4. For more detailed discussion of this complex issue see Soyer. • 5. Katz, 106–7. • 6. Simonsohn, vol. 2, 930. • 7. Bonfil, 26, 39–41, 47 • 8. Bonfil, 21. • 9. Giustinian, vol. 2, 42. • 10. Bonfil, 51–2. • 11. See Monaco, cited in Ait, 117; see also *Decrees*, vol. 1, 625–7. • 12. See his *DBI* entry, by Bruno Nardi; and Veltri. • 13. Grendler 1978. • 14. Archivio di Stato di Mantova, Archivio Gonzaga 586, fol. 10v, 15 February 1525. Gleason, 35–6. • 15. Ravid, 4, 14. • 16. Ferraro, 2–4, 11. • 17. Lewis, 25. • 18. Moore, 360. • 19. D'Este, 41–2, with bibliography. • 20. Ferraro, 65; for case-studies see Maglaque. • 21. N. Z. Davis, 60–61. • 22. Campbell and Chong,

107. • 23. Dursteler 2006. • 24. Williams 1995, 41–2; Guicciardini 1969, 176. • 25. Brummett, 33–5. • 26. Cook, 73. • 27. Campbell and Chong, 22–3; Setton, vol. 3, 25–33. • 28. Kunt, 22. • 29. Irwin, 136–9; Ágoston 2005, 58. • 30. Stinger 2005, 172. • 31. Guicciardini 1969, 334. • 32. Williams 1995, 42; Stinger 2005, 172; Kinross, 176–9. For further background on the Ottoman army and navy see Imber, Chapters 7 and 8. • 33. Meserve, 4–13. • 34. Giovio 2013, 23. • 35. Castiglione, 209. • 36. Machiavelli 1984, 10; for discussion see Bisaha, 177 and Malcolm, 159–83. • 37. Soykut, 17–18, 27, citing Scaraffia, 4; Dursteler 2006, especially the introduction. • 38. N. Z. Davis, 19–23, 54–57. • 39. N. Z. Davis, 62–3. • 40. BAV, MS Vat. Lat. 12275, fol. 371v. • 41. Perry, 34–5. • 42. N. Z. Davis, 153–90. • 43. N. Z. Davis, 69–71, 82–3. • 44. N. Z. Davis, 94. • 45. Leo Africanus, vol. 1, 12. • 46. Leo Africanus, vol. 1, 17. • 47. Leo Africanus, vol. 1, 103.

Chapter Thirteen

1. Guicciardini 1969, 321. • 2. Schilling, 149. Roper covers Luther's life from 1517 to 1521 at 95–193. • 3. Schilling, 150–52. • 4. Menchi, 186. • 5. On Alessandro see Fletcher 2016; for Ippolito see Rebecchini. • 6. Schilling, 158–9. • 7. Schilling, 155. • 8. Schilling, 157–9. The bull was *Exsurge Domine.* • 9. Schilling, 157–8. • 10. Schilling, 166, 180–81. • 11. With the bull *Decet Romanum.* • 12. Schilling, 167. • 13. Myers, 365. • 14. Schilling, 165, 172. • 15. Erasmus, vol. 8, 149–53. • 16. Cools et al., especially the essays by Marcel Gielis and Gert Gielis, 1–21, Raymond Fagel, 23–45, and Hans Hulscher, 47–66. • 17. Sanuto, vol. 32, col. 416, cited in Reiss 2005, 344. • 18. Valeriano 1.16, cited in Gaisser, 303. • 19. Clough 2005, 93–7. • 20. Reiss 2005, 345. • 21. Translation from Schilling, 163. • 22. Stinger 2005, 179. • 23. Partner 1976, 57–8. • 24. Reiss 2005, 347–8. • 25. Vasari 1912–14, online at https://ebooks.adelaide.edu.au/v/vasari/giorgio/lives/part3.43.html • 26. Reiss 2005, esp. 349–55. • 27. Bejczy, 95–6. • 28. Guicciardini 1763, vol. 8, 358; Guicciardini 1969, 442. • 29. Hallman; Fletcher 2016. • 30. Myers, 372, 380–81. • 31. Mullett, 135–7. • 32. Myers, 383. • 33. Michelangelo Buonarroti 1965–83, vol. 3, 1; translation from Reiss 2005, 359–60. For general background on papal patronage of art in this period see De Jong 2013 and for Clement in particular, Reiss 2020. • 34. Sherr 228, 230, 233, 246. • 35. Gaisser.

Chapter Fourteen

1. Vasari 1991, 317–18. • 2. Woods-Marsden, 123. • 3. Vasari 1912–14, vol. 8, 74–5 (Life of Giovanni da Udine), online at: https://ebooks.adelaide.edu.au/v/vasari/giorgio/lives/part3.64.html • 4. Rowland, 117; and Hall 2005b, 230–31. • 5. Markey, 14. • 6. Markey, 21. • 7. Online catalogue entry, at https://www.louvre.fr/en/oeuvre-notices/portrait-baldassare-castiglione-1478–1529. • 8. Partner 1976, 179. • 9. Talvacchia 2007, 146–7; Partner 1976, 169. •

10. Wolk-Simon, esp. figure 14.1. • 11. Michelangelo Buonarroti 1980 no. 5, p. 5. • 12. Vasari 1991, 433. • 13. Translations from Sebastiano's letters from Elam, 220. • 14. Online at https://ebooks.adelaide.edu.au/v/vasari/giorgio/lives/part3.9.html#pg4-183 • 15. Barbieri, 146–7. • 16. Elam, 221. • 17. Wallace. • 18. Vasari 1991, 300. • 19. Hope, 18. • 20. Jaffé and Bradley, 92–4. • 21. Hope, 15–16. • 22. David Jaffé, Nicholas Penny, Sorcha Carey, catalogue entries in Jaffé, 101–11. • 23. Vasari 1912–14, vol. 2, 142, cited in Barbieri, 144. • 24. *Carteggio* vol. 2, p. 32, no. 304, cited in Hirst, vol. 1, 126. • 25. Hirst, vol. 1, 175. • 26. Pisano; Biagioli. • 27. Knecht, 131. • 28. Translation from Kemp and Pallanti, 105–6. • 29. Knecht, 138–40, 427–8. • 30. Clayton, 240–41. • 31. Beatis, 132–3. • 32. Kemp 2006a, 2–19. • 33. Beatis, 182. • 34. Knecht, 431.

Chapter Fifteen

1. Giovio 1931, 325, cited in Sherer, 52. • 2. Mallett and Shaw, 143–4. • 3. Arfaioli, 10–11, 19–20; Oman 177–85. • 4. Le Gall, 23. • 5. Mallett and Shaw, 147–8. • 6. Parker, 42. • 7. Sanuto 1969–70, vol. 37, cols 159, 163. • 8. Sherer, 39–40. • 9. *Diario anonimo*, 21–4. • 10. *Diario anonimo*, 25–8; Taegio, 34 for the banquet. • 11. *Cronache dell'assedio*, 26. • 12. *Diario anonimo*, 28. • 13. *Cronache dell'assedio*, 70; Whistler, 5. • 14. Giovio, 1931, 258–9, cited in Sherer, 43. • 15. *Diario anonimo*, 28–9. • 16. Giovio 1931, 266, cited in Sherer, 49. • 17. Biblioteca del Museo Correr, Codice Cicogna 3473, Ducali di A. Gritti a F. Contarini. • 18. Giovio 2013, 387 and 699 n. 47. • 19. *Cronache dell'assedio*, 141. • 20. *Diario anonimo*, 30. • 21. Sherer, 58. • 22. *Cronache dell'assedio*, 223. • 23. *Cronache dell'assedio*, 228. • 24. *Diario anonimo*, 49–50; Sherer, 40; Guicciardini 1993, 35. • 25. Giovio 2013, 197. • 26. Le Gall, 111. • 27. *Correspondenz*, vol. 1, 150–52. • 28. Sanuto 1969–70, vol. 38, col. 5. • 29. Monluc, vol. 1, 52; translation adapted from Oman, 43–4. • 30. Sherer, 220 • 31. Guicciardini 1837, vol. 5, 157. • 32. Buchanan; Paredes. • 33. Le Gall, 118–27. • 34. Freeman, 95. • 35. Sanudo 1969–70, vol. 42, col. 637. • 36. DeVries 1999. • 37. Papo and Papo; Soykut 79–85.

Chapter Sixteen

1. Richardson 1999, 3–7. • 2. *Corresponding Renaissance*, 13–16; Richardson 1999, 107–12. • 3. Grendler 1989, 105, 88–9. On reading, see also Carlsmith. • 4. *Oxford Bibliographies: Renaissance and Reformation* (Manuzio, Aldo, entry by Craig Kallendorf). • 5. Richardson 1999, 21, 27–9. Lowry, 158 and 174, n. 96. For examples see *Primary Sources on Copyright*. • 6. Richardson 1999, 35–7. • 7. Castiglione, 90–91; Richardson 1999, 78–80. • 8. Richardson 1999, 84–5. • 9. Salzberg, 5. • 10. Richardson 1999, 142–3. • 11. *Letters and Papers* vol. 5, no. 1658; *State Papers*, vol. 7, 394. • 12. Epstein 2009, 271–4. • 13. Ravid, 24. • 14. Salzberg, 36. • 15. *Corresponding Renaissance*, 10. • 16. Cochrane 1980, 26. •

17. Cochrane 1981. • 18. Phillips 93–7; on liberty see also Baker. • 19. Stinger 2005, 176–7. • 20. Giovio 2013, 265. • 21. Kolsky, 18. • 22. Hale 1966, 120–21. • 23. Wiesner-Hanks; Kelly; Cox. • 24. Richardson 1999, 144; *Corresponding Renaissance*, 18. • 25. Richardson 1999, 145–7. • 26. Salamone, 504. • 27. Salamone, 508–9. • 28. Robin 2000. For biography, see *Corresponding Renaissance*, 91–2. • 29. King. • 30. Fedele, Introduction, and for the orations 159–64. • 31. On Costanza: Giovio 2013, 451; *Corresponding Renaissance*, 168–9. • 32. Giovio 2013, 517, 511. For context Robin 2012. • 33. *Pasquinate*, vol. 1, 437, no. 425. • 34. The poem is in Luna, fols 117r–118v. See for context Rabitti, 480–81; Milligan, 81–3. • 35. *An Anthology of Italian Poems*, 133–5. • 36. Ariosto 1909–13, vol. 3, 475. For context see Brundin 2016, 25–6. • 37. Brundin's entry for Colonna in the Oxford Bibliographies Online (Renaissance and Reformation) provides a useful introduction to her career: https://www.oxfordbibliographies.com/view/document/obo-9780195399301/obo-9780195399301-0077.xml • 38. Michelangelo Buonarroti 1980, 294, no. 88. • 39. Michelangelo Buonarroti 1980, 99, n. 147 • 40. Hale 2012, 306. • 41. Nagel, 391. • 42. *Corresponding Renaissance*, 215. • 43. Giovio 2013, 407. • 44. Oxford Bibliographies: Renaissance and Reformation (Gambara, Veronica, entry by Molly M. Martin). • 45. Gambara, 4, 5. • 46. D'Aragona, Introduction. *Corresponding Renaissance*, 192–3. • 47. McIver, 143. • 48. Eschrich, 75–7.

Chapter Seventeen

1. Talvacchia 1999, 120–21. • 2. Translation adapted from Romano 1988, 14. • 3. Talvacchia, 1999, 15. • 4. Waddington 2004, xxi–xxii. • 5. Richardson 1999, 91. • 6. Shemek, 2002. • 7. Rocke, 3–16. • 8. Talvacchia 1999, 18. • 9. Richardson 1999, 91–3. • 10. Verheyen, 1–2. • 11. Cellini, 71. • 12. Vasari 1991, 368–9. • 13. Maurer, 373, 375. • 14. Maurer, 376. • 15. Verheyen, 22. • 16. Verheyen, 13 and 31, citing Castiglione, 288. • 17. Vasari 1991, 372–3. • 18. Kemp 2006a, 14. • 19. Fletcher 2013a, 25. • 20. Bourne. • 21. Burke 2018, 15, 147–51, 132. • 22. On mistresses see Ettlinger. • 23. Bestor; Kuehn. • 24. Ferraro, 56–7. • 25. For further discussion see Fletcher 2016; Brackett. • 26. Burke 2018, 57, 128, 156–7. • 27. Romano 1988, 17. • 28. Ambrosini, 436. • 29. Storey 2005, 654–6. • 30. Translation from Pullan, 382, cited in Ruggiero, 53. • 31. Thomas, fols 39v–40r; *Street Life*, 78–9. • 32. *Street Life*, 106, 109. • 33. [Lorenzi], 108–9. • 34. Ambrosini, 429. • 35. Bonfil, 47. • 36. Barzaghi, 168, 177, 184. • 37. Newton, 16–18. • 38. Aretino 1994, 107, 111 • 39. Santore, 46–8. • 40. Rosenthal, 157, 82. • 41. Masson, 146. • 42. Aretino 1994, 115. • 43. Translation adapted from Masson, 37. • 44. *Corresponding Renaissance*, 174–6. • 45. *Corresponding Renaissance*, 159. • 46. Rosenthal, 86–7, 157. • 47. *Corresponding Renaissance*, 147. • 48. Aretino 1994, 129. • 49. Aretino 1994, 133–5. • 50. Aretino 1994, 16. • 51. Aretino 1994, 186. • 52. Aquilecchia, 460–61. • 53. Aretino 1994, 185. •

54. For the historiographical debate about the nature of the sack and the extent to which it was (or was perceived as) a watershed see Esposito and Pineiro, 126–7.

Chapter Eighteen

1. Clough 2005, 101–3. • 2. Cornelius de Fine, cit. and translated in Ait, 119. • 3. Guicciardini 1993, 79–82. • 4. Mallett and Shaw, 211. • 5. Reiss, 356. • 6. Hook 2004, 169. • 7. Cellini, 61, 65–6, 68. • 8. Cornelius de Fine; translation in Ait, 121; on Lutheran landsknechts see Sherer, 24. • 9. Ait, 112–14, 120. • 10. Cited in Partner 1976, 32. • 11. Clough 2005, 75–7. • 12. Hook 2004, 158–60. • 13. Esposito and Pineiro, 130. • 14. Levita, 100; N. Z. Davis, 247. • 15. N. Z. Davis, 247, 253. • 16. Esposito and Pineiro, 127–8; Sherer, 58; Esposito and Pineiro, 134. • 17. Esposito and Pineiro, 136; Reiss, 360–61. • 18. Reynolds, 143. • 19. Sanuto 1969–70, vol. 46, col. 231, cited in Reynolds, 147. • 20. Hook 2004, 210–11. • 21. *Letters & Papers* vol. 4, no. 4090. • 22. Vasari 1991, 271. • 23. Manfroni, vol. 3, 277–8, cited in Bicheno, 216–17. • 24. Sherer, 73. • 25. Tracy, 114. • 26. Parts of this discussion of the 'Ladies' Peace' were previously published in Fletcher 2018, which should be consulted for a full account and references. • 27. Giovio 2013, 369. • 28. Sanuto 1969–70, vol. 26, col. 474; vol. 39, col. 177; vol. 40, col. 291; vol. 25, col. 200. • 29. Giovio 2013, 371. • 30. Sanuto 1969–70, vol. 39, col. 305. • 31. Russell, 1992, 94–158. • 32. Setton, vol. 3, 323–6.

Chapter Nineteen

1. Castiglione, 31; Richardson 1999, 89. • 2. Castiglione, 88, 129. For a useful introduction see Motta. • 3. Burke 1995. • 4. Richardson 1999, 147. • 5. Talvacchia 2007, 118–21; Woods-Marsden, 129–30. • 6. Waddington 1993, 104. • 7. Lovett. • 8. Marguerite of Navarre, 396–8. Cartwright, vol. 1, 224–6, cited in Cockram, 101, n. 54. See also Clough 2005. • 9. Castiglione, 282, 286. • 10. Castiglione, 178; on Francesco Maria and Castiglione see Woodhouse, 18–19. • 11. Fantoni. • 12. Castiglione, 57. • 13. Parrott 2012, 44–5. • 14. Goldthwaite, 41–2. • 15. David Jaffé, Nicholas Penny, Sorcha Carey, catalogue entries in Jaffé, 101–11. • 16. Vasari 1991, 494. • 17. See the Uffizi catalogue entry, online at https://www.uffizi.it/en/artworks/portrait-of-francesco-maria-della-rovere • 18. Burke 2018, 128. • 19. Kolsky, Ch. 2, esp. 67–76. • 20. Kolsky, Ch. 3, esp. 107–8. • 21. Stras. • 22. Sicca and Waldman; Rawlinson. • 23. See his entry by William J. Connell in the *Oxford Dictionary of National Biography*. • 24. Vergil. • 25. Giovio 2013, 279. • 26. See the essays in Cresti et al. • 27. Kosior; Niiranen. • 28. Knecht, 124–5. • 29. Tracy, 121. • 30. Eisenbichler 1999; on Hogenberg see https://www.bl.uk/treasures/festivalbooks/BookDetails.aspx?strFest=0086 • 31. Fletcher 2016, 56–7. • 32. BAV, MS Vat. Lat. 12276, fol.

87r. • 33. BAV, MS Vat. Lat. 12276, fols 92r–93r. • 34. Meilman 2004a, 266–7. • 35. Freedman, 197. • 36. Gorse. • 37. Baker-Bates.

Chapter Twenty

1. Rubinstein, 75, citing Villari 1895–7, vol. 1, 483 ff. • 2. Pepper and Adams, 162; Hirst, vol. 1, 231–2. • 3. Pepper 2006, 49. • 4. Michelangelo Buonarroti 1980, 250–51, no. 47, a letter from Venice to his friend Battista della Palla who was still in Florence; Hirst, vol. 1, 236–7. • 5. Tracy, 122; Mallett and Shaw, 222. • 6. Sherer, 207. • 7. Wallace, 197–8. • 8. Baker, 232. • 9. Tracy, 132. • 10. *State Papers* vol. 7, 226. • 11. Partner 1976, 73, 84–5. • 12. Tracy, 125, 128, 104. • 13. Stein and Stein, 41. • 14. See his entry in the *Dictionary of Canadian Biography*, online at http://www.biographi.ca/en/bio/la_rocque_de_roberval_jean_francois_de_1E.html • 15. Otto, 34–5. • 16. Goldthwaite, 32. • 17. Brege, 209–10. • 18. Horodowich 2017, 31. • 19. Donattini, 67; for more specifics see Domenici 88–90. • 20. Markey, 17–19. • 21. Coniglio, 1–11; Maiorini, 71. • 22. Doria, 82–5. • 23. Cummins, 47, 53–4. • 24. Levin 2005, 44. • 25. *Relazioni* ser. 1, vol. 1, 22; Cicogna, 335, cited in Hillgarth 2000, 52. • 26. Kilian Leib, cited in Chastel, 108. • 27. Navagero, fols 25r–v. • 28. N. Z. Davis, 247, 253, 254. • 29. Montoiche, 359; Setton vol. 3, 396–8. • 30. Partner 1976, 180. • 31. Sherer, 28. • 32. Sherer, 7. Mallett and Shaw, 236–7. • 33. Setton vol. 3, 400–401, cited in Bicheno, 149. • 34. Setton vol. 3, 402. • 35. Ferraro, 66. • 36. Setton vol. 3, 425–7. • 37. Williams 1995, 48. • 38. Guilmartin 1974, 43–5. • 39. Chase, 71. • 40. Ascham, 49. • 41. Williams 1995, 48. On Henry VIII see Brigden. • 42. Markey, 20. • 43. Williams 1995, 49.

Chapter Twenty-One

1. For background see Wilson 2010; Oman; Hall 1997; Chase; Gaibi 1978. • 2. Sherer, 233. • 3. Pius II, 150–51. • 4. Mallett and Shaw, 209. • 5. Beretta Museum, online at http://www.beretta.com/en/world-of-beretta/private-museum • 6. Foley et al., 427. The design is in Codex Atlanticus fol. 56v, b. • 7. Morin and Held, 49. • 8. Morin, 84–6; *Documenti inediti*, 307–9. • 9. *Letters and Papers*, vol. 13, no. 828. • 10. Álvarez, 167, cited in Sherer, 1. • 11. Guicciardini 1969, 50–51. • 12. Giovio 1931, 425; Giovio 2006, 686, cited in Sherer, 181–2. • 13. Hale 1966. • 14. Tartaglia. • 15. Gelli, 67. • 16. ASF, Mediceo del Principato 633, fol. 11 (MAP Doc ID 9481). • 17. ASF, MdP 638, fol. 353 (MAP Doc ID 15371). • 18. *Lorenzo de' Medici at Home*, 38, 192. ASF, Guardaroba Medicea 7 (Inventario della Guardaroba del Duca Cosimo alla consegna di Giovanni Ricci da Prato), fol. 47r. • 19. Cellini, 159, 85–9. • 20. Benedetti, 175, 177. • 21. DeVries 1990. • 22. ASF, Guardaroba Medicea 43, Libro dellarme della guardaroba di S. E. I., p. 91bis. • 23. *Documenti inediti*, 324, 341. • 24. ASF,

MdP 3719, fol. 772 (MAP Doc ID 23877). • 25. ASF, MdP 3718, unnumbered folio (MAP Doc ID 23879). • 26. ASF, MdP 210, fol. 68 (MAP Doc ID 8471). • 27. *Letters and Papers*, vol. 1, no. 3496. • 28. Schwoerer, 126. • 29. ASF, MdP 1852, fol. 574 (MAP Doc ID 21465). • 30. ASF, MdP 522, fol. 199 (MAP Doc ID 19527). • 31. ASF, Guardaroba Medicea 7 (Inventario della Guardaroba del Duca Cosimo alla consegna di Giovanni Ricci da Prato), fol. 47r. • 32. Chase, 78. • 33. Smith, 81. • 34. Chase, 110. • 35. Chase, 74–5. • 36. *Italian Reports* 2002, 27–8. • 37. *Italian Reports* 2002, 59. • 38. See the essays in Raudzens for contextual discussion. • 39. Brooks, 136. • 40. Montaigne, vol. 3, 1030, cited in Grafton, 155. • 41. Horodowich 2017, 32.

Chapter Twenty-Two

1. Pastor, vol. 11, p. 11. • 2. Guicciardini 1969, 442. • 3. Pepper 1976. • 4. On Margaret see Steen; the details of her first marriage are now updated in Fletcher 2016. • 5. Mullett, 70–71. • 6. Mullett, 75. O'Malley 1995, 24. • 7. Arrizabalaga et al., 172. • 8. O'Malley 1995, 34; Mullett, 88. • 9. The bull was *Regimini Militantis Ecclesiae*. Mullett, 89–90. • 10. Comerford, 166. • 11. Mullett, 98. • 12. What follows is based on Audisio. • 13. Murphy 2007, 128–30. • 14. Mullett, 147. • 15. Menchi, 191. • 16. Murphy 2007, 132–8. • 17. Waddington 2006, 284. • 18. Menchi, 189. for further background on preaching in this period see Michelson. • 19. Thomas, 37r; *Street Life*, 76. • 20. *Street Life*, 76–8. • 21. Bireley, 46. • 22. Mullett, 32. • 23. Schilling, 403–4. • 24. O'Malley 2018, 51–69; Mullett, 33–6. • 25. O'Malley 2013, 70–71. • 26. Dandelet, 62–3. Levin 2002.

Chapter Twenty-Three

1. Nagel, 386. • 2. Nagel, 400–404. • 3. Nagel, 388–92. • 4. Waddington 2009, 181, 195–8. • 5. *Dizionario Biografico degli Italiani*. • 6. Falciani. • 7. Michelangelo Buonarroti 1963, vol. 2, 240–41. This is probably the drawing now in the British Museum. • 8. Michelangelo Buonarroti 1980, 161–2, no. 288. • 9. Brundin 2002; see also Brundin 2016, 33. • 10. Kristof. • 11. Esposito and Piniero, 128–9. Rice, 17; figures 10, 16, 18. • 12. Vasari 1991, 462; *Pasquinate*, vol. 1, 498, no. 462. • 13. Michelangelo Buonarroti 1980, 274, footnote. • 14. Michelangelo Buonarroti 1980, 283–5, no. 78. For discussion see the catalogue entry by Sefy Hendler in Falciani and Natali, 214–17. • 15. Translation from Meilman 2004b, 1; see also Vasari 1991, 507–8. • 16. Perlingieri, 35, 67. • 17. Perlingieri, 86–8. • 18. Garrard. • 19. Vasari 1912–14, online at https://ebooks. adelaide.edu.au/v/vasari/giorgio/lives/part3.25.html • 20. https://www. britannica.com/biography/Sofonisba-Anguissola • 21. Joannides, 122. • 22. Michelangelo Buonarroti 1963, vol. 2, xvii; the poem is in Michelangelo Buonarroti 1980, 71, no. 96. • 23. Michelangelo Buonarroti 1980, 255, no. 53.

• 24. Waddington 2006, 278, 287, 284. • 25. Giovio 1956, vol. 2, 122, translation from Richardson 1999, 100. • 26. Richardson 1999, 104. • 27. *Illustrations from the works of Andreas Vesalius.* On the attribution of the drawings to Kalkar, see Kemp 1970. • 28. Gentilcore, 191. • 29. Markey, 21. Gentilcore, 193–4. • 30. Grafton, 169. • 31. Horodowich 2005, 1040 n. 3. • 32. *Dizionario biografico degli italiani.* The dates of his birth and death are both uncertain. • 33. Eamon, 714; Burke 2002, 403. Roa-de-la-Carrera, esp. 59–60. • 34. Horodowich 2005, 1043. • 35. Groesen. • 36. Horodowich 2014, 841–77. • 37. Donattini, 66-67. • 38. Mullett, 15, 96–7, 194. • 39. The bull *Sublimis Deus.* • 40. Bireley, 156–7. • 41. Hsia, 197.

Chapter Twenty-Four

1. Fletcher 2016, 235. • 2. A useful English-language summary of the family's affairs is in Parrott 1997. • 3. Thomas, 39v; *Street Life*, 78. • 4. *Pasquinate*, vol. 2, 642, no. 567 and vol. 1, 480, no. 456. • 5. Dell'Orto; Parks. • 6. Bourne, and see above, Chapter Eighteen. • 7. Rocke, 229. • 8. Parks, 194. • 9. Wellman, 208–9. • 10. Dall'Aglio 2015, 160. • 11. Blockmans, 75–6. • 12. A useful English summary of the Siena war is provided in Richard. • 13. Cantagalli, lxvii. • 14. Cantagalli, lxxiii. • 15. Sozzini, 28. • 16. Sozzini, 88–9. • 17. Monluc, vol. 2, 55. For commentary see Eisenbichler 2012. • 18. Sozzini, 422. • 19. Sherer, 8. • 20. *Street Life*, 82 (sonnet no. 83). • 21. Thompson, 274. • 22. *Relazioni*, series 1, vol. 3, 348–9. • 23. Russell 1986, 133–223. • 24. *Relazioni*, ser. 1, vol. 1, 422–5, discussed at greater length in Fletcher 2015. • 25. Botero, part 6, p. 2, cited in Hillgarth 2000, 304. • 26. Morin and Held, 44, citing ASV, Collegio, Relazioni, b. 37, fol. 4rv. • 27. ASF, Miscellanea Medicea 39, inserto 15. • 28. ASF, Otto di Pratica del Principato, 121. • 29. Cellini, 241–2. • 30. Sherer, 47, citing Jütte, 26–7; see also R. C. Davis. • 31. ASF, MdP 3082, fol. 613 (MAP Doc ID 27923). • 32. For context, Milligan, 106–13; *Corresponding Renaissance*, 244. The text is in the 1597 edition, fols 3v–6v.

Chapter Twenty-Five

1. Richardson 1999, 43. • 2. Richardson 1999, 44. For background on the Inquisition and censorship see Black 2009, 158–207. • 3. Pattenden, 17. • 4. Pattenden, 22. • 5. Pattenden, 24–5. • 6. Waddington 2004, xxiii. • 7. Richardson 1999, 45. • 8. Menchi, 192–3. • 9. Sherer, 82–3. • 10. *Decrees*, vol. 1, 625–7. • 11. Roper, 389–96. • 12. MacCulloch 2004, 689–90. • 13. For bibliography see Bell's introduction in *Street Life*, 58–9. • 14. Bonfil, 70–71. • 15. *Street Life*, 18. • 16. Bonfil, 65–8. • 17. Arbel, 86–7. • 18. Bonfil, 63, 71. • 19. Robert C. Davis, 'Introduction', in Davis and Ravid 2001, vii–viii. • 20. Storey 2008, 1–2. • 21. Terpstra 1990. • 22. Battiferra degli Ammanati, 87–91. • 23. *Corresponding*

Renaissance, 196. • 24. *Corresponding Renaissance*, 196. • 25. Richardson 1999, 148. • 26. *Dizionario Biografico degli Italiani* (as Virginia Negri). • 27. Ferraro, 69–73. • 28. Medioli, 131. • 29. Medioli, 124–5. • 30. Riverso. • 31. Pattenden, 66. • 32. Pattenden, 106, 130. • 33. Hsia, 221–3. For more on the wider impact see Bamji et al. • 34. Mullett, 2–5. • 35. Mullett, 143-50. • 36. Menchi, 194-95; Ginzburg. • 37. Vasari 1991, 461. • 38. Cocke, 177–9. • 39. Pallucchini, vol. 1, 151–202. • 40. Vasari 1991, 508.

Chapter Twenty-Six

1. Williams 1995, 44. • 2. Crowley, 191–2. • 3. Bicheno, 151. • 4. Doria, 80. • 5. Chase, 94. • 6. Setton, vol. 4, 1004. • 7. Setton, vol. 4, 996. • 8. Inalcik, 186–7. • 9. *Battle of Lepanto*, xv. • 10. Setton, vol. 4, 1042. • 11. Guilmartin 1995, 317. • 12. Guilmartin 1974, 232–4. • 13. *Battle of Lepanto*, 313–15. • 14. Contarini, fol. 52r. • 15. *Battle of Lepanto*, xiii; 363. • 16. Contarini, fol. 52r. • 17. *Battle of Lepanto*, 75. • 18. Setton, vol. 4, 1100. • 19. De Jong 2003. See also the discussion in De Jong 2013, 119–61. • 20. *Battle of Lepanto*, 403. • 21. *Battle of Lepanto*, 73. • 22. Fenlon, 179. • 23. Bireley, 109–10; Mullett, 120–21. • 24. Humfrey, 204; Maurette. (I am grateful to Alex Bamji for drawing my attention to this essay.) • 25. Ovid, 6.382 ff.

Epilogue

1. Goldthwaite, 60 and 66–7, citing Burke 1974, 60–61. • 2. Chase, 80, citing Cardano, 189–90. • 3. Grafton, 203. • 4. Giovio 2013, 57. • 5. Botero, part 1, p. 2. • 6. Woolfson, 18. • 7. Arnold, 206. • 8. Molho 269–70, 279. • 9. Lasansky, 12–13, 125–9. • 10. Haskell, 107–27. • 11. Huxley, 178. • 12. Tim Butcher, 'The man who saved the Resurrection', BBC News, 24 December 2011, online at http://www.bbc.co.uk/news/magazine-16306893 • 13. For example, 'Italy: The real sick man of Europe', *The Economist*, 19 May 2005, online at https://www.economist.com/leaders/2005/05/19/the-real-sick-man-of-europe • 14. 'The Renaissance initiative', online at https://eu-renaissance.org/en. • 15. Foscolo, 129. • 16. Tobias Jones, 'Why Italy regrets its Faustian pact with tourist cash', *The Guardian*, 6 January 2019, online at https://amp.theguardian.com/world/2019/jan/06/cost-of-tourism-in-italy • 17. 'Italy joins China's New Silk Road project', BBC News, 23 March 2019, online at https://www.bbc.co.uk/news/world-europe-47679760 • 18. David Sanderson, 'Fresh doubt over world's most expensive painting', *The Times*, 13 April 2019, 1, 6. • 19. Machiavelli 2003, 164.

Index

Aachen 176–7

Abarbanel, Giuda *see* Leone Ebreo

Accolti, Cardinal Benedetto 276, 282

accountancy 210

Acre, Israel 164

Adrian VI, Pope (Adriaan Floreiszoon
    Boeyens) 178–81
    portraits 181

Africa 104, 167, 171–2, 266, 338
    colonisation 78, 92, 103
    slave trade 33, 34, 35, 78, 87, 91–2, 94,
        98, 104–5, 164, 165, 170–71, 227,
        266, 278, 305

Agnadello, Battle of (1509) 138–9, 144,
    145, 267

Agrippa, Cornelius: 'On the Nobility
    and Pre-eminence of the
    Feminine Sex' 215

Alba, Fernando Álvarez de Toledo, 3rd
    duke of 315, 340

Albania 23, 36

Alberini, Marcello 239

Alberti, Leon Battista 194

Albrecht of Brandenburg, Archbishop
    of Mainz 173

Albret, Charlotte d' 59

Alesio, Matteo Pérez de 302

Alexander VI, Pope (Rodrigo Borgia) 4,
    5–6, 7, 42, 46, 47, 48, 49, 50, 55–6,
    5, 58–9, 60–61, 62, 63, 65, 66, 67,
    72–3, 96, 107–8, 109, 127, 151, 155,
    161, 181, 281, 310, 345

Alexandria, Egypt 164, 166

Alfonso I, of Naples ('the Magnanimous')
    (Alfonso V, of Aragon) 22–3

Alfonso II, of Naples (*formerly* duke of
    Calabria) 24, 37, 43, 44, 47–8, 50,
    56, 57–8

Alfonso V, of Portugal 6–7, 16, 91

Algiers 269

Ali Pasha 337

Alidosi, Cardinal Francesco 112, 134, 179,
    249–50

Allegretti, Allegretto 278

alum, trade in 118, 129

Alviano, Bartolomeo d' 139

Amalfi 23, 105
    Battle of (1528) 242

Amalteo, Giovanni Battista 339

Amboise: Clos Lucé 192, 193

Amboise, Cardinal d' Georges 138

Ambrose, Saint 41

Americas, the/New World 43
    accounts of 95, 99, 100
    and African slave trade 98
    discovery of 6, 60, 92, 94–6, 98–100,
        343
    first diocese 178
    indigenous population 63, 94, 95
    plants 302
    and the Spanish 98, 101–2, 103, 104,
        105–6, 117, 119, 144, 278, 279, 302,
        303, 344
    and trade 91, 92, 94, 96, 97, 98
    and use of firearms 277, 278–9

Amsterdam 343

anatomy 301
Ancona 70, 309, 325, 326
Andrea di Ugoni 294
Andreini, Isabella 328
    La Mirtilla 328
Andros, island of 267, 333
Angela Greca 223
Angelico, Fra: San Marco frescoes 64
Angevins/house of Anjou 22
Anghiari, Battle of (1440) 25, 75–6
Anguissola, Sofonisba 213, 298–9, 328
    Bernardino Campi Painting Sofonisba
        Anguissola 299
    Lucia, Minerva, and Europa Anguissola
        Playing Chess 299
Anjou, house of 41
Anjou, John of 23
Anjou, René d' 23
Anna, archduchess of Austria 276
Anne of Brittany 32, 43, 58, 143, 286
Antwerp 30, 343
Aqquyunlu (Turkish rulers) 166
Aragon 4, 23, 33, 143
Aragona, Cardinal Luigi 193, 219
Aragona, Tullia d' 219, 327
    Dialogue on the Infinity of Love 219
Arbedo, Battle of (1422) 81
Arcimboldo, Giuseppe: Fire 344
Aretino, Pietro 152, 219, 222–4, 231, 251,
        295, 300, 301, 302, 323, 350
    La Cortigiana 126–7
    The Humanity of Christ 294, 295
    Il Marescalco 219, 223
    I Modi sonnets (The Sixteen Pleasures)
        223, 224, 228, 300
    Sei Giornate (Six Days) 224, 228, 230,
        232–3
Arezzo 70, 347
    Basilica of San Francesco frescoes 65
Argyropoulos, John 21
Ariosto, Ludovico 223, 273, 323
    Orlando furioso 212, 217, 223
Armenia 166
armies 83–5, 88–80
    see also weapons
Arno, River 74, 76, 259, 260

Arnolfini, Giovanni 29, 30, 118
Arnolfini Portrait (van Eyck) 29–30, 31
Articles of Schwabach 254
Artois 204
Ascham, Sir Roger 268
Al-Ashraf Tuman bay II 167
Asti 244
Athens, Don Manfred, duke of 76
Augsburg 95, 174, 261, 322
'Augsburg Confession' 261
Augustine of Hippo, St 16, 129, 285
Augustinian order 9, 64, 125, 126, 174, 240
Austria 45, 119, 137, 144, 313
Avalos, Costanza d' 216
Avalos, Fernando Francesco d', marquis
        of Pescara 115, 199, 200, 201, 215,
        216, 252, 273
Avignon 4, 37
    Papacy 330
Aybak 165
Azerbaijan 166
Azores, the 33, 60
Aztec civilisation 35, 278

Babur, Mughal emperor 169
Babylonian Talmud 210
Baglioni, Gianpaolo 111, 122
Baglioni family 110, 134
Bahri dynasty 165
Bale, John 108
Balkans, the 36, 37, 87, 167, 168, 245
    Mercenaries 49, 84, 138
Bandello, Matteo: novella 231
Bandinelli, Baccio 182
    Hercules and Cacus 259
bankers/banking 8, 30, 53, 86, 91, 92, 96,
        97, 98, 118, 134, 140, 148, 159, 162n,
        180, 181, 241, 263, 279, 324, 325, 346
    Medici 1, 25, 30, 93, 156
Barbari, Jacopo de': View of Venice 71
Barbaro, Nicolò 17, 18, 19–20
Barbarossa, Admiral Khair ad-Din 266,
        269
Barcelona, Treaty of (1529) 242–3, 255
Bardi and Cavalcanti (company) 96, 253,
        263, 276

Basel 285
Bassano 140
Bath and Wells, bishopric of 253
Battiferri degli Ammannati, Laura 327
Battista di Chino 274
Baviera, Il 188
Bayezid II, Sultan 46, 47, 73, 165
Beatis, Antonio de 193–4
Beaton, David 282
Beatrice of Aragon 36
Belgrade, Battle of (1521) 168, 204, 333
Bellini, Gentile 165, 166, 190
Bellini, Giovanni 190, 191
    Feast of the Gods 251
Bellini, Jacopo 190
Belluno 140
Bembo, Cardinal Pietro 104, 126, 140,
    219, 248, 282
    Gli Asolani 233
Benedetti, Alessandro 44, 49, 50, 275
Beneficio di Giesù Christo Crocifisso, Il
    (Benefit of Christ Crucified) 286,
    295
Benin 35
Benivieni, Antonio 51
Bentivoglio, Giovanni 111
Bentivoglio family 110, 112
Benzoni, Girolamo: History of the New
    World 279
Berardi, Giannotto 92, 93, 97
Berenson, Bernard 347
Beretta (company) 8, 271–2, 316
Beretta, Bartolomeo 271
Bergamo 113, 138, 301, 321
Bernardo di Bandino Baroncelli 40
Berni, Francesco 212
Bettona 329
Biagio da Cesena 331
Bibles 209, 285, 290
Bicocca, Battle of (1522) 197, 202, 216, 271
biographies 212, see also Giovio, Paolo;
    Vasari, Giovanni
Bisceglie, Alfonso, duke of 57–8, 59, 70
Bisenzio 309
Bisticci, Vespasiano da 23
Black Death (1348) 85–6, 160

Blanke, John 35
Boabdil, King (Mohammed XII of
    Granada) 3, 7
Boccaccio, Giovanni: Decameron 63, 126,
    213, 214, 323
Bohemia 36
Boiardo, Matteo Maria 50, 323
    Orlando innamorato 50, 212
Boleyn, Queen Anne 135
Bologna 45, 48, 70, 71, 100, 108, 109, 110,
    111, 112, 113, 115, 116, 125, 140, 213,
    218, 222, 248, 257, 264, 276, 283,
    290, 291, 328, 346
    Charles V's coronation (1530) 254–7
    Dominican priory 63
    Jesuits 283
    Julius II's statue 329
    population 85
    rebellion (1511) 249
    Santa Maria della Pietà 327
    University 208, 253
    women 326–7, 328
Bona of Savoy 41
'bonfires of the vanities' 67
Bonner, Edmund 247
bookkeeping, double-entry 210
Bordon, Paris: Portrait of a Man in
    Armour with Two Pages 83
Borgia, Cesare, Archbishop of Valencia
    6, 51, 56, 57, 58, 59, 69, 70–73, 80,
    107, 108, 121, 141, 154–5, 310
Borgia, Franceschetto 56
Borgia, Francisco, duke of Gandia 284
Borgia, Jofrè 56, 58
Borgia, Juan, duke of Gandia 56, 58, 59
Borgia, Lucrezia 56, 57–8, 59–60, 65,
    108, 111, 140, 141–2, 149, 150, 151,
    252, 345
Borgia, Cardinal Rodrigo see Alexander,
    VI, Pope
Borgia family 8, 12, 55, 169, 310
Borromeo, Cardinal Carlo 273
Bosch, Hieronymus 31
Boschetti, Isabella 224, 227
botanical specimens 301–2
Botero, Giovanni 316, 344

Botticelli, Sandro 9, 22, 40, 67, 88, 93, 188, 347

Bourbon, Charles, 8th duke of 236–7, 244

Bracchi, Cecchino 300

Bracciolini, Poggio 16, 17

Bragadin, Marc' Antonio 334, 335–6, 339

Brazil 7, 62, 92, 98, 99, 264

Brescia 113–14, 138, 139, 198, 214, 264, 274, 276, 294

Bretoa (ship) 92

Brittany 32, 43

Bronzino (Agnolo di Cosimo) 294, 295, 297, 327
    Christ Crucified 294, 295
    Medici portraits 297
    Portrait of Dwarf Morgante 297

brothels 229–30, see also prostitutes

Brue, Jörg 181

Bruegel, Pieter, the Elder 31

Bruges 29, 30

Brunelleschi, Filippo 9, 349

Bruni, Leonardo 32, 149
    History of the Florentine People 75

Bruno, Giordano 344

Brunswick 324

Bry, Theodor de: Voyages 303

Bucer, Martin 324

Buda 245

Buonvisi, Benedetto 118

Burckhardt, Jacob: Civilization of the Renaissance in Italy 10

Burgundy/Burgundians 29, 31, 32, 43, 83, 84, 143, 204

Burji dynasty 165

Busini, Giambattista 260

Butcher, Tim 348

Byzantine Empire 17, 18, 21, 163

Byzantium 293, see also Constantinople

Cabot, John (Giovanni) 6, 8, 96, 105

Cabot, Sebastian 96, 103

Caccini, Giovanni 276

Cadamosto, Alvise 77–8

Caesar, Julius 109

Cairo, Egypt 47, 165, 166, 167, 170

Cajetan, Tommaso de Vio, Cardinal 174

Calais 31

Calcione 275

Calixtus III, Pope 25, 55

Calvin, John/Calvinism 285, 286

Cambrai, League of (1508) 137–48, 243

Cambrai, Treaty of ('Ladies' Peace') (1529) 243, 244

Camerino, Giovanni Maria da Varano, duke of 150

Camerino 251

Campi, Bernardino 299

Canada 263

Canary Islands 33, 77, 94, 97

Canda 318

Candia see Crete

Cantelmo, Margherita 252

Cantino, Alberto 99

Capito, Wolfgang 324

Capo d'Orso, Battle of (1528) 242

Capponi, Niccolò 259–60

Capra, Galeazzo Flavio: 'On the Excellence and Dignity of Women' 215

Capri, island of 264

Carafa, Cardinal Gian Pietro see Paul IV, Pope

Carafa, Giovanni 328

Carafa, Cardinal Oliviero, 5

Carafa, Violante 328–9

Carafa family 328–9

Carbonariis, Giovanni Antonio de 96

Cardano, Girolamo: autobiography 343

'Cardinals' Conspiracy (1517) 133–5, 148, 322

Cardona, Ramón de 114, 115–16

Carew, Sir Nicholas 262

Carlos, Don, Prince of Asturias 315

Carpi, Alberto Pio da 171

Cascina, Battle of (1364) 75

Castellesi, Cardinal Adriano, bishop of Hereford 96, 132, 134, 253

Castelnuovo, Siege of (1539) 268

Castiglione, Baldassare 216, 248, 249, 323
  Book of the Courtier 8, 74, 81, 143,
    151–2, 170, 209, 217, 225, 233,
    247–50, 252–3, 258, 282, 319
  portrait (Raphael) 187
Castiglione, Zano, bishop of Bayeux 32
Castile 4, 22, 33, 163, 178, 179
Castro 308, 309
Cateau-Cambrésis, Peace of (1559)
    314–15, 321
Caterina di Meo Lippi 39
Caterina di Sanseverino 157
Catherine de' Medici see Medici,
    Catherine de'
Catherine of Siena, St 213
Cattanei, Vannozza de' 56
Catullus 209
Cavalieri, Tommaso 300
Celia Romana 231
Cellini, Benvenuto 75–6, 102, 224, 238,
    254, 274, 277, 297, 317
  Discourse on Architecture 192–3
Cellini, Cecchino 274
Cenami, Giovanna 29, 30
censorship 123, 211, 221, 302–3, 321, 323
Centurione family 93
Ceresole, Battle of (1544) 269
Cereta, Laura 37, 214
Cerignola 83
  Battle of (1503) 81, 197, 202, 271
Cervantes, Miguel de: Don Quixote 162
Chaldiran, Battle of (1514) 166
Chamberlain, Lady Ivy 347
chapmen 209
Charles I, of England 345
Charles V, Holy Roman Emperor 31,
    117, 178, 205, 235, 238, 243, 244,
    259, 261, 263, 282, 309, 311, 312
  African conquest 266, 269
  army 45, 198, 200, 262–3, 266, 269,
    312
  children 227, 307, 334, 338
  and Clement VII 242–3, 259
  coronation (1530) 225, 254–7
  elected emperor (1519) 143–4, 168,
    175, 176–7

  and Francis I and the French 143,
    145, 202, 203–4, 218, 243, 244,
    266–7, 269, 289
  guns 273, 277
  last years and death 313–14, 322
  and the New World 264, 269
  and Pope Paul III 290–91, 304
  portraits (Titian) 298
  relatives 102, 138, 204, 243, 315
Charles VII, of France 32
Charles VIII, of France 32–3, 41, 42, 43,
    44–6, 48, 49–50, 57, 58, 62, 69, 79,
    275
  and Savonarola 65–6, 68
Charles IX, of France 334
Charles the Bold, duke of Burgundy 32
Chigi, Agostino 187, 191
China 7, 10, 34, 96–7, 163, 207, 273–4, 278,
    304, 349
Chios, island of 6, 20, 93, 98, 117, 268,
    333, 335
Christianity
  and art 61–3
  and Islam 169, 170
  and Jews 169
  see also Roman Catholic Church
Cibo, Caterina 150–51
Cibo, Francesco 155, 156
Cibo, Cardinal Innocenzo 132, 276, 322
Cifuentes, count of 258
Cividale del Friuli 139, 160
Clarke, Tony 348
classical writers 7, 10, 16–17, 21, 35, 37, 57,
    65, 99, 100, 120, 122, 154, 209, 211,
    301
Claude of Brittany 244n
Clement VII, Pope (Cardinal Giulio de'
    Medici) 102, 120, 132, 176, 177, 178,
    179, 181–3, 190, 200, 202, 203, 221,
    222, 223, 235–6, 237, 238–9, 240,
    241, 242–3, 255–6, 257, 259, 261,
    262, 281, 282, 288, 304, 307, 308
Codex Vindobonensis Mexicanus I 102
Cognac, League of (1526) 205, 235, 242,
    256, 257
Colonna, Fabrizio 216

Colonna, Cardinal Pompeo: *Apology for Women* 215
Colonna, Prospero 197
Colonna, Vittoria 215–16, 217, 218, 219, 220, 247, 252, 257–8, 283, 294, 295, 300, 323, 326, 350
    poems 115, 216–17
    Rime Spirituali 217
Colonna family 5, 25, 58, 79, 235, 236, 239
Columbus, Bartolomé 101
Columbus, Christopher 4, 6–7, 8, 21, 40, 43, 60, 64, 92, 93, 94, 95–6, 97–8, 99, 100, 103, 104, 105, 278, 303, 343
Commynes, Philippe de 20, 24, 41, 49, 66
compasses 343
condotta system 146, 315
condottieri 70, 152, 216, 218, 219, 222, 223, 225, 250, 252, 260, 273
confraternities, Christian 86–7, 159, 327
Constantine I, Emperor 16, 19, 65
Constantinople 37, 73, 91, 97, 163, 165, 169, 203, 256, 269
    siege of (1452–3) 17–20, 31, 36
Contarini, Andrea 163
Contarini, Cardinal Gasparo 102–3, 163, 244, 282, 283, 285, 288,300
Contarini, Lorenzo 315, 316
convents 33, 64, 130, 131, 156, 208, 216, 252, 327, 328, *see also* nuns
conversos 3, 33, 325, 326
Córdoba, Gonzalo Fernández de 58, 79–80, 81, 83, 98
Corella, Michele (Don Michelotto) 59
Corfu 164, 335
Cornaro, Caterina, queen of Cyprus 164
Correggio 295
Correggio, Giberto X, lord of 218
Correggio, Niccolò 152
Corsi, Peter 276
Corsica 315
Corso, Rinaldo 295
Cortés, Hernán 117, 303
Corvinus, Matthias, king of Hungary 36
Costa, Cardinal Jorge da 5

cotton trade 164, 165
Counter-Reformation 227, 233, 258, 287, 294, 326, 327, 330, 338
courtesans 218–19, 223, 227–8, 230–32
Crema 139
Crespi, Treaty of (1544) 289
Crete 18, 164, 339
Cromwell, Thomas 9, 84, 148, 210, 247, 253
crusades 12, 20, 21, 23, 33, 131, 163, 167, 169, 187, 203, 268, 284, 341
Cuneo, Michele da 278
Cunha, Tristão da 92
curia *see* Roman Catholic Church
Cyprus 117, 163, 164, 334–5, 338

Damascus 166
Dandolo, Niccolò 334
Dante Alighieri 126, 327, 349
    Divina Commedia 63, 209
Delicado, Francisco: *La Lozana Andaluza* 229
Diane of France 307
Dianti, Laura 226, 227
Diez, Don Gonzalo 258
Dissolution of the Monasteries 287
Diu, Battle of (1509) 34, 165
Djem, Prince 46–7
Djerba, Battle of (1566) 333
Dolce, Ludovico 298
Dolfo, Floriano 226
Domenichi, Lodovico: *Rime diverse d'alcune nobilissime et virtuosissime donne* 219–20
Dominican order 63, 64, 65, 68, 174, 283, 330
Donation of Constantine 16, 23
Doria, Andrea 117, 242, 255, 257, 267–8
Doria, Filippino 242
Dossi, Dosso
    Alfonso d'Este 141, 251
    Bacchanal with Vulcan 251
Dovizi da Bibbiena, Cardinal Bernardo 226, 248
du Bellay, Jean 282
du Bellay, Joachim 314

du Bellay, Martin 144–5
du Prat, Antoine 138, 145
Dyck, Anthony van 299

Eck, Johannes 175
education 208, 214
Edward IV, of England 70
Edward VI, of England 287
Egypt 164, 278, *see also* Mamluk
    Sultanate
Eleanor, queen of Portugal 16, 244
Eleonora di Toledo, Duchess of
    Florence 264, 269, 297, 312, 327
Eliot, George 347
Elisabeth of Valois 299, 315
Elizabeth I, of England 32, 171, 249, 344
Elyot, Sir Thomas 252–3
    The Book of the Governor 252
Emili, Paolo 253
Empoli, Giovanni da 96–7
Enckevoirt, Cardinal Willem van 238
England/the English 21, 22, 31–2, 167,
    203, 204, 237, 248, 249, 313, 316
    ambassadors 256, 262
    Dissolution of the Monasteries 287
    gun industry 276
    mercenaries 84
    trade 91, 96, 97, 118
    see also Elizabeth I; Henry VIII
Equicola, Mario 252
    De Mulieribus (On Women) 252
Erasmus, Desiderius 109, 127, 178, 182,
    209, 239, 293, 323, 324
    Julius Exclusus 113
    New Testament translation 129
erotica 89, 218, 221–6, 228, 232, 277
Este, Alfonso I d', duke of Ferrara 51,
    59, 111, 114, 140, 141–2, 143, 191,
    225, 226, 251, 252, 273, 345
Este, Ercole I d', duke of Ferrara 40,
    65, 99
Este, Ercole II d', duke of Ferrara
    286
Este, Cardinal Ippolito I d' 51, 142, 273
Este, Cardonal Ippolito II d' 312, 332
    villa, Tivoli 10

Este, Isabella d', marchioness of
    Mantua 23, 48, 69, 107, 140, 149,
    151, 152–3, 190, 213, 218, 224, 227,
    237–8, 248, 252, 254, 309
Este, Suor Leonora d' 252
Este family 25, 60, 212, 345
Estouteville, Cardinal d' 55
Étaples, Treaty of (1492) 32
Ethiopia/Ethiopians 24, 35, 51, 100,
    304
Eyck, Jan van 29, 31
    Arnolfini Portrait 29–30

Famagusta, Cyprus 117, 334, 335–6, 340
Farnese, Alessandro, 3rd duke of Parma
    and Piacenza 299, 340–41
Farnese, Costanza 307
Farnese, Giulia 57
Farnese, Orazio 307
Farnese, Ottavio, duke of Parma and
    Piacenza 282, 307, 309, 340
Farnese, Pier Luigi, duke of Parma and
    Piacenza 274, 281–2, 291, 307–8,
    309
Farnese, Ranuccio (Paul III's son) 307
Farnese, Ranuccio (Paul III's grandson)
    307
Fausta, Livia 313
Fedele, Cassandra 214–15
Federico, duke of Mantua 224, 225
Federico, king of Naples 80
Feltre 160
Feltre, Bernardino da 161
Feo, Giacomo 154
Ferdinand I, Holy Roman Emperor 204,
    245, 254, 261, 313, 315
Ferdinand I, of Naples 1, 5, 36
Ferdinand II, of Aragon 3, 4, 6, 7, 33, 43,
    44, 60, 73, 80, 93, 100, 109, 122,
    137, 139, 143–4, 147
Ferdinand, Crown Prince of Spain
    (1571–8) 338
Ferrandino, King of Naples 47, 48, 79,
    80
Ferrante, King of Naples and Jerusalem
    23–4, 26, 41, 42, 43

Ferrara 10, 25, 26, 27, 59, 60, 111, 112, 138,
    139, 140, 146, 251, 260, 345
    Ducal Palace 141, 191
    dukes of see Este, Alfonso I d'; Este,
        Ercole I and II d'
    firearms and gun control 40, 273,
        275, 278, 317
    Jesuits 283
    Jews 326
Ferreri, Cardinal Antonio 111
Ferreri, Zaccaria 180
Fez, Morocco 170
Ficino, Marsilio 209
Filiberta of Savoy 133
Fine, Cornelius de 238–9
Fisher, Cardinal John 282
Flanders/the Flemish 22, 31, 83, 91, 97,
    179, 203, 314
Florence/Florentines 1, 2, 6, 9, 10, 39,
    41, 115–16, 132, 175, 181–2, 241,
    242–3, 250, 255, 261–2, 274, 281,
    323, 345, 346, 347, 350
    Accademia degli Umidi 295
    bankers 1, 25, 91, 93, 96, 156, 263
        and Battle of Anghiari (1440) 25,
        75–6
    Cathedral 67, 68, 349
    and Charles V 45, 46
    Council of 21, 330
    education/schooling 208
    firearms 317
    flood (1966) 348
    Fortezza da Basso 311
    Friday rebellion (1527) 236
    guilds 86
    historians/histories 211–12
    humanism 16–17
    Jews 161, 326
    Laurentian library 10, 189
        and League of Cognac 205,
        235 and League of Venice 49
        and Leo X 120, 132–4, 135, 158,
        187, 189 and Leonardo 69, 71,
        74, 75
    literacy 208 and Machiavelli
        69–70, 71, 111, 119, 120
    and Michelangelo 75, 76, 116, 189,
        190, 259–60, 262
    Museo dell'Opera del Duomo 349
    Museo Galileo 349
    museums 348–9
    Palazzo Vecchio 75–6, 269, 297
    Pazzi Conspiracy (1478) 26, 27, 37,
        40, 132
    population 85–6
    San Lorenzo 189
    San Marco 64, 65, 66, 67, 130
    Santa Croce 349
    Sassetti Chapel, Santa Trinità 62
    and Savonarola 64–8, 75
    secretaries 69, 120, 316
    servants 87
    siege of (1529–30) 260–61, 317
    and Siena 133, 134, 178, 311, 313, 315
    Signoria 67, 75, 120
    'Ten of War' 69–70
    and tourism 7
    Uffizi Gallery 349
    University 17, 21
    women 156, 157, 158, 213–14
    see also Medici family
Foix, Gaston de 113, 114
Foix, Odet de, viscount of Lautrec 242
Fontana, Lavinia 328
Fonte, Moderata
    La giustizia delle donne 326
    Il merito delle donne 326
foreshortening (painting technique) 22
Forlì 70, 154, 155
Fornovo, Battle of (1495) 49–50
Forster, E. M. 347
    A Room with a View 347
Forteguerra, Signora 313
Foscolo, Ugo 349
Francesco del Giocondo 77, 78, 97
France/the French 32, 42, 167, 237, 268,
    269, 281, 284, 310–11, 312, 314, 334,
    343
    ambassadors 109, 256
    arms production centres 271
    army 11, 45, 79, 80, 81, 82, 84, 138, 197,
        198, 201, 202–3, 242, 266–7, 313

and Canada 263
courtiers 247
explorers 96
Hundred Years War (1337–1453)
     21, 31
in Italy 11, 41, 72, 74, 80, 111–12,
     113–14, 117, 118, 134, 137, 138–9, 140,
     142, 144–5, 197–203
Jews 160
and League of Cognac 205, 235
and League of Venice 49
and Peace of Cateau-Cambrésis
     314–15
and Spain 8, 33
and Truce of Nice (1538) 267, 289
see also Charles VIII; Francis I; Henri
     II; Louis XII
Francis I, Pope 346
Francis I, of France 143, 144–5, 147, 168,
     177, 192, 193, 195, 198, 200, 201,
     202, 203 203–4, 218, 223, 237, 243,
     244, 253, 254, 263, 267, 269, 289,
     290, 295, 310
Francis II, of France 334
Franciscan order 64, 68, 161, 283, 294,
     303, 330
Franco, Veronica 228, 230, 231
Frederick II, Holy Roman Emperor 35
Frederick III, Holy Roman Emperor
     15–16, 17, 26, 255, 256
Frederick the Wise, elector of Saxony
     174, 175, 177, 178
Fregoso, Battista 99
Frescobaldi, Francesco 148
Friuli 69, 138, 139, 160
Fugger bank 181, 263

Galen 301
Galilei, Galileo 344, 349
Galle, Philips see Straet, Jan van der
Gallerani, Cecilia 226
Gallo, Antonio 99
Gama, Vasco da 92, 336
Gambara, Uberto 218
Gambara, Veronica 218, 220
Gambia 104

Gaoga, king of 278
Gardone Val Trompia 271, 316
Garibaldi, Giuseppe 346
Garigliano 83; Battle of (1503) 82, 148,
     197
Gedik Ahmed Pasha 37
Genoa/Genoese 25, 26, 42, 99, 105, 111,
     117–18, 140, 262, 299 315, 345
bankers 96, 97, 118, 134, 241,
     263, 279
Cardinals 5
colonies 6, 17, 20, 34, 268, 315, 333
explorers 6, see also Columbus,
     Christopher
in Holy League 335
and Iberia 97
Jews 161, 162
merchants 92, 93, 97–8, 264–5
population 85
ships 18, 19, 23, 242
and siege of Constantinople (1452–3)
     17–20
and slavery 34, 87, 93, 98
Gentileschi, Artemisia 328
     Judith and Holofernes 328
Geraldini, Alessandro 101–2, 104–5
Germany/Germans 2, 16, 17, 29, 31, 92,
     95, 119, 139, 144, 168, 176, 177, 178,
     207, 254, 256, 261, 263, 277, 287,
     313, 322, 348
bankers 92, 181
Ducal Guard 277
electors 168
firearms and gunpowder 271, 272,
     273, 275, 276, 277
Jews 160
landsknechts 84, 85, 89, 145, 146, 197,
     198, 199, 201, 238, 241, 313
peasants' uprising (1524–5) 203
princes 322
printmakers/printing 101, 207
troops 45, 84, 89, 245, 256, 265
see also Luther, Martin
Gherardini, Lisa 12, 77, 78
Gheri, Cosimo, bishop of Fano 308
Ghirlandaio, Domenico 40, 76, 188

Sassetti Chapel, Santa Trinità, Florence 62
Giberti, Gian Matteo, bishop of Verona 179, 182, 222, 239, 293, 330, 331
Gigli family 118
Gilino, Coradino 142–3
Giorgione 190, 191
Giotto di Bondone 9, 22
  Scrovegni frescoes 301
Giovanna, queen of Naples 22, 23
Giovanni da Maiano 253
'Giovanni delle Bande Nere' see Medici, Ludovico
Giovanni the Ethiopian 35
Giovio, Paolo 50, 135, 158, 266, 300–1
  Historiae Sui Temporis 103–4
  Life of Marquis of Pescara 273
  Life of Paolo Vitelli 273
  Notable Men and Women of Our Time 50, 52, 80, 83, 151, 169–70, 201, 212, 216, 218, 243, 244, 343
  La Vita di Alfonso da Este 141
Giraldi, Luca 263–4
Girolami, Raffaelo 261
Giulio Romano 182, 188, 221–2, 251
  Battle of Ostia 187
  Palazzo Te frescoes 224–5
Giulio Tedesco 272
Giustiniani Family 333
Gloucester, Humphrey, duke of 32
Goa 304
  Jesuit College 304
Goletta, La 266
Gonzaga, Elisabetta, duchess of Urbino 248
Gonzaga, Cardinal Ercole 152, 286, 295
Gonzaga, Federico, marquis (later duke) of Mantua 218, 223
Gonzaga, Ferrante I 238, 250, 258, 309, 327
Gonzaga, Francesco II, marquis of Mantua 49, 51, 107, 140, 151, 152, 226, 248, 250, 308, 309
Gonzaga, Cardinal Sigismondo 152
Gonzaga family 25, 345

Gramsci, Antonio 347
Granada, Spain 3, 4, 33, 60, 170, 265, 282
Granada, Treaty of (1500) 80
Grassi, Paride 107, 109
Graziani, Bartolomeo 319
Greco, El (Doménikos Theotokópoulos) 339
  Adoration of the Name of Jesus 339
Greece 18, 117, 167, 170, 333, 335
  ancient 7, 211, 226
Grimaldi, Bernardo 98
Grimaldi bank 241
Gritti, Andrea 114, 139
Gritti, Ludovico 205
Guicciardini, Francesco 27, 80, 210, 211–12, 239
  History of Italy 1, 6, 26, 29, 43, 48, 49, 55, 65, 80, 99, 104, 112, 114, 139, 142, 143, 146, 168, 173, 182, 202, 273, 281
Guicciardini, Luigi 236–7, 238, 239
guilds, Italian 86, 159, 188
Guinea 104
Guinigi, the 30
gun control laws 273, 275–6, 316, 318
gunpowder technology 11, 18, 34, 80–81, 272, 273, 274
Guoallite, Guedelha 92

Habsburgs, the 15, 31, 36, 43, 144, 204–5, 253, 262, 263, 273, 309, 322, 336, 341, 345
Hakluyt, Richard 171–2
  Principal Navigations 303
Hampton Court Palace, England 345
al-Hasan al-Wazzan see Leo Africanus
Hassan Pasha 334
Heemskerck, Maarten van 296
Heliodorus 187
Henri II, of France (duke of Orléans) 254, 307, 310, 311, 314–15, 322, 334, 340
Henry VII, of England 21, 31–2, 43, 96, 248
  tomb 32, 253

Henry VIII, of England 9, 32, 84, 112, 114, 135, 143, 163, 169, 171, 177, 237, 243, 253, 268, 269, 273, 276, 282, 290
Herodotus 100
Hispaniola 93–4, 103, 303
historians/histories 211–12; see Guicciardini, Francesco
Hogenberg, Nicolaus: festival book 255, 256, 257
Holy League 114, 335, 336, 337
Holy Roman Empire 8, 21, 25, 36, 43, 49, 84, 114, 118, 119, 137, 147, 167, 181, 268
   army 197, 198, 200, 202, 236, 262–3, 266
   Golden Fleece (order of chivalry) 344
   see also Charles V, Holy Roman Emperor
homosexuality 112, 226, 300, 308–9
Huguenots 334, 340
humanism/humanists 16–17, 21, 32, 75, 99, 100, 120, 122, 129, 143, 163, 169, 180, 209, 211, 251–2
   female 214
Hundred Years War (1337–1453) 21, 31
Hungary/Hungarians 36, 37, 38, 168, 204–5, 245, 256, 316, 333
Hurtado de Mendoza, Don Diego 277, 311, 312
Hurtado de Mendoza family 302
Hus, Jan/Hussites 175, 203
Huxley, Aldous: Along the Road 348

iconoclasm 293
illegitimate children 56, 153, 227
Imola 26, 70, 71, 153, 154–5
Imperia (courtesan) 228
Inca civilisation 35
India 35, 92, 100–1, 164, 264
   Jesuit missionaries 304
   Mughal Empire 169
Indonesia 35, 164
indulgences, sale of 126, 129, 135, 148, 173, 174, 175, 176, 329, 339

Innocent VIII, Pope (Giovanni Battista Cibo) 2, 3, 6, 25, 32, 42, 47, 56, 150, 155–6
Inquisitions
   Italian 286, 294, 331, 344
   Spanish 3, 4, 33, 163, 178–9, 265
Iran 166, 167
Iraq 146, 166
Isabella of Capua 327
Isabella of Castile 3, 4, 6, 7, 33, 43, 60, 73, 80, 93, 144 147
Isabella of Naples 41
Isabella, regent of Spain 267
Isabella Clara Eugenia, Infanta 299
Ischia, island of 216, 264
Islam/Muslims 34, 35, 37, 166, 167, 169, 170, 171, 293
Issogne, Castello di: fresco 88
Istanbul 47, see Constantine
Italian Communist Party 347
Italian Wars (1494–1559) 8, 22, 27, 29, 31, 32, 41, 43, 60, 69, 80–84, 87, 88, 103, 110, 114–15, 130, 140, 197, 205, 211, 215, 247, 274, 278, 321, 333, 344
   and libelli 210
   and women 149–58, 220
   see also mercenaries; Swiss mercenaries
Italy/Italians 2–3, 7–8, 9, 10, 22, 26–7, 38, 343
   ambassadors 16, 70, 102, 165, 248, 256, 312, see also under Venice
   economy 348
   employment 85, 86, 87
   and exploration 96–7, 98–101, 102–6, 343–4
   fashion houses 348
   houses and furnishings 87–8
   housing market 349
   independence of states 345
   Jews 4–5, 107, 159–63, 239, 323, 324–6
   literacy 207–8
   motor cars 348
   population 85–6
   soldiers 84, 85
Ivan the Terrible 277

Ivrea, Bonifacio Ferrero, Cardinal d'
    276

Jagiellon, Anna, queen of Poland 204
Jagiellon, Catherine, queen of Sweden
    254
Jagiellon dynasty 204
Jamaica 103
James I, of England 171
James II, of Scotland 20
James, Henry 347
Janissary troops 204
Jerome, St 129
Jerusalem 23, 35, 47, 163, 283
Jesuits 282–4, 304, 305, 331, 346
    Constitutions 283
Jews 169, 210, 230, 324
    in Italy 4–5, 107, 159–63, 239, 323,
        324–6
    in Sicily 160
    in Spain 3, 4–5, 33, 83, 242
Joanna (Juana) of Castile 144
John III, of Portugal 304
John of Austria see Juan, Don
Jonas, Justus 254
Jonson, Ben 273
Juan of Austria, Don 336, 338, 339
Juana 'la Beltraneja' 33
Julius II, Pope (Giuliano della Rovere)
    5, 51, 73, 97, 107, 108–13, 115, 116,
    122, 125, 127, 130, 131, 132, 139, 140,
    151, 155, 179, 210, 248, 250, 255–6,
    296
    portrait (Raphael) 181, 185–6
    tomb (Michelangelo) 110, 189, 297
Julius III, Pope (Giovanni Maria Ciocchi
    del Monte) 287, 321, 322
Julius Exclusus (?Erasmus) 113

Kalkar, Jan Stefan van 301
Katherine of Aragon 237, 268
Kelly, Joan 149
Knights Hospitaller/Knights of St
    John/Knights of Malta 47, 168,
    333, 335
Koron 165

'Ladies' Peace' see Cambrai, Treaty of
Landi, Giulio 105
Landriani, Lucrezia 153
landsknechts see Germany
Lannoy, Charles de, viceroy of Naples
    199, 200, 202, 235–6
Lansac, Louis de 312
Lanzol, Cardinal Juan Borgia 5
Laocoön 110, 180
Las Casas, Bartolomé de 102, 104
Lateran Council, Fifth (1512–17) 130–31,
    162, 210, 288, 321, 324
Latino, Juan: The Battle of Lepanto 336,
    338
La Tour d'Auvergne, Madeleine de 133
Legnago, Battle of (1510) 140, 142
Leo X, Pope (Cardinal Giovanni de'
    Medici) 1, 2, 26, 51, 109, 115–16,
    120, 131, 132–5, 137, 144, 148, 150,
    153, 157, 158, 167, 168, 170, 171, 179,
    180, 187, 188, 189, 192, 203, 281,
    296
    and 'Cardinals' Conspiracy' 133, 135,
        148, 322
    letters to 101–2, 104
    and Luther 126, 135, 173, 174, 175,
        177–8
Leo Africanus (al-Hasan al-Wazzan)
    170–71, 239–40, 266, 278
    Book of the Cosmography and
        Geography of Africa 171–2
León 147, 178
Leonardo da Vinci 8–9, 39–41, 69, 70, 71,
    73–4, 82, 99, 141n, 153, 185, 187,
    192–5, 199, 219, 254, 272
    Annunciation 40
    Battle of Anghiari 75, 76
    'Codex Atlanticus' 272
    equestrian monument to Francesco
        Sforza 39, 40
    erotic art 225–6
    Hercules 77
    Lady with an Ermine 226
    Last Supper 10, 40, 194
    Mona Lisa 8–9, 11, 12, 77–8, 187, 193,
        194–5

Salvator Mundi 77, 350
Treatise on Painting 71
Virgin and Child with St Anne 76–7
Virgin of the Rocks 40, 186, 294
Vitruvian Man 194
Leone Ebreo 162
Dialoghi d'Amore 162
Lepanto 165
Battle of (1571) 8, 9, 12, 332, 336–7,
338, 341
Leuven University 178, 238
Levant, the 91, 163
Levita, Elijah 239
Leyva, Antonio de, prince of Ascoli
257
libelli 210
Ligorio, Pirro 332
Villa d'Este 332
Linacre, Thomas 253
Lippi, Filippino
Carafa Chapel vault, Santa Maria
sopra Minerva, Rome 62
Lisbon 6, 77, 91, 92, 97, 99, 162, 263
L'Isle-Adam, Philippe de 168
Lithuania 36, 253
Livorno 312
Livy 211, see also under Machiavelli,
Niccolò
Lodi, Peace of (1454) 20
Lombardo, Julia 230–31, 284
Lomellino, Orazio 299
London
Crosby Hall 118
Italians in 253
Treaty of (1518) 167
Working Men's College 347
López de Gómara, Francisco: La
Historia generale delle Indie
Occidentali 302–3
Loredan, Leonardo 165
Lorenzetto (Lorenzo Lotti) 188
Lorqua, Don Ramiro de 72
Los Cobos, Francesco de 258
Louis II Jagiellon, king of Hungary 204
Louis XI, of France ('the Prudent') 32,
43, 115

Louis XII, of France (Louis of Orléans)
43, 58, 59, 69, 80, 109, 112, 113, 114,
137, 138, 143, 147, 286
Louise of Savoy 143, 203, 243, 244, 310
Loyola, Ignatius 282–3, 304
Spiritual Exercises 283
Lucca/Lucchese 26, 29, 30, 80–81, 118,
253, 319, 345
Jews 5
textiles 86
Lucia, Mona 327
Luna, María Enríquez de 56
Luther, Martin 9, 107–8, 123, 125–6, 127,
128–9, 170, 173–8, 179, 203, 210, 237,
238, 254, 284, 285, 289, 291, 301,
330
antisemitism 324
'Ninety-Five Theses' 135, 173, 289,
293
'On the Babylonian Captivity of the
Church' 176
'On the Freedom of the Christian'
176
On the Jews and their Lies 324
That Jesus Christ was Born a Jew 324
'To the Christian Nobility …' 175–6
Lutherans 179, 203, 221, 254, 287, 289,
295, 316, 321, 322
and Jews 324
Lyons 97, 192, 284, 295

Machiavelli, Niccolò 8, 12, 45, 69–70,
71–2, 80, 111, 116, 119, 120–21,
122–3, 146, 148, 154, 155, 190, 259,
261, 277, 323, 340, 346, 349, 350
Art of War 83, 119, 142, 210, 350
Decennali 209 10
Discourses on the First Decade of Titus
Livy 111, 118, 122, 209
Florentine Histories 119, 211
La Mandragola 210
The Prince 48, 105, 119, 121–2, 146–7,
170, 209, 233, 249, 279, 346, 347
Macron, Emmanuel 348
Madeira 33, 77–8, 91, 93, 97, 105, 164, 263
Madonna Lucrezia 213

Madrid, Treaty of (1526) 203–4
madrigals 182, 218
Magellan, Ferdinand 95, 103
maiolica 34
Majorca 266
Malacca 96
Malatesta, Baglione 260
Mali 35
Malta 333, 335
Mamluk Sultanate 34, 35, 36, 47, 163,
    165–7, 174
Manfredi, Astorre 71
Mannerism 11, 322
Mantegna, Andrea 61, 153, 190, 251
    Camera degli Sposi frescoes 22
    Triumphs of Caesar 345
Mantino, Jacob 163, 171
Mantua 8, 10, 21, 25, 26, 49, 137, 139, 152,
    153, 251, 256, 286, 289, 315
    Camera degli Sposi 22, 190
    Jews 4, 326
    Palazzo Te 221, 224–5
    studiolo 153
'War of the Mantuan Succession' 345
Manuel, King of Portugal 102
Manuzio, Aldo 209, 213
maps 6, 9, 35, 91, 95, 99, 343
Marcellus II, Pope (Marcello Cervini
    degli Spannocchi) 322
Marchionni, Bartolomeo 91–3
Marciano, Battle of (1554) 313
Margaret of Austria, duchess of Savoy
    31, 138, 243–4, 255n, 263
Margaret of Parma 188, 261–2, 269, 276,
    282, 307, 340–41
Marguerite de Valois, queen of Navarre
    (1492–1549) 203, 249
Marguerite of Valois, duchess of Savoy
    (1553–1615) 314–15, 340
Marignano, Battle of (1515) 144–5, 197
Marj Dabiq, Battle of (1516) 167
Maronite Christians 130
marriages 25, 31, 53, 56–7, 77, 94, 150, 155,
    166, 176, 214, 215, 223, 226–7,
    253–4, 285, 290, 326, 328
    and dowries 87, 156, 157

Marseilles 97, 267
Martin V, Pope 281
Martinelli, Biagio 256
Martire d'Anghiera, Pietro (Peter
    Martyr) 100, 102, 103–4
    De Orbo Novo 100
Mary, Virgin 97, 267, 327, 331, 339
    and immaculate conception 330
Mary I, of England 32, 243, 287, 312,
    322
Mary of Austria 204
Mary of Hungary 31, 255n
Matraini, Chiara 318–19
Maturanzio, Francesco 62
Maurice, Elector of Saxony 311
Maxentius 65
Maximilian, Holy Roman Emperor 39,
    43, 84, 137, 138, 139, 140, 144, 174,
    301
Mecca 35, 47, 165, 167
Medgyes, siege of (1534) 205
Medici, Alessandro de', duke of
    Florence 175, 227, 241, 259, 261,
    262, 268, 276, 277
Medici, Anna Maria Luisa, Electress
    Palatine 345
Medice, Bice de' 149
Medici, Catherine de', queen of
    France 175, 241, 254, 310, 312, 316,
    334, 340
Medici, Cosimo de' ('the Elder') 25, 64
Medici, Cosimo I de', duke of Florence
    (1519-74) 264, 268–9, 274, 275, 276,
    277, 295, 297, 300–1, 307, 311, 312,
    313, 315
Medici, Cardinal Giovanni de' *see* Leo
    X, Pope
Medici, Giovanni de' (son of Giovanni
    de' Medici and Caterina Sforza)
    see Medici, Ludovico ('Giovanni
    delle Bande Nere')
Medici, Giovanni de' (Il Popolano) 154
Medici, Giovanni di Bicci de' 25
Medici, Giuliano de' (Lorenzo the
    Magnificent's brother) 26, 93,
    181

Medici, Giuliano de', duke of Nemours (Lorenzo the Magnificent's son and brother of Leo X) 77, 115–16, 132, 133, 135, 151–2, 189, 248

Medici, Cardinal Giulio de' *see* Clement VII, Pope

Medici, Cardinal Ippolito de' 133, 182, 222, 227, 241, 259, 268

Medici, Lorenzino de' 268

Medici, Lorenzo de' ('the Magnificent') 1, 2, 23, 25, 26, 42, 64–5, 155–6, 168, 269, 274

Medici, Lorenzo de', duke of Urbino *see* Urbino, Lorenzo de', duke of

Medici, Ludovico ('Giovanni delle Bande Nere') 89, 154, 198, 201, 222, 269, 308

Medici, Piero de' ('the Unfortunate') 2, 7, 42, 45–6, 65, 66, 156, 157

Medici, Piero di Cosimo de' 115

Medici family 1, 2, 8, 12, 25–6, 30, 46, 66, 68, 76, 77, 115, 120, 122, 155, 156, 157, 158, 190, 203, 235, 241, 242–3, 259, 262, 346, 349

Medici Cibo, Maddalena de' 1–2, 155, 156, 173

Medici Ridolfi, Constessina de' 151

Medici Salviati, Lucrezia de' 156, 157

Medici Strozzi, Clarice de' 157, 219, 241

Medina 167

Mehmed II, Sultan ('the Conqueror') 17–20, 36, 37, 46–7

Melanchthon, Philip 129, 254

Melzi, Count Francesco 194

Mendoza, Cardinal Pedro 108

Menocchio (Domenico Scandella) 331

mercenaries 145–8, 197–8, 261, *see also* Swiss mercenaries

Mewtas, Sir Peter 273

Mexico 117, 263, 264

Michelangelo Buonarroti 8, 9, 76, 116, 127, 153, 182, 185, 189–90, 192, 215, 217, 257, 259–60, 261, 296, 298, 299, 300, 302, 349

Battle of Cascina 75–6

Battle of the Centaurs 76

Brutus 297

Campidoglio piazza 296

Christ on the Cross 295

David 12, 76

Deposition (Florentine *Pietà*) 296

illustrated menus 88

Last Judgment 241, 294, 296–7, 300, 331

Madonna of the Steps 76

Pietà 76

St Peter's, Rome 296

San Lorenzo, Florence 189, 259, 261, 262, 297

Sistine Chapel frescoes 11, 62, 110, 189

Slaves 297

sonnets 217–18, 295, 300

statue of Julius II 112

tomb of Julius II 110, 189, 297

Milan/Milanese 2, 6, 16, 23, 41, 57, 79, 197, 262, 263, 344

and Battle of Anghiari (1440) 25, 75–6

and Battle of Arbedo (1422) 81

Cathedral (Duomo) 40

and Charles V 269, 309

dukes of 52, *see* Sforza family

and Francis I 145, 198, 237

Index of Prohibited Books (1538) 321

Jews 5, 161, 326

in League of Cognac (1526) 205, 235, 242, 256, 257

in League of Venice (1495) 49

and Leo X 180

and Leonardo 39, 40, 74, 192

and Louis XII 59, 69, 80, 137, 138

and Peace of Vercelli (1495) 79

plague 198

population 85

Santa Maria delle Grazie 10, 40

surgeons 275

see also Sforza family

Milvian Bridge, Battle of (312) 65

Minerva, Monte: massacre 37

Minorca 266

Mirandola 111

Mirandola, Count Antonio Maria della 58

Mirandola, Count Lodovico della 152

missionaries 303–4
    Jesuit 282–4, 304
mistresses 226–7, 232
Modena: Este library 99
Modesti, Jacopo 116
Modon 165
Mohács, Battle of (1526) 204, 244
Moncada, Fabrizio de 299
Moncontour, Battle of (1569) 338
moneylending 159, 162, 324, 325
Monferrato 26, 251, 256, 315
Monferrato, Bonfacio, Paleologo,
    marquis of 251, 256
Monluc, Blaise de 202, 313
Montaigne, Michel de 278–9
Monte Cassino 348
Montefeltro, Agnese di 216
Montefeltro, Federico da, duke of
    Urbino 70
Montefeltro, Guidobaldo da, duke of
    Urbino 58, 248
Montefeltro family 70
Montemurlo, Battle of (1537) 268, 312
Monterotondo, lord of 276
Monti di Pietà 162, 324
'Monuments Men' 347
'Moors', the 3, 78, 83, 242, 265, 274
More, Thomas 282
Morgante (dwarf) 297
Morocco 33, 170
Morone, Cardinal Giovanni 287, 322–3
Moroni, Andrea 301
Muffel, Nikolaus 17
Mughal empire 169
Mühlberg, Battle of (1547) 289, 298, 311
Murano, Island of: St Peter Martyr 338–9
Muscovy, Grand Duchy of 36
musicians/musical instruments 31, 86,
    182, 191, 218, 252, 254, 346
Muslims see Islam
Mussolini, Benito 347, 349
Mustafa Pasha, General 335

Nancy, Battle of (1477) 32
Naples, kingdom of 1, 2, 4, 6, 8, 10,
    22–4, 26, 33, 41, 42, 47–8, 49,
    73, 79–80, 90, 98, 109, 139, 162,
    216, 242, 263, 311, 314, 315,
    322, 346
    archive 348
    Castel dell'Ovo 48, 79
    Castel Nuovo 24, 48, 62, 79, 82
    Jews 326
    population 265
    University 208
    viceroys of 264, 269, 312, see also
        Lannoy, Charles de
Napoleon Bonaparte 345, 346
Nassau, Henry, count of 256
Navagero, Andrea 265
Navarino 165
Navarre 33, 138, 283
    Henry III, king of 340
    John III, king of 59, 73
Naxos, island of 267, 333
Negri, Francesco 108
Negri, Paola Antonia 327–8
Nelli, Plautilla 213
Nelson, Lord Horatio 346
Nemours, Giuliano de' Medici, duke
    of see Medici, Giuliano de',
    duke of Nemours (Lorenzo the
    Magnificent's son and brother
    of Leo X)
Nepi 309
Netherlands 22, 84, 85, 138, 168, 296, 334,
    340
New World, the see Americas, the
Nice, Truce of (1538) 267, 289
Nicholas V, Pope 15, 16, 21, 34, 60
Nicodemus 296
Nicosia, Cyprus 334, 335
Norris, Henry 135
Notaras, Loukas 37
Novara, Battle of (1513) 121, 144
nuns 19, 50, 130, 213, 214, 224, 226, 252,
    328, see also convents

Ochino, Bernardino 286, 295
Orley, Bernhard van: tapestries 202
Orsini, Clarice 155
Orsini, Gerolama 307

Orsini family 25, 57, 58, 59, 72, 108, 151, 157

Orsini Medici, Alfonsina 2, 65, 149, 156–7, 158

Orvieto 48, 57, 240, 241
    Cathedral frescoes 241

Osiander, Andreas 324

Osman, Ottoman emperor 169

Otranto 36–7, 38, 264, 331

Ottoman Empire/Ottomans/Turks 8, 9, 17 *and n*, 21, 27, 34, 46–7, 55–6, 63, 69, 106, 112, 117, 129, 243, 244–5, 253, 264, 267–8, 269, 281, 283, 289, 310, 311, 315, 331
    and Battle of Lepanto (1571) 8, 9, 12, 332, 333, 336–7, 338, 341
    and Battle of Mohács (1526) 204, 244
    carpets 30–31
    conquest of Constantinople 17–20, 31
    in Hungary 158–9, 204–5, 245
    invasion of Cyprus 334–6, 340
    invasion of Puglia 36–8
    Italian attitudes towards 169–70
    firearms 277–8
    and Leonardo 73–4
    and Mamluks 166, 174
    and Silk Roads 34
    traders 87, 164, 165
    and Venice 164–5, 172
    see also Süleyman, Sultan

Oviedo, Gonzalo Fernández de 303

Pacioli, Luca 192, 210

Padua 21, 138, 140, 301
    botanical garden 10, 301–2
    Capella degli Scrovegni 301
    Jesuits 283
    Scuola del Santo 191
    University 32, 100, 208, 214, 253, 301, 344

Palermo 264

Palestrina 239

Pallavicino, Argentino 219

Pallavicino family 151

Panciatichi, Bartolomeo 294–5

Panciatichi, Lucrezia 295

Panciatichi family, the 294, 295

Pannartz, Arnold 207

Paoli, Giovanni 264

Papacy, the/popes 2–3, 23, 24, 27, 106, 108, 177, 205, 210, 235, 330, 335
    finances 129–30

Papal States 2–3, 24–5, 42, 58, 73, 110, 111, 114, 129, 176, 210, 250, 251, 259, 261, 291, 317, 345, 346
    Jews 324, 326

Paré, Ambroise 275

Paris 30
    The Louvre 345
    St Bartholomew's Day massacre (1572) 340
    University 283

Parma 144, 151, 251, 307, 309, 335

Paros, island of 267

pasquinades 210, 216, 308, 309

patrons/patronage
    art and architecture 1, 31, 53, 76, 77, 78, 130, 190, 195, 250–51, 252, 258, 277, 298, 300–1
    of explorers 6, 103
    humanist 32
    papal 59, 61, 110, 182, 185, 261, 283, 288
    Spanish 257, 299
    women 155, 156, 157, 219

Paul, St 344

Paul II, Pope (Pietro Barbo) 25

Paul III, Pope (Alessandro Farnese) 57, 274, 281–2, 283, 287, 288–91, 296, 297, 299, 304, 307, 308, 309, 310, 321
    and Jews 325
    portrait (Titian) 298

Paul IV, Pope (Cardinal Gian Pietro Carafa) 282, 288, 309, 322–3, 328–9
    and Jews 325–6

Pavia 198, 199, 262, 263
    Battle of (1525) 235, 236, 255, 269, 271
    Jews 161
    Siege of (1524–5) 198–203, 205
    surgeons 275

Pazzi Conspiracy (1478) 26, 27, 37, 40, 132, 156
Pazzi family 26
Pendinelli, Stefano, Archbishop of Otranto 37
Peretti family 318
Persephone in Hades 180
Peru 263, 302
Perugia 110, 111, 134, 307
    Baglioni wedding massacre (1500) Jews 5
    money-changers' guild frescoes (Perugino) 62
    Rocca Paolina 309
Perugino (Pietro Vannucci) 40, 153, 185, 187, 188
    frescoes 62
Pesaro 56, 70
Pescara, marquis of *see* Avalos, Fernando Francesco d'
Peter Martyr *see* Martire d'Anghiera, Pietro
Petrarch 209, 327, 347
Petrucci, Cardinal Alfonso 133–4, 135
Petrucci, Cardinal Raffaele 135
Philip I, of Castile (the Fair) 243
Philip I, landgrave of Hesse 324
Philip II, of Spain 287, 299, 313, 314–15, 327, 334, 339, 340
Philip, Count Palatine 256
Philip the Good, duke of Burgundy 29
Philip the Handsome, duke of Burgundy 143
Pia, Emilia 248
Piacenza 140, 144, 151, 309
Piccolomini, Enea 312
Piccolomini, Signora 313
Pico della Mirandola, Giovanni 62
Piedmont/Piedmontese 244, 266, 269, 315, 316, 344
Piero, Ser 39
Piero della Francesca
    The Legend of the True Cross 65
    Resurrection 348
Piero di Cosimo
    Building of a Palace 188

Pigafetta, Antonio 95, 103
Pinello, Francesco 97–8
Pinturicchio (Bernardino di Betto) 61
    Belvedere casino, Vatican gardens 61–2
    Castel Sant'Angelo tower and loggia 62–3
    frescoes, Borgia apartments 61, 62
Piombino, Jacopo V, lord of 151
Pisa 10, 74, 75, 76, 117, 259, 276
    botanical garden 302
    Cathedral pulpit (Pisano) 62
    'Little Council' 130, 132
Pisana, Camilla 232
Pisano, Giovanni: Pisa Cathedral pulpit 62
Pistoia 274
pistols 272–3
Pitigliano, Count of 275
Pius II, Pope (Enea Silvio Piccolomini) 20–21, 23, 24, 25, 55, 62, 68, 118, 271
Pius III (Francesco Piccolomini) 73, 325
Pius IV, Pope (Giovanni Angelo Medici) 289, 323, 329
Pius V, Pope (Antonio Ghislieri) 337, 338, 339
Pizan, Christine de 213
    The City of Ladies 213
plague 89, 179, 198, 211, 239, 240, 241, 290
Plantagenets, the 21
Plato 100
Pliny the Elder 99, 171
    Natural History 35, 301
Plutarch 154, 211
Po, River/Po valley 10, 45, 110, 140, 141, 199
poets/poetry
    French 314
    Latin 67, 209, 213
    men 1, 20, 21, 23, 24, 50, 126, 152, 209, 210, 100, 212, 213, 271–28, 222, 248, 273, 293, 295, 319
    women 215–17, 218, 219–20 294, 295, 318–19, 327, 349, 350

Poggio a Caiano 156–7, 241
Poitiers, Diane de 310
Poland 36, 215, 253, 286, 287, 316
Pole, Cardinal Reginald 273, 282, 285,
    288, 322
Polesella, Battle of (1509) 141
Pollaiuolo, Antonio del 194
Polo, Marco 34
Polsine 140
Pontano, Giovanni Gioviano
    23–4, 62
Pontormo (Jacopo Carucci) 297
Porretta 226
Portugal/Portuguese 35, 60, 61, 83, 91,
    92, 104, 117, 165
    colonialism 33–4, 77–8, 96, 97
    conversos 325
    embassy to China 97
    Inquisition 160
    Jesuit mission 304
    Jews 4, 160
    in New World 302
    see also Lisbon
pox/syphilis[?]/'the French disease'
    51–2, 142–3
Prato 116, 260
Preveza, Battle of (1538) 268, 333
Primaticcio, Francesco 254
printing 11, 131, 163, 174, 175–6, 207,
    209–11, 221, 343
    in Mexico 264
    Venetian 9, 104, 163, 207, 209, 213,
        224, 279, 302–3, 327
    and women 213–15
Propertius 209
prostitutes 52, 229–30, 261, 326, 329
Protestantism/Protestants 9, 107, 108,
    129, 131, 176, 254, 284–5, 286–7,
    289, 290, 293, 294, 296, 300, 322,
    323, 324, 330, 331, 344
    see also Luther, Martin; Lutherans
Provence 4, 266
Ptolemy 99
    Geography 99
Puglia 36–8, 50, 264
Purgatory 53, 126, 129, 284, 330

querelle des femmes 213
Querini, Marc'Antonio 334
Querini, Marco 334
Querini, Vincenzo 265

Raimondi, Marcantonio 188, 221–2
    I Modi 221, 223, 228
Ramusio, Giovanni Battista 303
    Delle navigationi e viaggi 303
Rangoni, Ercole 223
Rangoni, Guido 219
rape 12, 19, 37, 63, 116, 154, 227, 228, 261,
    308–9, 329
Raphael (Raffaello Sanzio) 153, 182, 185,
    187–8, 189, 190, 192, 221, 226, 298,
    300
    Baldassare Castiglione 187
    papal apartments 185, 186–7
    Pope Julius II 181, 185–6
    School of Athens 187
    Sistine tapestries 181, 188
    workshop 188–9, 221
Ravenna 109, 115
    Battle of (1512) 114, 115, 116, 140, 141,
        216
Reconquista 3, 282, 337
Reformation, the 285, 344
'Renaissance' 10–12
Renée of France 286
Rhodes, island of 47, 168, 179, 333
Riario, Girolamo, lord of Imola 153, 154
Riario, Ottaviano 70, 155
Riario, Cardinal Raffaele 4, 132, 134, 162
Riario Sforza, Caterina 70, 153–5, 269
Riccio, Pier Francesco 274
Richard III, of England 21, 44
Ridanieh, Battle of (1517) 167
Ridolfi, Emilia 151
Ridolfi, Cardinal Niccolò 297
Ringmann, Matthias 95
Risorgimento 346
Robbia workshop, della: Adam and Eve
    187
Roberval, Jean-François de 263
Romagna, the 59, 70–71, 72, 73, 79, 80,
    137, 139, 218, 310

Romagnano, Battle of (1524) 198
Roman Catholic Church 9, 18, 36, 37,
     52–4, 63–4, 128, 129, 346
     College of Cardinals 25, 128, 133, 134,
          135, 282, 329
     curia 25, 67, 118, 128, 130, 131, 132, 134,
          171, 179, 180, 181, 219, 222, 238, 241,
          288, 293
     Index of Prohibited Books (1538,
          1559, 1564) 321, 323
     reforms 2, 9, 54, 63, 65, 67–8, 110, 127,
          130, 131, 135, 137, 152, 175, 178, 181,
          182, 281, 285–6, 287, 288, 290, 293,
          294, 295, 305, 307, 321, 324, 326,
          330, 332, 339, see also Counter-
          Reformation; Luther, Martin;
          Trent, Council of
     sacraments 290, 330
     and sex industry 230
     and slavery 94, 304–5
     spirituali 285–6, 287, 294, 295
     see also Papacy, the
Roman Empire 16, 17, 36,344, 347
Rome 2, 3, 4, 8, 9, 16, 17, 24, 25, 37, 46,
     47, 48, 115, 126, 127, 128, 262, 265,
     266, 274, 281, 287–8, 296, 321, 337,
     346
     biographies 212
     Cancelleria 176
     Carnival procession (1513) 112
     Castel Sant'Angelo 46, 62–3, 134,
          153–4, 155, 170, 237, 238, 240, 282
     courtesans 229
     English Hospital 148
     ghetto 325
     historians 212
     Inquisition 321, 322
     Jews 4, 325
     literacy 208
     Luther's visit (1511) 125–8
     Nero's Golden House 196
     Palazzo Colonna 338
     Palazzo Farnese 296n, 308
     Palazzo Medici Lante della Rovere
          157
     Palazzo Venezia 347

Piazza Navona 3, 4
plague 240, 241, 290
population 85
printing 207
Roman College 284
Sack of (1527) 153, 233, 236–41, 247,
     255, 265, 296
St James, Piazza Navona 3
St Peter's 15, 16, 110, 127, 131,
     188, 255
San Pietro in Vincoli 17, 110,
     186, 189
San Silvestro in Capite 126
San Stefano degli Abissini 35
Santa Maria dell'Anima 181
Santa Maria della Strada 283
Santa Maria Maggiore 338
Santa Maria sopra Minerva (Carafa
     Chapel vault) 62
Scala Sancta 17, 125
Sistine Chapel 5, 11, 22, 62, 127, 131–2,
     181, 188, 189, 296, 302
statue of Pasquino 210
Trajan's Column 187
Villa Giulia (Etruscan Museum) 322
'Villa Madama' 188
Ronciglione 309
Rosselli, Cosimo 188
Rossi, Properzia de' 213, 298
Rossini, Gioacchino 349
Rosso Fiorentino (Giovanni Battista di
     Jacopo) 254
Rousseau, Jean-Jacques 346
Rovere, Francesco Maria della, duke of
     Urbino 112, 114, 132, 133, 134, 152,
     179, 227–8, 235, 236, 239, 249, 250,
     256, 308
     portrait (Titian) 251
Rovere, Cardinal Giuliano della see
     Julius II, Pope
Rovere, Guidobaldo II della, duke of
     Urbino 249, 251
Rovere Orsini, Felice della 108, 151
Rubens, Peter Paul 75
Ruskin, John 347
Russians 277

Sabbioneta 10
Sadoleto, Jacopo 282
Safavid Empire 36, 166, 167
St Quentin, Battle of (1557) 314
St Vincent (ship) 92
Salaì (Gian Giacomo Caprotti) 194–5
Salt War (1482–4) 27
Saluzzo 315
Salviati, Cardinal Giovanni 156, 201
Salviati family 156
Sampson, Richard 262
San Miniato 259, 260, 261
Sancia of Aragon 56, 58
Sangallo, Antonio da, the Younger 181, 188, 260, 309
   Pozzo di San Patrizio 240
Sangallo, Aristotele del 75
Sansepolcro: monastery 348
Santi, Giovanni 185
Santorini, island of 267
Sanudo, Marin 17, 35, 49–50, 114, 135, 139, 155, 202
São Jorge da Mina 93
Sardinia 267, 315
Sauli, Cardinal Bandinello 134
Savelli family 151
Savona 110, 137
Savonarola, Girolamo 63–8, 76, 107, 108, 120, 127, 131, 174, 178, 210, 287, 323, 330
   'On the Decline of the Church' 63
Savoy 41, 47, 132, 133, 266, 269, 284, 326, 335
   dukes of 156, 256, 315
   see also Louise of Savoy
Schianteschi, Guglielmina 158
Schmalkaldic League (1531) 289, 298, 311
Schönberg, Nikolaus von 282
schools 208
Schwarz, Berthold 273
scientific investigation 301
Scillacio, Nicolò 100
Scorel, Jan van 181
sculpture, classical 11, 12, 110, 180, 226

Sebastiano del Piombo 181, 182, 189, 191–2, 257, 258
   Andrea Doria 257
   Christ Carrying the Cross 258
   Pietà 258
   Victoria Colonna [?] 257–8
secretaries 251–2
Selim I, Ottoman Emperor 167, 168
Selim II Sultan, Ottoman emperor 333–4, 335, 337
Seminara, Battle of (1495) 79
Seville 92, 93, 97, 162
Sforza, Cardinal Ascanio 5, 26, 42, 51, 58
Sforza, Bianca Maria 39
Sforza, Bona, queen of Poland 36, 215, 253–4
Sforza, Francesco I, duke of Milan 16, 41
   equestrian monument to (Leonardo) 39, 40
Sforza, Francesco II, duke of Milan 197, 199, 259, 266
Sforza, Galeazzo Maria, duke of Milan 26, 41, 153
Sforza, Gian Galeazzo, duke of Milan 5, 26, 41, 49, 215, 254
Sforza, Giovanni 56, 57, 58
Sforza, Ludovico ('il Moro'), duke of Milan 1, 26, 39, 40, 41, 42, 43, 49, 50, 57, 69, 80, 145, 155, 197, 226
Sforza, Massimiliano, duke of Milan 144, 145, 197
Sforza family 26, 79, 144, 175
   coat of arms 348
Shakespeare, William 344
shipbuilding 268
Sicily 35, 48, 89, 267, 276, 313, 315, 335, 346
   Jews 160
Siena/Sienese 10, 20, 26, 41, 118–19, 133, 134, 178, 277, 278, 311–12, 315
   Jesuits 283
   Jews 326
   Monte dei Paschi 162n
   Piccolomini Library 21, 62
   Siege of (1554–5) 311, 313
Sifanto (Sifnos) 333
Sigismund I, of Poland 253

Signorelli, Luca: Orvieto frescoes 241
Silk Roads 34, 163, 349
Sistine Chapel 11, 22, 62, 189, 302
    Last Judgment)Michelangelo) 11, 241,
        294, 296–7, 300, 331
    Raphael's tapestries 181, 188
Sixtus IV (Francesco della Rovere), Pope
        3, 25, 26, 33, 37, 97, 108, 134, 153
slaves/slave trade/slavery
    African slave trade 33, 34, 35, 78, 87,
        91–2, 94, 98, 104–5, 164, 165,
        170–71, 227, 266, 278, 305
    in the Americas 9, 87, 92, 105, 304
    Hispaniola slaves 93–4
    Italian traders 12, 34, 87, 93, 98, 164
    Muslim slaves 170, 266
    oarsmen 242, 336
    Ottoman slave-owners 19, 20, 87, 337
    Ottoman slaves 204, 266, 339
    Portuguese traders 33–4, 91–2
    and Roman Catholic Church 87, 93,
        94, 304–5
    Spanish traders 94, 103, 304–5, 344
    see also Mamluk Sultanate
Society of Jesus see Jesuits
Soderini, Cardinal Francesco 134
Soderini, Piero 75, 158
Songhai Empire 35
Soriano, Battle of (1497) 57
Sozzini, Alessandro 313
Spain/Spanish 9, 21, 33, 49, 61, 72, 114,
        118, 134, 263, 302–3, 313, 335, 346
    ambassadors 4, 7, 109, 258, 265
    army 78, 81, 82–3, 84, 85, 89, 90, 98,
        114, 115–16, 117, 197, 198–201, 242,
        261, 269, 273, 278, 311–12, 314,
        315–16, 324, 344
    'Black Legend' 33, 107
    Cardinals 72, 73, 238
    conquistadors 98, 117, 278, 279
    courtiers 247
    Eight Years War 334
    Inquisition 3, 4, 33, 163, 178–9, 265
    Jews 3, 4–5, 33, 160, 161, 163, 324
    mercenaries 147
    merchants 97, 98

    and New World 98, 101–2, 103, 104,
        105–6, 117, 119, 144, 278, 279, 302,
        303, 344
    patronage 257, 299
    population 32
    Reconquista 3, 43, 282, 337
    and slavery 94, 103, 304–5, 344
    and Treaty of Tordesillas (1494) 60
    see also Ferdinand, king of Aragon;
        Isabella of Castile
Sperulo, Francesco 141
spice trade 92, 164, 166
Spoleto 58, 151
Sri Lanka 164
Strabo 21, 100, 171
stradiots 49, 84, 114, 138
Straet, Jan van der, and Galle, Philips:
        Nova Reperta 343
Strasbourg 285, 286
Strozzi, Agostino 252
Strozzi, Filippo 157, 219, 232, 241, 297, 312
Strozzi, Piero 310, 312, 313, 316
Strozzi family 120, 235
Stuart, Bernard 51
Stufa, Luigi della 158
Subiaco, monastery of 207
Suetonius 211
    Lives of the Caesars 57
sugar trade 77, 91, 93, 164, 165, 263–4
Süleyman, Sultan 144, 168, 179, 203, 204,
        244–5, 266, 267, 268, 281, 333
surgeons/surgery 275, 301
Sweynheym, Conrad 207
Swiss mercenaries 84, 85, 138, 144, 145,
        197, 201
    pikes 79, 81, 84, 145
syphilis 283
Syria 130, 163
Szapolyai, János, king of Hungary 205,
        245

Tacitus 100
Tarabotti, Arcangela 328
Tariffa delle puttane di Venegia, La 230
Tartaglia, Niccolò 274
Tenochtitlán 278

Tetzel, Johann 173, 174
Theatines 282
Thomas, William 287–8, 308
Thucydides 211
Tibullus 209
Ticino, River 199
Timbuktu, Mali 170
Tintoretto (Cacopo comin) 338, 339
Titian (Tiziano Vecellio) 153, 190, 191,
    218, 251, 257, 294, 298, 301, 332, 347
    Allegory of Prudence 332
    Allegory of the Battle of Lepanto 332,
        338
    Allocation of Alfonso d'Avalos 298
    The Andrians 191
    Assumption of the Virgin 191
    Bacchus and Ariadne 191
    Death of Actaeon 332
    Duke Federico Gonzaga 257
    Duke Francesco Maria della Rovere 251
    The Flaying of Marsyas 332, 339–40
    Laura Dianti 226, 227
    A Man with a Quilted Sleeve 191
    Mary Magdalene 218, 294
    Nicolò Zen 303
    Pope Paul III 298
    Sacred and Profane Love 191
    Three Ages of Man 332
    Venus of Urbino 227–8, 251
    Worship of Venus 191
Tivoli 239
    Villa d'Este 10, 332
Tlaxcalán 117, 278
Toledo, Garzia di (Garcia de) 312
Toledo, Don Pietro di (Pedro Álvarez
    de), viceroy of Naples 264, 312
Tordesillas, Treaty of (1494) 60
Torres, Luis de 93–4
Torrigiano, Pietro 189–90
    Henry VII's tomb 32, 253
Toscanella, sack of 48–9
Toscanelli, Paolo dal Pozzo 6, 40, 91
tourism 7, 345, 347, 349
Trent, Council of (1545–63) 130, 131, 182,
    222, 289–91, 294, 301, 310, 321, 323,
    326, 327, 329, 330–31

Trento: Jews 161
Trevisan, Angelo 101, 103
Treviso 138, 139, 160, 303, 321
Tridentine reforms see Trent, Council
    of
Trieste 139
Tudor dynasty 31–2
Tunis 240, 266, 287
Turin 45, 140, 256, 266, 267, 275, 315
Turin, siege of (1536) 275
Turks see Ottoman Empire

Uccello, Paolo 160–61
Udine 139, 160
Udine, Giovanni da 181, 182, 186, 187, 188
UNESCO World Heritage sites 9–10
universities 10, 32, 52, 129, 130, 208, 347
    American 7
    Bologna 208, 253
    Florence 17, 21, 120
    Granada 336
    Leuven 178, 238
    Naples 208
    Padua 32, 100, 208, 214, 253, 301, 344
    Paris 283
    Pavia 199
    Venice 62
    Vicenza 62
Urbino 8, 10, 26, 70, 132–3, 147, 179, 248,
    251, 253, 335
    Corpus Domini monastery 161
    Ducal Palace 61, 70, 248–9
    dukes of see Montefeltro, Federico
        and Guidobaldo da; Rovere,
        Francesco Maria and Guidobaldo
        II and below
Urbino, Eleonora, duchess of 152
Urbino, Lorenzo de' Medici, duke of
    132, 133, 156, 157, 158, 175, 177, 189,
    190, 227

Valdés, Juan de 285
Valla, Lorenzo 23
Vallabio, Bernardino: Cronichetta
    113–14
Vanni, Pietro (Peter Vannes) 253

Varano, Giulia 150–51
Varchi, Benedetto 308
Varthema, Ludovico de 100–1
Vasari, Giorgio 269, 297, 338
    Lives of the Artists 39, 61, 64, 67, 77,
        180, 185, 185–6, 189, 190–91, 192,
        195, 212, 213, 224, 251, 296, 298,
        299, 300, 332, 350
Vassy: massacre of Huguenots (1562)
    334
Vatican 56, 58, 131–2, 179, 346
    apartments 46, 186–7, 189, 221
    'banquet of the chestnuts' 73
    Belvedere 110
    Belvedere casino 61
    Borgia apartments 61, 62, 65, 107
    Library 10
    Sala Regia 338
    sculpture garden 180
Vaudès, Pierre (Peter Waldo) 284
Venezuela 92, 99
Venice/Venetians 2, 10, 44, 50, 72, 79,
        99, 117, 119, 151, 198 200, 215, 250,
        259, 265, 271, 303, 344, 345
    ambassadors and diplomats 72, 81,
        101, 103, 166, 244, 265, 314, 315
    architecture 34, 163
    artists 190–92, see also Titian
    Barbari's view of 71
    Biblioteca Marciana 10
    Cardinals of 5, 282
    censorship 321, 323
    colonies 164
    Columbus' crew 93
    convents 328
    courtesans 230–31, 233
    doges 75, 119, 139, 165, 205
    and fall of Constantine (1453) 17–20
    fleet 276, 336–7, 339
    ghetto 139, 160, 161, 325, 326
    glassmaking 86, 164
    Great Council 71
    and Holy League 114
    illegitimate children 227
    Incurabili hospital 283
    Inquisition 286, 327, 331

    interest in India 100–1
    Jesuits 283
    Jews 4, 139, 159–60, 161, 163, 326
    and League of Cognac (1526) 205,
        235, 242, 256, 257
    and League of Venice (1495) 49
    and Leonardo 69
    and Mamluks 165, 166
    maritime trading 77–8, 105, 106, 117,
        163–5, 166
    marriages 328
    and Ottomans 17, 36, 164–5, 172,
        244–5, 267–8, 283, 333–8
    Palazzo Ducale 191, 339
    population 85, 209, 230
    printers/printing/publishers 104, 163,
        207, 209, 213, 224, 279, 286, 302–3,
        321, 323, 327
    prostitutes 229, 230
    and Salt War (1482–4) 27
    Santa Maria dei Frari 191
    SS Giovanni e Paolo monastery 331
    servants 87
    shipbuilding 164
    slave trade 87, 164
    and tourism 349
    troops 113, 114, 142, 144–5, 239, 251
    University 62
    and 'War of the League of
        Cambrai' (1509–10) 137–40
    writers 213, 214, 219, 223–4
Venier, Sebastiano 336
Venus of Urbino 11, 12
Vercelli, Peace of (1495) 79
Vergerio, Pier Paolo, bishop of
    Capodistria 286–7, 300
Vergil, Polydor 253
    History of England 253
Verona 137, 138, 140, 182, 331
domestic service 87
Veronese, Paolo
    The Allegory of the Battle of Lepanto
        338–9
    Feast in the House of Levi 331–2
Verrazzano, Giovanni da 96
Verrocchio, Andrea del 39–40

Vesalius, Andreas 301
   De Humani Corpis Fabrica 301
Vespucci, Amerigo 36, 92, 93, 94, 99,
   105, 343
   Mundus Novus 95
   Soderini Letter 95
Vespucci, Bernardo 36
Vespucci, Simonetta 93
Vicenza 95, 137, 138, 140, 160, 289
   University 62
Vich, Don Jerónimo de 258
Vienna 245, 341
Vigo, Giovanni da: *Practica copiosa in
   arte chirurgica* 275
Vijayanagara, India 101
Villafranca, Battle of (1515) 144
Visconti, Chiara 200
Visconti, Filippo Maria, duke of Milan
   41
Visconti Sforza, Bianca Maria 41
Vitelli, Paolo 273
Vitelli family 72
Viterbo 20–21, 192, 242
Viterbo, Egidio da (Giles of Viterbo)
   125, 130
Vulgate, the 129

Waldensians 284–5, 331
Waldseemüller, Martin 95–6
Warbeck, Perkin 32
Wars of the Roses 21, 31
weapons
   arquebuses/arquebusiers 81, 85, 197,
      201, 202, 272, 273, 274, 275, 277, 317
   cannons 18, 40, 45, 90, 141–3, 166,
      198, 201, 238, 251, 257, 261, 268,
      273, 278, 336
   crossbows 80
   halberds 81
   handguns/firearms 166–7, 271–9,
      316–18, 343
   pikes 79, 81, 82, 84, 145
   pistols 272–3
   see also gunpowder technology
Welser, the (banking family) 92, 263

Weyden, Rogier van der 31
witchcraft 331
Wolsey, Cardinal Thomas 134, 138, 144,
   167, 237, 243, 253
women
   artists and sculptors 213, 298–9, 328
   and honour 145
   and Italian Wars 70, 138, 149, 313
   literacy 208
   patrons 155, 156, 157, 219
   portrayal of 226
   and power 149–58
   and *querelles des femmes* 213
   in religious circles 326–8, *see also*
      nuns
   treatment of 37, 252, *see also* rape
   Waldensian 284
   and witchcraft 331
   writers and poets 209, 212–13, 214–18,
      219–20, 293, 294, 295, 301, 317,
      318–19, 327, 328, 349, 350
   see also courtesans; marriage;
      mistresses; prostitutes
workshops, artistic 188–9
World War, Second 347–8
Worms, Diet of (1521) 177–8
Wyatt's rebellion (1554) 287

Xavier, St Francis 304

Yaunis Khan, Battle of (1516) 167

'Zaffetta, La' (Angela del Moro) 12,
   227–8
Zamora, Bishop Antonio de 240
Zen (*or* Zeno), Cardinal Giovanni, of
   Venice 5
Zen, Nicolò 303
Zen, Pietro 166
Zheng He 34
Zimbabwe 35
Zorzi, Alessandro 101
Zuan Bianco *see* Giovanni the
   Ethiopian
Zwingli, Heinrich 129